Human Institutions

Human Institutions

A Theory of Societal Evolution

Jonathan H. Turner

ROWMAN & LITTLEFIELD PUBLISHERS, INC.
Lanham • Boulder • New York • Oxford

ROWMAN & LITTLEFIELD PUBLISHERS, INC.

Published in the United States of America
by Rowman & Littlefield Publishers, Inc.
A Member of the Rowman & Littlefield Publishing Group
4501 Forbes Boulevard, Suite 200, Lanham, Maryland 20706
www.rowmanlittlefield.com

P.O. Box 317, Oxford OX2 9RU, United Kingdom

British Library Cataloguing in Publication Information Available

Library of Congress Cataloging-in-Publication Data

Turner, Jonathan H.
   Human institutions : a theory of societal evolution / Jonathan H.
Turner.
      p.   cm.
   Includes bibliographical references and index.
   ISBN 0-7425-2558-9 (cloth : alk. paper)—ISBN 0-7425-2559-7 (pbk. :
alk. paper)
      1. Social institutions.   2. Social evolution.   I. Title.
HM826 .T87   2003
306—dc21   2002151047

Printed in the United States of America

To all of my grandchildren:

Ghislaine
Katherine
Mitchell
Kristen
Mati
Joshua
Michelle

(and the unnamed
one on the way)

Contents

Preface

Many years ago, my first book—*Patterns of Social Organization: A Survey of Social Institutions*—outlined the evolution of human institutions, with particular emphasis on their dynamic interchanges. Twenty-five years later, I wrote *The Institutional Order,* which expanded coverage in light of more recent literatures and with even more attention to institutional interchanges. In this book, I integrate these descriptions of human social institutions with a theory of macrodynamic processes. I argue that the original core human social institutions—economy, kinship, religion, polity, law, and education—are the outcome of macrolevel forces that have generated selection pressures on human populations; and out of people's efforts to meet these pressures, they have successively created kinship, economy, religion, polity, law, and education. The forces driving the formation of these institutions are population, production, reproduction, regulation, and distribution. I see these as "forces" because they push individual and collective actors to organize in certain ways. These social forces thus explain how and why the social universe at the macro level of social organization reveals particular kinds of institutional systems.

Other forces drive the formation of the meso and micro levels of social reality, and so, I believe that each level of human social organization reveals its own distinctive forces causing the formation of structures unique to the micro, meso, and macro domains of the social universe. To be sure, meso structures are composed of micro encounters; and institutions are constructed from the corporate and categoric units of the meso level. Still, we cannot explain the macro level of social organization by those forces generating structures at the meso and micro levels of reality. Macro reality—that is, the universe of social institutions—requires explanation by forces operating primarily at this level.

Chapters 1 and 2 of the book explain my theoretical position and enumerate the abstract laws of population, production, reproduction, regulation, and distribution. In developing these laws, I try to obviate problems of traditional functional analysis by viewing each force as a variable—that is, as a property of the social universe that varies by degree—rather than as a functional need or requisite. Variations in the valance of each force are, to some extent, explained by the other forces but also by additional properties of social organization. The relationships among these properties can be expressed in formal propositions that, I believe, explain why and how institutions formed and, later, differentiated. Chapter 3 defines the elements of each core institution and enumerates the selection pressures that have pushed humans to create various institutional systems. Chapters 4 through 7 examine the selection pressures generated by macrodynamic forces at four basic stages of human evolution: hunting and gathering, horticulture, agrarian, and industrial/post-industrial. Chapter 8 explores the interchanges among institutional systems as they have become increasingly differentiated from each other during societal social evolution.

In the end, I hope that this book provides new conceptual and theoretical insights into the process of human social evolution over the last twenty thousand years. The materials are not new, but the way of analyzing them is. Indeed, I am trying to revive "the Old Institutionalism" (i.e., functionalism) because "the New Institutionalism" is more about mesolevel processes than macrodynamics. Sociology needs an analysis of institutions, per se, rather than a view of institutions as merely "environments" for organizations. The old-style functionalists were essentially correct in viewing long-term evolution as revolving around the differentiation of institutions. Unfortunately, their mode of analysis was flawed because they did not explain the forces driving the formation of institutional systems. In these pages, I try to overcome this problem and, thereby, provide a theoretical explanation of *why* humans created the institutional core over the history of human evolution.

ACKNOWLEDGMENTS

The research for this book was supported by a grant from the Academic Senate, University of California, Riverside. I am most grateful for the continued support of the senate, which has supported all of my work over the last years.

Chapter One

Institutional Analysis

For unknown millennia, perhaps as many as two hundred and fifty, humans lived as hunter-gatherers. The mode of social organization was probably not dramatically different than humans' hominid ancestors who had first moved onto the African savanna and, as a result, were forced to develop stronger social ties if they were to survive (Turner 2000). As hunter-gatherers, the structure of human societies was simple, consisting of nuclear families of parents and their offspring organized in small bands that moved about a territory in search of food. If there was a more complex structure, it consisted of the common culture among bands within a territory, and possibly weak ties among members of different bands. Then, anywhere from twenty thousand to fifteen thousand years ago, a few bands began to settle down, leaving their more nomadic ways behind; as people stayed in one place, populations began to grow, forever changing the nature of human societies.

In hunting and gathering, the economy is folded into kinship, with the sexual division of labor directing gathering and hunting activities. Similarly, to the extent that it existed, religious activity was conducted within kinship, although at times specialized practitioners could be found in some bands. Political activity was very recessive because most bands did not have leaders, although certain individuals had influence because of their skills. The first laws were, for the most part, coextensive with traditionalist kinship rules, and adjudication was generally a community activity of the band as a whole. Similarly, education was conducted exclusively within kinship and the band.

Thus, among the first societies, the institutional systems that dominate modern societies—economy, polity, kinship, religion, education, law, science, medicine, sports, and others—were not highly visible outside the structure and culture of kinship and band. The last twenty thousand years of human evolution have, therefore, involved the differentiation of distinctive institutional systems; and today, any society is composed of a series of institutional complexes that organize virtually all human activity. None of these complexes would have ever emerged if humans remained hunter-gatherers; and so, it is with the establishment of permanent settlements and their subsequent growth that institutional differentiation was initiated. When or why institutions became distinctive is for some less interesting than the fact that they exist today, but if we are to understand institutional systems in the modern world, it is necessary, I believe, to explain why they evolved in the first place. This line of inquiry takes us into a search for the forces that pushed humans to create new institutional systems from the simple structures of hunter-gatherers.

Institutions are an important topic because they are the structures that enable human populations to adapt to their environment. We can define social institutions, therefore, *as those population-wide structures and associated cultural (symbolic) systems that humans create and use to adjust to the exigencies of their environment.* Without institutions, humans do not survive, and societies do not exist. Institutions are thus fundamental to the viability of humans as a species.

THE INSTITUTIONAL DOMAIN OF REALITY

Despite the fact that many subfields in sociology are dedicated to the analysis of human social institutions, conceptualizing institutions as a distinct level of social reality remains problematic. Typically, it is the organizational units from which institutions are constructed that receive most attention. For example, sociologists study family rather than kinship systems, firms more than economies, churches more than religion, governmental organizations more than polity, medical professionals more than medicine, agents of law enforcement more than law. Even when the broader structural and cultural environments of organizational forms are examined, there is a tendency to conceptualize these in rather vague terms. Indeed, the "new institutionalism" in organizational theory is more about organizations in their cultural environments than it is about the specific dynamics of the institutional systems, per se (e.g., Scott 1995; Powell and DiMaggio 1991). I do not want to push this point too far, since indeed, some scholars do study institutions as a whole and as an emergent property of human social organization. Still, there can be little doubt that there is a mesolevel bias in studying institutions.

One way to overcome this mesolevel bias in institutional analysis is to conceptualize the levels at which human societies unfold as they grow and develop. Each level, I argue, is driven by its own distinct set of forces, creating structural and cultural forms that are unique to a given level of reality. The question about which level of social reality is paramount has occupied theorizing in sociology for several decades (Turner 1983; Turner and Boyns 2001b). Some are microchauvinists, proclaiming that all reality is ultimately constructed from interpersonal processes; others are macrochauvinists, arguing that all microlevel processes are constrained by larger-scale sociocultural formations. In a sense, both positions are correct to this extent: social and cultural structures at the macro level were produced by human beings in interaction and are sustained by face-to-face interaction; and conversely, all encounters of face-to-face interaction are embedded in more macro social structures and cultural systems and, hence, are constrained by these systems. But such arguments are more metaphorical than theoretical. What is needed is the clear recognition that human societies unfold at three levels of organization, each with its own forces driving the operation of structural and cultural formations (Turner 2003a, 2000, 1999). While this assertion is analytical, I argue that it is more than a conceptual convenience. Rather, the macro, meso, and micro levels of social reality *are* just that: real. One can see distinct structures at each of these levels, and the goal of sociological theory is, in my view, to explain the forces driving their formation. True, the levels are interrelated and embedded in each other: organizations are composed of micro encounters, and institutional systems are structured from mesolevel structures like organizations; and conversely, the formation of mesolevel structures and culture is constrained by the institutional domain in which they are nested, while encounters are circumscribed by the mesostructures in which they are lodged. We must, however, do more than simply assert this to be the case; it has to be demonstrated.

In this book, I analyze the initial emergence and subsequent development of the core social institutions of human society—economy, kinship, religion, polity, law, and education. In the very beginnings of human society, these institutional systems were fused within kinship units and bands comprising the meso level of social reality. But even at this early stage of human evolution, the forces that ultimately drive institutional evolution were at work, but at relatively low valences because the scale of human society was so small. But as this scale increased, these forces became more powerful, driving humans to create new institutional systems. As these systems emerged, the nature of social reality as operating at three distinctive levels was ever more evident.

LEVELS OF SOCIAL REALITY

Sociocultural Structures at the Micro, Meso, and Macro Levels of Reality

In figure 1.1 the basic structures and attendant cultural formations of the micro, meso, and macro levels of reality are portrayed. At the micro level, the encoun-

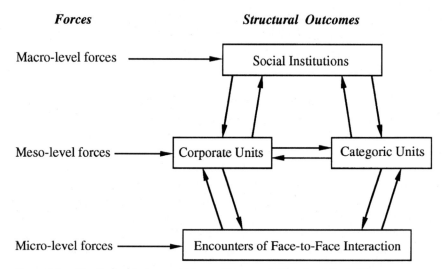

Forces   ***Structural Outcomes***

Macro-level forces ⟶ Social Institutions

Meso-level forces ⟶ Corporate Units ⟷ Categoric Units

Micro-level forces ⟶ Encounters of Face-to-Face Interaction

Figure 1.1.   The Embeddedness of Macro, Meso, and Microlevel Social Forces

ter is the basic structural unit; at the meso level, corporate and categoric units are the key structures; and at the macro level, institutions are the essential structures. An *encounter* is an episode of mutual awareness among individuals punctuated by communication that shapes the ebb and flow of face-to-face interaction. As Erving Goffman (1967, 1961) emphasized, there are (1) *focused encounters* where individuals face each other and actively engage in mutual communication and (2) *unfocused encounters* where individuals sustain mutual awareness and implicitly communicate in ways that keep them from focusing on each other as they move about public spaces. Thus, at the micro level, we need explanations of the dynamic of face-to-face interaction in focused and unfocused encounters, and such explanations must examine the fundamental forces that drive human interaction (Turner 2002).

At the meso level, two structural forms emerge: corporate and categoric units (Hawley 1986). A *corporate unit* is typified by a division of labor organized to pursue ends or goals, however clear or vague. The basic forms of such corporate units are groups, organizations, and communities. A *categoric unit* is formed by the distinctions that people make and use: gender, age, class, ethnicity/race, region, and the like. Members of these social categories share certain distinguishing characteristics that mark them for differential treatment by others.[1] As the arrows in figure 1.1 indicate, corporate and categoric units can be related. Many categoric distinctions in human societies follow from positions in corporate units—for instance, student, worker, father, scientist, and the like. Conversely, categoric unit membership can be the impetus to corporate unit organization, as has been the case in the Civil Rights and women's movements. Thus, when engaged in mesolevel analysis, scientific sociology needs to develop theories of the forces driving the formation or operation of corporate and categoric units.

At the macrolevel of reality, institutions are the essential structures. Institutions and their corresponding systems of cultural values, ideologies, and norms allow populations as a whole to adapt to the environment, both the biophysical and sociocultural. Macrolevel analysis will, therefore, revolve around developing theories about the forces that drive the formation of institutional systems as populations adapt to the biological, physical, and sociocultural environments in which they must be sustained (including those created by the very act of social organization). Institutional analysis is, therefore, inherently evolutionary because it explores how humans create population-wide structures and cultural systems that enable them to survive in the environment, often an environment of their own making.

Forces Operating at the Micro, Meso, and Macro Levels of Reality

Table 1.1 lists the forces that I see as driving each level of social reality (2002). By forces, I mean properties of the social universe that push individual and collective actors to create particular kinds of structures and cultural formations. I deliberately use the term *forces* in order to emphasize my "hard science" view of how sociology should explore the social universe (Turner 1995). Just as gravity or any of a number of fundamental forces examined by physicists drive the formation and operation of the physical universe, so the social universe is to be understood by the operation of fundamental forces. Similarly, the biotic world is driven by the forces of evolution, such as natural selection, gene flow, mutations, and other elements of the modern synthesis in evolutionary biology. Granted, invoking the notion of "forces" is somewhat pejorative, but I do so to emphasize the commonality of the social universe with other domains of reality. Unlike so many in sociology, I do not see any fundamental differences among the social, physical, and biotic worlds to justify a science of sociology that is different than any other "hard science."

The study of human social institutions, therefore, must begin with an analysis of the forces driving their formation. As is evident in table 1.1, I see five macrolevel forces as operating in creating, sustaining, and changing the institutions of society: population, production, reproduction, regulation, and distribution. Correspondingly, mesolevel analysis examines the forces driving the formation of corporate and categoric units: segmentation, differentiation, and integration. And, the microlevel analysis explores the forces shaping the

Table 1.1.   Forces of the Social Universe

Macrolevel Forces

1. Population	The absolute number, rate of growth, composition, and distribution of people.
2. Production	The gathering of resources from the environment, the conversion of resources into commodities, and the creation of services to facilitate gathering and conversion.
3. Distribution	The construction of infrastructures to move resources, information, and people in space as well as the use of exchange systems to distribute resources, information, and people.
4. Regulation	The consolidation and centralization of power along its four bases (coercion, administrative structures, manipulation of material incentives, and symbols) in order to control and coordinate members of a population.
5. Reproduction	The procreation of new members of a population and the transmission of culture to these members as well as the creation and maintenance of sociocultural systems that sustain life and social order.

Mesolevel Forces

1. Segmentation	The generation of additional corporate units organizing activities of individuals in the pursuit of ends or goals.
2. Differentiation	The creation of new types of corporate units organizing activities of individuals in pursuit of ends or goals and new categoric units distinguishing people and placing them into socially constructed categories.
3. Integration	The maintenance of boundaries, the ordering of relations within corporate and categoric units, and the ordering of relations among corporate and categoric units.

Microlevel Forces

1. Emotions	The arousal of variants and combinations of fear, anger, sadness, and happiness.
2. Transactional needs	The activation of needs for confirmation of self, positive exchange payoffs, trust and predictability, facticity or the sense that things are as they appear, and group inclusion.
3. Symbols	The production of expectations (normatization) with respect to categories of people present, nature of the situation, forms of communication, frames of what is included and excluded, rituals, and feelings.
4. Roles	The presentation of sequences of gestures to mark a predictable course of action (role making) and the reading of gestures to understand the course of action of others (role taking).
5. Status	The placement and evaluation of individuals in positions vis-à-vis other positions and creation of expectation states for how individuals in diverse and differentially evaluated positions should behave.
6. Demographic	The number of people co-present, their density, and their movements, as well as the meanings assigned to number, density, and movements of individuals.
7. Ecological	The boundaries, partitions, and props of space as well as the associated meeting of boundaries, partitions, and props.

dynamics of encounters: emotions, transactional needs, status, roles, symbols, and demography/ecology. Although table 1.1 defines these basic forces for each level of reality, my goal in this book is to examine only those of the macro realm.

FORCES OF THE MACRO REALM

Institutions are generated, sustained, and changed by population, production, reproduction, regulation, and distribution. Each of these forces constitutes a basic contingency of human existence, pushing individual and collective actors to build particular kinds of social structures and cultural systems. And, the larger a population becomes, the more likely are multiple institutional systems to evolve in response to the operation of these forces. There are many complicated and, indeed, rather problematic issues in visualizing the macro realm in this way, but before addressing these issues, let me offer a brief summary of what these forces are.

Production

In order to survive biologically, humans must gather resources from the environment and convert them into usable commodities that sustain life. This process of production is fundamental to human organization, and it drives a great deal of activity in all societies. Out of this activity comes the institution of the economy, and more indirectly, virtually all institutional systems that depend upon environmental resources. Traditionally, economists talked in terms of "elements of economies," such as land, labor, capital, and entrepreneurship. I follow this older tradition but redefine and supplement this list. In my view, variations in production and, hence, economies stem from the following elements (Turner 1997, 1972): (1) *technology* or knowledge about how to manipulate the physical and social environment, (2) *physical capital* or the implements, including money that can buy these implements, used in gathering resources and converting them into commodities, (3) *human capital* or the knowledge and skill possessed by people, (4) *property* or socially constructed rights to possess and use objects of value, and (5) *entrepreneurship* or the mechanisms for organizing technology, physical capital, human capital, and property systems for gathering resources and converting them into commodities. It might be noted that I have not mentioned distribution of goods and services as a part of production, although it is an essential dynamic of the economy. As is evident below, I see distribution as a distinctive force, above and beyond its effects on the economy, per se.

Population

Demographic factors are not typically seen as a force in the formation and evolution of human social institutions. Yet, early sociologists such as Auguste
Comte (1830–1842), Herbert Spencer (1874–1896), and Émile Durkheim
(1893) all saw population size and its rate of growth as the driving force of
human evolution. As populations grow, they argued, the differentiation of
social structures and culture accelerates. I think that their respective insights are
essentially correct: *institutional differentiation began with growth of human populations*. For, as populations grow, new kinds of *logistical loads* are placed on a society—loads for securing more resources, for coordination and control, for
distributing resources, and for finding ways to sustain social structures. These
loads pressure people to find solutions to new problems that are emerging, and
from these pressures come patterns of institutional differentiation.

Not only is the absolute size of a population and its rate of growth a driving
force of human organization, but so are the diversity, distribution, and movement of a population's members. Diverse populations pose more logistical
loads than homogeneous ones, all else being equal; and so populations that can
be distinguished culturally and that can be differentiated into diverse types of
categoric units above and beyond age and sex distinctions push actors to
develop new institutional systems or to change older ones. Similarly, the distribution of populations in space has an enormous impact on institutional evolution. If a population is large but distributed across vast territories, pressures for
institutional evolution are less intense than is the case when the same population is densely settled in a comparatively small area. Under these latter conditions, differentiation of institutional systems will accelerate. Moreover,
movements of populations in space have effects on institutional systems. If
immigration into a society exceeds emigration (out migration), this ratio of
immigration-to-emigration will increase the size of the total population and
generate pressures for differentiation; and if immigration is to already dense
settlements, then these pressures are that much greater.

I should pause briefly to note that terms such as *logistical loads* and *pressures*
are vague. I will seek to clarify these terms and introduce the notion of *selection*
as a key mechanism later, but for the present, let me ask that this vagueness be
endured. My eventual goal is to expand the notion of natural selection to
human populations, emphasizing that forces driving the formation of institutional systems do so by generating *selection pressures* that push actors to develop
new forms of social organization, if they can, in order to sustain their viability
in a given environment (Turner 2001c, 1995). Sometimes these pressures over-
whelm a population, causing it to disintegrate or be conquered by a better-
organized society; at other times, by rational planning, diffusion of culture,

experimentation, trial and error, and just pure luck, new institutional forms are created as a means to manage selection pressures. The most primal of these pressures historically has been population growth as it creates new problems of how to sustain this larger population in the environment. Without the pressures of a growing population, humans may have stayed hunter-gatherers forever, but once growth forced humans to settle down in more permanent settlements, institutional evolution was thereafter inevitable. Population forces have continued to exert pressures on institutional differentiation, but as we see below, institutional differentiation generates new kinds of selection pressures that force further institutional development. Let me leave the argument at this point, only to pick it up later in this chapter.

Regulation

In order to survive, individuals and corporate units organizing people's activities must be coordinated and controlled. Mechanisms must be discovered to control deviance and conflict, to coordinate actions, and to allocate resources; and as the valences for production and population increase, selection pressures for regulation also increase. As we will come to appreciate, higher valences for regulation generate selection pressures for the mobilization of power. Power is thus the basic element of regulation.

Power is the capacity to dictate, to varying degrees, the actions of others, whether individuals or collective units. There are four bases of power: (1) *coercive* power, or the ability to force physically others to do what an actor with power desires; (2) *symbolic* power, or the capacity to use appeals to values and ideologies to regulate the actions of others; (3) *material* power, or the use of incentives or disincentives—that is, giving or taking away material resources—to secure conformity to one's desires; and (4) *administrative* power, or the use of organizational systems to monitor and control actions of others.

Many have analyzed combinations of these bases of power (e.g., Turner 1995; Mann 1986; Blalock 1989; Collins 1975; Etzioni 1961). My view is that there are two important dimensions along which power varies. One is what I term the *consolidation* of power, and the other is the *centralization* of power. *Consolidation* refers to which bases of power are mobilized to what degree as a means of controlling and regulating the actions of others, whereas *centralization* denotes the degree of concentration of decision-making prerogatives among actors. Consolidation of any combination of power—whether coercive, symbolic, material, or administrative—inevitably leads to some degree of centralization, but there can be large differences in how centralized various configurations of consolidation are. For example, when power is consolidated principally around the coercive and administrative bases, it will generally be more centralized than when it is consolidated on the material and symbolic bases. Moreover, different configurations or profiles of consolidation and varying degrees of centralization yield varying types of institutional systems, especially the polity. For instance, a high degree of mobilization of the symbolic and coercive bases along with high degrees of centralization produce systems like those in postrevolutionary Iran or Taliban Afghanistan; a moderate degree of centralization based upon high levels of material and symbolic power, coupled with the strategic use of coercive and administrative bases, generates institutional systems like the Western democracies.

A theory of institutions, then, must specify how regulation as a force increases and sets into motion power dynamics, especially the conditions under which power is centralized or remains relatively decentralized and the conditions under which varying profiles of consolidation emerge. For most of human evolution, regulation as a force remained at low levels, escalating with interpersonal conflicts within bands and perhaps occasional clashes between bands of hunter-gatherers. But once humans settled down, the valences for regulation continually increased, thereby creating selection pressures for the mobilization of power along all its bases and for varying degrees of centralization of power.

Distribution

For a population to sustain itself, it must distribute information, resources, and people. I separate distribution from the analysis of the economy because I believe it to be a much more generic force of human organization than just the distribution of economic goods and services. Distribution of economic goods and services, to be sure, is an important aspect of distribution, but noneconomic resources, and most particularly, human bodies and information are also distributed outside the purely economic arena. There are two dimensions to distribution: (1) *infrastructure,* or the physical facilities for moving material resources, people, and information about a territory; and (2) *exchange,* or the process of giving up some resources to secure other resources. Obviously, exchange distribution depends upon infrastructural facilities, such as roads, ports, communication and transportation technologies, and conversely, exchange activity often leads to the development of distributive infrastructures to encourage and facilitate trade, especially as markets using money and credit evolve.

Like any other force, the analysis of distribution involves specifying the conditions under which distributive infrastructures expand and exchange distributions accelerate. Production is certainly one such condition, but political consolidation and centralization of power are another, as is population growth, and other forces. Thus, distribution is a force driving virtually all other institutional systems, either holding their evolution back or accelerating their development to the point where the institutional systems of a large number of societies become intertwined in a world system.

Reproduction

Evolution was defined by Charles Darwin (1859) as "descent with modification" by which he meant that individual members of a species survive by reproducing themselves under the pressures of natural selection. Today, it is recognized that such descent involves the passing on of genotypes, with those genes promoting fitness or reproduction surviving in the gene pool. Social evolution is, however, more Lamarckian because human actors often have the capacity to alter structures, or create new ones, under selection pressures. Moreover, humans cannot survive biologically without being socialized into a culture and acquiring those skills necessary to occupy positions and play roles in social structures. This is not to deny, of course, that there are not inertial tendencies in socialization and in sociocultural systems that can be seen as the equivalent of genotypes, and hence, as subject to the forces of natural selection (Hannan and Freeman 1977). Indeed, human history is filled with societies whose structure and culture were so rigid as to make them vulnerable to Malthus's "four horsemen." Still, even if efforts fail, social organization can be changed by acts of agency in an effort to promote fitness in physical-biological-sociocultural environments. Humans can create new social structures and cultures, and they can resocialize the young into these sociocultural systems. As a result, human reproduction is mediated by patterns of sociocultural organization that, to some extent, insulate genotypes from the forces of biological evolution.

At the most fundamental level, human social institutions cannot exist without people, and so, biological reproduction is perhaps the most driving force of all behind patterns of social organization. Thus, human social institutions initially evolved under selection pressures for biological reproduction, but since this reproduction cannot occur outside of human groupings, reproduction also involves the replication of social structures and systems of culture to provide the haven within which biological reproduction and subsequent socialization can occur. While biological descent with modifications is no doubt occurring to humans on a very gradual scale, it is the descent with often dramatic modifications of social structures and cultural systems organizing human activity that is even more evident. For in the end, the viability of humans as a species depends upon the creation as well as replication of sociocultural systems and, then, the socialization of all new members to a population

into these systems. For most of human history, hunting and gathering populations reproduced themselves without dramatic alterations (perhaps for as long
as 230,000 years); and while the cultures and the specific social structures of
hunter-gatherers varied somewhat, they all conformed to a basic form of small
bands of nuclear families wandering defined territories in search of food. Only
when human populations began to settle in more permanent communities and
grew in numbers did the "modification" portion of "descent" begin to accelerate. Reproduction has thus become more about sociocultural change than
stasis, but such changes are to some extent driven by the necessity of creating
sociocultural systems that are adapted to the environment and that, as a result,
enable humans to reproduce those structures and cultural systems necessary for
biological reproduction.

From an evolutionary perspective, then, we need to understand the conditions under which reproductive forces drive the formation of new institutional
systems, above and beyond those devoted solely to biological reproduction.
Substantively, this process involves moving beyond the nuclear family units (of
mother, father, and offspring) typical among hunter-gatherers to more complex
kinship systems and, eventually, to non-kin structures and cultural systems like
education involved in social reproduction of individuals who can participate
in complex cultures and social systems. But reproduction involves more than
differentiation of new kinds of socialization systems, such as the institution of
education; it also pushes individual and collective actors to reproduce all sociocultural systems and to modify them in ways that facilitate adaptation to the
ever more complex environments of developed societies. For example, political policies that seek to sustain cultural traditions and social structures, laws that
specify behaviors, appeals to supernatural forces that reinforce particular norms,
biomedical discoveries and practices that sustain health, and many other patterns of action in institutional systems are partially responses to the force of
reproduction. Thus, reproduction extends its driving force well beyond socialization processes into virtually all practices that operate to sustain social structures and culture or to change them in ways that enhance adaptation.

Forces, Institutions, and Environments

As is perhaps obvious but nonetheless fundamental, the environment within
which adaptation occurs changes as societies become more complex or differentiate new institutional systems. The physical-biological parameters of society
always exert pressures on human populations, particularly if their institutional
systems cause environmental degradation or natural events dramatically alter
the availability of resources, but as societies become more complex, new institutions become part of the environment to which all other institutions must

adapt. Moreover, the institutions of other populations are also part of the environment; and as populations grow and as institutional differentiation accelerates, the sociocultural environment often poses as many problems of adaptation as the physical–biological environment. Thus, many of the selection pressures that drive institutional differentiation and development come from other institutions, those within a society and/or those of another society.

This pressure for populations to create institutional systems in order to adapt to their own sociocultural environments drives human evolution more than other species. More fundamentally, any given force driving institutional formation and change will be influenced by variations in the other forces. For example, the level of production is very much related to the level of consolidated power emanating from regulation or the scale of infrastructural and exchange distribution. Thus, we can analyze the relations among institutions at two levels. One level traces out the interconnections among various institutions, as is the case when we examine the relationship between the polity and economy, kinship and polity, law and economy, and so forth. At another, more fundamental level, we can examine the relationships among the forces that generate these relations among institutional systems. For instance, the degree of centralization of power along coercive and administrative lines will influence the level of production differently than will centralization along the material or symbolic bases; or the differentiation of reproductive structures like schools for socialization will have effects on the symbolic bases of power and the level of human capital formation on production.

The important point here is that most institutional analysis, when it occurs at all, is typically conducted at the first level. When the second level is also pursued, I think that our understanding of institutional dynamics is greatly increased. Hence, in the chapters to follow, I pursue both levels, the first being primarily descriptive and the second more theoretical. In the next chapter, I offer some preliminary laws on the dynamics of macrolevel forces that can guide the more descriptive portions of subsequent chapters. Before doing so, however, I need to return to the issue of selection pressures.

FUNCTIONAL NEEDS, HUMAN AGENCY, AND SELECTION PRESSURES

The Ghosts of Functionalism?

Some of the macrodynamic forces that I propose sound very much like the needs or requisites of old-style functional theorizing (e.g., Spencer 1874–1896; Durkheim 1895, 1893; Radcliffe-Brown 1952; Malinowski 1944; Parsons 1951). The logic of functionalism is to posit a list of basic needs that all societies must meet if they are to survive in an environment and, then, to analyze social structures and processes in terms of how they meet, or fail to meet, these needs (Turner and Maryanski 1979; Turner 2001c). Thus, it is a short step from my view that population, production, reproduction, regulation, and distribution are the basic forces to the view that these are the functional requisites of human societies, with particular social institutions like economy (production and distribution), polity (regulation), or family and education (reproduction) functioning to meet these requisites. However, there are some important differences, if only in emphasis, between traditional functionalism and my approach (Turner 2001c, 1997, 1995). First, the forces of population, production, regulation, reproduction, and distribution are not static need states; rather they are *variable states* that, depending upon their valences, exert varying degrees of pressures on humans to organize along certain lines. Second, as will be evident, I make explicit what is often left implicit or ignored in functional theorizing: the mechanism of *social selection* whereby need states generate selection pressures to which people and collective actors respond, sometimes successfully and, at other times, unsuccessfully. The emphasis on selection pressures shifts the entire analysis away from categorizing institutions on the basis of which functional need they meet to one where the level of a force, as it generates selection pressures, pushes agents to act in certain ways; and this line of reasoning makes no assumptions that these agents do so successfully. In fact, history tells us that all societies eventually collapse or are conquered because they fail to respond to these selection pressures.

The Critique of Functional Logic

The basic critique of all functional arguments is that they do not specify how human agents create social institutions. Instead, the critics argue, functional theories simply crosstabulate functional needs and the institutional systems that meet these needs without ever telling us how, and through what processes, this correlation between a need state and institutional system came about. While the critique is typically overdrawn, it has some merit. Among the various criticisms that can be summarized, let me focus on the one developed by rational choice theorists who seek to explain institutions as the outcomes of decision-making processes of rational actors (Hechter 1987; Coleman 1990).

There are variations in the exact argument but all rational-choice explanations of institutions begin with the assumption that individuals are rational, seeking to maximize utilities and minimize costs in pursuing various lines of conduct. Ultimately, institutions arise from both negative and positive "externalities" (bad and good outcomes, respectively) experienced by individuals. When individuals experience negative externalities, they seek to create structures so that these negative consequences go away or are minimized and, if possible, so that positive outcomes ensue. There is, then, a demand for a jointly produced good—a pattern of cooperative organization—that eliminates the negative externalities and provides positive reinforcers to individuals. If the production of a joint good takes collective effort, with each individual making a contribution, the problem of "free riding" emerges. Free riders enjoy the benefits of the jointly produced good but do not contribute their fair share of effort in its production; and since it is rational for each actor to free ride (in order to maximize utilities and minimize costs), all actors may free ride; and when this occurs, the joint good will not be produced—thus, escalating negative externalities once again. To avoid free riding, control systems must be created to monitor and sanction potential free riders, but monitoring and control are costly; and so, the demand for the joint good—in this case, a new pattern of cooperative behavior that forms the basis for an institutional system—must be high and the costs of monitoring and sanctioning must not be so high as to impose new kinds of negative externalities. Indeed, institutions often emerge as mechanisms to overcome the costs involved in monitoring and sanctioning free riding in other cooperative spheres.

The arguments of rational choice theorists are more detailed, and the goal is to specify the nature of the negative externalities and how these motivated agents to give up some of their rights to create constraining patterns of social organization (Coleman 1990). The logic of this argument is often juxtaposed to that of functionalism and seen as a superior form of explanation because it provides a mechanism by which problems and pressures translate into actions that generate and sustain institutional systems. It is possible, I believe, to mediate between these logics; and the key is the concept of *selection pressure*.

Macrodynamic Forces and Social Selection

Most sociological analyses invoking the notion of selection borrow from Charles Darwin's (1859) view as it filtered through Émile Durkheim's analysis of *The Division of Labor in Society* (1893). For Durkheim, population size and growth increase material density, as do communication and transportation technologies that "reduce the space" between individuals. Increased material density, Durkheim continues, magnifies the moral density or rates of interaction among individuals. And, as material and moral density increase, competition for resources escalates, with the most fit staying in a given resource niche, and with the less fit migrating to new niches in order to secure resources. Figure 1.2 summarizes Durkheim's argument. Hence, specialization of activities in the social world, as opposed to speciation in the biotic world, is the result of these dynamics. And, unlike Darwin (1859) who held out the possibility for the extinction of species not able to adapt to an ecological niche, Durkheim had a more optimistic view that competition would lead to specialization of individuals in ever more diverse resource niches instead of their extinction. In contrast, Spencer (1874–1896) argued more in line with Darwin, when he coined the phrase *survival of the fittest,* but Spencer's real contribution to the notion of selection does not reside in his Darwinian-sounding pronouncements.

What Spencer argued in his *The Principles of Sociology* (1874–1896) is what all functional theories imply: selection pressures are set into motion when a population faces problems of adaptation to an environment; and many of these pressures exist because there is an absence of relevant structures or cultural symbols to deal with these problems. Thus, rather than density-competition setting selection into motion, Spencer emphasized that problems of adaptation to the environment typically arise from a lack of structures (no density) or the existence of ineffective structures. In fact, most selection in human societies is of this kind: a new problem emerges forcing actors to consider alternative ways of dealing with the problem; and by thought, borrowing, diffusion, trial and error, innovation, or luck, they create a sociocultural pattern that resolves the problem and, as a result, facilitates adaptation. For example, we can see Spencerian selection today in the problems of integrating the world system or, more specifically, the global economy; and these problems are forcing nations and other international actors to think of ways and to build structures that can resolve the problems emerging from globalization. It is very much in the balance whether these and additional efforts—such as the World Bank, International Monetary Fund, United Nations, Group of Seven/Eight advanced industrial nations, and the like—will be enough to maintain some equilibrium in the global economy; there is no inevitability that agents will hit upon solutions to problems that work.

All functional theories in the social sciences imply this logic, but unfortunately, they generally bypass explanation in terms of a selection process, sometimes Durkheimian but more often Spencerian. When individuals encounter problems of adaptation to their environments—a kind of "negative externality" in rational choice terms—they begin to cast about for solutions in the face of the selection pressures they are experiencing. One kind of selection pressure comes from density in a resource niche and competition for resources in this niche, but another stems from the lack of appropriate structures to manage a problem. Since humans are rational in the minimal sense of trying to avoid punishments, they will generally try new options. Sometimes they succeed,

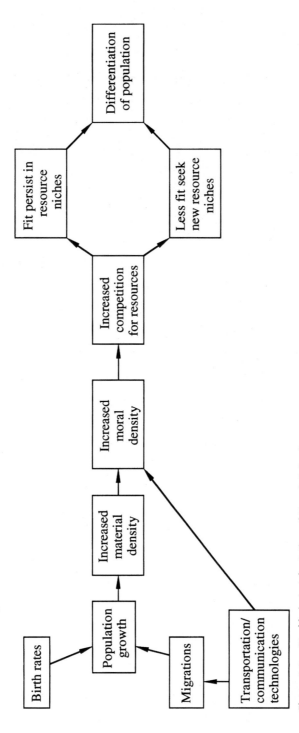

Figure 1.2. Durkheim's Adaptation of Darwin's Logic

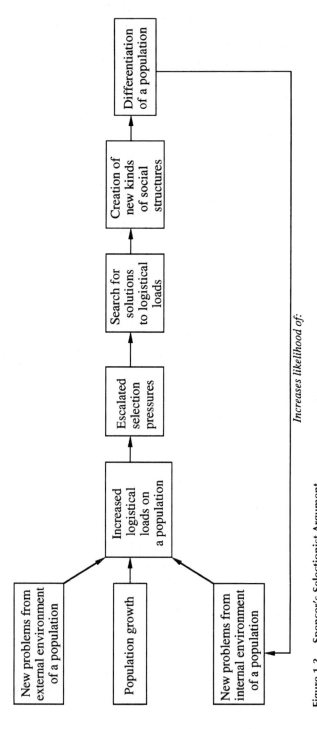

Figure 1.3. Spencer's Selectionist Argument

and at other times, they fail; but in the long run of human evolution, they have at least managed many adaptive problems by creating new institutional systems that, ironically, may resolve one problem but set into motion new kinds of selection pressures.

One way to view Spencerian selection pressures is in terms of first-order and second-order selection (Turner 1995). *First-order selection* pressures emerge with problems of adaptation to the external environment of a population. The source of these pressures can come from the physical and biotic environments as well as the sociocultural systems of another population. Whatever their source—environmental degradation, war-making from another society, natural disaster—agents must deal with events external to their society. *Second-order selection* comes from the sociocultural environments created by the growing complexity of society itself—for example, internal conflict stemming from inequality, market collapse because of fraud, increasing rates of crime, and poor coordination of economic units. These kinds of selection pressures come from inside the society as a result of its increasing differentiation and complexity. This line between first-order and second-order selection is not always so clear, but in general terms, the first institutional systems emerged in response to first-order selection, but once these systems were created and evolved in complexity, they began to generate second-order selection pressures that led to the alterations of existing institutional systems and/or the development of new ones.

In sum, then, the concept of selection can be expanded to reconcile agent-based and functional theories of institutional development. The functional needs or requisites facing human populations need to be reconceptualized as forces, pushing on both individual and collective agents to solve a problem of adaptation. These forces are universal in that they are always present, but they always reveal *varying levels* of intensity when populations of humans adapt to their environments. For example, among hunter-gatherers the forces of production and reproduction are much more intense than the other forces, and hence, the selection pressures that these generated led to the emergence of nuclear kin units in bands with the division of family labor also serving to define the simple economic roles of men and women. With the emergence of horticulture, selection pressures from population and regulation increased, leading to the differentiation of polity and other institutional systems. Over the course of human history, then, the valences of forces have caused varying profiles of selection pressures; agents try to respond to these pressures, if they can, by considering alternatives that can eliminate the negative externalities that they are currently experiencing or that they anticipate may come about in the future. Out of these responses to negative externalities, as fueled by selection

pressures stemming from the operation of macrolevel forces, humans have successively created the institutional systems of society.

CONCLUSION

In the chapters to follow, I develop a theory of macrodynamic forces and, then,
illustrate this theory with descriptive accounts of the major stages in human
evolution: hunting-gathering, horticulture, agrarianism, and industrial and
post-industrial societies. My emphasis is on the core institutional systems that
first emerged in human evolution: kinship, economy, polity, law, religion, and
education, although one could make the case that science, medicine, and education differentiated at about the same time. In figure 1.4, I have schematically
arranged the basic model of the forces driving human evolution. I see population size and growth, relative to land mass and resources, as the ultimate driving
force of evolution because it has intensified the values of other forces. Together
these forces have generated selection pressures, some Darwinian and others
Spencerian.

My goal is to offer more than a descriptive account of institutional evolution
from hunting and gathering to the present; others have already performed this
exercise in many guises and, at the same time, presented theoretical arguments
on the driving forces of evolution (e.g., Lenski 1966; Nolan and Lenski 2001;

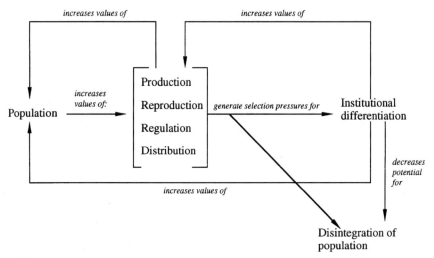

**Figure 1.4. Macrodynamic Forces of Selection Pressures for Institutional
Differentiation and Development**

Sanderson 1995a, 1995b). I also seek to present an alternative theory of the macrolevel forces that drive the formation of institutional systems. In the next chapter, I present this theory in its broad contours as a series of elementary principles on macrodynamics.

NOTE

1. The concept of *categoric unit* is similar to the notion of *nominal parameter* developed by Peter M. Blau (1994, 1977) in that both concepts emphasize that the categorization of individuals influences the nature of interaction, or in Blau's theory, rates of interaction.

Chapter Two

A Theory of Macrodynamic Forces

In the course of human history, institutions have emerged as responses to selection pressures imposed by the fundamental forces driving the macro level of social reality. A theoretical explanation of institutional evolution thus requires a set of theoretical principles on the dynamics of these forces, and in particular, on those properties of human populations that increase or decrease the value of each force. In this chapter, I lay out what I see as some of the elementary theoretical principles that explain the operation of each macrolevel force. Many of the conditions that raise or lower the values of any one force are the other macrodynamic forces, although additional properties of societies are also introduced. Since the evolution of human institutions beyond hunting and gathering was initiated with population growth, let me begin here and, then, move to the analysis of production, power, distribution, and reproduction.

POPULATION DYNAMICS

The Law of Population

Thomas Malthus ([1798] 1926) was the first to conceptualize the relationship among population growth, carrying capacity of the environment, and potential for societal disintegration. His famous "four horsemen"—war, disease, pestilence, and famine—underscore the problems faced by growing populations. One "solution" to these problems is to expand productivity and to create new forms of political regulation. In this way the carrying capacity of the environment can be increased. Alternatively, a population must find ways to cut its rate of growth, and Malthus posited that economic growth can work to lower birth rates and, hence, population growth. In very modern-sounding terms, he posited what has become known as the "demographic transition." As production expands, people's standards of living rise, and as their expectations for consumption escalate, additional children are seen as cutting into consumption. As a consequence, birth rates begin to decline. More recent demographic theorists like Esther Boserup (1981, 1965) have rephrased Malthus's argument by positing a relationship between population growth, competition for resources, and demands for innovations that can increase production so as to support the larger population. This line of argument takes us to the notion of selection pressures, because "demand" for innovations under conditions of competition is simply one way to state that population growth generates selection pressures for new kinds of social structures. Moreover, as demands for increased production are realized, rising normative standards of living cause individuals to have fewer children in order to meet these standards.

Herbert Spencer (1874–1896) and Émile Durkheim (1893) both pursued similar lines of argument. For Spencer, population growth increases logistical loads on a population for securing sufficient resources to sustain the larger population, for assuring that social structures and cultural systems can be reproduced, for coordinating and controlling the larger population, and for distributing resources and information among members of the population. For Spencer, these logistical loads generate selection pressures that cause the differentiation of new kinds of productive, reproductive, political, and distributive structures; and as these differentiate, the larger social mass can be sustained in its environment, as emphasized in chapter 1. Spencer thus posited a form of selection that has been underemphasized in sociology: selection for new structures in the absence of structures that can manage increasing logistical loads. This is why I term this process *Spencerian selection*.

Émile Durkheim (1893) added a more Darwinian twist to the argument: population growth or any force that increases material and moral density (such as transportation and communication technologies that "reduce the space" between individuals) increases competition and selection pressures that cause actors to seek resource niches in which they can sustain themselves. While Durkheim tended to have a rather rosy view of how differentiation would eventually lead to reintegration of a society along "organic" lines, his discussion of the pathologies of differentiation—forced divisions of labor (or inequality), poor coordination, and of course, anomie—signals that disintegration is possible as differentiation increases. Yet, unlike Spencer who saw that the necessary institutional differentiation in the face of population growth may never occur in the first place or be unsuccessful when it does (thus hastening disintegration), Durkheim assumed that the new institutional forms would somehow magically emerge.

In a variety of fields over the course of two hundred years, then, the basic insights about population dynamics have been revealed. And in new traditions, such as Christopher Chase-Dunn's (2001; Chase-Dunn and Hall 1997) analysis of world system dynamics, population pressures are a crucial force driving this system. In other works (Turner 1995:22), I have tried to synthesize these long-standing ideas about population in analytical models and formal propositions. My latest thinking on population dynamics can be summarized by the following principle or "law."

$$N = \{[(N_D) \times (N_{ST})] \times [(+/- P) \times (DF_{MS, MY}) \times (=/+ DF_{CP}) \times (+/= PO_{CL})]\} + (TS)$$

where:

N = the size of the population

N_D = the density $(_D)$ of population (N)

N_{ST} = the proportion of population (N) residing in permanent settlements $(_{ST})$

P = the level of production (gathering of resources and their conversion into commodities)

$DF_{MS,MY}$ = the differentiation (DF) of market systems $(_{MS})$ using money and other financial instruments $(_{MY})$

DF_{CP} = the level of differentiation (DF) among corporate $(_{CP})$ units organizing people's activities

PO_{CL} = the level of consolation $(_{CL})$ of each base of power (PO)

TS = the amount of territorial space (TS) inhabited and controlled by a population

The equation above and those to follow require some clarification. Equations like this one are "quasi math" but they are sufficient to delineate key relationships without the complicated notations in conventional mathematics. The equation argues, first of all, that the size of a population (N) is related to the multiplicative relationship between the proportion of a population in permanent settlements (N_{ST}) and overall density of the population (N_D) throughout its territory. As populations urbanize, they generally grow because they attract immigrants and indigenous migrants who will maintain high birth rates for a time after moving to urban areas. This effect on population size is related in a positively curvilinear pattern with increases in production (P) that enable larger, densely settled populations to support themselves; and in turn, increasing production is multiplicatively related to the differentiation and development of markets using money ($DF_{MS,MY}$) for the distribution of goods and services between rural and urban areas, as well as within dense settlements. And once these settlements can secure resources, they can grow and, thereby, increase the size of the population. A larger population can only be supported by increases in structural differentiation of corporate units (DF_{CP}) to house diverse activities and by increases in the consolidation of power (PO_{CL}) to coordinated diverse structural units; and once differentiation and capacities for political regulation are in place, these operate as a stimulus to further population growth, at least until the demographic transition sets in with very high levels of production (hence, the positively curvilinear relation, symbolized by the $(+/-)$ sign, between production to population size). These two blocks of variables—that is, $[N_D, N_{ST}]$ and $[P, DF_{MS,MY}, DF_{CP}, PO_{CL}]$—are multiplicatively related to each other in their effects on the size of a population; and, together, they are influenced by how much territory is available to a population (TS).

At this point, I should pause and note some of the signs on the variables in the equation: as just indicated, a $(+/-)$ sign indicates a positive curvilinear relationship, with population size increasing with increases of production until raised standards of living initiate the second phase of the demographic transitions under conditions of very high levels of production; a $(+/=)$ sign indicates that the consolidation of power will lead to increases in size of the population during initial consolidations of each base of power, eventually leveling off with further consolidations of various bases of power; a $(=/+)$ sign signals a lagged positive relationship in which initial increases in one variable have no effect (signaled by "$=$") on another until a certain threshold is reached, and then, the relationship turns positive $(+)$; a (x) sign emphasizes that relationships are multiplicative in the sense that the variables interact in terms of their effects on population growth beyond their additive effects alone; no sign indicates a positive relationship; and just to fill out the other logical possibilities for equations, a $(-)$ sign indicates a negative relationship between variables, while a $(-/+)$ sign denotes a negative curvilinear relationship in which the relationship is initially negative but eventually turns positive; a $(=/-)$ relationship indicates a lagged effect, with no effects until some threshold is reached in the signed variable and, thereafter, with the relationship turning negative. This kind of notation is not standard, but it communicates to the nonmathematically inclined key relationships. An equation like the one above allows me to communicate in a parsimonious way the complicated relationships among forces and properties of the social universe. Let me briefly expand upon the argument in more discursive terms.

Settlements and Population

When humans began, some 15,000–20,000 years ago, to establish more permanent settlements, they did so because of the ready availability of resources, typically fish near rivers, lakes, or other bodies of water. Once settled near resources the population generally began to grow, particularly since its members no longer needed to pack up and move about a territory. Eventually population growth and intensive hunting and gathering activities in an area depleted resources, forcing humans to turn to horticulture and, at times, to herding in order to generate enough resources to maintain the growing population. But the key event was the initial settlements, because once committed to this form of subsistence, populations would grow with access to resources, and as they grew, settlements expanded. Moreover, new settlements would be created as older ones became full, thereby raising the overall level of density among members of a population across its territory. Thus, the interaction effect between settlement densities and the proportion of people in stable communities is perhaps obvious but, nonetheless, fundamental because once settlements are established, they provide the structural base for further growth, whether through higher birth rates or immigrations, if production and distribution can expand to sustain individuals in urban areas. Thus, settlement patterns are multiplicatively related to production and distribution; without expansion of the latter, urban communities cannot survive. Once this dynamic relation between urbanization and production/distribution was initiated, population density increased.

Production and Population

In order to support a larger and more densely settled population, new modes of production become essential. If production cannot be expanded to meet population growth, then settlements are abandoned, as was the case for the Anasazi in the southwest United States and the Incas of Peru who, because of ecological changes, simply could not produce sufficient food to support the population. Thus, increased production will allow the population to grow, but eventually, high levels of production and escalating standards of living initiate the demographic transition. As individuals become oriented to the consumption of ever more varieties of consumer goods, they eventually come to see larger numbers of offspring as working against this consumption; and as a consequence, birth rates begin to decline. And so, the relationship between population and production is positively curvilinear ($+/-$).

Markets and Population

Population growth depends not only on increased production but also the capacity to distribute goods (and eventually services as well) to larger numbers of individuals. Markets become the key force in this process because they allow goods to flow to those not directly engaged in production, and as money and other financial instruments such as credit emerge, markets can function even more effectively in allowing economic resources to flow to those engaged in other kinds of activities. Urbanization of a population will eventually force market development because, as settlements get larger, many individuals are no longer engaged in actual production of food; and this fact generates selection pressures for markets that distribute food and other necessary goods to those living in urban areas. Once markets using money exist, they allow individuals and collective actors to express new preferences (with money as a generalized marker of value) and, as a result, diversify demand in markets, which, in turn, provides a stimulus to new modes of production. This mutually reinforcing cycle between market development and increased production allows a population to grow further, thereby escalating selection pressures for enhanced production and distribution.

Corporate Units and Population

Production, market distribution, and the consolidation of power are multiplicatively related to the differentiation of meso structures because, without the capacity to expand the division of labor and to house labor or human capital in new kinds of corporate structures, production is limited. Initially, population growth can be managed by segmentation, or the reproduction of similar corporate units. For example, a horticultural population can grow and expand production, to a point, by adding more kinship units such as lineages, clans, and submoieties. Thus, the relationship between production and differentiation of corporate units is lagged and positive ($= / +$); that is, segmentation of units can, for a time, provide the necessary structural skeleton for the larger social mass and the needed structural forms for expanded production, distribution, and regulation, but as population and production expand, selection pressures will operate to differentiate *new kinds* of corporate units engaged in a variety of activities beyond production, such as marketing, political regulation, religion, and education. If these do not emerge, then population growth will be arrested or the population will disintegrate and de-evolve back to simpler systems of corporate units.

Power and Population

Without the capacity to coordinate and control larger numbers of individuals and the more complex structures organizing their activities, population growth will lead to disintegration. The consolidation of power along all four bases— coercive, symbolic, material, and administrative—becomes ever more necessary as selection pressures from regulation as a macrolevel force mount for increased control capacity. Thus, for the population to continue to grow, without causing disintegration, the consolidation of power is necessary. As the history of human societies so clearly documents, however, societies often fail to achieve the right balance among the bases of power, thereby assuring their disintegration from within or their conquest from without. For power to be consolidated, it becomes necessary to generate an economic surplus, above and beyond subsistence needs. The bracketing of production, market expansion, differentiation of corporate units, and consolidation of power in a multiplicative relationship (in terms of their combined effect on population size) emphasizes that without additional resources and capacities to distribute them across diverse structural units, it is not possible to sustain the corporate units involved in production and consolidation of power. Furthermore, this block of variables will operate to concentrate populations in settlements which, in turn, will create settlement structures that can sustain a larger population (hence the multiplicative relationship in the above equation between population settlement and density, on the one hand, and production, markets, corporate unit differentiation, and consolidation of power, on the other.

Territorial Space and Population

It is obvious but still fundamental that a larger territory, all other things being equal, can encompass a larger population. True, variations in resources, ecology, and geography can alter this relationship somewhat, but generally, a small territory cannot accommodate large numbers unless a population has access to the resources of another population. And even here, there is eventually only so much space that can accommodate so many people, no matter what the level of productivity and exchange distribution with other societies. Thus, the Netherlands cannot be a large society, no matter what its level of productivity, unless it engages in territorial expansion, as it has done at times in its history. China and the United States, in contrast, can accommodate large populations, as long as the other forces listed as variables in the equation above are operative at high levels. Moreover, with a larger territory, segmentation of structures can absorb growing numbers of individuals without differentiation that will introduce increased complexity, with such complexity setting into motion selection pressures for expanded production, market development, and political regulation. Even with segmentation of similar units in a larger territory, selection pressures will typically lead to expanded production and distribution as various settlements specialize in somewhat different economic activities. Moreover, larger territories present greater logistical loads for not only internal regulation but also for defense of borders. And so, even if segmentation in larger territories proceeds, pressures for differentiation also build, and as the units organizing a population differentiate, a larger population can be supported.

Other Demographic Forces

I emphasize the absolute size of a population as a critical force in macrolevel social organization. While population size and rate of growth are paramount forces driving much human activity, there are other demographic forces to consider. As the equation emphasizes, the distribution of a population is an important demographic force. Urbanized populations generate different selection pressures than rural ones because, once a large proportion of the population lives in dense settlements, new modes of production, distribution, and regulation become necessary; and these lead to differentiation, which provides a structural base that can support a larger social mass. Another demographic force not explicitly incorporated into the equation is the diversity of the population. Diverse populations, as defined by varying locations in different kinds of corporate units and by categoric distinctions such as ethnicity and social class, generate more selection pressures for coordination and control than do more homogenous populations; and as new modes of production, marketing, political regulation, and corporate unit differentiation emerge, the structural base to support a larger population is in place.

Still another demographic force is movement of a population. When individuals are mobile, migrating to new regions and urban/rural areas or emigrating/immigrating across a society's borders, the density and size of a population is typically changed. Migration to urban areas increases the values of the first block of variables in the equation, and a net increase of immigration over emigration directly increases the size of the population and generally the overall density of the population (since immigrants often go to urban areas). In turn, mobile populations, per se, increase logistical loads for production, distribution, and regulation; and if they increase size and density, these logistical loads and the selection pressures that these loads generate increase that much more. When these pressures cause the expansion of production, distribution, and regulation as well as differentiation of new kinds of corporate units, they provide the structural base for further population growth. Thus, there are many ways to conceptualize population as a force in human evolution, but in general, the size and rate of growth of the population capture much of what is needed to explain the emergence of new institutional formations.

PRODUCTION DYNAMICS

The Law of Production

Production is a force that drives individuals to gather resources from the environment and convert them into life-sustaining commodities, but as institutional differentiation occurs, the diversity of resources gathered and goods produced goes far beyond what is essential for maintaining life. Instead, forces driving other institutional systems and corporate units from which these institutions are built dramatically expand the demand for new kinds of goods and, eventually, services. As I note in chapter 1, the basic elements of production are (1) *technology* or knowledge about how to manipulate the environment, (2) *physical capital* or the implements used in gathering and converting resources into commodities and, later, into the liquid resources like money used to buy implements, (3) *human capital* or the dispositions and skills of humans engaged in gathering and production, (4) *property* or definitions of how to control resources, both material and symbolic, and (5) *entrepreneurship* or the mechanisms by which technology, physical capital, human capital, and property are coordinated in the gathering and conversion of resources.

A principle on production, then, needs to explain variations in these elements. The equation below represents my best effort to develop such a principle:

$$P = (N) \times [(TE) \times (CA_{PH}) \times (CA_{HU}) \times (NR)] \times (DF_{CP}) \times (DF_{MS,MY})$$
$$\times [(+/=PO_{CL}) \times (+/-PO_{CT})]$$

where:

P = the level of production (gathering of resources and their conversion to commodities)

N = the size of the population

TE = the level of technology or knowledge about how to manipulate the environment

CA_{PH} = the level of physical ($_{PH}$) capital (CA) or implements used in production

CA_{HU} = the level of human ($_{HU}$) capital (CA) or skills of individuals engaged in production

NR = the level of access to natural resources in the environment

DF_{CP} = the degree of differentiation (DF) of corporate ($_{CP}$) units

$DF_{MS,MY}$ = the degree of differentiation (DF) of market systems ($_{MS}$) employing money and other financial instruments ($_{MY}$) for the distribution of goods and services

PO_{CL} = the level of consolidation ($_{CL}$) of the coercive, symbolic, material, and administrative bases of power (PO)

PO_{CT} = the level of concentrated power along all bases of power

This is a complicated proposition, but it captures the forces driving production in human populations. The equation argues, first of all, that the level of production (P) is a positive function of population size (N) as it pushes actors to increase the level of technology (TE), physical capital (CA_{PH}), human capital (CA_{HU}), and access to resources (NR). In turn, these variables are all multiplicatively related to each other in their effects on production. That is, these elements mutually accelerate each other's values so that an increase in one will increase the others, thereby increasing production. This is a fairly obvious set of relations, but essential nonetheless.

The other forces enumerated in the equation are the key as to whether or not these multiplicative relations will actually increase production. There must be some entrepreneurial mechanisms to organize these elements for them to increase production, and the equation visualizes one of these mechanisms as the differentiation of new corporate units (DF_{CP}), some of which can organize new modes of gathering and converting resources (as well as other kinds of activities like market, political, and religious activities). My argument is that structural elaboration, per se, is critical, even if this differentiation of corporate units is not initially used in production. Another entrepreneurial mechanism is the differentiation of market systems employing money and credit ($DF_{MS,MY}$). Until markets using money and credit exist and until differentiated corporate units organizing technology, capital (both human and physical), and property systems are in place, the scale of production will be limited. It is only when technologies, capital, labor, and property become subject to market distribution among differentiated corporate units that production can begin to accelerate to high levels. These markets can vary in terms of how much the "laws" of supply and demand operate, but once markets of any kind are in place, they provide a means for the distribution of knowledge, resources, and people to larger-scale productive activities organized in corporate units.

Markets distributing the key elements of economic activity will not, however, prove effective in the long run unless they are regulated by centers of power. Thus, the consolidation of each base of power (PO_{CL}) is essential, as are moderate degrees of centralization of power (PO_{CT}). These two power forces feed off each other, with consolidation of a base of power causing some centralization of that base (but not necessarily other bases). After a certain threshold in production and market activity is reached, selection pressures for regulation through consolidation of all bases of power may begin to escalate. Centralization of power is a distinctive dimension of power as a macrodynamic force. Without some degree of centralization of the bases, unregulated entrepreneurial activity can be exploitive, definitions and enforcement of property rights can be chaotic, and markets can become too speculative and unstable, especially if money and credit are not regulated. Yet, too much centralization often leads to elites usurping for privilege the economic surplus that could otherwise be invested in entrepreneurial activity encouraging the development of new technologies, physical capital, and human capital. This is why I indicate by the (+ /−) sign that the relationship of centralization to the consolidation of power and to all other variables in the equation is curvilinear. I should emphasize that, in particular, consolidation and moderate centralization of power are critical to reformulating definitions of property in ways that make them a dynamic element of production. Without symbolic power to legitimate definitions of what is property and who has rights to property and without the capacity to administer and enforce these rights, property is not easily transferred in markets and, instead, is hoarded by elites to maintain privilege and, hence, less dynamic productive activities. Of course, markets also concentrate property, but not to the extent of nonmarket distributions. Let me now look at each variable in the equation more systematically.

Population and Production

As I note earlier, a growing population generates selection pressures for expanded production; and reciprocally, increased production will allow a population to grow in a cycle that ends with the demographic transition or with the disintegration of the population. This same growth can also exert pressures for the segmentation and perhaps differentiation of new kinds of corporate units as well as the consolidation and centralization of power which, as the equation emphasizes, also affect production. Other demographic forces can also be important, particularly the distribution of the population. Until human and physical capital can be concentrated in space, production will remain somewhat limited. But with urbanization, the large-scale corporate units housing more complex divisions of labor can coordinate human and physical capital, thereby increasing production.

Technology, Capital, Resources, and Production

Access to natural resources is critical to production. Environments vary in terms of how plentiful resources are, but to a very great extent, technologies or knowledge about resources and how to gain access to them, along with the formation of physical and human capital to gather and convert them, determine resource levels of a population. Hunter-gatherers knew nothing about most of the resources that industrial societies use, even if they were sitting under their feet; and so, it is fairly obvious that access is relative to technology and capital formation. Moreover, as I discuss below, market dynamics are also critical in gaining access to resources. When technologies and capital, both physical and human, and property flow through markets, they can be imported and increase access to resources, or the resources themselves can be imported from other populations. In either case, the level of resources available for production increases.

Corporate Units and Production

For production to expand, non-kin corporate units must eventually emerge because as long as production occurs within kinship, even within fairly large kin units like those of unilinear descent systems, it will be limited. Distinct entrepreneurial units dedicated solely to production must differentiate from kinship to organize technologies, physical capital, and human capital; and such organization cannot emerge without clear and stable definitions of property rights to own and coordinate elements of production (i.e., technology, physical capital, and human capital). Thus, corporate units engaged in purely economic activity depend upon property rights sanctioned by the consolidation and centralization of power. If centers of power do not create laws defining and enforcing property rights, however, these rights will not operate as a stimulus to economic activity; rather, they will tend to preserve elites' traditional privileges and, hence, perpetuate a relatively static economy as capital is channeled to elite consumption and as power is used to stifle change-generating technological innovation. Thus, as centers of power extend their influence, additional corporate units must be created to regulate both production and distribution. Without distinct types of corporate units devoted to production and the consolidation of power, then, the overall level of production will be limited. Consolidation of the bases of power, coupled with moderate centralization, is most likely to encourage the formation of entrepreneurial corporate units, while allowing for the regulation of these productive corporate units.

Markets, Money, and Production

As Fernand Braudel (1982, 1977) emphasized in his history of commerce in Europe, markets exist at different levels. The "lower" markets consist in ascending order of (1) person-to-person barter, (2) person-to-person exchange using money, (3) peddlers who personally make goods and sell them for money while extending credit, and (4) shopkeepers who sell with money and credit goods that they do not make. At the "upper" level are (5) fairs with relatively stable locations where higher volumes of goods are bought and sold with money and credit, (6) trade centers where brokers and bourgeoisie sell goods and services, including credit and other financial instruments, and (7) private markets where merchants are engaged in high-risk and high-profit speculations in trade revolving around long chains of exchange between buyers and sellers. Markets are thus limited by the availability of stable money and credit, but once relatively free markets using money and credit emerge, production will increase. Money allows individual and collective actors to express preferences with a generalized medium of value—money. Once actors can express their individual preferences in markets without the need to have a particular good to barter for another good, aggregate demand increases and becomes more diversified. In turn, as demand diversifies, markets can differentiate, thereby creating new niches in which buyers and sellers compete. Such competition is Darwinian, with the more successful surviving and the less successful either ceasing to operate or moving to a new resource niche, but in the end market activity escalates, thereby creating demands for higher levels and more diversity of goods and, eventually, services to facilitate production and distribution. Credit accelerates these trends because now a buyer does not have to possess the money in hand, only the ability to pay lenders back at some future date.

Once money, credit, and free market systems are widely dispersed across the territories housing a population, production can expand; and increasingly, production revolves around generating services that can facilitate distribution—such as banking, insuring, and underwriting. Eventually, markets begin to buy and sell stocks and other financial instruments marking ownership of corporate units within both the productive and distributive sectors of a society. Speculation in these instruments becomes another higher-level market beyond Braudel's typology, around which bundles of financial services are bought and sold.

Of course, for most of human history, markets did not exist; and even when they emerged around fifteen thousand years ago, they stayed at the lower level in Braudel's typology. Only over the last few thousand years have higher-level markets appeared, and as a result, production was limited until recently in history. Once markets begin to spread, however, they have multiplicative effects on all of the variables in the equation above. Power must be consolidated and centralized to regulate the increased volume of transactions and to assure that money, credit, and other financial instruments are not misused. The differentiation of corporate units dramatically expands in order to organize the increased variety and volume of goods and services being produced and distributed. Further, the multiplicative effects among the elements of the economy are accelerated because technology, physical capital, and human capital can be bought and sold in markets that, in turn, generate a dramatic expansion in definitions of property which, themselves, become subject to market forces. Once market forces expand trade, access can potentially be gained to resources in remote regions and with the territories of other populations.

Power and Production

Power cannot expand without the productive outputs that exceed the subsistence needs of a population. As production increases, it not only provides the surplus resources beyond subsistence that, via taxation, can be used to sustain bases of power, but increasing production also generates selection pressures for new forms of regulation. Once production and distribution occur outside kinship, pressures for the regulation of corporate units, markets, money, credit, and other financial services build. At first, traders generated their own codes and enforcement procedures, as was the case of the Hanseatic League in northern Europe, but eventually, selection pressures mounted for the consolidation and centralization of power, as was the case among the merchants of Venice and as is currently the situation in the global economy. There is, of course, no inevitability to this mobilization of power to regulate distributive and productive forces, but once it exists, it has positive effects on all those variables in the equation on production. Regulation of markets sustains the money supply and monitors abuses of markets; consolidation of the administrative and material incentive bases of power generates new kinds of corporate units; regulation allows for integration of the population within territories whose members, in turn, increase demands for expanded production; and the multiplicative relations among technology, physical capital, and human capital are accelerated with moderate degrees of regulation, especially as polity expands and clarifies definitions of property that, in turn, regularize the development and distribution of technology and capital.

REGULATION DYNAMICS

The Law of Regulation

Regulation is a force that drives actors to increase the capacity to control and coordinate members of a population and the units organizing their activities; and the higher the valences for regulation, the greater are the selection pressures for the mobilization of power. Power, in turn, is the capacity of one set of actors to dictate the actions of another set of actors. As I have emphasized, there are two dimensions of power: (1) consolidation and (2) centralization. As societies become more complex, problems of coordination and control escalate, increasing the values of regulation and, hence, selection pressures for the mobilization of power. For most of human history as hunter-gatherers, power was not mobilized because values for regulation as a force were very low. When hunter-gatherers settled down or when they found themselves in conflict over territory, however, regulation as a social force increased, setting into motion selection pressures favoring those populations that could consolidate and, to the degree necessary, centralize power. Thus, regulation as a social force remained recessive during hunting and gathering modes of production and social organization, but once selection pushed populations to develop new mechanisms for coordination and control, power became a dominant property of human populations, thereby changing forever the nature of institutional evolution. With power, institutional differentiation and development could proceed because there was an enhanced capacity to coordinate and control diverse actors within and between institutional domains.

$$RG = \{(PO_{CL}) \times [(N) \times (P) \times (DF_{MS,MY})]\} +$$
$$\{[(PO_{CL}) \times (+/= PO_{CT})] \times [(I) \times (TH_{IN})] \times (TH_{EX})]\}$$

where:

RG = the capacity for coordination and control of a population.

PO_{CL} = the degree of consolidation ($_{CL}$) of all bases of power (PO)

N = the absolute size (N) of a population

P = the level of production (P)

$DF_{MS,MY}$ = the level of differentiation (DF) of market systems ($_{MS}$) of distribution using money, credit, and other financial instruments ($_{MY}$)

PO_{CT} = the degree to which power (PO) along all bases is centralized ($_{CT}$)

I = the degree of inequality (I) in the distribution of valued resources among members of a population

TH_{IN} = the level of internal ($_{IN}$) threat (TH) stemming from actual conflict, or perceived potential for conflict among organizational units and/or subpopulations

TH_{EX} = the level of external ($_{EX}$) threat (TH) stemming from actual conflict with other populations, or perceived potential for such conflict

This equation argues that there are two blocks of forces and properties of social systems that increase the level of regulation (RG). One block denotes those variable properties of a society that increase the consolidation of the four bases of power (PO_{CL})—coercion, symbols, administration, and manipulation of material incentives, while the other block specifies those conditions that increase the centralization of power across the four bases.

1. Consolidation is the process of mobilizing bases of power, but the particular profile of consolidation can, of course, vary because rarely is each base equally mobilized. There are, however, some configurations that are more likely than others. For example, coercive mobilization is often accompanied by high levels of administrative mobilization, whereas symbolic and material mobilization often occur together with moderate amounts of administrative mobilization and only strategic use of coercion. No one base, by itself, can regulate a population; other bases are almost always activated but it is the relative proportions of activation that make a difference in how the institution of polity and, by extension, law become structured. For our present purposes, we

need not worry about these empirical details; what is required is a general principle on those forces and properties of societies that mobilize power along any or all of its bases. In the first block of variables, the consolidation of power is multiplicatively related to the size of the population (N), per se, and to the multiplicative relation between growing production (P) and expanding markets using money, credit, and other financial instruments ($DF_{MS,MY}$). As production increases, stimulating the expansion of markets, and vice versa, selection pressures for regulation of markets and the corporate units engaged in production also increase. These pressures mount as money and credit are used in markets. Equally important, the surplus wealth generated by production and market activity, especially markets using money, provides the resources necessary to support all bases of power (PO). The coercive base can be mobilized by other means, such as kin loyalties, but larger-scale mobilization of this base ultimately depends upon the ability to pay officers of coercion and to finance their operations. Similarly, the administrative base can be organized along kinship lines or patterns of personal loyalties, but in the end, the base can only expand when its incumbents are hired for salaries in labor markets. The material incentive base can, for a time, operate through manipulation of redistribution of the products of production, such as food surpluses, or through the allocation of plots of land, but for this base to control larger populations, selective taxation, patronage, and other forms of bestowing material well-being depend upon the use of monetary resources that can only be generated on a large scale when markets are operative. Finally, the symbolic base of power can operate effectively through charisma and abilities of leaders to manipulate symbols, but still, without financial resources and systems of distribution, appeals to symbols will not reach larger populations.

2. The second block of variables in the equation on regulation (RG) denotes the properties of societies that increase the degree to which power is centralized, or concentrated (PO_{CT}). Consolidation of power initiates centralization (PO_{CL}), but these effects of consolidation alone cannot generate high levels of centralization. Additional properties of a society must also come into play: inequality (I), internal threats (TH_{IN}), and external threats (TH_{EX}). These are all multiplicatively related because concentrated power is used to extract resources and, hence, increase inequality; inequality poses threats that require more centralization of power to regulate tensions and conflicts over resources; and centralized power and inequality often lead centers of power to create external threats to justify more centralization of power. Similarly, internal threats can be magnified to legitimate the use of power. But, both external or internal threats alone will cause centralization of power, and once this process of centralization is initiated it is used to regulate a population to a higher degree.

I could have written the equation in a simpler form: $RG = (PO_{CL})$ x $(+/= PO_{CT})$. That is, the capacity to regulate is a joint function of the multiplicative relation (positive, but then leveling off) of consolidation on centralization of power. But such an equation does not offer a sense for what forces increase consolidation of power or what properties of societies beyond consolidation increase centralization of power. At times, I have (Turner 1995) written the two blocks as separate equations—that is, $PO_{CL} = (N)$ x $(P$ x $DF_{MS,MY})$ and $PO_{CT} = (+/= PO_{CL})$ x $[(I)$ x (TH_{IN}) x $(TH_{EX})]$. I want to emphasize, however, that the force pushing for the consolidation and centralization of power is regulation and that this force generates selection pressures on the mobilization of power, and so, I have written out the more complicated equation emphasizing how consolidation and centralization stand in multiplicative relations with other forces and properties of social systems to increase regulation. Let me now backtrack and examine each block of variables in more detail, beginning with the first block.

Population Growth and the Consolidation of Power

Historically, population growth among settled hunter-gatherers led to some degree of consolidation, often in the form of "Big Men" who would assume the reins of power, using a combination of coercion, symbols, manipulation of material incentives, and a small cadre of lieutenants to administer and monitor decisions (Johnson and Earle 1987). With population growth, however, the logistical problems of coordinating and controlling the larger social mass generated selection pressures for even more consolidation of power. After segmentation reaches its limits in structuring activity, growing populations are likely to differentiate and urbanize; and as they do so, control problems become that much greater, generating additional selection pressures to find a way to coordinate and control diverse activities. At first, the authority and descent systems of kinship could be used, but eventually pressures for further consolidation led to the formation of the state.

Production, Distribution, and the Consolidation of Power

As populations grow, selection for new forms of production ensue; and if societies of the past were to remain adapted to their environments, gathering and conversion of resources into goods shifted toward horticulture and, eventually, to agriculture. As production expands, new systems for distribution begin to emerge, at first on a small scale (barter) and, over time, ascending up Braudel's scale of lower to higher markets, and beyond Braudel's scale to metamarkets dealing in financial instruments (e.g., money, stocks, bonds, derivatives). These demographic, productive, and distributive forces have all generated selection pressures on a population for coordination and control. Large populations, if they are to remain a coherent society, needed to be coordinated within a territory; and if power could not emerge, they generally de-evolved to smaller and less complex societies, or were conquered by more organized populations. Historically, production initially expanded within kinship systems, mobilizing power relations among kindred to coordinate and control individuals. Growing populations that could not develop more complex kinship structures using descent rules to connect families together as productive units often had a difficult time adapting to the environment, and without mobilizing each base of power to some degree, coordination of kin would be difficult. As production moved outside kinship, the problems of controlling independent corporate units escalated, dramatically increasing selection pressures for the consolidation of power. Similarly, distribution within and between kin units would require some degree of political control, but once markets began to use generalized media of exchange such as money and credit, selection for their regulation increased, eventually causing more consolidation of power. And, as distribution reaches very high levels to even a global scale, these pressures escalate dramatically. Indeed, the global system is currently experiencing selection pressures to find some way to consolidate power to coordinate world trade within the limits imposed by high degrees of consolidated power within nation-states. Moreover, once high volume and velocity markets using money exist, the political legitimacy of polity (a symbolic basis of power) increasingly depends upon a stable currency (i.e., low inflation) and stability in market forces (e.g., managing the business cycle, or keeping accounting practices transparent and banking practices honest).

Consolidation and Centralization of Power

To consolidate any base of power is, to a degree, to centralize power. As leaders seek to increase their hold on coercive, symbolic, material, or administrative power, they create structures for making decisions and, in doing so, centralize each base. Once some degree of consolidation exists along each base, leaders of each respective base often form coalitions, or, alternatively, engage in conflict, with the winner pulling together under a more centralized power those who have lost in the struggle. For example, historically in Europe, the Roman Catholic Church mobilized several bases of power but confronted emerging states doing the same thing; and out of their struggle over several centuries a more centralized profile of all bases of power emerged. More recently, religious leaders in Iran in the 1980s were able to translate their control of symbolic bases of power into the capture of coercive and administrative bases in the aftermath of the Iranian revolution; and in the end, power was centralized around religious elites, although their hold on power is growing more tenuous in recent years. Thus, consolidation of power, per se, will centralize power along each base to some extent, but more fundamentally, initial consolidation typically leads to competition and struggle among leaders of varying bases, and out of these processes, power becomes more centralized, at least up to a certain point. For power to be highly centralized, other dynamics must come into play, with inequality and threats being the most important.

Inequality, Internal Threats, and Centralization of Power

Inequality will almost always lead to the centralization of power, particularly its coercive and administrative bases, as a means to control the tension and potential conflict among members of various social strata. When inequality is high, the level of internal threat to elites increases, leading them to extract resources to finance social control. Ironically, these practices only increase inequality, thereby escalating threat. And if this cycle of inequality-threat-centralization of power, followed by more inequality-threat-centralization, continues, very authoritarian regimes emerge. For a time, manipulation of symbols and, perhaps, material incentives can keep a lid on rising threats, but to the extent that centers of power must rely upon large coercive and administrative structures to maintain order, they must constantly usurp resources to pay their agents and, as a consequence, increase inequality and threat.

External Threat and Centralization of Power

Threats from outside a society will lead to the centralization of power so that resources can be mobilized to deal with the threat. Sometimes the threat can be bioecological, but more typically, threat comes from competition and/or conflict with another population. As competition or conflict increases, power is concentrated along all bases. Symbols are mobilized to encourage members of a population to make sacrifices to deal with the enemy; material incentives are directed at plans and programs to combat the enemy; administrative control is tightened to assure that resources are directed at the enemy; and coercive forces are mobilized to not only deal with the external threat, but to control internal threats that might emerge among segments of the population as power is ever more centralized.

As mentioned earlier, internal and external threats are often related. Centers of power have frequently engaged in warfare or manufactured external enemies in order to deflect attention from the inequalities and abusive practices used to maintain order, but as Max Weber (1922) and, more recently, Theda Skocpol (1979) have documented, when these leaders lose a war, their legitimacy soon unravels and internal conflict is likely to follow. So, it is always a high stakes game when centers of power seek to manufacture external enemies as a way to bolster their symbolic base of power and to justify their policies aggravating inequalities. These dynamics can also work the other way around: prolonged conflicts, whatever their origins, can aggravate internal threats as inequalities increase and as the abusive practices of centers of power are resented by, potentially, both elites and those lower in the stratification system. For, to mobilize a society's resources for external activities involves the use of power to extract and focus resources on enemies; and as centers of power do so, they demand sacrifices from many segments of a population who, over the long haul, come to resent centers of power, initially withdrawing legitimacy from the state and, later, perhaps mobilizing to counter the coercive and administrative control of the state. Thus, once power is centralized to deal with threats, the longer the threat persists without clear resolution, the more likely is internal threat to escalate.

DISTRIBUTION DYNAMICS

The Law of Distribution

As emphasized in chapter 1, distribution revolves around two elements: (1) the *infrastructure* for moving people, resources, and information about a population; and (2) the *exchange* of resources. The two are, of course, related with an extensive distributive infrastructure encouraging exchange, and with exchanges in markets pushing for an expanded infrastructure that can extend the reach of markets. Still, these two elements of distribution are distinctive because other properties of societies can accelerate or retard either, somewhat independently of each other. For example, a centralized political system may desire transportation facilities for moving military equipment and personnel rapidly without much consideration for the effects of these facilities on markets; indeed, free markets may be viewed suspiciously by authoritarian regimes. The equation below summarizes the key forces that increase the overall level of distribution—both infrastructural and exchange distribution.

$$DS = \{[(N) \times (+/-P) \times DF_{MS,MY}) \times (CA_{PH,MY})] \times [(PO_{CL}) \times (+/-PO_{CT})]\} \times DF_{CP}$$

where:
DS = the volume, velocity, scale, and scope of distribution
N = the size of the population

P = the level of production

$DF_{MS,MY}$ = the level of differentiation (DF) of market systems ($_{MS}$) using money and other financial instruments ($_{MY}$)

$CA_{PH,MY}$ = the level of physical ($_{PH}$) capital (CA) formation, including liquid capital or money and other financial instruments ($_{MY}$) that can purchase physical capital

PO_{CL} = the degree of consolidation ($_{CL}$) of the four bases of power (PO)

PO_{CT} = the degree of centralization ($_{CT}$) of all bases of power (PO)

DF_{CP} = the level of differentiation (DF) among corporate units ($_{CP}$) organizing the activities of members of a population

The multiplicative relations among the variables in the first block of the equation—that is, population size (N), production (P), market differentiation ($DF_{MS,MY}$), and the formation of physical capital (CA_{PH})—interact and accelerate the level of distribution of resources, information, and people (DS). The relation between population growth (N) and production (P) in their mutual effects on distribution (DS) is curvilinear ($+/-$) because very high levels of population growth eventually exceed the capacity of production to support all members of the population; or, alternatively, population growth begins to drain surplus production as demands for social welfare programs use up capital that could be reinvested in production or that could be deployed to stimulate markets or build out infrastructures. When population growth or any force stimulates expanded production, the differentiation of market systems (DF_{MS}) occurs, and the formation of physical capital (CA_{PH}) increases. Exchange distribution encourages infrastructural development while generating the surplus wealth that, as capital, can be used to expand production and to build out distributive infrastructures. In turn, as populations grow, production expands, markets develop, and surplus capital is created, the second block of variables in the equation is activated—that is, the consolidation (PO_{CL}) and centralization (PO_{CT}) of power. As production and capital formation rise, capital is taxed and used to consolidate power (PO_{CL}) and, thereby, coordinate larger numbers of individuals and new productive units; and as centers of power do so, they generally expand the distributive system. Consolidation of all bases of power (PO_{CL}) causes moderate degrees of centralization of power (PO_{CT}), which in turn becomes a crucial condition for the differentiation of market systems and, indirectly, for the development of distributive infrastructures. As markets become more complex, some external regulation by centers of power is more essential, and eventually, infrastructural development becomes so expensive that it can only be financed by centers of power with the capacity to tax economic surplus. In turn, as centers of power encourage exchange distribution and build out infrastructures, production and capital formation increase; and all of these forces together increase the level of distribution, especially as these forces also influence growth in the population. Too much centralization of power around its coercive and administrative bases, however, will lead to over-regulation of both production and distribution, thereby mitigating the dynamic relationship between production and distribution (hence, the positively curvi-linear relationship $[+/-]$ between centralization of power and distribution). Too little regulation can cause chaos in many forms—for example, corruption, deep business cycles, and overspeculation. Thus, when centralization occurs primarily around the symbolic and material incentive bases, with moderate lev-els of centralization around the coercive and administrative bases, sufficient regulatory power exists to mitigate against chaos while encouraging entrepre-neurial activities in both production and exchange distribution.

The level of differentiation of corporate units (DF_{CP}) is also critical in increasing distribution (DS). As population growth, production, and capital formation affect the consolidation and centralization of power, the overall level of differentiation among members of a population increases. Larger populations must find new structural formations within kinship and, later, outside of kin-ship to coordinate the expanded division of labor. Rising production similarly generates new kinds of corporate structures to coordinate more workers. Capi-tal formation such as this stimulates markets, and the building of distributive infrastructures further expands the number and diversity of corporate units. And, both the consolidation and centralization of all bases of power cause new organizational formations to emerge. As new specialized corporate units emerge, exchanges between them dramatically increase the level of distribu-tion, especially since many of these new structures are not directly engaged in gathering or converting resources and, hence, must pursue exchanges to receive them. Now let me examine each of the variables in the equation in more detail.

Population Size and Distribution

Independent of any other force, a larger population poses more distributive problems than a smaller one. Thus, as populations grow, logistical loads for distributing resources and information increase, setting off selection pressures that expand distribution. Such is especially likely to be the case when popula-tion growth is accompanied by structural differentiation in which individuals playing specialized roles or corporate units engaged in specialized activities must exchange resources in order to remain viable in their respective environ-ments. And, to the degree that population growth causes production to expand and power to be mobilized, then the effects of a growing population are that much greater as new outputs from production require distribution and as new forms of consolidated and centralized power begin to regulate exchanges and infrastructural development.

Yet, if population growth is too rapid or too great, productive outputs are distributed as welfare, and hence, cannot be used as capital reinvestments to stimulate more dynamic markets or even infrastructural development. Such is especially likely to be the case when the consolidation of power involves extraction of productive resources to feed corrupt elites who, in turn, distribute just enough material incentives to sustain a potentially restive population. Under these conditions, population growth works against expansion of markets and infrastructural development because elites will rely upon traditional and conservative modes of taxation and patronage. Population diversity only aggravates these roadblocks to market activity, especially if diversity is correlated with high levels of inequality into patterns of ethnic stratification.

Population density will increase market activity over what it would be with low density because, unlike a rural population, which can often be self-sustaining, people in urban areas must purchase sustenance in local markets in order to survive. Such market activity tends to fall into the lower levels discussed by Braudel; and these kinds of markets are not highly dynamic, nor do they generate pressures for their own expansion in the same way as high-level markets using money and financial instruments do. Moreover, densely settled and poor populations pose social control problems for polity, thus forcing the use of capital resources for sustaining the coercive base of power.

Production and Distribution

There is an obvious relationship between production and distribution; the more that is produced, the more goods that must be distributed. I have separated production and distribution because they reveal somewhat different dynamics, despite their close affinity in most economic theorizing. As production expands, it exerts selection pressures for new distributive structures. These pressures lead to the development of infrastructures for moving goods and commodities about a population, as well as to the differentiation of market systems. Once markets become highly differentiated and dynamic, however, they begin to exert more influence on production in the sense that market demand drives production rather than production pushing market formation.

Thus, a certain threshold of production is necessary to set into motion these endemic dynamics of markets. Without high levels of production, there is simply not enough to distribute to stimulate markets beyond lower-level barter and trade, but as the volume and variety of goods increase, markets using money and credit emerge. Once these kinds of markets are in place, they will often expand to ever higher levels in Braudel's scheme, culminating in complex metamarkets. For such higher-level markets to operate, however, distributive infrastructures for moving resources, commodities, services, and information across long distances must be in place; and once infrastructures are built, they stimulate more differentiation of markets, thereby creating demands for expanded production. It is these feed-forward and feed-back relations that make production and markets stand in a multiplicative relationship to each other in their effects on distribution.

Markets and Distribution

Markets allow for the exchange of commodities and services. As they differentiate, they move up Braudel's hierarchy of markets, eventually using money, credit, and other financial instruments. Exchange with money is revolutionary in that it allows individuals and corporate units to express their preferences as demand in markets without the need to have a commodity to exchange (as is the case in barter). Instead, a generalized medium of exchange—that is, money—provides a common yardstick for determining value; and as the use of money and later other financial instruments are institutionalized, markets become more dynamic. They can exchange goods and services more rapidly; they can exchange a much wider variety of goods; and they can expand into new territories.

Once individual and collective actors can express preferences with money, and indeed borrow money, aggregate demand increases, but more significantly, the diversity of demand increases, stimulating the differentiation of markets that, in turn, creates niches of resources that entrepreneurial activity by individuals and corporate units can seek to exploit. Moreover, as money and financial instruments become part of any transaction, markets for services dramatically expand; and these services become essential for not only maintaining markets but production as well.

As an outgrowth of these processes, metamarkets are generated (Collins, 1990). Media of exchange in one market become the goods exchanged in a metamarket. Thus, money becomes subject to market forces (i.e., is bought and sold), as do other financial instruments such as stocks, bonds, mortgages, derivatives, and futures. Once metamarkets differentiate, production increasingly revolves around services (e.g., brokerage, banking, insuring, accounting, advising, advertising) that, in turn, differentiate markets even more while allowing metamarkets to operate. As production shifts to services, markets begin to use money and financial instruments even more, and as a result they differentiate considerably beyond what is possible when only hard goods are being produced. Moreover, these services become increasingly important in the expansion of markets beyond a population's borders in patterns of long-distance trade.

Once production revolves around services as much as commodities, speculation in metamarkets increases, with the consequence that markets can collapse from overspeculation. As these high-level markets fall, their contraction is felt in all other markets down Braudel's typology of higher-level to lower-level markets. For example, if a stock market collapses, this contraction will eventually decrease aggregate wealth and, hence, demand for all goods and services which, in turn, will lower production and the number of goods and services that can be distributed. Moreover, if metamarkets extend beyond a population's territorial borders, collapse can set off chain reactions that decrease wealth in trading partners and, thereby, demand in external markets. Thus, ironically, production of services drives the expansions of markets, but as the scale, scope, and velocity of these markets increase, they become vulnerable to overspeculation as well as normal cyclical downturns that appear endemic to all markets, thereby lowering production for a time. Yet, even with contraction in markets and de-evolution to lower-level market activity, markets will generally expand in the long run when the production of services becomes as prominent as the production of goods and commodities. For as corporate units are organized to produce services, they have interests in constantly seeking new clients for their services; and as they do so, they exert constant pressure to expand markets and to build out infrastructures to reach ever more numbers of people within and outside a population's borders.

Physical Capital and Distribution

Without capital, not only will production be limited but the differentiation of market systems using money and other financial instruments will also be constrained. There must be physical facilities for high-volume and -velocity exchanges—ports, roads, trading centers, warehouses, communications systems, and the like—and until production reaches relatively high levels, there will be insufficient capital surplus to build infrastructures. And, of course, without surplus capital, reinvestment in new technologies and production systems cannot occur. Moreover, unless there is surplus production, power cannot be sufficiently mobilized to finance the expansion of infrastructures. In fact, while a certain amount of privately financed infrastructural development occurs during early phases of market differentiation, it is the polity that eventually must see this development as essential to its interests, such as making war or encouraging production, that can then be taxed to support governmental activities.

Liquid physical capital is essential in infrastructural expansion because the capacity to finance projects depends upon having resources to pay human capital, buy materials, and reward entrepreneurs. When liquid capital is scarce, however, more traditional forms of organizing distributive activity will dominate (e.g., feudal tenure systems, slavery); and while traditionally organized labor can be used to construct infrastructures, the need to reproduce traditional ties of domination and subjugation imposes limits on how dynamic these efforts can be, although the infrastructures built by agrarian populations like the ancient Romans or Egyptians can be both extensive and impressive in scale. At some point, however, without liquidity of capital and market activity freed from traditional patterns of social relations, limits of infrastructural development are reached and, indeed, even the maintenance of existing infrastructures becomes more difficult. Thus, there is a mutually reinforcing effect between markets using money and the flow of liquid capital that can be used in more efficient ways of organizing large-scale infrastructural projects. If there is no liquid capital, then infrastructure will be limited; but as the amount of money and credit available increases with higher-level market activity, new facilities for accelerating and extending exchange can be built. Thus, market differentiation is, on the one hand, a stimulus to infrastructural growth but, on the other hand, an outcome of such growth.

Structural Differentiation and Distribution

Exchanges occur between individuals and collective units. Thus, the more differentiated are corporate units organizing members of a population's activities, the greater will be the volume of exchange as corporate units seek the resources necessary to sustain themselves. High degrees of differentiation among corporate units come from the interrelated dynamics of population growth, production, physical capital formation, and market systems as well as the consolidation of power. A larger population requires more structural forms to organize activities in a more complex division of labor; increasing production will generate new kinds of corporate units, especially as physical capital and market systems differentiate demand. And all of these combined create resource niches within which organizations seek resources; and from the Darwinian competition among them, new kinds of corporate units are generated as they move to new niches in search of resources or create new resource niches to support themselves. Similarly, the consolidation of power, especially along the administrative base but along all other bases as well, will create new kinds of regulatory corporate units, thus directly expanding the diversity of corporate units organizing activity and seeking resources in markets to sustain themselves. More indirectly, to the extent that the consolidation and centralization of power facilitate production, physical capital formation for infrastructural development, and market distribution, political systems encourage further differentiation of corporate units through their effects on production and distribution.

We need not see Adam Smith's "invisible hand of order" as a necessary outcome of this relationship between differentiation and market development; indeed, just the opposite of "order" has often been the case historically. But once differentiation increases, units must seek resources, including human capital, to sustain themselves; and as they do so, the level of distribution among the individual members of a population as well as the corporate units organizing their activities accelerates dramatically. Units must often seek members in labor markets or clients and members in other markets; necessary supplies, commodities, and services must often be purchased in markets; and even symbolic goods and services must be secured in markets. And, each member of all the diverse corporate units must, in turn, use resources to secure what is necessary to maintain self or household. Thus, differentiation is a prime force behind distributive activity in a society.

REPRODUCTION DYNAMICS

The Law of Reproduction

To survive, members of all species must reproduce themselves. Because humans can survive only in social structures coordinating their activities, reproduction involves considerably more than passing on genes; it also revolves around creating, sustaining, and, if necessary, changing sociocultural formations. Thus, reproduction as a force generates many of the selection pressures driving institutional evolution. The equation below offers a principle on those forces influencing the level of reproductive activity among members of a population.

$$RE = \{[(N) \times (P) \times (DF_{MS,MY})] \times [(PO_{CL}) \times (+/-PO_{CT})]\} \times (DF_{CP})$$

where:

RE = the level of reproductive activity and structures organizing this activity among members of a population

N = the size of the population

P = the level of production

$DF_{MS,MY}$ = the differentiation (DF) of market systems ($_{MS}$) using money and financial instruments ($_{MY}$)

PO_{CL} = the degree of consolidation ($_{CL}$) of all four bases of power (PO)

PO_{CT} = the degree of centralization ($_{CT}$) among all bases of power (PO)

DF_{CP} = the level of differentiation (DF) among corporate units ($_{CP}$) organizing the activities of members of a population

This equation argues that the level of reproductive activity (RE) and the number as well as diversity of structures organizing this activity increase with initial population growth (N) as this growth accelerates production (P) and differentiation of market systems using money ($DF_{MS,MY}$). These three forces stand in a multiplicative relationship to power, causing the consolidation of power (PO_{CL}); and consolidation, in turn, accounts for the initial centralization of power ($+/-PO_{CT}$). As is the case for differentiation, the two sets or blocks of variables revolving around, respectively, population, production, and distribution, on the one hand, and the consolidation and centralization of power, on the other, increase the overall level of differentiation of corporate units (DF_{CP}); and as this differentiation occurs, reproduction (RE) increases because each differentiated unit must reproduce itself in its own way, and incumbents in each structure must acquire the unique culture of the unit as well as the skills to occupy positions and play roles in the unit. Now, let me isolate each variable in the equation for further discussion.

Population and Reproduction

As populations grow, reproduction becomes more problematic. A growing population signals, of course, that individuals are able to reproduce themselves biologically, but the capacity to absorb all these bodies into the broader social structure and culture can increasingly prove difficult. Historically, initial growth of human populations led to the expansion of kinship structures into more complex forms, but these most always produced tensions as large numbers of kin had to live in proximity to each other. Thus, internal conflicts among kin often caused problems in reproducing the kinship system so essential to the biological and social reproduction of individuals. Moreover, as populations became even larger, expanded production and the consolidation/centralization of power increased inequalities to the point of generating conflict that, in turn, threatened reproduction of the entire institutional order.

Thus, the size of a population has always generated enormous selection pressure from reproduction as a macrodynamic force. The population must expand the basic system for biological reproduction—that is, kinship—and find new ways to integrate the more complex social structures and cultures that come with large numbers of individuals having to find niches as adults in the broader society. And the institutional systems created to manage the larger population—particularly economy and polity—increase problems of reproduction in two senses: individuals must find slots in the economy in order to survive, and the ever-increasing complexity of the economy and the consolidation/central-ization of power themselves pose problems of how they are to be reproduced.

Production and Reproduction

As populations grow, selection pressures on production mount. As production expands in response to these pressures, new problems of sociocultural repro-duction escalate, even as sufficient levels of resources allow the larger popula-tion to survive biologically. In a larger, more complex economy, individuals will require additional training for more specialized positions in corporate units, and as inequality increases with economic growth (and centralization of power that results from economic growth), problems of finding niches in the economy increase, as do resentments of those who are denied access to those positions that increase material well-being, prestige, and other forms of cultural capital and power. As these tensions mount, conflicts increase, posing problems of how the structure and culture of the entire society are to be reproduced, thereby generating selection pressures for new systems of reproduction.

Market Systems and Reproduction

The expansion of market systems will increase inequality (Lenski 1966) until very high levels of market development are reached—thereby aggravating the problems of reproduction discussed above. But markets are systems that differ-entiate a population not only by social class but also by the number of special-ized positions in wider varieties of corporate units. Thus, markets create new positions for which increasingly specialized training is required, thus expanding the number and variety of reproductive structures—e.g., primary and second-ary schools, universities, trade schools, technical institutes, and the like. The total volume of activity geared toward reproduction increases, especially as kinship systems begin to cede over many socialization functions to non-kin corporate units. Moreover, as markets develop, a labor market is created as the principal mechanism for moving individuals from reproductive structures to positions in the increased number and variety of corporate units.

As labor markets expand, structures increasingly come to rely upon educa-tional credentials for placement of individuals in positions. Markets thus become more involved in the process of supplying individuals who will ulti-mately occupy positions in all institutional spheres and who, as a result, will be very much involved in reproducing the corporate units of each institutional sphere.

Power and Reproduction

As population, production, and markets all grow, the consolidation and centralization of power become essential for coordination and control of relations
within and between individuals and the corporate units in which they are
incumbents. As a consequence, power becomes a principal mechanism of
reproduction because it will regulate structures so that they reproduce social
relations, while at the same time, it will finance new reproductive structures
outside of kinship, such as schools.

Power will also regulate production and distribution processes necessary for
reproduction. For example, the amount of physical capital available for economic activity, the scope of the distributive infrastructure, and the dynamics of
markets will increasingly be subject to some regulation by centers of power
and the administration of law. As power is used in this way, it has reproductive
consequences for a society's ability to sustain itself in its environment.

Differentiation and Reproduction

The more differentiated are the structures organizing individual and societal
activities, the more complex is the process of reproduction. Each structure will
channel resources to sustain itself in its local environmental niche, especially if
it must compete with other units in a resource niche. Equally fundamental is
the differentiation of new reproductive structures to train individuals to occupy
positions in very diverse kinds of structures; and as differentiation of corporate
units increases, kinship becomes increasingly inadequate to provide the necessary socialization for incumbency in corporate units. As a result, a wide variety
of distinctive educational structures devoted to social reproduction are differentiated from kinship. Thus, the level of differentiation among corporate units
will dramatically increase selection pressures for the expansion of reproductive
structures.

FORCES, SELECTION, AND
INSTITUTIONAL EVOLUTION

The theoretical principles on population, production, distribution, regulation,
and reproduction presented in the equations above are, to say the least,
abstract, as is the effort to summarize the relations among the variables in the
equations. Yet, if we are to develop more general theoretical principles on the
evolution of human social institutions, it is necessary to move beyond descriptions of institutions to explanations of why they would emerge in the first place

and, subsequently, develop during the course of societal evolution. Of course, we need to use these principles to explain actual empirical events, but it is best to start with a theory of the forces driving these events, now and in the past.

I have emphasized that, at each level of social organization, there are distinctive forces driving the formation of the structures and the attendant culture unique to each level. At the macro level, institutional systems are the basic structures, as is the culture of these structures. And, while institutions are ultimately composed of corporate and categoric units, as well as the focused and unfocused encounters by which these meso structures are sustained, we need to remain at the macro level to understand how institutional systems evolve. The forces operating at the macro level generate selection pressures on populations whose members seek to find solutions to the problems posed by these pressures. At first, selection pressures came from the biophysical environment, but as the complexity of social structure and culture increased, selection pressures came from the very sociocultural systems that had been used to increase adaptation to the biophysical environment. Thus, as institutional systems evolve, they constantly create new environments generating new kinds of second-order selection pressures that push institutional evolution toward ever more complex formations. Ironically, as the scale and complexity of institutional systems has increased, they have caused environmental degradation generating a new set of biophysical selection pressures on institutional systems. Thus, even as humans have created sociocultural environments to which they must respond, they have come full circle back to issues faced by the earliest hunter-gatherers who had to find a way to sustain themselves in the biophysical environment.

In the chapters to follow, I review the emergence and development of the core institutions that first enabled humans to adapt to the biophysical and, increasingly, the sociocultural environments of their own creation. We start with hunting-gathering and, then, move through horticultural, agrarian, industrial, and post-industrial societies, exploring the emergence, differentiation, and development of six core institutions: economy, kinship, religion, polity, law, and education. As becomes evident, these institutions are universal because they represent the earliest responses to selection pressures generated by macrodynamic forces—population, production, distribution, regulation, and reproduction.

Initially, selection for production and reproduction dominated the institutional order of hunter-gatherers, but as human societies became larger and more complex, other macrodynamic forces—population, regulation, and distribution—generated selection pressures. Indeed, at different stages of societal evolution, a somewhat different configuration of selection pressures has dominated, indicating that macrodynamic forces exert varying degrees of pressure on human organization at different points in the history of human societies. And, by the time industrial and post-industrial societies emerged, all of these forces placed pressure on all institutional systems.

Macrodynamic forces put pressures directly on each institutional system, but there are also indirect effects. Because institutions are interrelated, the forces driving any one institution may exert their effects through this institution as it influences the organization of another institution. For example, regulation influences the economy primarily through its effects on the polity and law which, in turn, regulate economic activity; reproduction influences the economy through its effects on kinship and education; distribution has direct effects on the economy as markets are created, but much of this effect operates through pressures on polity to build out infrastructures; and so on for each set of reciprocal relations among institutions. Thus, we will have to be attuned to the mutual effects on institutional systems on each other because it is through these interdependencies among institutions that macrodynamic forces often operate.

CONCLUSION

Much analysis of societal evolution emphasizes a "master force," such as technology (e.g., Lenski 1966), energy transfers (White 1959; Freese 1997), or population (Spencer 1874–1896; Chase-Dunn 2001) as having historically driven the movement of societies from simple to more complex forms. None of these kinds of explanations is wrong, per se, but just incomplete. The analysis of societal evolution requires, I believe, a theory of macrodynamics consisting of abstract principles about the forces driving the formation and change of institutions (Turner 1995). Societal evolution has, at the macro level, revolved around the emergence and transformation of institutional systems, and these systems represent responses to the selection pressures generated by five fundamental forces: population, production, reproduction, distribution, and regulation. These are not functional needs, as traditional functional analysis might argue, but rather, they are forces that push actors in certain directions. They set in motion selection pressures on actors to find solutions to problems or face the prospects of societal disintegration. Since virtually all human societies except the newest nations have collapsed at some point in their histories, there is no guarantee that individuals and collective actors can respond adequately to selection pressures. Still, over the long course of human evolution, the complexity of human societies has increased, or to phrase it another way, the level of differentiation and development of social institutions has increased. So, some societies at some places and times in history have been able to respond to selection pressures posed by macrodynamic forces.

Not only has much analysis of societal development been mono-causal, even more has been atheoretical. That is, descriptive accounts of societal evolution have been offered, and with the exception of the "master force" presumed to drive social transformations, descriptions rather than explanations of stages in societal evolution have been offered. Not all analysts have so restricted their approaches in this way, but many have. My goal is to build on previous theoretical approaches by offering a general theory of the macrolevel forces that explain, I believe, the evolution of human social institutions and, by extension, all of the meso and micro structures from which institutional systems are built. Before tracing the history of institutional evolution, however, we need a review of the basic elements that make up each institution and of how selection has pushed actors to create and use these elements to build institutional systems.

Chapter Three

The Institutional Core

Human social institutions emerged in response to selection pressures generated by macrodynamic forces. As institutions evolved, they were constructed from meso structures—at first groups and later organizations and communities—that could address problems posed by increases in the values and valences of these macrodynamic forces. In this chapter, my goal is to outline the basic elements of the core institutional systems and assess the kinds of selection pressures that caused them to emerge in the first place. Later, we can explore how institutions evolved during the movement from hunting and gathering through horticulture and agrarianism to industrial and post-industrial societies.

ECONOMY

Selection Pressures and the Economy

All life forms must secure resources from their environment, convert them, if necessary, into usable substances, and then distribute these substances to life-sustaining parts. These activities emerge as a consequence of the selection pressures generated by production and distribution. When life forms must be organized to survive, however, group members' activities are coordinated in the pursuit of resources; and once groupings of individuals gather resources, the process of converting these resources and distributing them to members of the group moves from being an individual act to an *economy* whereby cultural codes and group structures organize gathering, conversion, and distribution.

Gathering, conversion, and distribution of resources are thus fundamental to the survival of a species; and in the case of humans, these processes reveal a structure—that is, the organization of distinctive types of status positions, normative expectations, enacted roles, and embellishments from cultural value

57

premises and beliefs. All other institutional activities and forms are guided by the economy, but we do not want to go so far as to assert that the economy determines the profile of all other institutions because other institutional systems have important effects on the economy. We *can* say this much: if we know how economic activity is organized, we can make fairly accurate predictions about the structure and operation of other institutions.

Elements of Economic Organization

Because the economy is so directly tied to the forces of production and distribution, the elements of all economies are the same for those outlined for production and distribution. To review briefly from the last chapter, economies reveal certain basic elements (Turner 1995, 1972): (1) *technology*, or knowledge about how to control and manipulate the natural and social environments; (2) *physical capital*, or implements used to gather, produce, and distribute, as well as the liquid resources like money that can buy such implements; (3) *human capital*, or the number as well as the distribution of characteristics (knowledge, skill, motivations) among those who occupy positions and play roles in the economy; (4) *property*, or the socially constructed right to own, possess, and use physical and symbolic objects of value; and (5) *entrepreneurship*, or the way in which (1), (2), (3), and (4) are *organized* for gathering, producing, and distributing (Parsons and Smelser 1956). The economy as an institution can thus be defined *as the use of technologies, physical and human capital, entrepreneurial structures, and property systems for the gathering of resources, the conversion of resources into usable commodities, and the distribution of these commodities to members of a population.*

The first economies were very simple, and most of these elements revealed very low values. Technology revolved around knowledge of how to exploit environments for their surface plant and animal life, physical capital consisted of digging sticks and perhaps bows and arrows, human capital involved the skills and energy used to gather plants and hunt animals, property did not exist except in the sense of a home range among various bands of hunter-gatherers, and entrepreneurship was organized by the kinship system in which division of labor in the nuclear family also determined how gathering, converting, and distributing resources was to occur. Thus, the economy was fused with kinship in the first human societies, although it is relatively easy to distinguish between economic and family activities of kin members within small bands. Still, kinship was humans' first social structure, and all institutional systems were embedded in the culture and structure of kinship for most of human history.

Population growth exerted selection pressures for increased economic outputs and distribution. At first, kinship could be used as the principal entrepreneurial and distributive structure, but as populations grew larger, non-kin structures for organizing the economy became necessary. Some of these non-kin structures emerged in response to selection pressures outside the economy proper. Regulation generated selection for polity and law as a means to coordinate and control the larger population; reproduction created selection for more explicit religious structures and, eventually, the schools of the educational system; and distribution increased selection pressures on infrastructures and markets to move people, information, and resources among the larger population. Thus, the very selection pressures coming from the mutually escalating causal effects among population, production, and distribution that led to the expansion of kinship also caused the emergence of new institutional systems as the capacities of kin structures to organize a population were exceeded.

Once the economy became more differentiated from kinship, new entrepreneurial structures began to organize technology, physical and human capital, and property. Indeed, the scale of the economy was limited by its embeddedness in kinship, where the norms of kinship dominated over those for economic organization. With non-kin corporate units within the economy proper (e.g., guilds, manorial estates, shops, banks, chartered corporations, businesses) and outside the economy (e.g., the state, religious bureaucracies, townships and cities), the dynamic potential for economic development increased because these corporate units were less restricted by kinship as primarily a reproductive rather than a productive structure. Moreover, as new entrepreneurial systems responding to selection for increased distribution emerged (e.g., markets, infrastructures for transportation/communication), the dynamism of the economy increased even more. Indeed, because markets distribute productive outputs while at the same time moving the elements of the economy (technology, physical capital, labor, and property) into new entrepreneurial combinations, they became ever more the engine that pushed production as economies moved out of agrarianism into industrial and post-industrial forms. Yet, even as the economy differentiates and develops, it nonetheless responds at the most basic level to selection pressures stemming from the forces of production and distribution.

Yet, second-order selection pressures stemming from the differentiation of other institutional systems like polity, religion, law, and education from kinship also begin to push economic development. These other institutional systems all depend upon surplus economic outputs for their support because these systems cannot sustain themselves without physical capital, especially liquid capital, and markets for distributing human capital. For as the corporate units comprising each institutional domain grow, they become bureaucratized and, thereby, depend upon liquid revenue streams to pay labor and to maintain infrastructures. And, as the viability of these structures depends upon economic outputs, the corporate units of each institutional domain place pressures on the economy for continued development. Thus, as the economy became fully differentiated from kinship, differentiation of each institutional domain generated additional selection pressures on the economy.

KINSHIP

During hunting and gathering, all institutional formations were discernible only by the distinctive types of activities of family members as they sought food (economic), raised their children (education), addressed the supernatural (religion), and resolved disputes (law). Other institutions, such as polity, were hardly visible even in this minimal sense of observable activities among family members. In very global terms, the history of human development over the last 15,000 years has revolved around two trends in kinship: (1) the initial elaboration of kinship from its simple form in hunting and gathering societies to accommodate the selection pressures generated by increased size and complexity of society as humans discovered horticulture, and then with further evolution, (2) the differentiation of new institutional systems outside of kinship, and a corresponding reduction in the scale of kinship back to the simple form evident with hunter–gatherers (Blumberg and Winch 1977; Turner 1997, 1972).

Selection Pressures and Kinship

Systems of kinship emerged and have persisted in human populations for the simple reason that they have facilitated survival. Kinship was selected because it increased fitness. All species must reproduce themselves, and sex and sexual drives are the evolved mechanisms assuring that the appropriate parties get together, while assuring a minimal level of genetic diversity. Without sex drives, members of a species would not regenerate themselves, but sex among humans is never unregulated. For the ancestors of humans, or hominids, a major roadblock to kinship existed: males and females are promiscuous, and hence, no stable kinship structure among mothers, fathers, and children existed. One can see this structure today in humans' closest relatives—chimpanzees—who reveal no permanent bonds between adult males and females. Only mother and her offspring endure, but her children transfer from the troop at puberty (Maryanski and Turner 1992). But, as hominids were forced to adapt to the African savanna, where they could no longer enjoy the protection of the forests, selection favored tighter-knit group structures. By looking at the brain, the footprints of selection are clearly evident (Turner 2000): the spetum, which is responsible for sex drives, has additional areas for pleasure among humans; and I would speculate that these areas enhanced male-female bonds in ways that allowed for the emergence of nuclear families. Once males and females formed more permanent bonds beyond the act of sex, and once growth of the brain expanded the capacity for culture, these bonds could be normatively regulated.

Norms could now specify "appropriate" persons, times, places, ways, ages, and circumstances where sex can occur—although the specific content of norms naturally varies from society to society (Davis 1949; Murdock 1949). However, the key breakthrough was that, whatever variations existed, a family structure came into existence, and the norms of this structure emerged under additional selection pressures. First, sex drives can lead to competition among individuals for sex objects, and out of such competition arise jealousies, anger, and perhaps murder. Furthermore, since males tend to be physically stronger than females, sexual dominance and exploitation of females by males can also occur, leading to more anger, frustration, and hostility. Such a situation can create tremendous personal anxieties as well as threaten the survival of the human species, since newborn children depend for a long time on the physical and emotional support from parents (or surrogates). Building upon the inherited legacy from their ape and hominid ancestors, humans developed implicit "understandings" about how competition for sexual objects was to be mitigated and how more enduring physical relations among adults were to be established. Initially these understandings were probably not consciously or deliberately instituted, but over time, because of their success in mitigating sexual conflict and in establishing enduring sexual relations, they persisted. As they persisted, these implicit understandings became translated into binding norms about sex and mating that combined with other norms arising out of similar processes to form a kinship system.

Second, the newborn are biologically helpless. A baby cannot feed, clothe, shelter, or protect itself; and for brief periods, neither can the mother, especially if she must care for the infant. Through processes similar to those delineated above, norms originally emerged to assure the protection of biologically helpless members of the species. Societies have different kinship norms regarding who and how many people are to protect the infant, but with some exceptions, the biological father and mother were designated to be the primary caretakers of infants, although in many societies the cast of protectors can be much more extensive and include grandparents, aunts, and cousins. The biological support functions of kinship can, moreover, include taking care of the incapacitated, aged, and diseased.

Third, social systems regenerate themselves not only through biological reproduction of the species but also through social reproduction in which the young acquire through socialization those personality traits necessary for par-

ticipation in the social positions of society. For once social structures are used
to meet selection pressures for reproduction, the nature of reproduction
changes as the young must learn how to participate in the culture and structures organizing social activity. All known societies have evolved structures
having consequences for social reproduction, and the most prominent of these
structures was the family. The father and mother are usually intimately
involved but sometimes aunts, uncles, grandparents, and other relatives do as
much or more to assure social reproduction.

Fourth, humans can experience a wide range of potentially disruptive emotions—such as fear, frustration, uncertainty, anger, and jealousy—which can
generate tremendous anxiety and tension, while immobilizing individuals and
disrupting social relations. These kinds of emotional states are, no doubt, one
of the costs of having a big brain that can remember, think, and embellish more
primal emotions. Thus, with large brains, selection pressures mounted to find
solutions to the emotional overloads that can come with being human. Selection initially worked to enhance human's emotional capacities for bonding
(Turner 2000), and the family was the easiest route to providing the social and
emotional support that humans needed to perform social roles effectively.

Fifth, after years of biological and social support as well as socialization of
the young, the issue of how and where to insert the young adult into the wider
society appears. This issue has been one of the most fundamental for all populations because it involves the transition from child to adult. Without this transition, social reproduction cannot occur. Such a transition raises questions of
where the young adult will go in a society, how this decision will be made,
and what criteria will be employed in making it. Through varied historical and
evolutionary processes, two basic ways of resolving the problem have developed (Davis 1949; Stephens 1967): (1) Insert the young into the wider society
on the basis of *ascription*, where a child's adult status in the society is determined
at birth and where children assume the occupational, religious, political, and
legal status of their families or their birth order and status of their parents within
a larger kinship system. Because social placement is determined at birth, family
support and socialization are directed toward preparing youth for this predeter-
mined slot in the wider society. (2) Insert youth into the larger society on the
basis of *performance*, where role performance in key activities becomes the criterion by which one is inserted into various statuses. In turn, such performance
is a reflection of inherited and socialized personality traits; and because kinship
circumscribes both biological inheritance and socialization, it has had far-
reaching consequences for social placement in nonascriptive, performance-ori-
ented societies, although performance systems almost always have intermediary
structures, like a school system, that become the arbitrators of performance.

Sixth, the kinship subsystem has had far-reaching consequences for organizing and coordinating much societal activity. As noted earlier, among hunters and gatherers the respective economic roles of males and females were dictated by the family division of labor. Or, as was evident for horticultural societies, kinship is the principle by which most economic activity is organized; and in these systems, what is true of the economy is also the case for political, legal, religious, and educational activity. Thus, kinship has often been very much involved in the coordination of activities in human populations.

In sum, then, kinship has represented a solution to a whole series of fundamental selection pressures on humans—sex and mating, emotional support, biological maintenance, socialization, placement, and social coordination—that have arisen under the forces of production, reproduction, and regulation. We can, therefore, provisionally define the institution of kinship as *those marriage and blood ties organized into structures and mediated by cultural symbols that regularize sex and mating, provide biological support, reproduce societal members, offer social support, engage in social placement and, at times, coordinate societal relations.* We will, however, want to expand upon this definition after reviewing the elements of kinship organization.

Elements of Kinship Organization

Kinship is a set of norms specifying relationships among (1) those who are related by blood (or who share genes) and (2) those who are related by marriage. These norms specify who is *to be considered* kinfolk as well as who is to marry whom and how, who is to be related to whom and how, who is to live with whom and where, who is to perform what duties and how, who is to have authority over whom, and who is to inherit property, authority, and other resources. Norms that so fundamentally organize people's lives are heavily infused with values, or imperatives about what *should* occur. These value elements give norms a moral quality, increasing the chances that people will abide by them. Populations that could not develop normative agreements and underlying value premises over such matters did not persist and reproduce themselves, and so the basic types of normative systems that have emerged are worth more detailed review because they have been so essential to human survival.

Norms of Family Size and Composition If one maps out the genealogy chart of kinsmen on both sides of a couple's respective families, the potential size of the family becomes quite large. And in some societies where just about everyone is related in some way, a few large kinship groupings would be virtually coextensive with the total society. Many Polynesian societies came close to doing just this because kin ties could be traced for just about everyone in a village, district, or even the total society. As Raymond Firth noted in his description of the Tikopia, virtually everyone could trace kin relationships in a community numbering well over a thousand so that "the whole land is a single body of kinfolk" (Firth 1936:234). Kinship ties have often been less extensive, however, because specific norms limit the scale and scope of family. One set of such norms that has evolved is those regulating the size and composition of family groupings, creating three general structural forms: (1) nuclear, (2) extended, and (3) polygamous.

1. The *nuclear* family is small and contains only father, mother, and their children. Immediate relatives are excluded from the household or living unit. This nuclear form was the dominant type in both the earliest societies, hunting and gathering, and as we will see in later chapters, it is also the type most prevalent in the complex industrial and post-industrial societies of the West.

2. The *extended* family is large and includes several nuclear units, thereby bringing other relatives to a household. In this way, not only parents and their children, but grandparents, great-grandparents, aunts, cousins, and others can potentially become part of an extended household unit. The degree of extendedness of families can vary greatly, with family members living within one house or a compound of houses. Yet regardless of how concentrated their residence, the members of the family perceive themselves as a discrete unit that must control and coordinate activities. Their perceptions of themselves as a distinct unit are often bolstered by the fact that extended families own and work property upon which their subsistence depends.

3. A *polygamous* family unit is one in which plural marriage and residence are allowed. The most common form of polygamy is *polygyny*, where norms permit inclusion of several wives (and their children) in a single house or where norms allow each co-wife to occupy a dwelling of her own clustered together within a family compound or homestead. Norms allowing women to have multiple husbands are termed *polyandry*. Where polygyny or polyandry have existed, families tended to be large, but even in societies that have permitted polygamous families, monogamous marriages have often been more common because most males in societies allowing polygamy could not afford multiple wives.

Norms of Residence   Once two people get married, they confront the problem of where they are going to live. There are three logical possibilities: (1) alone and where they wish; (2) with the groom's family or community; or (3) with the bride's family or community. Respectively, these three possibilities are labeled neolocal, patrilocal, and matrilocal residence norms.[1] Generally, matrilocal or patrilocal residence rules are most pronounced for extended and polygamous family units. Since these types of families connect multiple adults together, there needs to be a residence rule specifying who is to move into whose household. For example, if a kinship system is composed of extended families and has a patrilocal residence norm, then the married couple lives not only in the groom's community but most likely in his parents' home or compound. The reverse would be the case for a matrilocal residence rule in a kinship system composed of extended families. And in systems with a polygamous family unit, residence norms also tend to be either matrilocal or patrilocal, since multiple spouses will be recruited from different families and villages, typically moving to the household and village of the single spouse. There can be other residence rules, such as the avuncular, which requires that a married couple move to where the mother's brother (or the uncle of their children) lives. Here, the mother's brother will have considerable authority over the male and his children (Ember and Ember 1983:249–59, 1971). Thus, while most human populations have had neolocal, patrilocal, or matrilocal residence rules, considerable variation can occur.

Norms of Family Activity   Most kinship systems display clusters of norms concerning family activities. These rules revolve around three major concerns: (1) household tasks, (2) child care, and (3) socialization of the young.

1. Just what the task obligations of males and females are within the family is usually spelled out by norms, although the specific norms vary from society to society. Frequently males are required to engage in economic activity, with females involved in household or domestic tasks, but equally often in the history of human societies females have engaged in as much or more economic activity than males. Children in most kinship systems assume the status of student apprentice, acquiring the skills of their parents.

2. There are numerous ways to bring up a child, and rarely is this decision left up to the complete discretion of parents (or other kin). Just how a child is to be fed, clothed, and sheltered is usually specified by kinship rules, which establish minimum standards for child care. Should the adults responsible for this care not meet these standards, child care then becomes the responsibility of designated kin or, in societies with a developed political system, the responsibility falls to the state and its welfare agencies.

3. In all societies there are general norms indicating how children are to be socialized. The ways love, affection, discipline, and instruction are administered by adults are greatly circumscribed by kinship norms, although these have displayed great diversity in the course of humans' evolutionary history. Parents generally socialize their young, but in many kinship systems one parent is excluded from socialization. For example, a mother's brother (or child's uncle) in an avuncular system may be more responsible for a young male's socialization than the biological father. And other arrangements excluding a parent from socialization have existed in the world's kinship systems.

Norms of Dissolution   Even when there are clear and powerful kinship rules, marriages in all societies may become unstable, with the consequence that societies have provided ways for their dissolution. In general, there are three types of rules in kinship systems governing dissolution: (1) conditional rules, (2) procedural rules, and (3) rules of dependence.

1. Conditional rules indicate the conditions under which dissolution is pos-sible. The conditions appropriate for dissolution differ greatly from society to society; among them are lack of female fertility, mutual incompatibility, infidelity, criminal offense, and mental cruelty. Conditional rules can be either broad or narrow and encouraging or discouraging.

2. Procedural rules indicate how dissolution should occur. They can be simple (moving belongings out of a spouse's house) or exceedingly complex (going to court, pleading a case, and establishing guilt).

3. Dissolution usually involves children (and sometimes other dependent members, such as the elderly). Kinship rules tend to insure that these dependents are cared for and socialized.

Norms of Descent   With birth one inherits two separate bloodlines, and this fact raises the question of whose bloodline—the male's or the female's—is to be more important. The norms specifying which side of the married couple's family is to be more significant are termed *rules of descent*,[2] and there are three general types: patrilineal, matrilineal, and bilateral. In a *patrilineal* descent system, a person belongs at birth to a special group of kin on the father's side of the family. This group includes siblings (brothers and sisters), father, father's siblings, father's father and his siblings, and father's brother's children. In such a system, the mother's kin are not important; for it is to this special group of male kin that an individual owes allegiance and loyalty, and it is these kin who will protect, socialize, and eventually place into society an individual. It is from these kin that the succession of authority and inheritance of property and wealth will pass. In a *matrilineal* system the mother's instead of the father's kin would assume this important place in the life of the young. *Bilateral descent* systems assign influence to both sides of the family, but where bilateral descent exists, it is almost always *truncated* so that both mother's and father's kin are equally recognized and respected but neither kin group exerts much influence or power over the children. In this way, conflicts between the two sides of the family are mitigated.

Unilineal descent rules (that is, patrilineal or matrilineal norms) divide up a particular residential unit, since one member of the family (either wife or husband) must be an "outsider" (Stephens 1963:105). For example, in a patrilineal descent system, father and children generally belong to the same descent grouping, with the mother as an outsider. Aside from dividing up a particular family group or household, descent norms also divide societies into "segments" (Murdock 1949). In a unilineal system one belongs to a patrilineal residential unit and then to other patrilineally reckoned units in the village, community, and perhaps territory. In this way various residential units within some geographical territory are linked together through a patrilineal descent system or the male bloodline. Such linkages are usually referred to as *lineages*. Frequently they own property and can be considered a kind of "corporation" that can engage in wars, feuds, and economic competition and be subject to legal liability. When several lineages are connected by a descent norm, a *clan* can be said to exist. And when clans are linked together by descent norms, a *moiety* is formed and represents the largest unilineal kin grouping. Many historical societies have been divided into moieties, each with their constituent clans, lineages, and residential family units. The extensiveness, clarity, and scope of such descent groupings have varied tremendously in the history of human societies, although these more complex forms reached their zenith in the horticultural era. The descent rule in these societies, as it laced together kindred, was the principal basis of societal organization and integration.

Norms of Authority   In all kinship systems there are rules of authority. These rules concern who makes the important and ultimate decisions affecting the welfare of a particular family or larger kin group such as a lineage or clan. But even where rules clearly specify authority, others in the family may still exert considerable informal decision-making powers. Yet the rules of a kinship system usually endow specific statuses with authority. These rules are two general types: (1) patriarchal, and (2) egalitarian.

1. In *patriarchal* kinship systems, the father makes major decisions for his family or residential unit. Eldest and/or most-able males make decisions governing the larger kin grouping embodying all kin wherever their residence may be.

2. In *egalitarian* systems, there is usually a division of labor in decision making, with males making major decisions in some areas and females in others. Besides patriarchy and egalitarianism, there is a third type, at least logically, revolving around matriarchy, but such systems do not invest women, per se, with ultimate authority but rather the authority has historically resided with her male kin who, because of the modest but decisive strength differences between males and females, have been in a better position to force conformity. Thus, the authority resides in the female's side of the family more than in the female herself, although in modern single-parent households, women may have full authority, albeit authority under difficult circumstances. Such systems have been, however, comparatively rare.

Norms of Marriage   Almost all societies require a mother to be married. Marriage sets up a series of mutual obligations between husband and wife concerning domestic duties, child rearing, and sex, while at the same time it perpetuates the kin grouping. Aside from the general rule requiring marriage of all mothers, most kinship systems have norms concerning whom one may, or may not, marry. The three most prominent types of marriage rules have been (1) incest taboos, (2) norms of exogamy, and (3) norms of endogamy.

1. *Incest taboos* are norms prohibiting sex and marriage among close kin. Some of these have been universal or nearly so: mothers and sons, fathers and daughters, and siblings may not have sex or marry. Usually more distant kin (aunts, uncles, cousins, nieces, or nephews) are also covered by an incest taboo. The effect of such rules is that they force people out of their immediate residential kin group in search of partners.

2. Often marriage rules are also *exogamous* and prohibit marriage to members of one's community or larger kin grouping—thus forcing marriage with partners from other communities, lineages, regions, clans, or moieties.

3. At times marriage rules are also *endogamous*, requiring marriage within certain groups—usually a social class, kin group, caste, or village. Coupled with incest (and perhaps exogamy) rules, endogamous norms severely restrict the pool of potential mates. In contrast, some kinship systems have few explicit rules of marriage. Mothers are "encouraged" to be married; incest rules apply only to close blood kin; and explicit norms of exogamy or endogamy do not exist.

We are now able to revise our earlier, provisional definition of kinship. Kinship can be viewed as *those normative systems, infused with values, that specify the size and composition, residence patterns, activities, authority relations, and lines of descent within those units organizing blood and marriage ties in ways that have consequences for regularizing sex and mating, socializing the young, providing biological and social support, placing the young into the broader social structure and, at times, coordinating other institutional activities.*

As humans' first social structure beyond the band, kinship was charged with coordinating many other institutional activities. Indeed, once humans had hit upon using blood and marriage ties to organize responses to selection pressures, these ties were used after hunting and gathering to organize economy, religion, polity, law, and education. Of course, the complexity of the normative rules increased in order to respond to the myriad of selection pressures coming from all macrodynamic forces, but kinship proved to be workable in organizing institutional activities for ever larger populations. At some point, however, the limits of kinship as a regulatory structure were reached, and as a result, institutions differentiated from kinship and developed their own organizational and cultural forms; and once freed from the constraints of blood and marriage ties, institutional systems could not only differentiate, they could develop. And, as these processes occurred, kinship de-evolved back to the nuclear family system that had organized the first human societies.

RELIGION

Neandertals, one branch of later hominids, began to populate the earth at least 250,000 years ago. One of the most interesting habits of Neandertals was that they buried their dead, and around these burial sites have been found the remains of ritual and perhaps worship: pollen from bouquets of flowers, skulls placed on sticks, paintings marking entrances to burial caves, and stones arranged in patterns around graves. Just what these artifacts mean can never be known for sure, but they suggest concern about the afterlife and the nonempirical world of beings and forces existing in a special realm. In a word, they suggest religion among hominids whose brain was equal and, in fact, sometimes larger than contemporary humans (whether or not Neandertals are the immediate ancestor to modern humans or a closely related species is still debated).

Religion was thus one of the earliest human inventions, and except for many hunting and gathering societies, which often do not have religion, it is nearly universal in all known human societies where people are settled in territories, a fact that argues for religion as an important activity for humans psychologically and for their organization into society. Why, then, did humans create visions of another realm inhabited by special forces and/or beings to whom ritual appeals were owed? The general answer resides in the additional power that is given to activities that are believed to be sanctioned by the supernatural. Before exploring the selection pressures that led to the emergence of religion, however, let us first see what makes religion a distinctive kind of institutional activity (Turner 1972:342–46; Wallace 1966; Kurtz 1995:51–101). All religions reveal certain common elements: (1) a concern with the sacred and supernatural, (2) rituals, (3) beliefs about the nature of the supernatural, and (4) cult structures.

Elements of Religious Organization

The Sacred and Supernatural   All religions involve a notion of the sacred, or the special qualities imputed to objects and events that have been touched by supernatural forces or that symbolize the supernatural. Because the sacred arouses intense emotions, it gives religion tremendous influence in mobilizing and controlling human action in a society (Durkheim 1912). Although there are some notable exceptions (Wuthnow 1988:474), religions usually contain assumptions about the supernatural, or a realm lying outside the everyday world and having the capacity to bestow sacredness on things and events. This other world is conceived as being occupied by forces, beings, spirits, and powers that in some way alter, circumscribe, and influence this world's happenings and occurrences. Sometimes the supernatural is a series of forces who are all-seeing and -knowing. The "mana" of many traditional societies was such a force that could change, alter, intervene in the world, and bestow sacred power on objects, but which itself was not an object but only a vague and diffuse source of power underlying natural events. Frequently the supernatural is conceived of as a set of personified beings, or gods and deities. And sometimes the supernatural is seen as a spirit having the form of animals and other living creatures (Swanson 1960:8). Whatever its form, the supernatural has been viewed by the members of a society as influencing events in the natural world.

Ritual   Rituals are *stereotyped* sequences of behavior directed to evoke the powers of the supernatural (Goode 1951:38–50). The content of ritual varies tremendously and can involve such forms of behavior as prayer, music, dancing, singing, exhortation, reciting a code, taking drugs, eating, drinking, making sacrifices, and congregating (Wallace 1966:52–70). Basically there are two types of rituals: calendrical and noncalendrical. *Calendrical rituals* are enacted on a regular schedule—whether at the day or night, at the waxing and waning of the moon, at the beginning or ending of seasons, at eclipses and positions of planets and stars, or on the birthdays of supernatural beings. In contrast, *noncalendrical* rituals are performed sporadically, on special occasions, or in times of crises. Some noncalendrical rituals such as the puberty rites or *rites de passage* of many societies follow somewhat of a cycle and occur at certain more or less determined times in the life of an individual, but the time, place, and period of the ritual are not precisely set by the calendar. Whether calendrical or noncalendrical, rituals serve to link the natural and supernatural worlds by activating the emotions of individuals toward the sacredness of the supernatural (Collins 1988; Durkheim [1912] 1965). Much of what is observable about a religion is, therefore, seen in ritual activities of a community of worshippers (Wallace 1966:71; Goode 1951:48–52).

Beliefs   All religions reveal conceptions of the supernatural and sacred realms, defining the meaning of rituals (Goode 1951) while rationalizing their performance (Wallace 1966). Religious beliefs usually become part of the broader culture of a society and generally consist of two components, (1) a cosmology and (2) a system of values.

Cosmology. A *cosmology* is a set of beliefs concerning the nature of a universe, including the natural and supernatural. A cosmology often includes a *pantheon* or group of supernatural beings or forces that in varying degrees affect and alter social processes in the natural world. In many religions, the beings and forces in the pantheon are listed in terms of a hierarchy of their power and influence—from the most powerful god, through lesser gods, to mortals who are godlike. A cosmology also contains a body of myths that describe the historical events leading to the current hierarchical ordering of supernatural beings and that describe the origin, career, and interaction of gods with ordinary or only quasi-sacred mortals. In some literate societies these myths are codified into basic texts, such as the Old Testament, the New Testament, and the Koran. Cosmologies typically include *substantive beliefs* about planes of existence lying outside the natural world—heaven, hell, nirvana, and other realms in the supernatural. Yet, in many simple religions, the cosmology is not well developed, consisting of a series of entities and forces who reveal no clear hierarchy and who inhabit only a vaguely conceived supernatural realm.

Values. Religious values guiding, justifying, and sanctioning ritual are usually very similar to the more secular values of a society's culture that regulate everyday activity. Values indicate what is right and wrong, proper and improper, and good or bad; and religious values are frequently codified into a religious code, such as the Ten Commandments in Christianity, the Ethics of Confucius in Confucianism, or the Noble Eightfold Path in Buddhism. Such values provide a highly general and overarching framework within which many secular values and specific norms in a society operate.

Cult structures   A *cult* is a corporate unit where those rituals made meaningful and justified by supernatural beliefs are enacted. As such, the cult is the most fundamental corporate unit in the *institution* of religion in any society; and as we will see, the structure of cults can vary from a worldwide system (such as the Catholic Church) with a vast bureaucracy to a small and exclusive group of tribesmen engaged in a common ritual addressed to the supernatural. In all cults, the other elements of religion are instantiated: a set of common beliefs about the sacred and supernatural; a set of rituals designed to appeal to the supernatural; and a membership or community of worshippers who share the cult's beliefs about the sacred and supernatural and who engage in its rituals. Thus, it is at the cult level of social organization that beliefs and rituals about the sacred and supernatural become integrated. Cults can vary tremendously with respect to their size, degree of bureaucratization, existence of professional clergy, reliance on lay clergy, degree of centralization, stability of membership, and exclusiveness of membership (Wallacer 1966:84–101).[3] Religion in any society is, therefore, a distribution of cults; and except for the simplest societies, such as hunter-gatherers where cults and family-bands are fused, a variety of cult structures manifesting somewhat dissimilar beliefs and rituals is evident among a population.

In sum, then, the basic elements of all religions involve: beliefs about the sacred and supernatural, or a realm lying beyond mundane activities and composed of beings and forces that are viewed as influencing ongoing social action in a society as well as processes in nature; stereotyped behaviors or rituals that arouse emotions, sustain beliefs, and provide links between the natural to the supernatural world; and cult structures, consisting of a community of individuals who share beliefs about the sacred and supernatural and who engage in common rituals directed toward the sacred forces, entities, or beings of the supernatural.

Selection Pressures and Religion

As we will come to appreciate in later chapters, religion is often a source of conflict and societal disintegration, but if this were its only consequences, it would never have emerged in the first place, nor would it have persisted to the present, even in the face of intense pressure for the secularization of social life. Religion was thus selected as a solution—albeit a most problematic one—to problems of organization revolving around (Turner 1972:346–49): (1) reinforcing institutional norms, (2) regulating socialization and social placement, (3) legitimating tension-producing inequalities, and (4) alleviating personal anxiety and tension. Each of these sources of selection pressures is briefly examined below.

1. Under selection pressures generated by the force of reproduction, religious rituals and values typically reinforce concrete norms guiding role behavior within the economic, familial, and political institutional spheres (Swanson 1960; Luckmann 1967; O'Dea 1970, 1966; O'Dea and Aviad 1983; Goode 1951; Durkheim [1912] 1965). Values give institutional norms special—perhaps even sacred—significance and thus increase the probability of conformity. Religious rituals, particularly in traditional societies, frequently permeate and circumscribe crucial role behaviors (Wallace 1966:216–46). For example, among the Tikopia—a small, island society where fishing was one major economic activity (Firth 1936)—religious rituals assured adequate preparation of fishing canoes for often dangerous expeditions into the sea; the overhauling and caring for canoes were viewed by the Tikopian native as an extension of ritual obligations to the deities to secure food offerings. When work was performed as much for the gods as for human subsistence, the speed, energy, harmony, and coordination among workers increased greatly (Firth 1936:90–95; Goode 1951:107–9). Similar consequences of religion were evident in reinforcing and maintaining the Tikopian kinship system. For example, the patrilineal descent system of the Tikopians was reinforced by the fact that the dwelling of the oldest male ancestor was maintained as a temple for ritual performances directed at gods and ancestors (Goode 1951:200), with patriarchal authority norms being reinforced by the exclusion of young women from certain religious rituals.

In more economically developed societies, the reinforcing consequences of rituals for institutional processes decline, but religious beliefs, especially values, have frequently been the cultural underpinnings of many specific institutional norms. Indeed, when the religious code of the dominant religious cult in an industrial or post-industrial society is compared to the basic postulates and statutes of that society's legal system, it is clear that religion still exerts considerable influence on the normative system of a population. For law codifies many basic cultural values, particularly those articulated by religions, and thereby mediates between religion and other institutional spheres.

2. Again, under selection pressures from reproduction but also from regulation, religion reinforces kinship norms, especially those regulating socialization and placement of the young into the broader society (Luckmann 1967). More specifically, religious rituals in many societies guide first the birth of a child and then mark with sacred significance his or her passage through adolescence, adulthood, and marriage. The religious rituals surrounding these status transitions, or *rites de passage*, regularize socialization and maturation, while impressing upon their recipient the new normative rights and obligations attached to each new status. To exceed these rights or not live up to the obligations becomes difficult when sanctioned by the supernatural. In this way religion helps assure commitment on the part of maturing actors entering new adult status positions. Among horticultural and early agrarian populations of the past, religious rituals were extremely elaborate and of great significance to the members of a society, whereas in industrial and post-industrial societies their impact tends to decline.

3. Societies revealing some degree of differentiation also display inequalities with respect to wealth, prestige, and power, thereby creating problems of regulation and, hence, selection pressures for the legitimization of such inequality. Religion in pre-industrial societies not only had far-reaching consequences for legitimating political and other forms of activity, it also worked to legitimate the broader stratification system. This legitimating function reached its peak in the precolonial era in India where the Hindu cosmology revolving around karma and reincarnation became a justification for a rigid caste system of stratification. Those born orthodox Hindus (i.e., Brahmans) were entitled to elite caste positions, since the gods in controlling their reincarnation had placed them in an elite family. As Hinduism spread across India, non-Hindus were absorbed into inferior caste positions because the non-Hindu tribes were ritually "impure" and ignorant of basic Brahman beliefs. Although rarely as extreme as in precolonial India, religion in most traditional systems legitimated not only the institution of the polity but the broader stratification system in a society.

Moreover, as Max Weber ([1922] 1978:491–92), recognized, religion's effect in supporting stratification varies for different social classes. For those high in the stratification system, religion legitimates their station as right and proper, whereas for those lower in the system, religious beliefs typically hold out promises of a better station—or salvation—in the next life *if* beliefs are sustained and rituals practiced. It is this latter effect of religion that led Karl Marx ([1843] 1963:441) to declare religion as "the opium of the people" because it encouraged them to accept their situation in the present (with false promises for a better future). It is thus no coincidence that, in the history of human societies, religion became more complex and concerned with control of earthly social patterns when stratification intensified during the agrarian stage of societal evolution. In Guy Swanson's (1960) famous study of the emergence of high gods in fifty different types of pre-industrial societies, for example, he found that the supernatural becomes ever more interested in everyday morality as the level of stratification increases. Similarly, Underhill (1975) developed a much larger sample of pre-industrial societies and found that the presence of a high god is related to societal complexity, a finding he interpreted in a Marxian tone as indicating that active high gods emerge when the economic system begins to generate stratification.

Even in more industrial societies, studies have supported the notion that religiosity tends to be associated with political conservatism, a conservatism that legitimates political regimes and systems of stratification (Sanderson 1995a:483; Glock and Stark 1965). But since a smaller proportion of the population in industrial societies is religious, the effects of religion on sustaining stratification are reduced. Yet, even though the direct influence of religion has declined, it is not difficult to see the religious roots of widely held beliefs that are often used to legitimate inequalities. For example, in the United States the "Protestant Ethic" is very much alive in Americans' distrust of the welfare system that "gives money to those who do not work" or in Americans' belief that those who "do not work" should not enjoy the same benefits as those who do. Or, to illustrate further, the intense identification of Americans' sense of self-worth with occupation and their concern with work and being "productive" reflect the continuing power of the "Protestant Ethic."

Thus, under the impetus of regulation as a macrodynamic force, religion in all societies has consequences for social integration and control, whether through reinforcing institutional norms or legitimating inequality (Goode 1951:222–23), but this fact should not obscure the potentially *dis*integrative consequences of religion for a society: new, emergent religious cults in a society can become a revolutionary collectivity. The sacralization of institutional norms can generate rigidity in behavior, which can become a liability when changes in the social and physical environment of a society require flexibility (O'Dea 1966). Religion can legitimate in the short run a ruthless political regime or oppressive stratification system, which in the long run can create divisive and disintegrative strains in society, while generating disincentives for innovation (Childe 1953, 1952, 1951). Thus, as regulation generated selection pressures for the use of power to coordinate and control a population, it forced actors to create not only polity but religion as a symbolic base for legitimating centers of power. But, as power is used to regulate, it can also be used to sustain privilege and promote inequalities that in the longer run will increase the disintegrative potential of a population—thereby raising the values for regulation as a macrodynamic force.

4. In all societies, people experience uncertainty, concern over the unknown, powerlessness, unpredictability, and anxiety—a byproduct of having a large brain that can remember the past, ponder the vicissitudes of the present, and worry about the future. In providing a cosmology of the sacred and supernatural, religious beliefs have had the ability to alleviate or mitigate these multiple sources of tension; and in prescribing ritual behavior, religion has provided solutions to the individual and collective tensions among the members of a society. In horticultural and agrarian societies where economic uncertainty was a constant condition of social life, selection pressures emanating from reproduction and regulation would push people to find ways of reducing negative emotions. One solution to these pressures was the expansion of religion. In advanced industrial and post-industrial systems where many economic uncertainties have been eliminated for at least some sectors of society and where selection pressures for expanded reproduction led to the emergence of new kinds of reproductive systems, such as education, the alleviating consequences of religion are less far-reaching, but among many segments of the population in these societies—the poor, disenfranchised, the aged, and alienated—religion still provides an interpretation and answer to their fears and uncertainties. For example, many of the fundamentalist movements and small, sectlike cults emerging in industrialized and urbanized societies appeal to those who for various reasons cannot adjust, or feel marginal to, post-industrial social structures (Loftland and Stark 1965; Glock 1964). Yet, as has been clear in the United States, fundamentalists have become politically active, giving voice to those who feel marginalized and, thereby, reducing their sense of marginality; and as fundamentalists influence political decisions, they represent a "solution"— albeit a contentious one—to selection pressure emanating from regulation as a macrodynamic force. Moreover, in recent decades, studies in the United States have shown that fundamentalist beliefs need not be a reaction or barrier to broad participation in a post-industrial society (Wuthnow 1988:484). Thus, as beliefs alleviate anxieties and manage tensions, they do not necessarily involve retreat from modernity but, instead, appear to give people a sense of meaning as they engage in the secular activities of a post-industrial society.

We are now in a position to define religion as an institutional system (Turner 1972:349). Religion is *a system of beliefs and rituals pertaining to the sacred and supernatural which are organized into cult structures that have consequences for reinforcing norms, legitimating inequality, guiding socialization and social placement, and managing variable sources of tension and anxiety in a society.* Despite the commonalities of all religion specified in this definition, the nature of beliefs, rituals, and cult structures has varied enormously as human populations moved from hunting and gathering through horticulture and agrarianism to industrialism and post-industrialism. Indeed, despite the apparent religious activity of Neandertals, many hunting and gathering populations did not have religion, but once the values of reproduction and regulation as macrodynamic forces increased, selection favored the emergence and, later, the clear differentiation and development of religion as an institutional system.

POLITY

Hunting and gatherings populations do not reveal a polity because the conditions generating high values for regulation—population growth, increased production, inequality, exchange distribution, and threat—generally do not exist. Perhaps leaders emerged to regulate and coordinate activities when hunter-gatherers found themselves in conflict with other populations, but typically hunter-gatherers did not consolidate or centralize the bases of power because the valences for regulation were low and could be managed by the band and nuclear family. Indeed, among the Eskimos, people are reluctant to bestow real power on leaders, and the same is the case with the bushmen of the Kalahari desert in Africa who have leaders without any power to enforce their decisions (others follow them by choice because they are perceived to have special skills, for example, in activities like the hunt).

Elements of Political Organization

The key elements of all political systems are (1) leadership and decision-making and (2) consolidation of power. Leaders are individuals who are given the right to make decisions for other members of a population. For leaders to do more than give advice, however, they must consolidate the bases of power. They must have the capacity to monitor conformity to decisions (administrative base); they must have the ability to enforce conformity to decisions (coercive base); they must be seen as legitimate and able to use ideologies and beliefs to inspire conformity (symbolic base); and they must have at their disposal material resources to encourage some actions or discourage others (material incentive base). The more leaders can mobilize all bases of power, the greater will be their ability to make binding decisions on members of a population.

Selection Pressures and Polity

Selection favored the emergence of leaders as populations settled down and grew because the problems of coordination and control increased dramatically as the valences of regulation increased. Those settled populations that could produce leaders were better able to coordinate and distribute resources for meeting societal goals and were more efficient in controlling the activities of actors, both individuals and collective. As a result, they were more likely to adapt to their biophysical and sociocultural environments. Those populations that could not agree upon leaders who would be given the rights to make decisions soon scattered and de-evolved back to hunting and gathering or were conquered by populations who had effective leaders.

Conflict within or between populations dramatically escalates these selection pressures for leaders because without the ability to control conflict internally or to win wars externally, a population ceases to be viable in its environment. We can see the transition from essentially leaderless hunting and gathering populations to the emergence of leaders in what are often termed "Big Men" societies (Johnson and Earle 1987). Typically, when hunter–gatherers have settled near water and, as a result, can sustain themselves on fishing, gathering, and perhaps trade with other populations, Big Men emerge to take control of decision making. They do so by their personal charisma and by forging effective alliances that allow them to outcompete potential rivals. Big Men define the goals of the society, assign tasks to others, tax economic surplus but with the obligation to redistribute it back to the population, resolve disputes among individuals or kin groups, and generally maintain order. Big Men thus evidence all the features of leadership and decision making of all polities.

Leadership is effective, as noted above, if leaders can *consolidate power* along each of its bases—coercion, symbols, material incentives, and administration. Big Men, for example, often used coercion to gain power and, if necessary, to ward off rivals; and they typically developed a set of symbols, often religious, to legitimate their right to hold power. They also manipulated material incentives by using their power to hoard resources that they would then redistribute to members of the society. And they often organized the beginnings of administrative structures in the delegation of tasks to loyal followers who would monitor and enforce decisions made by the Big Man. Big Men systems of polity were, in a sense, selected only under unique conditions: when hunting-gathering populations settled into more permanent communities. Under these conditions, selection pressures become immediately more intense, punctuating the evolution of Big Men. But this system was only a temporary solution to selection pressures from regulation as a macrodynamic force.

As humans began to garden rather than hunt and gather resources, leadership was increasingly lodged within a kinship system organized around rules of descent. Thus leaders of larger kin groups, such as clans (systems of relations among lineages composed of several families) and moieties (linkages among clans), also become political leaders who used their fellow kinsmen to administer decisions and enforce conformity to them, with the values and norms of the kinship system as well as religion providing the symbolic base of power. And since kin leaders assigned gardening plots and redistributed the products of horticultural activity, they also manipulated material incentives. Thus, except for Big Men systems, which only existed in verdant environments with a renewable supply of game, the elaboration of blood and marriage ties, or kinship, was the easiest route to resolve the intense selection pressures of how to consolidate power to coordinate and control, allocate tasks, and distribute resources. Selection worked on what it was given—nuclear families created by marriage and involving two blood lines. The elaboration of kinship along blood and marriage ties provided a more stable structural and cultural base than Big Men systems for assigning leaders and consolidating bases of power to control larger numbers of individuals. These kin-based polities, however, revealed their own tensions because kin authority among adults is always resented. Still, compared to Big Men systems, these kin-based polities were more stable and could use power to control, coordinate, and regulate members of a population in pursuit of societywide goals.

Thus, we can define the institution of polity as *the consolidation and centralization of power in the hands of leaders who possess the capacity to make binding decisions on members of a population and, in so doing, coordinate activities, allocate tasks, distribute valued resources, and maintain social control.* Of course, the form that polity takes varies with other forces, particularly as population growth, production, exchange, and conflict increase (see equation on regulation in chapter 2). As long as these forces reveal low values, polity is recessive; but as their valences rise, regulation as a macrodynamic force increases selection pressures for the consolidation and centralization of power.

At some point in this process, the state emerges as a basic form of polity in which larger administrative structures organize all bases of power under control by leaders. But whether or not a state exists, polities vary along a number of dimensions such as: the configuration among the four bases of power used by leaders, the degree of centralization of leadership, the mechanisms for the transfer of power to new leaders, the amount of participation of the members of the population in the selection of leaders, the span of control exercised by leaders, and many other variables (Turner 1972:265–66). Despite these variations, however, the basic structure of polity remains the same: leaders making decisions because they have consolidated power in response to selection pressures stemming from problems of coordination and control.

As populations became larger and as new institutions differentiated, the values for regulation escalated even more because problems of coordination and control among the corporate units organizing activity within institutional domains increased. Relations within institutional domains—kinship, economy, law, religion—and between these domains generate new kinds of second-order selection pressures for the use of power for coordination and control as well as resource allocation. And, as power is consolidated and centralized in response to these selection pressures, inequalities increase and generate additional second-order selection pressures for controlling the conflict-potential inhering in stratification. As all of these second-order pressures mount, polity is forced to expand and differentiate the legal system.

LAW

As human populations have grown and differentiated, problems of regulation have escalated beyond the capacity of polity alone to coordinate and control activities of individual, corporate, and categoric units. Problems of resolving disputes among diverse individual and collective actors, controlling rising rates of deviance, enforcing agreements among parties, legitimating the growing concentrations of power, mitigating against the episodic conflict potential of inequality, codifying cultural ideals and values into a workable set of rules for an ever more diverse population, and specifying the relations between those in power and those subject to power, all escalate. If these problems cannot be resolved, they can tear a society apart. Indeed, it is these kinds of problems emanating from the force of regulation that have led to the disintegration of human populations as coherent societies, indicating that solutions to these selection pressures have often been ineffective, or just temporary stopgaps in the face of mounting disintegrative pressures (Turner 1995).

One response to these selection pressures has been to consolidate and concentrate power, but power creates its own integrative problems that set into motion additional or "second order" selection pressures to find a mechanism for legitimating power and inequality while coordinating and controlling members of a population. For those populations who remained viable in their environment, the solution to these selection pressures has been the evolution of law.

Among simple hunter-gatherers, law was recessive because many of the problems of coordination and control could be managed through face-to-face negotiation among members of small bands. As populations became larger and more differentiated, however, new problems of coordination and control emerged. Moreover, power became more consolidated and centralized which, in turn, increased tension-generating inequalities. Under these conditions, the visibility and scope of the legal system became essential in the face of rising disintegrative potential. By late agrarianism and early industrialization, then, the legal system had become one of the most visible institutional complexes in human societies.[4]

Elements of Legal Systems

A legal system is composed of a number of basic elements (Turner 1997, 1980, 1974, 1972): (1) a body of rules or laws, (2) a capacity to adjudicate disputes in accordance with laws, (3) a set of procedures for creating new rules or eliminating old ones, and (4) an ability to enforce laws.

Body of Laws   Rules that specify how individuals and collective actors are to behave, above and beyond the day-to-day normative agreements among individuals and corporate units, can be considered laws. Since humans could not write for most of their history, laws do not need to be written down but they must be understood by all. Moreover, laws not only specify what is appropriate or inappropriate; they also indicate that these rules should be obeyed and that a failure to do so invites intervention by third parties (Malinowski 1922; Moore 1978; Hoebel 1954; Turner 1980). A body of laws consists of two fundamental types of rules: First, there are *substantive rules* for (a) regulating relationships among members of a population and (b) defining deviant behavior and, then, controlling such behavior. Second, there are *procedural rules* indicating just how substantive rules are to be used by third parties to regulate what are viewed as important relationships and what are defined as deviant acts. Although the differentiation of laws from regular norms, along with the distinction between substantive and procedural laws, would be difficult to discern in most hunter-gatherer populations, these features of laws emerged from time to time, indicating that an implicit legal system was buried just beneath the surface of daily activity. As societies moved beyond hunting-gathering and became larger and more complex, these characteristics in the body of laws became manifest and began to regulate more and more aspects of social life (Turner 1980).

The body of laws in a population always instantiates, to some degree, the traditions, values, customs, institutional norms, and other cultural systems, especially the culture of elites who are most influential in deciding what the laws will be (Black 1976). Yet, to the degree that the body of laws only represents the culture and interests of the powerful and privileged, it will be less effective in regulating, controlling, and coordinating the larger mass of the population; and as a consequence, coercive force or the threat of its use more than the moral imperative of law will be used to control members of a society. In hunting and gathering populations, law was very much fused with custom, tradition, values, and culture (Lowie 1966; Gurvitch 1953); and hence, it was effective when needed. In advanced post-industrial societies, law also tends to reflect broadly held cultural customs, traditions, values, beliefs, and institutional norms that are amalgamated into a "civic culture," which, in turn, is translated into broad legal postulates (both substantive and procedural) guiding the formation and adjudication of laws. It is the societal types between these beginning and current end points of societal development—that is, from advanced horticulturalism through agrarianism to early industrialism—that the greatest amount of discordance between the body of laws and the culture of the broader masses could be found. For, in these societies inequality has been greatest with law often used as a tool by the powerful and wealthy to exploit economically the masses and to control their protests (Marx 1965; Pashukanis 1978; Cain and Hunt 1969; Davis 1962; Duke 1976). It should not be surprising, therefore, that these societies are subject to periodic collapse from within because of internal strains or to conquest from without. Thus, even as the consolidation of power has escalated with societal development, power itself begins to generate second-order selection pressures which, if met, lead to an effective legal system and which, if unmet, increase the disintegrative potential of the society.

Management of Disputes and Deviance   A legal system develops mechanisms for dealing with disputes and deviance in accordance with laws. Such management involves appeals to a third party who listens to claims and, then in accordance with an interpretation of law, renders a judgment of who is at fault and why, as well as what should be done to the offending party. These are the essential features of a court and, in particular, the key role of a judge, but in most societies of the past, these features of courts were not well developed (Black 1993:97–122). For example, in a review of anthropological ethnographies, Katherine Newman (1983:50–103) develops a typology of "court" systems in pre-industrial societies. In some hunter-gatherer societies, there was no third party available for resolving disputes; in slightly more developed societies, third parties of high-prestige individuals were available but were not defined as necessary by procedural rules and were not given any power to reach a verdict (only the giving of "advice" was possible). In somewhat more developed hunter-gatherer systems, disputants were supposed to approach third parties, or their representatives were to do so, but these parties still could not make binding decisions (they could only suggest compromises that would activate informal, interpersonal pressures by band members on disputants). In even

more developed hunter-gatherers, such as Big Men systems, and in simple horticultural populations, mediation could involve true adjudication by leaders or
councils of elders rendering decisions or verdicts that were binding on the disputants who increasingly were represented by others (such as fellow kinsmen
acting as "lawyers"). In the subsequent evolution of horticultural systems,
councils became more restricted to elites, and chiefs now had increased power
to render verdicts, with the more complex of these systems having an appeals
process from local councils/chiefs to paramount chiefs and restricted councils
of elites. And, in advanced horticulture and agrarianism where a state existed,
a system of courts often with full-time judges and bureaucratic organization
would emerge. From this base, industrial and post-industrial societies now
reveal a structure of courts revolving around (a) judges, juries or panels, law-
yers/barristers, and litigants/defendants, (b) division of adjudication into criminal and tort (civil) systems as well as specialized administrative, military, and
other restricted forms of adjudication, (c) full bureaucratization of record keeping and other administrative functions, and (d) hierarchical ordering of courts
culminating in a supreme tribunal.

Thus, the evolution of courts and related functions has occurred incremen-
tally and slowly in human history. Political leaders and elites have been reluctant to turn their decision-making power over to an autonomous legal system,
but as the volume and diversity of disputes and the rates of deviance have escalated, elites had to create adjudicative structures or watch their societies disintegrate (Turner 1980, 1974; Parsons 1962; Bredemeier 1962). As this process
occurred, courts often had to articulate new laws or mandate their enactment
in order to manage ever-emerging problems of coordination and control.

Creating New Laws   There is always a legislative element in a legal system
whereby particular parties are given the right—indeed, often the mandate—to
enact new laws as circumstances require (Evan 1990; Turner 1980, 1974, 1972;
Lloyd 1964; Davis 1962; Sawer 1965). Among hunter-gatherers, prestigeful
persons could suggest new rules, but these individuals had no capacity to
impose these rules on others. It is not until some degree of power was consolidated and concentrated in Big Men, kin heads, village chiefs, and councils of
elders that a true legislative function existed in which new laws could be
enacted. As power became more consolidated, this legislative function was
more pronounced, especially as the complexity of social relations and rates of
deviance increased. Eventually, legislative bodies are elected by the citizenry in
industrial and post-industrial societies, but this transition occurs only with late
agrarianism; and even with industrialism, legislative bodies are often little more
than "rubber stamps" for those holding dictatorial power. Thus, except in
those legal systems that allow some court decisions to serve as law-making, as

is the case in the United States and England but less so in continental Europe (Vago 1994:10–13), the legislative process remains solely within the polity.

Enforcement of Laws and Court Decisions   Ultimately, if laws and court decisions are to have the capacity to coordinate, regulate, and control, they must be obeyed. Historically, moral persuasion, informal sanctions, shaming, and other noncoercive techniques could operate effectively on members of small populations revealing minimal differentiation of only age and sex categories and low levels of inequality with respect to only prestige and honor. As populations became larger and more complex, however, laws and decisions had to be enforced by coercion if necessary (Newman 1983). Since the polity rarely relinquishes its claim to a monopoly of force—indeed, it seeks to legitimate through law and ideology its right to have a monopoly on the use of force— the enforcement of laws and court decisions comes from the polity rather than the courts. Courts can have enforcement agents of their own, but these never rival the coercive force of political leaders. As long as the capacity to make decisions on disputing parties or to force deviants to change their behavior overlapped extensively with polity—as is the case with chiefs, kings, and councils of elites who fill both court and legislative functions—there was little conflict between the emerging legal system and the more developed political system. Enforcement simply came by edict of political leaders. However, when there is a separation of courts from political decision-makers and when legislative bodies have some autonomy from political leaders in the administrative branch of government, a potential dilemma emerges because legislators and judges have no real coercive power. Instead, they must draw upon the coercive power of political leaders at the top of the administrative system to enforce laws and court decisions; and if conflict between these leaders and the emerging legal system occurs, the autonomy and viability of the legal system can be undone by political fiat backed by coercive force.

Thus, as the legal system has historically differentiated from the polity, it has remained partially embedded in the polity and had to rely upon the latter's coercive base to enforce decisions and judgments. This reliance has included the capacity of the court and legislative systems to have their decisions against political leaders and administrators backed by the coercive base of power lodged in the very polity that is being regulated by laws and court decisions. Only if a viable civic culture exists—one infused with accepted legal postulates about the relationship between the state and the population—has the legal system been able to exert this influence on polity. In return, for giving the legal system this autonomy, law provides polity with much of its symbolic base of power.

Selection Pressures and Legal Systems

Selection pressures, stemming from the operation of all macrodynamic forces, have led humans to develop legal systems (Turner 1972:214–15). We can group these pressures into three categories: (1) structural coordination, (2) legitimating power and inequality, and (3) preserving, codifying, and integrating cultural symbols.

Structural Coordination   Actors in a population, whether individuals or corporate units, must be minimally coordinated by the consolidation of power. Populations that could not create laws to coordinate actors, resolve disputes, and manage deviance did not survive, whereas those that could became more fit in their environment.

The use of power to create law has major consequences for establishing, maintaining, or reestablishing coordination in a variety of ways. (a) The legal subsystem specifies and enforces appropriate action in crucial areas of interaction among actors. Laws, courts, and enforcement as well as administrative agencies regularize interaction and give it predictability. (b) Law also provides procedures for settling disputes and conflicts when they arise. The legal subsystem provides an alternative to violence and vengeance by allowing disputing parties to settle their sources of conflict in courts. In this way law restores coordination when it breaks down. (c) Law checks deviance that could pose a serious breakdown in coordination and control. By specifying what is deviant and providing negative sanctions for such deviance, the legal system controls behavior in critical spheres. Such control facilitates coordination by increasing conformity and hence the predictability of social action.

Legitimating Power and Inequality   The consolidation and centralization of power inevitably increase inequalities that, in turn, dramatically increase second-order logistical loads and, hence, selection pressures from regulation as a macrodynamic force. Those without resources have always, over time, become resentful, potentially mobilizing for conflict that can cause disintegration and reduce fitness. The evolution of law represented one mechanism to mitigate against this disintegrative potential arising from inequalities. Legal subsystems have always legitimized power, giving some the right to control others and, in the process, bestowing upon elites wealth and privilege. As power is consolidated, intense selection pressures emerge to find ways to legitimate symbolically the use of the other bases of power, particularly as inequalities increase. Sometimes inequality is explicitly written into laws and enforced by courts and police, but frequently the legitimization is more subtle: Police differentially enforce the same laws for the rich and poor; the wealthy have the knowledge and financial resources to press effectively their interests in courts; or administrative agencies in the legal system push the interests of the rich more than the poor. And so, once a legal system exists, it always legitimates and reinforces inequality and stratification—sometimes successfully but often times unsuccessfully.

Preserving, Codifying, and Integrating Cultural Symbols   Every society has a cultural system, or storehouse of customs, traditions, values, lores, beliefs, technology, and dogmas. As this storehouse of culture becomes complex, selection pressures emanating from regulation and reproduction build to find mechanisms for specifying key relations in terms of values and beliefs and for integrating elements of culture. Without law as a mediator among elements of culture, cultural conflict can ensue. And so, much of the cultural inventory of a population, especially basic values and beliefs, is reflected in the codes and statutes of a legal system (Weber [1922] 1954) that operates as a reproductive force in helping sustain cultural continuity. For example, basic American values of equality, justice, humanitarianism, and individualism are preserved and codified in the Constitution, as well as in a wide number of national and state codes and statutes. Similarly, before the collapse of the Soviet Union, basic values of collectivism were codified in the Soviet constitution and legal system, while being imposed on satellites of the union (which was one of the reasons for the low levels of legitimacy given to the Soviet polity by its western and southern satellites).

Law does more than preserve and codify; it integrates values and other cultural components into concrete and specific structural situations. Law specifies in certain crucial situations just exactly how values, beliefs, customs, and traditions are to be realized in day-to-day interaction among actors (Luhmann 1982); and in so doing, it operates as a symbolic base of power. This relationship between law and culture can be highly dynamic in any rapidly changing society where new values, beliefs, and ideologies often come into conflict with the old, thereby forcing legislation and decisions by courts to reconcile changing values not only with each other but with concrete interaction situations that are affected by the conflict (Gurvitch 1953). If reconciliation of these sources of cultural conflict cannot occur, as is often the case, the disintegrative potential of a society increases. Thus, the legal system of a changing society seeks to resolve many—but never all—of the conflicts resulting from a lack of cultural integration, especially as these conflicts disrupt basic social relations (Friedman 1969a, 1969b). For example, in the United States at the turn of this century, the values of rugged individualism and laissez faire came into conflict with emerging values of collectivism and social welfare. The conflict was particularly acute in labor-management relations as labor sought to bargain collectively with management determined to preserve old laissez faire values. In the long run, a host of labor-management laws partially resolved this integrative crisis. Similarly, in the face of widespread poverty, conflicts between American values of rugged individualism, on one side, and humanitarianism on the other were mitigated with the emergence of a host of welfare laws at both the national and state levels, although Americans still remain highly ambivalent about welfare to the poor. Similar examples of the integrative impact of law on culture and society can be found in all societies, especially those undergoing rapid cultural and social transformation.

As problems of structural coordination, legitimating power and inequality, and integrating culture have escalated in human history, law has been used as a "solution," at least temporarily until the disintegrative potential in these problems overwhelms the legal system and centers of power. All forces—population growth, regulation leading to the consolidation and centralization of power, reproductive demands on culture, production and distribution requiring new modes of coordination—have generated a broad array of selection pressures that pose problems that only law can resolve. Indeed, the scale of society will be greatly limited without an active legal system (Parsons 1966). Thus, we can define law as an institutional system as *the system of rules and rule making, rule mediating and interpreting, and rule enforcing that addresses problems of structural coordination, legitimization of power and inequality, and cultural preservation, codification, and integration.*

EDUCATION

For most of human history, people have learned what they needed to know through participation in familial, economic, religious, political, and legal activities. They learned by watching or doing, and occasionally, by explicit instruction. Almost imperceptively and, indeed, often episodically learning gradually changed, at least for some in society: Future shamans, magicians, priests, and other religious practitioners became apprentices to those already practicing these vocations. Somewhat later came apprenticeships in trades, crafts, arts, and closed professions or guilds. Much of this training was embedded in kinship, although non-kin apprentices would often learn their trade in patrimonial families composed of kin and non-kin. Similarly, families involved in commerce would teach their children how to read, write, and calculate. And at times, low-prestige private schools would emerge to teach the basics of literacy to some of the masses seeking careers in commerce and government. For elites, private tutors would give them the cultural capital—languages, classics, literature, history, poetry, and other nonvocational knowledge bases—necessary to mark them off from the masses and middle classes. And over time, private and elite preparatory schools began to house and train the children of elites. Eventually, true universities were to emerge, at first to train literate members of the middle classes in professions such as law and medicine and, later, to instruct elites in nonvocational fields of learning such as science.

Still, most instruction occurred through apprenticeships, family instruction, and private tutoring right up to the beginnings of the industrial era, although schools and universities were evident in the most advanced agrarian societies. With industrialization, however, the scale and scope of education increased, and education began to reach larger numbers of people in the population. This sudden growth was the last spurt of a long-term evolutionary trend as the complexity of societies escalated selection pressures arising from reproduction as a social force.

Elements of Educational Systems

The institution of education, as distinct from general socialization and learning in kin structures, increasingly evolved into: (1) a system of formalized instruction, (2) an explicit curriculum, and (3) a pattern of ritualized passage. As education has become ever more differentiated as a distinct institutional system, these three elements have become correspondingly more pronounced, although it is difficult to mark the transition from an educational system embedded in other institutions to one clearly differentiated from other institutional domains.

Formalized Instruction   Education involves two distinct status positions: teacher and student. The more explicit the distinction between teacher and student, and the more formally organized their interaction in terms of time and place of instruction, the more they are part of the institution of education. For most of human history, however, learning was not institutionalized in a distinct educational system. Among hunter-gatherers or simple horticulturalists, adults might have paused or set aside a time for formal instruction in handcrafts, religious rituals, or other activities, and on these occasions, the institution of education could be seen but only as a fleeting set of activities buried in other institutional systems like kinship, economy, or religion. With advanced horticulture and agrarianism, more permanent instructor-student relations emerged in apprenticeships for a wide variety of crafts, private tutelage of elites, religious instruction for future members of the priesthood, merchant family instruction in literacy and arithmetic, closed guilds requiring specific periods of instruction for professionals, and even private schools that could range from places for acquiring literacy to universities imparting high culture or professional skills. Under these conditions, education has become more formalized, marking its first beginnings as a distinct institutional system.

Explicit Curriculum   Education as an institution revolves around a curriculum, or subject matter that is to be taught by teachers to students. Again, for most of human history, the curriculum remained buried in the ongoing socialization of the young and learning by adults in their daily lives, but as instruction became more explicit in apprenticeships, tutelage, guilds, families, and schools, the formalization of the teacher-student relationship was associated with a more clearly stated and delimited subject matter, whether this emerging curriculum be trade skills, literacy, arithmetic, or languages and cultural markers of elites. As the curriculum of formalized instruction became more clearly defined, then, education was further differentiated as an institutional system.

Ritualized Passage   Throughout history, most formal instruction, even that revolving around a curriculum in schools, did not involve mandatory attendance, grades, examinations, or degrees (Collins 1977). Rather, students' observable proficiency in a skill was an indicator of their progress. Yet, the beginnings of what eventually became the capstone of a fully differentiated educational system could be found when apprentices were declared practitioners, when guilds admitted their trainees to full membership, when student-priests became full-fledged priests, when low status schools pronounced that a student could read, and at other points of passage that denoted progress through a curriculum. As education became further institutionalized, these points of passage were ever more ritualized along several dimensions: (1) attendance at formalized instruction became more mandatory, (2) proficiency was more subject to grading and examinations, and (3) progress through the curriculum was denoted by standardized degrees or other markers of progress. The more ritualized is formal education along these dimensions, the more it is institutionalized.

In sum, then, the emergence of education as a distinctive institution revolves around formalized relations between teacher and student, explicit and delimited curriculum, and ritualized passage through the curriculum. Until the beginnings of the nineteenth century, the vast mass of the population in human societies remained untouched by the institutionalized system of education. Indeed, it had been a recessive institutional form, barely or only episodically distinguishable from activity in the more developed economic, kinship, and religious institutional systems. Thus, although education is now a prominent institutional form in most human societies, this high visibility of education is very recent. Given its late arrival as a distinct system, we might conclude that education is not one of the core institutional systems. Yet, education was always present in human organization, moving periodically outside kinship and, then, by fits and starts becoming ever more distinct as a system of corporate units providing formalized instruction of a curriculum marked by *rites de passage* and credentials. This emergence, differentiation, and development of education occurred as a response to selection pressures arising from several macrodynamic forces.

Selection Pressures and Education

Selection pressures for the social reproduction of the population were relatively low in agrarian societies; and as a consequence, education tended to be either

(1) oriented to acquiring practical economic skills through apprenticeships, low status primary schools, and family socialization or (2) nonvocational and concerned with acquiring cultural capital through private tutors, elite preparatory schools, and universities in order to mark status differences among strata in the system of inequality (Collins 1977; Bourdieu 1984; Bourdieu and Passeron 1977). Education began to change when the developing state, under selection pressures emanating from regulation as a social force, sought to use education to instill a civic culture in order to (a) consolidate its symbolic base of power and (b) train bureaucrats to sustain the administrative and coercive bases of power. Surprisingly, economic changes associated with industrialization were less important forces on education because most occupational skills could be acquired through apprenticeships and on-the-job training. Indeed, even today, some have argued that education has less to do with acquiring vocational skills than it does with marking social status and maintaining political loyalties.

Thus, the selection pressures that have operated to expand education as a distinct institution of formalized instruction of a curriculum, at least initially, have emanated primarily from regulation as the state has sought to consolidate symbolic, administrative, and coercive bases of power and to legitimate symbolically inequalities and, only secondarily, from production and reproduction in efforts to expand human capital and technology. These selection pressures are, of course, intimately connected, because the polity, economy, and stratification have mutual effects on each other. As these mutually interconnected forces have played themselves out historically, and most particularly in the industrial and post-industrial era, diverse sets of selection pressures have pushed for the expansion of educational systems. These selection pressures can be grouped as follows: (1) social reproduction, (2) cultural storage, (3) social placement, (4) conflict management, and (5) social change.

Social Reproduction The differentiation among institutional systems has increased the values of reproduction as a social force. Each institutional domain has its own culture and set of positions that individuals must be qualified to occupy. Thus, as the complexity of societies has increased, problems of reproduction have escalated, generating selection pressures for the differentiation and development of education. And so, as education evolved as a formal system of instruction (in schools), imparting a particular curriculum, and establishing a highly ritualized passage through the system, it has important effects on reproducing members who can participate in, and fit into, other institutional spheres. This reproduction occurs along several dimensions, including: (1) economic, (2) political, and (3) cultural.

Economic reproduction. For most of human history, economic skills were learned through formal and informal tutelage within kinship or, if distinct non-kin units performed economic activity, through on-the-job training or apprenticeships. With post-industrialization, however, economic reproduction becomes much more complex, forcing the development of a large system of formal educational structures if the economy is to remain dynamic. The more developed an educational system, the greater is its effect on imparting trade skills, cognitive knowledge, interpersonal skills, and motivational dispositions appropriate for participation in the economy.

Political reproduction. As political power is consolidated and centralized into a distinct system of corporate units comprising the state, selection pressures for legitimating and, hence, reproducing the state increase. The expansion of education by the polity can be viewed as a reproductive strategy to consolidate its symbolic base of power. The state began to finance schools in the agrarian era in order to expand literacy among those who might become its bureaucratic functionaries, but such initiatives did not massify the educational systems. Rather, as states have sought to consolidate their symbolic base of power, they have supported schools to impart the "civic culture" (values, goals, beliefs, histories, mythologies, heroes) that is used to legitimate power (Ichilov 1990; Boli, Ramirez, and Meyer 1985; Ramirez and Boli 1987; Anyon 1980). These efforts by polity revolve around imparting to individuals a conception of themselves as "citizens" who will contribute to the goals of the polity and, at the same time, who will enjoy as consumers the beneficial outcomes of state actions (Ramirez and Boli 1987:154). In so doing, the state has attempted to blend its symbolic and material incentive bases of power, thereby reproducing relations of power in the society.

Cultural reproduction. Informal tutelage was sufficient to reproduce the culture of a population for most of human history. As societies became more complex, however, and as the culture of diverse institutional spheres differentiated, education as an institutional system differentiated in response to growing selection pressures from reproductive forces. Although schools impart the basic ideologies contained in the economic and political culture of society, they also teach students the broader societal culture and the professional-bureaucratic culture of the school system itself (Gramsci 1972; Apple 1988, 1982a, 1982b, 1979, 1978; Giroux 1990a, 1990b, 1981). Thus, much of what schools teach is cultural—language, science, history, art, music, literature, civics, mathematics—and so the schools are involved in reproducing the culture of a society. Although this culture is disproportionately influenced by the forces of production and regulation as they drive the formation of the economy and polity, schools also have an impact on the broader culture of a population; and the more complex this culture has become, the more intense have been selection pressures on education.

Cultural Storage   For most of human history, culture was stored in people's heads and, then, taught to each new generation. But as societies grew and differentiated, culture became more complex, especially as the use of writing spread. Increasingly, in order to reproduce culture, schoollike structures emerged to, first of all, store culture and then, pass it on through formalized instruction. When culture is unwritten, it cannot be highly complex because of the limitations of human memory, and as a consequence, selection pressures from reproduction on formal education are less intense, but, once a written language existed, the capacity to expand systems of symbols escalated dramatically. As culture expanded, it could no longer be stored in the minds of people. Selection for new ways to store culture increased, and in response, education expanded. Today, culture must now be assembled in texts, computer algorithms, files, and other compilations; and these compilations of symbols must, in turn, be stored in a way that they can be retrieved (Turner 1972). Although much storage and retrieval occurs outside educational structures, education nonetheless becomes an important cultural warehouse. For the collective knowledge of instructors, libraries, computer facilities, and research staffs house much of a population's culture. Moreover, this culture is stored in ways that it can be retrieved, if desired or needed, and passed on to new generations via the reproduction activities of the educational system.

Social Placement   The transition to adulthood always has involved rituals marking through *rites de passage*, with these rituals underscoring that not only has the individual reached biological maturity but also a new level of social maturity in the acquisition of the necessary knowledge and skills to be defined as an adult. For most of humans' evolutionary history, acquiring the necessary knowledge and skill occurred in kinship or in various forms of non-kin tutelage. For elites this tutelage assured their membership in status groups of high prestige; for the non-elite, economic skills in the expanding division of labor were learned. Thus, whether embedded in kinship or extended to non-kin units, education has always had effects on the placement of individuals in the broader social structure. Such placement operates at two different, although increasingly interrelated, levels: (1) membership in status groups, and (2) incumbency in occupational positions.

Status groups. In advanced horticultural and agrarian societies, low-status primary schools that taught the rudiments of literacy, apprenticeships and guilds that gave individuals a craft or profession, and kin-based instruction that imparted the necessities for commerce were all involved in placing individuals in the larger occupational structure. The specific occupations of these nonelites became the criterion for their placement in a status group—whether merchant, artisan, government scribe, or priest—that could be distinguished by lifestyle, demeanor, speech, and other forms of cultural capital. In contrast, the private tutors, preparatory schools, and scholastic tracks of universities were involved in sustaining the distinctiveness of elites without reference to a vocation. Thus, there was a clear separation between status group membership based upon occupation and income, on the nonelite side, and status group membership based on acquired culture, on the elite side. Indeed, education in music, poetry, rhetoric, history, classics, literature, and other nonvocational pursuits, coupled with the demeanor styles that such nonvocational pursuits generated, became an important marker and gatekeeper of class divisions between elites and nonelites (Collins 1977). Thus, once distinct social classes emerged in human societies, selection for ways to distinguish their members culturally from each other led to the expansion of school systems.

Occupations. Much of the early growth of educational systems came not so much from efforts to achieve a better vocation, but rather from a desire of nonelites to claim greater prestige because of their educational achievements. Often children of wealthy merchants were sent to school, or were given private tutoring, in a self-conscious effort to emulate the cultural styles of elites, whereas at other times education was used by the less affluent to gain an increase in respectability (Collins 1977). And in a few instances, education has been used, as was the case among the *philosophes* in eighteenth-century France, to mobilize new cultural symbols that challenged those of the elite (indeed, the teachings of the *philosophes* legitimated the French Revolution of 1789, while becoming the broad principles behind the U.S. Constitution).

Vestiges of this division between education for status group membership remain even in post-industrial societies—for example, education in "prep schools" as well as Ivy League and other elite private colleges in America, "public" schools (really private schools) as well as Oxford and Cambridge universities in the United Kingdom. In the more recent history of education, the distinctions between education for entrance to status groups and occupations have become blurred. As the middle and lower classes have sought "cultural capital" as a source of prestige and respectability, and as the state has expanded education at all levels, the same educational credentials affect *both* vocational placement in an occupation or profession and status group membership. This crossover effect began slowly, as is illustrated when top government officials in England were recruited from the ranks of elite school graduates or as is evident when law and business schools at Ivy League and other elite universities feed the upper echelons of corporate law and business. Once this connection between educational credentials and occupation is established for elites, nonelites can begin to pressure the state to provide educational opportunities facilitating higher occupational and status group memberships.

If the stratification system, and its corresponding series of status groups, have remained strong, then a "sponsored-mobility" pattern where the young are sorted early into vocational or college-bound tracks and schools will be most evident. Such a system gives enormous advantage to the children of elites who have the resources to sponsor their performance in schools and examinations. In contrast, if strata and status groups are more fluid and flexible, then a "contest-mobility" system prevails, giving many more opportunities to greater varieties of young to pursue higher education and delaying as long as possible the sorting of young into college-bound and vocational tracks. There are always political pressures toward a "contest-mobility" system as individuals seek the credentials that gain access to both better occupations and status group affiliations. And this connection between advancement in schools and occupation as well as status group membership becomes ever more visible as employers (initially the state and educational system itself as employers but eventually economic employers as well) begin to use credentials as the main criterion for hiring.

As these placement effects of a growing educational system develop, the system itself becomes more ritualized in marking passages, since grades and test scores are increasingly used to determine how far students can go in school and, hence, where they will be placed as adults in society. And as passages become ritualized, the possession of educational credentials becomes the primary resource of the young in highly competitive labor markets. And, as the labor market and credentialing activities of the educational system become ever more interdependent, the social placement consequences of education become more pervasive and profound.

Conflict Management Whenever education has existed, it has been implicated in conflict, especially if it has increased inequalities of status group membership or economic opportunities. Yet, in the transition into industrial and post-industrial societies, regulation as a force has pushed polity to expand the educational system and the credentials determining people's life chances in labor markets. In so doing, polity has used education to manage conflicts emanating from the regulatory problems inherent in inequality and stratification. Much class and ethnic conflict has now been transformed and transmuted into debates over access to the cultural capital and credentials offered by the educational system. Thus, access to schools rather than transformations in economic and political arrangements is more likely to become the salient issue when educational credentials, job placement, and status group membership become associated; and as this deflection of tension occurs, potentially more serious conflicts are avoided, or at least mitigated when they come. In this deflection conflicts also become more ideological (Gramsci 1972; Apple 1988; Giroux 1990a, 1990b), focusing on inclusion of ethnic cultures and their histories, on special programs to help the culturally disadvantaged, on better pedagogy in order to reach effectively more diverse student populations, on the fairness of the testing system, on teacher cultural biases, and on a host of related issues that skirt around more basic class, gender, and ethnic inequalities.

It is this effect of education on regulatory problems that brings polity into education. If the schools can be expanded and if their incumbents can come to believe that access to an education is more equally distributed, then those who do not perform well in the system can be stigmatized for their personal failings or limitations, while the broader patterns of societal stratification can escape criticism. One does not need to view this process critically or cynically because expansion of education does increase opportunities for mobility by nonelites *if* the labor market is able to place credentialed graduates in positions corresponding to their educational attainment. Of course, when the educational system produces a surplus of credentials relative to jobs, then the conflict potential is escalated, although only if graduates blame the economy or polity. In fact, because of their inculcation into the economic and political culture, graduates frequently do not protest or mobilize for conflict; instead, they often blame themselves or migrate to countries with a more robust labor or human capital market. And so, ironically, societies whose economies cannot absorb their overeducated graduates become exporters of educated labor to more developed societies, as has been the case, for example, with India (at least until its recent spurt of economic growth).

Social Change   In industrial and post-industrial societies, educational systems are almost always viewed by the state as a vehicle for implementing social change. Indeed, developing societies in the process of industrialization expand the educational system not only in order to create "new citizens" but also to raise the skill level of human capital so as to stimulate further economic development. There is now a world-level ideology associating education and social progress (Ramirez and Boli 1987), an ideology that has encouraged the rapid expansion of educational systems in all parts of the world. This expansion has also been encouraged and financed by such trans-societal sources of funding as the World Bank, which propagates the ideology that economic growth and education go hand in hand and which also advocates a particular model of how education should be structured. As a consequence, there is now convergence in how schools are organized in the developing world.

Polity in fully industrial and post-industrial societies also uses the educational system to implement social changes. For example, as noted above, special programs in schools are often used to increase equality of opportunities for formerly disadvantaged groups. More indirectly, polity can fund "Big Science" in research universities in an effort to develop new knowledge that will be adopted in change-producing technologies.

Thus, because polity can control schools, coupled with the fact that schools are involved in the socialization of citizens and human capital as well as in the production of knowledge and symbol systems, the state views the schools as a vehicle for implementing policies. Other institutional systems—kinship, religion, and economy—are less easily managed, or are managed at unpredictable costs and with uncertain outcomes, by state intervention. Hence, the state is more likely to use an institutional system that it can control to generate social change.

At times, however, education is used to generate social change that is not sanctioned by the state. This more "subversive" use of education can occur in private schools (although these usually support the status quo because they are generally funded by elites and religion), in state-financed schools removed from administrative supervision, and in schools where democratic ideals of the broader society create a normative climate emphasizing "academic freedom." An instance of this latter pattern is found in American higher education, where classrooms are often used for political mobilization and ideological conversion of students against social inequalities and supporters (e.g., corporate America, government) of the status quo. Conversely, schools in some Islamic societies teach religious fundamentalism that may be at odds with state policies. If such transformative efforts actually threaten the state, however, use of the material base of power (cutting off funds, for example) and even the coercive base are likely to ensue.

Education is the last of the core institutions to differentiate in human history, and we are now in a position to define education as an institution, distinct from learning that occurs through activities in other institutions. Education is *the systematic organization of formal student-teacher instruction, revolving around an explicit curriculum and involving ritualized student passage, that has consequences among the members of a population for social reproduction, cultural storage, social placement, conflict management, and social transformation.*

CONCLUSION

In this chapter, I seek to outline the basic elements of each of the core institutional systems that have become differentiated from kinship over the last twenty-five millennia. I begin with the economy, only because humans cannot survive without production. Similarly, they cannot survive biologically without reproduction. And both of these forces have placed in our ancient past heavy selection pressures on humans to forge new kinds of bonds in nuclear families grouped into small bands. This system was enormously adaptive because humans radiated all over the globe during their first 230,000 years on earth. For most of human history, then, production and reproduction of humans have been the driving forces, but once population as a force increases in valence, new selection pressures are generated, activating the remaining macrodynamic forces—regulation and distribution—while increasing the valences for production and reproduction. Thus, as humans settled into more permanent communities, populations grew and the successive differentiation of the core institutional systems ensued. Evolution has not always been lineal because de-evolution back to hunting and gathering has, no doubt, occurred. For example, it is likely that Australian aborigines are former horticulturalists from New Guinea who, when coming to Australia, reverted back to hunting and gathering in response to the severe ecology of inland Australia.

Over time, each institutional system has differentiated from kinship, and as institutions have become distinctive domains with their own cultures and systems of corporate as well as categoric units, the analysis of institutions involves not only an explanation of the forces causing this differentiation and development but also an analysis of how institutional systems become reintegrated in patterns of mutual influence. The term *integrated* is not meant to imply a smooth operating equilibrium or a stable system of institutions but, rather, to denote the fact that as institutions become distinct they reveal patterns of mutual influence that need to be explored (see chapter 8). Thus, as we begin our review of the prominent stages in human evolution from hunting and gathering to post-industrialism, we need to examine how institutions differentiated, developed and, once separated, became reintegrated. And, as we come to appreciate, many of the selection pressures operating on a given institution come from the forces pushing the operation of other institutions.

NOTES

1. These definitions differ somewhat from those commonly employed by anthropologists. Frequently when a newly married couple does not move into one of their parent's family compounds, but still lives within the same community, this is referred to as a neolocal residence pattern. In the definitions offered here this would be either a matrilocal or patrilocal pattern. For us neolocality pertains to norms allowing for the free choice of residency by married couples.

2. For references on unilineal descent systems, see: Fox (1967), Radcliffe-Brown (1952), Keesing (1975), Ember and Ember (1983), Fried (1957), and Fortes (1953).

3. Sociologists have made a wide variety of typologies pertaining to the organization of religious activity. Probably the most influential typology was Weber's two polar types of religious organization: the church and sect. These were developed in more detail by Weber's student Ernst Troeltsch ([1911] 1960), who viewed a *church* as a large, conservative, elite-based ascriptive and dominant religious organization. At the polar extreme to a church was a *sect*, which was viewed as a small, voluntary, quasi-rebellious religious order. Numerous amplifications of this typology have been made (Yinger 1970; Wilson 1969; Pfautz 1955; Becker 1950; Wuthnow 1988:495). Generally, sociological typologies of religious organization include, from least to most organized: cult, sect, established sect, church, denomination, ecclesia (Salisbury 1964:96–97; Moberg 1962:73–99; Johnson 1960:419–

39). While useful in analyzing religion in modern societies, these distinctions do not allow us to grasp either the subtleties or complexity of traditional religious organization. For this reason I have abandoned a sociological classification in favor of a more anthropological one (Wallace 1966). This classification will allow us to put in a comparative perspective modern religious organization. Thus, as noted above, cult structure is a generic term encompassing all *specific* forms of religious organization, whether a cult (in the sociological sense), sect, established sect, church, denomination, or ecclesia.

4. The approach taken in this chapter is functionalist, but with a conflict theory slant. I draw from my own work (Turner 1980, 1974, 1972; Fuchs and Turner 1991) and William M. Evan's (1990:222–23) theoretical model, and also, elements of Black's (1993) theory. For reviews of theoretical approaches to the sociology of law, see: Rich (1977), Selznick (1968), Reasons and Rich (1978), Vago (1994), Evan (1990, 1980, 1962), Chambliss (1976), Black and Mileski (1973).

Chapter Four

Institutional Systems of Hunter-Gatherer Populations

The human ancestral line emerged between five and eight million years ago. This first ancestor looked like an ape, because it was a kind of ape who sought to survive in the predator-ridden African savanna. Somehow these animals and their kind had to find food, fend off predators, and reproduce themselves in an environment that was not hospitable or safe, especially for primates whose ancestors had evolved in the now dwindling arboreal habitat of trees. Natural selection first worked on the body of this animal, making it upright by five million years ago so that it could see above the grasses where danger lay, run from and after prey, and use its dexterous hands to carry food, throw objects at predators, and perhaps even make crude tools. Natural selection also worked on social organization, creating the bonds, attachments, and solidarities that would enable this vulnerable-looking ape to face danger collectively and, equally important, to organize the quest for food and the reproduction of their kind (Maryanski and Turner 1992). Organization was thus to be the key to this apelike animal's success; and the more these *hominids*, or those primates on the human line, could organize their activities, the greater were their chances of survival.

Survival for each of the successive species of hominids would be a momentous achievement, since apes were in decline five million years ago, and as we now know, only four genera of apes—gibbons, orangutans, chimpanzees, and gorillas—are still with the human descendants of these first hominids. If we count humans as an evolved ape, then just five genera have survived the last eight million years—five out of many hundreds. Apes are thus one of the great failures in the evolutionary record.

Yet, hominids beat the odds, probably because they became better organized. At some point, natural selection favored ever more intelligent hominids who could forge tighter-knit social bonds and attachments. But even as the brain got larger, patterns of social organization remained simple—at best, bands of a few dozen males, females, and offspring. Perhaps they had families, but at first, only the mother and her offspring could be seen as "family." Later, males became more attached to mothers and their offspring as natural selection heightened human emotions and transformed what had been highly promiscuous sexual relations between males and females into more enduring social bonds (Turner 2000). Even as this transformation into the first families of mother, father, and offspring occurred, the structure of the band housing these families was still very simple: clusters of nuclear families wandering together in search of food to gather or kill. Apparently, this simple structure, coupled with the intelligence of its incumbents who could use fire and make tools, was sufficient for hominids to prosper. By two million years ago, descendants of the first hominid—*Homo habilis* and, later, *Homo erectus*—had been able to migrate out of Africa and populate much of the globe.

And so it remained for the rest of hominid evolution. At some point, perhaps as long as 250,000 years ago, *Homo sapiens sapiens* or modern humans could be found in Africa and the Middle East. Even if this date is wrong, there is no doubt that by 100,000 years ago, the threshold to being fully human was crossed, but long before full-fledged humans emerged, gathering and hunting bands had been the basis of survival for several million years.

Human hunting and gathering societies were typically small, usually consisting of a band of fifty to eighty people. Bands tended to be autonomous, although each remained in contact with others sharing the same language, culture, and region. The largest single grouping of hunters and gatherers ever discovered in the archeological record was a settlement numbering about 400 to 600 people in a highly fertile area of France. A band of hunters and gatherers wandered a region or territory, often in a somewhat circular pattern. The band would settle for a time—perhaps several weeks—in one area, extract the available resources, and then move on to exploit a new location. Eventually, when resources replenished themselves, the band might return to its starting point and initiate a new round of movement to and from favored locations. Band members appeared to have a sense for their own and others' home range, and as a result, they tended to wander within a delimited area, respecting the home ranges of others, although conflict between bands may have been frequent if resources became scarce. Equally often, however, the band may have dispersed for a time (and even permanently) when resources in an area diminished, with some members seeking a new area to exploit. This demographic and spatial profile required low population densities so that the environment would not be overtaxed. The bands themselves sought to maintain their population size to an optimal level through a combination of infanticide, abortion, and birth control (which included women nursing children for prolonged periods and maintaining a low lever of body fat and weight; see Kolata 1974).

Hunter-gatherers were thus the prototypical social form in which all nascent institutional systems were housed. Human social evolution has involved the successive differentiation from band and nuclear families all of the core institutions—economy, religion, polity, law, and education. In a sense, it is not meaningful to talk about institutions among hunter-gatherers because there is only one clear-cut institution: kinship. Selection pressures arising from the force of population, production, reproduction, distribution, and regulation led to the formation of the nuclear family, clustered into small bands. Thus, all of the macrodynamic forces worked through two simple corporate structures—bands and nuclear families—and few categoric distinctions—age and sex classes. Since hunting and gathering bands were, in essence, mesolevel structures, macrodynamic forces were at low valences, revolving primarily around creating a sufficiently stable structure that could respond to pressures for production and reproduction, while meeting low-level valences for distribution and regulation. If a species cannot find food and reproduce itself it is soon selected out, as were most species of apes. Indeed, the only ape to survive to the present day in the open-country African savanna was the hominid line, with rival lines dying out over the last eight million years. Today, all other species of apes live in the forest or woodlands because, unlike humans and their hominid ancestors, they are not sufficiently organized to survive in open-country conditions.

KINSHIP

The nature of kinship is very much connected to the type of economy. In hunting and gathering bands, kinship was very simple: nuclear family units of mother, father, and offspring, at times connected together to form a larger unit of several nuclear families. In this kinship system, marriage was relatively unconstrained, although rules of incest and, at times, exogamy and endogamy applied. Dissolution of marriages was also relatively simple, with minor rituals allowing marriage partners to separate. Relations within the nuclear family were egalitarian, although men and women engaged in very different activities, and only men tended to garner high prestige for skill in their activities. Residence varied and could be neolocal, bilocal (both mother's and father's sides), or patrilocal, but even if there was a clear residence rule, bilateral and truncated descent rules prevailed, indicating that family lines were not emphasized.

Thus, as table 4.1 summarizes, the kinship system of hunter-gatherers was composed of norms of bilateral/truncated descent, neolocal residence (with some bias toward bilocal or patrilocality), nuclear families (at times joined in

Table 4.1.   Structure of Kinship in Hunting and Gathering Societies

Size and composition	Predominantly nuclear units of mother, father, and children
Residence	Neolocal, bilocal, and patrilocal
Activity	Clear division of labor: males hunt, and females gather and do domestic chores
Descent	Usually bilateral, but truncated
Authority	Egalitarian, although considerable variability exists (with some systems giving males more authority over women)
Marriage	Incest prohibited; exogamy and endogamy; considerable freedom of choice; divorce easily effected

extended families), free choice in marriage guided by rules of incest (and at times, exogamy and endogamy), easy dissolution, egalitarian authority, and a division of labor in which males hunted and females gathered. It is in this division of economic labor that the seeds of the institution of the economy can be found.

ECONOMY

Hunter-gatherers revealed only minimal levels for each of the basic elements organizing their economic activity (Maryanski and Turner 1992:83; Turner 1972). Technologically, they possessed limited albeit highly useful knowledge about how to exploit the environment. This knowledge revolved around such practical matters as how to gather various food sources at different times of the year; how to hunt with spears and, for some, bows and arrows; and how to search for hidden water sources in times of drought.

Physical capital formation in the economy was also extremely limited, consisting of the equipment for hunting (spears, bows and arrows) and gathering (e.g., digging sticks and baskets) and perhaps a few utensils for preparing food. Human capital was strictly divided between men and women, with men performing almost all the hunting and with women doing virtually all the gathering, which normally involved picking or digging for food, as well as carrying it back to camp for processing. Many hunters and gatherers did not appear to work hard in order to meet their nutritional requirements, even under extreme environmental conditions (Sahlins 1972:1–32; Lee and DeVore 1968; Woodburn 1968). Yet, their work could be tedious; and there was probably great variability in difficulty and arduousness of their labor. In general, men normally provided far less food with their labor than women, primarily because hunting was not always successful. When successful, however, a short term (and perishable) economic surplus might emerge. Women and their offspring were much more likely to secure the necessary food among hunter-gatherers, but there was generally considerable variability in how many hours they needed to spend in gathering fruits, nuts, berries, roots, and other edible foods. Some have argued that hunters and gatherers generally lived what has been called a "leisure-intensive" lifestyle (Eibl-Eibesfeldt 1991:55), although these populations could be subject to environmental changes that might put them on the brink of starvation.

Entrepreneurship, or the organization of other economic elements, was performed by the band and nuclear kinship units. Consisting of mother, father, and children, the nuclear family unit was organized for two explicit ends: the procurement of food and the procreation/socialization of the young. The band as a whole might also be seen as an entrepreneurial unit, since it sought to organize nuclear families in ways that facilitated movement to available resources. But unlike the corporate units of more complex societies, the bands were not elaborate, hierarchical, or highly constraining. They were simply places where individuals had considerable freedom to choose when and how they would pursue their various lines of activity.

Finally, property as an element of economic organization was minimal. The physical capital—spears, bowls, bows and arrows, digging sticks—was usually defined by hunter-gatherers as private property; and at times, the home range or territory of the band as a whole was defined as their collective property. Understandings about how to distribute a hunting kill evoked a sense of property (for example, the person who actually made the kill would get the most valued parts), but most resources were shared among members of the band.

Table 4.2.   Economy in Hunting-Gathering Societies

Technology	Practical knowledge of: indigenous plant resources including, at times, seeding and harvesting; animal resources and hunting; seasonal effects on availability of plant and animal resources. Knowledge of how to make tools—spears, digging sticks, hatchets, bows and arrows, baskets, and at times pottery
Physical Capital	Hunting equipment; digging implements; cooking utensils
Labor	Clear sexual division of labor; males hunt, and females gather
Entrepreneurship	Band and nuclear family units organize economic activity
Property	Personal possessions. At times, collective territory. No material inequality, although rules about how to distribute a hunting kill can be seen as early definitions of property

In this kind of simple economy, all institutional structures were folded into, or fused with, the nuclear family units and the band. Just as the economy was embedded in kinship and band, so other institutional systems, such as religion, polity, law, and education, were coextensive with kin and band. Indeed, as emphasized above, the history of human societies has been one of differentiating new institutional systems as populations have grown and as the economy has expanded. We should remember, however, that for most of our history as a species, humans' biological nature was conditioned by hunting-gathering economies. We are, at our evolutionary heart and soul, hunter-gatherers who have created complex social structures and systems of culture over the last fifteen thousand years. The first step along this developmental path was, as we see in the next chapter, the adoption of a new mode of economic organization: horticulture.

RELIGION

Among the attempts to delineate stages of religious evolution (e.g., Bellah 1970, 1964; Habermas 1979; Luhmann 1984; and Wallace 1966), I find Wallace's (1966) discussion of pre-modern religions the most useful. To classify religions into types, we need to select some common dimensions that can serve as a point of reference for both comparing religions and recording their evolutionary development. Three dimensions follow from the definition of religion presented in chapter 3: (1) the nature of religious beliefs about the supernatural, (2) the nature of rituals, and (3) the nature of cult structures.

Among most hunter-gatherer bands, religion was comparatively simple, if it existed at all. Spirits and beings inhering in the empirical universe (sea, sky, plant life) were often postulated, but in many cases they were not perceived to exert extensive control over the world, nor were they always worshipped as sacred in a highly intense way. There were no cult structures, save for the individual who may have practiced rituals that evoked feelings and emotions about spirits and beings.

Among hunter-gatherers revealing a more developed religion, part-time shamans emerged to act as mediators to the supernatural (Wallace 1966; Norbeck 1961). In these *shamanic religions*, the cosmology displayed some degree of definition and complexity (Bellah 1964:364–66). Supernatural beings were objectified and viewed as clearly distinct from the natural world, and some of these beings were believed to control and influence the worldly activities of individuals. Usually gods had specified and delimited spheres of influence, and the relationships among gods could be the source of considerable speculation, often creating an incipient hierarchy or pantheon of relations among gods.

Religious myths delineating the history of gods could also exist, but their complexity varied considerably. Yet, these religions did not display a well-articulated system of values or moral codes of conduct.

This form of belief system can be illustrated by briefly noting some salient features of the traditional Eskimo or Inuit religion (Turner 1972). The Eskimo pantheon was composed of a varied mixture of lesser beings who were personified as the souls of preeminent humans and animals. Also, there were various minor and local spirits regulating the behavior of individuals. Usually particular kin groups had a set of ancestral souls and spirits with whom they had to reckon, and frequently some myths surrounded the emergence and persistence of these local beings and spirits. Higher up in the pantheon were two primary gods—the Keeper of Sea Animals and the Spirit of the Air—but the mythology, division of powers, and the hierarchy of control among these higher, societywide gods remained somewhat vague and blurred. Thus, the traditional Eskimo religious belief system marked a clear-cut distinction between at least some aspects of the natural and supernatural, but the internal differentiation of the cosmology into a complex and clear pantheon accompanied by supporting myths had only been initiated in this simple shamanic religion.

The fairly clear differentiation between the natural and supernatural in shamanic religions encouraged the development of rituals through which gods and humans interact. The locus of such rituals is the cult structure, but the cult structures in shamanic religions were loosely organized; and following Wallace (1966:83–90), two general types of cult structures were evident: *individualistic cults* and *shamanic cults*. In *individualistic cults*, there was no distinction between religious specialists and laymen because members of the cult engaged in appropriate rituals addressed to the supernatural without a religious specialist as an intermediary. *Shamanic cults* displayed a more differentiated structure, with part-time religious practitioners serving as intermediaries between laypersons and the supernatural, with these intermediaries assuming this status on the basis of family ascription, specialized training, and inspirational experience with the supernatural. General norms required that for a fee the shamans act as magicians, witch doctors, medicine men, mediums, spiritualists, astrologers, and diviners. Depending upon the society, the nature of religious beliefs, and the needs of the client, shamans could usually perform at least several of these services.

It is thus with shamanic cults that the first religious division of labor emerged in human societies, and perhaps it is here that religion began to differentiate from kinship as a distinct institution responding to selection pressures generated by the forces of reproduction and, perhaps, regulation. The shaman represented a religious specialist who was clearly differentiated from lay clients, but shamanic cults remained loosely organized, rarely revealing clear boundaries, places of worship, or stable membership. In fact shamanic cults displayed a transient clientele who had little sense of religious community and who, despite sharing beliefs and rituals, had relatively low mutual identification and solidarity. Furthermore, there were few if any calendrical rituals required of cult members; rituals were apparently performed only when needed.

Eskimo cult structure and organization reflected most of these conditions. Generally there were two individualistic cults and one shamanic cult organizing religious beliefs and rituals (Wallace 1966:89). One of the individualistic cults was termed the Spirit Helper Cult, and within this cult individuals sought the particular spirits, souls, and beings of their locale or of their kin grouping, because people inherited patrilineally certain Spirit Helpers who were seen as guiding and helping individuals in their daily activities and to whom appeals were made by wearing little statuettes of walrus tusks, bags of pebbles, and remains of shellfish. To secure help from the spirits, individuals also had to observe certain taboos, especially with respect to *not* killing the creatures being represented in this ancillary appeal. What is important about this cult is that there were no regularly scheduled rituals, with individuals seeking the help of their ancestral and local spirits by themselves. The second individualistic cult—the Game Animal Cult—had a more clearly established set of norms that cut across both local kin groups and larger communities. Certain societywide taboos existed, ostensibly to inhibit behavior that would offend major game animals—for example, the flesh of land and sea animals was never to be cooked together, since to do so would bring illness and starvation (Wallace 1966:90). These and other norms were believed to prevent giving offense to the souls and spirits—the Keepers—who controlled and regulated the supply of game upon which the Eskimos depended for survival. Violations of norms had to be openly confessed; and if violations on the part of one individual persisted, he or she was banished from the community. Through ritual conformity to norms, the community believed that it could avert potential disaster. Thus the Game Animal Cult of the Eskimos displayed a more clear-cut structure than the Spirit Helper Cult because it was societywide and because it had clear-cut norms that were ritually observed and that, when violated, brought sanctions from the community. Actual ritual behavior was still enacted by individuals without the assistance of an intermediary (hence, it remained an individualistic cult). The most complex cults among the traditional Eskimos were led by shamans who were seen as having a special ability to get the attention of a Spirit Helper. For a fee the shaman would call upon Spirit Helpers to assist clients suffering ill health or bad fortune, with the shaman's task being one of discovering from a Spirit Helper the supernatural entity who had been offended, the taboo that had been broken, or the ritual that had not been performed by the client. Once diagnosed, the shaman underwent a spiritual trip to rectify the illness or misfortune. In the shamanic cult of coastal villages there was one quasi-calendrical ritual ceremony performed by the shaman: his annual spiritual trip to the ocean's bottom to persuade and entice Sedna—the Sea Goddess and Keeper of Sea Animals—to release from her domain a sufficient number of animals so that the communities and villages could survive for the ensuing year.

Table 4.3.   Religion in Hunting and Gathering Societies

Belief system	Conception of a supernatural realm of beings and forces, but not clearly organized into a cosmology; some mythology; no clear religious value system
Rituals	Some calendrical rituals, but most rituals performed ad hoc as needed; shaman directs some rituals, but many performed by individuals on their own
Cult structure	None that can be distinguished from band or its nuclear units; occasional "festivals" when bands come together

   In sum, then, shamanic religions—as exemplified by the Eskimo and other small groupings of hunter-gatherers—can be viewed as the most basic religious type, once some degree of religious evolution has occurred. The religious belief system, while distinguishing the sacred and profane as well as the supernatural and natural, does not display a clearly differentiated and systematized cosmology and value system. Structurally, cult organization evidences at most a clear differentiation between shaman and layman, although much religious activity still occurs within individualistic cults. Yet, we should remember that this level of religious development is the extreme, about as far as hunter-gatherers went in differentiating religious activity. Eskimo or Inuit populations realized this level of religious evolution because they were often semi-settled along the coasts of oceans. Most other hunting and gathering bands had much less religion, or none at all, because they were smaller and more nomadic.

POLITY

In most hunting and gathering populations, a polity did not exist because it was not needed. Values for regulation as a macrodynamic force were too low to generate intense selection pressures for leadership and consolidation of power. Leadership tended to be somewhat ad hoc, arising if required for a specific purpose but soon dissipating. Among some hunting and gathering populations, a headman was differentiated, but as was typical, his powers were very limited. For example, among the !Kung-san of Africa the headman's main duties revolved around directing migrations and some economic activity, while performing certain necessary religious ceremonies for the society's welfare (Fried

1967:87), but these leaders possessed no sanctioning power or capacity to use force.

Among some hunting and gathering populations, however, a more visible leader could be found. Such was especially likely to be the case when hunter-gatherers began to settle down, usually near waterways or bodies of water where fishing could provide an ample economic surplus to support a larger population. Under these conditions, a "Big Man" took power in order to coordinate economic activities, promote defense, negotiate peace or wage war, and regulate exchange. The Big Man became the village spokesperson with outside groups, negotiating trade, performing ceremonies, striking political agreements, and if necessary, pursuing war. Internally, the Big Man often "owned" the land, or had rights to its economic outputs; and he usually had the right to distribute the resources to other members of the population or, as was often the case, to sponsor prestige-giving festivals and to engage in trade with other populations (Johnson and Earle 1987; Maryanski and Turner 1992:114; Sahlins 1963). Thus, if a stable surplus existed and if a population grew, even hunter-gatherers could begin to consolidate and centralize power, but in a real sense, this development was premature because normally hunting and gathering populations were small, nomadic, and leaderless. When they were able to produce a stable surplus and, thereby, become more sedentary, valences for regulation increased and set into motion selection pressures for leadership and consolidation of power.

Thus, Big Man societies were an evolutionary cul-de-sac, but they point to the basic conditions that cause the values of power and population as forces to increase and set into motion selection pressures for polity. These conditions were, however, more consistently evident with the spread of horticulture among the world's populations.

Table 4.4 summarizes the consolidation and centralization of power among both nomadic and settled hunter-gatherers. Nomadic were more typical than settled populations; and so, very little power was ever mobilized among hunter-gatherers until populations settled and grew, thereby raising the values for population and regulation as macrodynamic forces. Leadership and power were simply not needed among hunter-gatherers. Moreover, since hunter-gatherers reveal very little, if any, inequality and, hence, internal threat, selection pressures from this source did not push actors to create polity. And, because production does not generate a surplus, and distribution occurs within the context of kinship, there are few selection pressures from these two macro-dynamic forces to cause leadership to emerge and consolidate power. Yet, if hunter-gatherer bands or groups of bands in a territory found themselves in conflict, leadership may have emerged in response to external threats. Still,

Table 4.4. Polity in Hunting and Gathering Societies

	Nomadic	Settled or Semi-Settled
Centralization of decision-making and leadership	Some individuals may be followed because of their prestige and expertise, but no compulsion to conform to directives. Most decisions are made by individuals or by nucleated kin groups	Sometimes, settled hunting and gathering populations develop "Big Men" who possess power to direct activities
Consolidation of bases of power		
Material incentives:	None for most hunter-gatherers	In Big Men systems, leaders often use their control of trade, land, and economic surplus to manipulate others
Symbolic:	Those with prestige can often get others to follow them	Same as nomadic, although Big Man systematically seeks to garner prestige through manipulation of material incentives
Coercion:	Not utilized in most hunting and gathering societies	Big Man and his allies or kindred in semi-settled populations often use coercive force
Administration:	None	Big Man and his allies or, at times, his kinsmen can become a "quasi staff" among more settled populations

there is not enough evidence in the lost record of hunter–gatherer populations of the earth to know for sure how common conflict occurred and how it influenced leadership in bands or sets of bands.

Thus, nomadic hunter-gatherers do not reveal a polity, except on rare occasions where leadership is required. With settlement, however, polity emerges in more stable forms and leaders begin to consolidate and centralize power in order to respond to selection pressures emanating from regulation for coordination and control as well as selection pressures stemming from regulation and distribution for the allocation of resources. Big Men systems represent one path, perhaps a transitional one on the way to full-blown horticulture, but as power is consolidated and used to respond to selection pressures, kinship is once again the structural unit that houses power, at least during the early stages of horticulture. So, even as concentrations of power emerge and mark a distinctive institutional form, the polity remains for a time embedded in kinship.

LAW

Some hunter-gatherers did not have all elements of a legal system because rules invoking the possibility or appropriateness of third parties to resolve disputes did not exist. These systems generally had rules that allowed for self-redress by an individual for perceived wrongs. For example, among the !Kung-san of Africa, one of the last remaining hunter-gatherer societies, "when a dispute arises between members of the band . . . the only remedy is self-help" (Schapera 1930:152); and a person may seek "vengeance" for serious offenses. Yet, individuals in these self-help systems typically possessed a sense of proportion about the seriousness of an offense and the intensity of the self-help response. For instance, illicit sexual relations would be viewed tolerably, perhaps only inviting a weak rebuke among some hunter-gatherers, but among others, adultery was viewed more severely (Newman 1983:60). Among the Mataco of South America, for instance, infidelity gave the injured party the right to impose sanctions, but if jealousy led to murder of the offending party, this act was considered too extreme and invited a harsh penalty in the form of an avenging "blood feud" by the victim's family (Fock 1974:224–25). In fact, the original infidelity was forgotten because of the greater severity of murder.

Other sanctions among hunter-gatherers included shaming rituals by the band against offenders, rituals to send illness to offenders, contests designed to humiliate offenders, and other less physical forms of retaliation (Newman 1983:59–65). Yet, at times, the punishment for violations of the law or loss of a dispute could be quite physical. For example, among the Australian aborigines, an aggrieved "plaintiff" and his kin could hurl spears at the "defendant" who was armed with a shield. When the defendant was wounded, the punishment was over (Sawer 1965); and while the defendant did not usually die, he was nonetheless hurt, often severely. What is evident in these examples is the existence of rules carrying special significance and sanctions for their violation as well as explicit procedures for enforcement of violations of these rules through self-help. Such is a legal system at its most elementary level; and it is from this primordial base that legal evolution must have begun many thousands of years ago.

A somewhat more developed legal system among hunter-gatherers involved the intervention of a third party into the self-redress process—thereby signaling the beginnings of a judge and court. The third party was usually a high prestige man who could be called upon to advise disputing parties about what they should do, but he did not have the power to make them follow his advice. Yet, his prestige and his capacity to shame litigants (over their disrespect of the customs and moral codes) gave him considerable influence.

At times, this advisor role could be expanded to that of mediator, in which the third party negotiated settlements between relatives of the litigants who acted as "lawyers" for the disputing parties (Kroeber 1925:89; Newman 1983:70–73). At other times, the third parties were the representatives of the litigants themselves who came to constitute a primitive court. For example, among the Yurok of California (Kroeber 1926), an individual feeling cheated by another would engage the assistance of two nonkinsmen, as would the other charged with the offense. These assistants would then assume the status of judge, or as they were known to the Yurok, "crossers." Procedural laws indicated just how these "crossers" were to behave; and after hearing the evidence offered by the litigants and their pleas pertaining to substantive law, the "crossers" would render a decision in accordance with a rule of punishment known by all (Hoebel 1954:24). Here was a primitive court, *analytically* very similar to those in modern systems: the litigants were their own lawyers, but clear-cut judge statuses were created to interpret grievances in light of unwritten laws.

A somewhat more developed system of mediation was found in Big Man societies where there was some capacity to dictate solutions to disputes by withholding material incentives or by using coercion. These types of legal systems were far less prevalent than the advisor and self-help pattern, but data from enough of them indicate that once some power was consolidated, the legislative component of law clearly emerged. For example, Llewellyn's and Hoebel's (1941:127–28) reconstruction of the Cheyenne Indians—who had reverted from horticulture back to hunting and gathering with the arrival of the horse in North America and with their relocation onto the plains—provides a good illustration of what transpires with Big Man systems, or in the case of plains Native Americans, with chiefs (who were, in essence, Big Men rather than heads of unilineal kin units). To go on the warpath a Cheyenne warrior borrowed, without asking, the horse of another Cheyenne warrior. When the horse was not returned, the aggrieved warrior went to a court (as a litigant) composed of "warrior chiefs" (high prestige warriors) who sent for the culprit. The "defendant" confessed, agreed to restitution, and even offered to make the aggrieved warrior his blood brother. The matter as a court action was then settled, but the chief or Big Man then assumed a legislative role, proclaiming: "Now we shall make a new rule. If any man takes another's goods [note: not just horses, but any goods] without asking, we shall go over and get them back for him. More than that, if the taker tries to keep them, we will give him a whipping." Thus new substantive and procedural laws were enacted by the chief, as both judge and political legislator.

Among hunter-gatherers, then, we can see the beginnings of a legal system: A body of laws existed, although only just distinguishable from other normative agreements; and there was an incipient distinction between substantive and procedural laws indicating, respectively, what laws were violated and how violations were to be managed. There could be no court in purely self-help systems, save for the "court of public opinion," but once advisors were used and once individuals or their relatives made a case to the advisor, the positions of judge, litigants, and lawyers could be found in their most rudimentary form. Enforcement was mostly self-help among hunter-gatherers but it was action constrained by rules that "punishments must fit crimes." The law-making or legislative component was the most recessive component of the legal system of hunter-gatherers, although decisions or advice given by mediators were remembered and used again to settle similar violations of rules or disputes among parties. And when a Big Man emerged—as was the case of "chiefs" among the Cheyenne—power was consolidated and more explicit law-making and enforcement ensued.

Table 4.5 summarizes these emerging elements of a legal system among hunter-gatherers. Even without the explicit consolidation of power by leaders, law is evident in even the simplest population because it is essential to coordination and control. But, without the surplus to support leaders and without more intense selection pressures stemming from regulation (as these pressures escalate with population growth), transitory leadership roles serving as the equivalent of judges and courts are sufficient to maintain order in hunter-gatherers. Only when power becomes more consolidated, then, does a clearly differentiated legal system become evident. But the sporadic instances where the system emerged among hunter-gatherers reveal the kinds of selection pressures that push actors, when they must, to create the institution of law.

EDUCATION

Education as a distinctive institutional system does not exist among hunter-gatherers. Reproductive forces pushing hominids to form kinship were sufficient in meeting the selection pressures for a stable source of socialization. However, the elements of education can be seen when the young are given explicit instruction in various skills and cultural lore by elders, but these activities are hardly distinct from adult roles in the kinship system. Indeed, as I emphasize in chapter 3, education does not become a clearly differentiated structure until rather late in human evolution, because kinship is adequate to manage the selection pressures posed by the forces of production and regulation. Thus, as is evident in table 4.6, education is completely embedded in kinship during hunting and gathering, as we will see, for most of human history up to late agrarianism and early industrialization.

Table 4.5. Law in Hunting and Gathering Societies

	Nomadic	Settled or Semi-Settled
Body of Laws		
Substantive:	Few laws that can be distinguished from day-to-day norms, but norms do specify proscriptions and prescriptions	Same as nomadic, but some norms will be more "rule-like" because of Big Man's or headman's claims to property, trade, and other prerogatives
Procedural:	Some norms specify what is to be done when violation of important norms occur	More likely to be rules specifying what is to be done with violation of important rules, especially those involving headman's prerogatives
Legislation of Laws	No explicit body or person to legislate rules, although high prestige individuals may suggest rules	Headman is, at times, likely to try to legislate new rules, although his capacity to get conformity is based upon his prestige and personal charisma
Courts		
Judge:	No one is authorized to manage violations of rules, except for those who feel that their rights have been violated. Prestige leaders may at times offer suggestions about how to resolve disputes	Same as nomadic, although Big Man may assume role of advisor and make suggestions about how to resolve disputes. At times, these suggestions carry moral authority
Jury/Council:	None	None, although at times Big Man and his allies can act as a council that considers disputes and grievances
Enforcement of Laws	"Redress" system of enforcement in which harmed individuals must seek compensation or punishment on his or her own. Most disputes resolved by simple face-to-face discussions. Violence in the form of feuds and revenge can occur, but is rare because unresolvable disputes usually lead to a breakup of the band	Most disputes resolved by normal face-to-face discussion. Aggrieved parties, even with favorable advice from Big Man, must still use redress and seek enforcement of rights on his or her own. Feuds and revenge are more frequent, but usually mediated by the Big Man

Table 4.6.   Education in Hunting and Gathering Societies

Instruction	Most learning comes by observation and practice. Occasional instruction by adults within family and band units
Curricula	Hunting and gathering technologies, religious beliefs and rituals, band-kinship history
Ritualized passage	Typically a ceremony marking general transition from childhood to adulthood

KEY INSTITUTIONAL INTERCHANGES

Because institutional differentiation is only incipient among hunting and gathering populations, the dynamic relations among institutions are not so evident as they are later in societal evolution. We cannot trace with any detail, therefore, the mutual influences among institutions for hunter-gatherers, but we can, I believe, see the dim outlines of the interchanges among institutions that will become ever more evident with societal evolution and institutional differentiation. Thus, my goal here is only to set the stage for what must become an important facet of institutional analysis—interchanges among institutions—as societies become more complex.

Kinship and Economy

When kinship and economy are clearly differentiated from each other, the basic interchange is for kinship to provide human capital for the economy and for the economy to generate consumer goods to sustain family members (see chapter 8). When economy is embedded within kinship, however, kinship rules provide all elements of the economy: the technology lodged in family members' brains, physical capital or the implements of gathering produced by family members, human capital consisting of the learned skills of family members, definitions of property, and entrepreneurship provided by the structure of kinship. Some of these effects of kinship on the economy might be seen as somewhat distinct, such as technology and physical capital, but in fact the norms of the kinship system as they dictate what family members are to do and what they should learn determine the level of technology, physical capital, and all other economic elements. The reverse relationship of the effects of the economy on kinship, however, remains much the same throughout societal evolution: economy provides the resources necessary to sustain life and the social structures built up by human activity.

Over the course of human evolution, as institutions differentiated from kinship, the effects of kinship on the economy were successively reduced. Even in the role of providing human capital, kinship has had to give up functions to formal educational systems that have also differentiated from the economy. Similarly, technology is developed by actors within the economy itself, or by other institutions such as science and education. The same is true with physical capital, and even human capital is trained within specific corporate units devoted solely to economic activity. Polity and law provide definitions of property and enforce property rights; and the distribution of all economic elements is increasingly the purview of markets and infrastructures regulated by law and polity.

Thus, in hunting and gathering, the forces of production and reproduction generated selection pressures on hominids and their human descendants producing nuclear kinship systems and bands. Kinship proved to be an amazingly effective response to pressures for production and reproduction (and regulation as well) for millions of years among hominids and, for two hundred thousand years, among humans as well. Thus, by simply strengthening male-female bonds over what they are evident among apes (where strong ties are virtually absent, except among gibbons/siamangs), a very efficient structure was created that resolved problems posed by selection pressures and, as we will see for horticulture, that could be altered to organize key economic elements into more complex patterns.

Kinship and Religion

The basic interchange between kinship and religion is evident among hunter-gatherers, even without clear differentiation between the two systems. Religion provides beliefs and rituals that can alleviate tension and anxiety, while reinforcing critical kinship norms as sanctioned by supernatural forces, entities, and beings. In return, kin members provide commitments to beliefs and a willingness to practice rituals that sustain religion. Yet, when religion is not clearly differentiated from kinship, kin members assume many of the positions that become the exclusive domain of religion when it is fully differentiated.

Kinship and Polity

When kinship and polity are differentiated, kinship provides loyalty to political elites, which allows them to consolidate and centralize power, while the polity allocates power within kinship units, often through law. When a polity does not exist, however, and when leadership is, in essence, not required because of low values for regulation, this fundamental relationship between kinship and polity is hardly observable. Moreover, when polity did evolve with horticulture, kinship still provided the structural framework within which power was consolidated and centralized. That is, power essentially flowed through hierarchies of kin units as organized by descent rules. Until the state as a political formation emerged with advanced horticulture, kinship provided virtually all the bases of power for leaders. Only with high degrees of differentiation between kinship and polity did these far-ranging effects of kinship on polity recede. Thus, among leaderless hunter-gatherers, there was no interchange between kinship and polity because regulation was not a driving force. But, if Big Men emerged in settled hunter-gatherers or if previously leaderless bands engaged in conflict or confronted other environmental crises, such as a dramatic change in the ecology of a population, the values for regulation increased as a macrodynamic force and set into motion selection pressures for power that could be used to order relations of authority within kinship units, thus establishing the fundamental relationship between these two institutions.

Kinship and Law

When law is a distinct institution, it provides for kinship external rules and procedures governing family organization, while kinship socializes commitments to the general tenets of the legal system. This general relationship held even in simple, leaderless hunting and gathering populations because rules of kinship were enforced and adjudicated, although the processes by which this occurred were situationally evoked. Still, despite the ad hoc and transient nature of legal system activity among hunter-gatherers, the fundamental relationship between the two institutions was evident.

Kinship and Education

Because education does not differentiate from kinship in hunting and gathering, the fundamental relationship is obscured. As differentiation occurs, education assumes many of the socialization functions of family, while kinship provides the financial (via taxes) and cultural (via socialization) resources necessary for the schools to operate. But like all else in hunting and gathering societies, the folding of institutions into kinship obscures this relationship, and kinship was the major structure within which all education—indeed, most socialization—occurred among hunter-gatherers.

Economy and Religion

Religion can provide mechanisms for alleviating strain, tension, and uncertainty associated with economic activity, especially if it is dangerous (as in fishing offshore) or if the environment is undergoing significant changes that decrease resource availability. At the same time, religion may reinforce critical norms of economic activity, although these are still lodged within kinship. In the long run, economic surplus will provide the resources essential for the differentiation of a distinctive religious system, but among hunter-gatherers this effect of the economy was not so evident because a separate set of religious practitioners did not have to be supported outside the economy and kinship. As hunter-gatherers settled, however, distinctive religious practitioners emerged, and at times, may have been supported in roles outside kinship or economy. Once this process began, a new structural base beyond band and kinship was laid down for subsequent religious evolution.

Polity and Economy

Polity provides the physical capital for the economy, while the economy provides the resources necessary to sustain polity. Only with Big Men systems was this relationship evident among hunter-gatherers, as the Big Man allocated individuals or kin units to various economic activities and as he taxed some or all of the economic outputs, only to redistribute these outputs primarily because they were typically perishable and had to be redistributed before they spoiled. This redistribution garnered prestige for the Big Man (a kind of symbolic power) and provided a material incentive base of power. However, among leaderless hunter-gatherers, where no polity exists, this relationship between economy and polity did not exist.

CONCLUSION

This is the first of four chapters on the most visible stages of societal evolution: hunting and gathering, horticulture, agrarianism, industrialism, and post-industrialism. There are, of course, variants of these stages, such as herding and fishing societies, that can be considered offshoots of simple horticultural forms. It is from the structural base described in this chapter that all other institutions evolved. The forces of production and reproduction are dominant in this stage, although the other macrodynamic forces were operative at very low values. When populations begin to settle down and grow, the valences for other forces suddenly increased and began to drive institutional development.

I place population as a primary force because it changes the valences of all other forces. When populations are small, homogeneous, and spread out over large territories (lowering density), this force exerts relatively little pressure, allowing production and reproduction to be accommodated by simple nuclear families in small bands. As populations grow, however, the values of production, reproduction, regulation, and distribution as forces are raised. More food must be produced and distributed; more control and coordination through the consolidation of power will have to exist; more extensive socialization of individuals into more diverse sets of specialized roles will have to occur. As the values for all macrodynamic forces increase, selection pressures drive actors to find new solutions to new sets of problems, and among those populations that survived the threats posed by these problems, differentiation and development of institutional systems previously embedded in kinship among hunter-gatherers became increasingly evident. The first major evolutionary step toward this new institutional order was horticulture.

Chapter Five

Institutional Systems of Horticultural Populations

Horticulture is simple farming and gardening without the benefit of the plow or nonhuman sources of energy. Humans only slowly eased into horticulture because it involves considerably more human capital (in terms of time and energy spent) than hunting and gathering. Indeed, when members of the few remaining hunting and gathering populations were asked why they did not adopt horticulture, they generally replied that it was too much work. Some hunter-gatherers clearly understood how to plant because they would often cast seeds about as they left an area, hoping that they would grow into easy food sources when they returned in their cyclical wanderings about a territory. Thus, it was not the technology, or knowledge of how to plant, garden, and harvest, that was so novel to humans; rather, it was their willingness to expend so much effort to maintain gardens that represented the key breakthrough. Humans did not jump into horticulture, given the first opportunity; they were forced to adopt this technology once their numbers increased as a consequence of settling in one place. The most likely scenario is that settled communities hunted and gathered all of the food in an area but were now too large to pick up and move, as had previous generations. As a consequence, selection pressures from population and production forced them to reorganize into horticultural modes of production. Once this step had been taken, the nature of human societies was changed forever.

Horticultural systems varied enormously in size, from 100–150 people in simple systems to many thousands in complex systems.[1] Horticulturalists often had to resettle as they depleted the soil or as overpopulation forced them to seek new resources. In fact, many horticultural techniques are very hard on the ecosystem, leading to serious depletion of the soil's fertility. Some horticulturalists may have reverted back to hunting and gathering, but once populations

grew, the amount of available territory declined, and horticulturalists were typically in constant warfare with their neighbors. Thus, once trapped in horticulture, it may have been difficult to escape.

ECONOMY

In terms of the elements of economy, horticulturalists differed considerably
from hunting and gathering populations. Technologically, they had practical
knowledge of: (1) planting, harvesting, grinding, and storing grains as well as
cooking; (2) breeding, fertilizing, and crop rotation (in more complex systems);
(3) tool making, initially with stones and later in more complex systems with
metal; (4) masonry; (5) pottery-making with kilns, which later led to metallurgy, or annealing, smelting, casting, and eventually alloying.

Physical capital included tools, pottery, storage facilities, city walls and,
slowly, negotiable capital, at first with barter of hard goods but eventually with
money. Human capital revealed a clear division of labor, with females doing
most of the gardening and with males increasingly involved in specialized
trades and occupations (weapon-making, pottery, house and boat building,
bartering and commerce, metal-working, leather-making, masonry), although
women could also pursue some trades such as weaving. The level of skill and
energy output of human capital thus increased significantly with horticulture.
Entrepreneurial structures also changed, and dramatically so. In simple systems,
more complex kinship structures linking nuclear families together into larger
kinship units organized much of the economy; and even in more advanced
horticultural populations, these large and more complex kinship systems still
organized activity. Villages and eventually larger cities also ordered the economy in terms of distributing gardening plots, trade specialization, barter and,
eventually, commercial systems using money. Markets where goods and services were bought and sold (either through barter or money) also began to
appear as a prominent way to structure distribution and, consequently, gathering and production as well. True political leaders could now be found, and
these leaders dictated the distribution of land and economic roles of kin members.[2] For some populations, a "Big Man" political system emerged in which
an individual and usually his fellow kinsmen accumulated foodstuffs and then
redistributed this surplus through elaborate feasts; and in this manner the Big
Man gained prestige and, at times, power (Johnson and Earle 1987). Although
such systems were more typical of hunter-gatherers like the "Indians" of the
Pacific northwest who were in the process of settling down, Big Men could
also be found among simple horticultural populations, such as those in Polynesia (Sahlins 1963).

Table 5.1. Horticultural Economies

	Simple	Advanced
Technology	Practical knowledge of herding, farming (planting, harvesting, storing, grinding, and cooking of grains), tool-making (initially with stone, then with metals), pottery-making (with kilns, which later led to annealing, smelting, casting, and eventually, alloying)	Practical knowledge of herding, breeding, farming, fertilizing, and crop rotation, tool-making with metals (with exceptions, such as ancient China), pottery-making, metallurgy, and masonry
Physical Capital	Tools, pottery, houses, storage sheds, negotiable items used (in most cases) in barter; unstable economic surplus; little ability to hoard perishable commodities	Tools, pottery, houses, storage sheds, walled cities, and the beginnings of liquid capital or money; stable economic surplus, which could be used in exchange and hoarded
Human Capital	Clear division of labor between males and females (with females doing most of the tending of gardens); specialized occupational "trades" in weapon-making, pottery, house-building, boat-building, and bartering; some use of proto-slaves captured in war	Clear division of labor between males and females; increased level of specialization in trades and occupations, especially in masonry, metal-working, weaving, leather-making, pottery-ceramics, boat- and house-building, and commerce; frequent use of slaves captured in war
Entrepreneurship	Community/village structure; kinship units in villages are principal organizing structure, although village leaders/headman often allocate gardening plots and other resources, extracting some of the product to redistribute to village members; at times, a few trade specialists	Community structure; kinship and headman are principal organizing structure at village level, with leaders and headman involved in resource allocation and redistribution; increased number of trade specialists; in larger core cities, merchants and markets become major entrepreneurial mechanisms

Table 5.1. (Continued)

	Simple	Advanced
Property	Emerging system of property; moderate inequality in distribution of property; headmen, religious specialists, heads of kin units, some craft specialists and paramount chiefs receive surplus material goods (food, lodging, weapons, land), although redistribution requirements on political leaders mitigate degree of material inequality. Some stratification in terms of material property, but not developed into homogeneous ranks or social class; clear differentiation of headman and religious elites from others; if there is a dominant kin group (lineage or clan), then some differentiation among kin grouping; also, at times, village differentiation, with one village dominating others; vast majority of population forms a single class, with distinctions by kin group, sex, age, and at times, craft specialization being salient but not producing distinctive social classes. Slavery could also create a distinct class	Hardening system of private property, with high inequality; headmen, religious elites, paramount chiefs, military elites, successful craft specialists, and especially king and his court receive surplus material goods; accumulation of wealth becomes possible as more material surplus becomes durable and redistribution requirements begin to recede. Several homogeneous subpopulations in a hierarchy of ranks and beginnings of class system; political leaders and their kin constitute distinctive grouping, as do religious specialists; military elites and economic specialists can become distinctive sub-groupings; slaves, where found, constitute a distinctive class; vast majority of population forms a single class, with distinctions by kin group, sex, and age being salient but not producing distinctive social classes; however, craft specialties and other economic positions can produce identifiable classes, and ethnic distinctions can also create a new basis of class formation

Property became more clearly defined with horticulture. In simple systems the headman or chief could theoretically own everything and received most productive output, but this leader was also required to redistribute what was given to him. Similarly, in Big Men systems, the leader usually had to give away most of what he and his kinsmen had accumulated if he was to maintain his standing. In larger and more complex horticultural systems, political and religious elites as well as those engaged in market activity could claim private property, as could individuals with respect to their personal possessions. As claims to private property were allowed, inequality and stratification became prominent features of human society (Turner 1984; Lenski 1966). Rights to land, physical capital, human capital (whether as slaves, apprentices, or wage workers), and occupations were increasingly becoming the basis for stratifying the members of the population (usually leaving a large mass with little property). Such inequality was aggravated by the widespread, although highly variable, practice of slavery among horticulturalists.

Table 5.1 summarizes the basic structure of simple and advanced horticultural economies. By the time a more advanced system emerged in human history, the basic structure began to rival that of simple agrarian economies, but as long as human power was the primary source of energy, the system remained horticultural. It was only with the advent of nonhuman sources of power that full agrarianism began to emerge in human evolution.

Institutional differentiation began to accelerate with horticulture. Even as kinship expanded and became the basic structure organizing the population, especially in simple horticultural systems, the beginnings of separate spheres of economic, political, religious, legal, and educational activity could be seen. Once differentiation was initiated, it operated to encourage population growth, forcing expanded efforts at gathering, producing, and distributing which, in turn, furthered the process of institutional differentiation and development. Thus, with advanced horticulture, the core institutional systems of human populations were differentiated or, as was the case with education, on the verge of becoming a distinctive institutional system. Still, even with this new potential for differentiation, kinship was for most horticultural systems not only the dominant entrepreneurial structure for the economy but also the principal regulatory structure for the society as a whole.

KINSHIP

The nature of kinship is very much connected to the type of economy. In hunting and gathering kinship was very simple: nuclear family units that, at times, were connected together; marriage was relatively unconstrained, although rules of incest and, at times, exogamy and endogamy applied; dissolution of marriages was simple; relations were egalitarian, although men and women engaged in very different activities, and only men tended to garner high prestige; residence varied and could be neolocal, bilocal (both mother's and father's sides), or patrilocal, but even if there was a clear residence rule, considerable flexibility prevailed; and descent was bilateral and truncated, indicating that family lines are not emphasized. When human populations began to grow, however, population, production, and regulation as macrodynamic forces set into motion selection pressures favoring new ways to coordinate economic activity in order to support the larger population (M. Cohen 1977; Binford 1968). Members of populations adopting gardening faced a dilemma: how were they to build more complex structures to sustain themselves? The solution was to increase the salience of the descent norm specifying whose side of the family was to be more important and, then, to build the organization of the society around kinship principles that followed from the descent rule. Thus, nuclear families were connected together into lineages, lineages into clans, and clans into one of two moieties (which divided a society in half). There were other mediating structures, but the goal was to connect nuclear families into ever-larger systems of descent and authority.

Without the capacity to build bureaucracies and other structures coordinating larger numbers of individuals, kinship was the only and perhaps the easiest solution because it involved elaborating on a structure that already existed. And so, with the emergence and expansion of horticultural technologies, unilineal descent systems grew as a mechanism to coordinate and regulate physical and human capital (Harner 1970). The result was for the size and composition of family units to grow, being connected into extended units in accordance with a patrilineal descent in the vast majority of cases or, in a lesser number of cases, matrilineal descent. Residence would then follow the descent rule, being either patrilocal or matrilocal, although there were exceptions. Authority would become male dominated or patriarchal in both descent systems (since men on average are somewhat stronger than women), although in the matrilineal-matrilocal system, it was the males on the female's side of the family who would generally exercise authority. Marriage became much more regulated, not only by incest rules but also by rules of exogamy (having to choose partners outside one's lineage, clan, or moiety) and, frequently, by rules of endogamy (where partners must be chosen inside a specific lineage, clan, or moiety). In these larger kin units, the division of labor between males and females, as well as between generations, became much more explicit and rigid.

Such a system served as a functional equivalent of bureaucracy because it could organize and coordinate large numbers of people in an authority system. This form of kinship was, however, riddled with tension because generations of kin were packed together, forcing them to manage potentially volatile out-bursts. Feuds, external warfare (perhaps displacing internal aggression), and sporadic fighting within and between kin units were very typical of these kinds of kinship structures, as one might expect when kinfolk were forced to live together in large numbers within a rigid system of authority and highly pre-scribed activities (Maryanski and Turner 1992:91–112).

With advanced horticulture (see right side of table 5.2), sufficient economic surplus could be produced to support nonkin organizational structures, and kinship as the principal organizing structure of society was about to be replaced with the advent of agriculture by manorial estates composed of more nucleated tenant farmers, administrative bureaucracies attached to the state, and new cor-porate structures such as guilds, cartels, and companies. These alternatives could organize far greater numbers of people, and they allowed people to escape the "cage of kinship" (Maryanski and Turner 1992). Under these changes, kinship began its odyssey back to the more isolated nuclear family system of hunters and gatherers. The descent rule lost much of its salience, except for the inheritance of property and titles, and the construction of lin-eages and larger structures like clans and moieties became increasingly less via-

Table 5.2.   Structure of Kinship in Horticultural Societies

	Simple	Advanced
Size and composition	Nuclear units connected to nuclear units	Connected nuclear units, but some re-nuclearization evident
Residence	Patri- or matrilocal, but mostly pat-rilocal	Residence rule begins to break down, especially as migration to urban centers occurs; but patrilocal bias continues
Activity	Clear division of labor between males and females in economic, community, political, religious, and domestic tasks	Same as simple system
Descent	Unilineal, generally patrilineal; organized to the lineage and clan level, and at times, to the moiety level	Descent rule begins to break down, but still regulates inheritance of wealth and power in kinship units that remain linked
Authority	Male-dominated	Male-dominated
Marriage	Incest prohibited; considerable exogamy and endogamy; dissolu-tion allowed	Incest prohibited; exogamy declines; and endogamy becomes increasingly based on social class as much as kinship

ble. Larger families composed of members from more than one nuclear unit remained but were not essential, and they were often converted to patrimonial structures of kin and non-kin workers or apprentices. Residence retained some of the patrilocal bias of horticultural systems, but neolocality became ever more frequent as people migrated to new lands or emerging urban areas. Authority remained patriarchal, and activities of men and women were strictly divided, but as the extended family began to decline in prevalence and as neolocal residence became possible, intergenerational authority and division of labor were less explicit and restrictive. Incest rules remained for marriage partners, but rules of exogamy and endogamy declined and, then, disappeared. Marriage dissolution often became more difficult, however, as males made divorce difficult to achieve as a means for controlling women.

These transformations were well under way with advanced horticulture, but still, kinship was the key organizing structure for all institutional systems. I have typified this as the "cage of kinship" because it constrained individuals' options to a very high degree and forced them to live in what were often tension-filled units. It is not surprising, therefore, that given the chance to live in alternative arrangements, humans quickly abandoned the most restrictive aspects of kinship once the economy could support new kinds of social structures.

POLITY

Kin-based Polities in Simple Horticulture

As human populations grew and settled down, the descent rule of kinship was used to create a way of organizing this larger population. The first true polities were thus lodged in unilineal descent structures, with the leaders of the descent group—whether a lineage, clan, or moiety—being the political leader for that grouping. As descent groupings came into conflict or competition, some of these groupings were more successful than others; and as a result, the head of the dominant grouping, usually a clan or moiety, became the chief or paramount chief among other local heads or chiefs, with the latter assuming the role of the paramount chief's lieutenants. When this process occurred historically, polity was no longer tied to each village but began to consolidate villages into a larger political system (Kirch 1980).

The bases for this kind of centralized polity involved a consolidation of (1) coercion by fellow kinsmen and their allies, (2) symbolic legitimization through the beliefs and rituals of communal and, later, ecclesiastic religious structures, (3) use of kinship rules of descent, authority, and residence to create an administrative structure, and (4) extraction through taxation or tribute of the material surplus produced in economic activity and then its redistribution (often with some skimming to support the privilege of elites in more advanced horticultural systems). In simple kin-based polities, this consolidation of power was highly effective, although the use of the kinship system to organize social life inevitably created strains among kinfolk forced together by descent and residence rules and subordinated to each other by descent and authority rules (Maryanski and Turner 1992:91–112).

Table 5.3.   Polity in Horticultural Societies

	Simple	*Advanced*
Centralization of decision-making and leadership	Headman or chief at village level empowered to make decisions in consultation with other kinsmen and, perhaps, religious special-ists. At times there is a paramount chief who, in consultation with village heads, makes decisions for larger network of villages	Explicit king or chief empowered to make decisions for all commu-nities and kin units, sometimes in consultation with local village/kin leaders and religious specialists
Consolidation of bases of power		
Material incentives:	Headman can extract economic production of kin units but also must redistribute economic out-put in ways that enhance his power	Developed taxation system that the king or chief can use to manipulate conformity from other elites who, in turn, control villages and kinsmen
Symbolic:	Prestige that comes from redistri-bution by chief, kinship descent and authority rules as they define leaders, and sanctioning by supernatural beings and/or forces	Prestige that is attached to king and chief, but less reliance on redistribution and more on pomp and ceremony of office. Religious beliefs become as important and, often, more important than kin-ship rules (descent and authority) for legitimation of king or chief
Coercion:	Chiefs have coercive capacity, enforced by their allies and kinsmen	Dramatically escalated coercive power, often from a standing army of kinsmen and non-kin recruits. In highly advanced sys-tems, a professional army
Administration:	Chiefs and paramount chiefs have staff comprised of allies and kinsmen. Lineages, clans, and at times moieties become adminis-trative conduit of decisions	Kinship begins to be replaced by more bureaucratic system of administration, but kinship and village leadership still an impor-tant conduit of administration

If this kin-based polity sought to conquer its neighbors and extend its territorial holdings, the balance in the consolidation of power began to change as
further strains on the kinship system mounted in efforts to use kinship principles to control the larger territory. For when larger territories were conquered,
their surplus was often extracted and their peoples subordinated through coercion rather than religiously legitimated kinship rules. New patterns of political
control were adopted as the inadequacies of kinship to rule became increasingly evident. Chiefs now became kings; and extraction of surplus without full
redistribution to those who produced this economic surplus increased inequalities and, thereby, made the legitimization of privilege more problematic.
Moreover, the administration of power now involved more than kindred, who
may still have held the elite positions in the polity but who had to turn over
the tasks of administering coercion, extracting surplus, and controlling tensions
to non-kin. As this process occurred in human history, the beginnings of the
state became evident (Carneiro 1987, 1981, 1970; Service 1975; Evans et al.
1985).

Advanced Horticulture and the Emergence of
the State

With the greater economic surplus provided by more advanced horticulture
and, later, early agrarianism, the consolidation and centralization of power
began to shift. Power was now concentrated in a monarch; and the bases of
power were consolidated in a somewhat new pattern: coercion was organized
in a more clear-cut militia or standing army in order to control conquered
territories, thwart hostile actions by the nobility, and repress peasant uprisings;
legitimization came from religion, but the emerging conflict between religious
leaders and the nobility created selection pressures for new bases of legitimization in tradition and law; administration was increasingly turned over to non-
kin functionaries who were organized in quasi-bureaucratic structures; and
material incentives were used primarily to keep the nobility in line with the
monarch's wishes, creating vast inequalities between the nobility and the rest
of the population, particularly the peasants who produced the surplus that was
extracted to support the power and privilege of the monarch and nobility
(Lenski 1966; Turner 1984).

Once this pattern of consolidated power existed in human history, it tended
to increase inequalities because the need to coerce potential dissidents and the
escalating requirements for administering the appropriation of material surplus
were expensive, thereby increasing the costs of running the state and, hence,
the need to extract ever more surplus to meet these costs (Fried 1978, 1967).
Given the problem of legitimating this inequality as tensions with the ecclesias-

tical cults of religion mounted, the reliance on the coercive and administrative bases of power further skewed the consolidation of power away from the symbolic base and the use of material incentives toward coercion and tight administration (Turner 1995). These trends were well under way with advanced horticultural systems, but they did not fully replace kinship as the organizing principle of power until full agrarianism was in place.

LAW

The legal system among simple horticulturalists was often much like the advisor-mediator system of hunter-gatherers. Yet, a greater potential for law-making existed, because power was being consolidated in kin-heads, village chiefs, councils of elders, and religious specialists. For example, the chiefs of the Bantu-speaking Tswand of South Africa possessed considerable law-making authority. They could lay down edicts and declare old laws obsolete (Schapera 1956). To illustrate this power of law-making, Hoebel (1954:278) relates that in 1934 a young married man died childless; and according to kinship rules, the young man's unmarried younger brother was supposed to take up with the widow and "seed" her with children. He would not do so, however, with the result that his father took up sexual relations with the widow—substituting for the derelict son. This situation did not sit well with the father's wife, who appealed to the district council (she is now litigant, the council is now a court of law) to have her husband stopped. The council ruled against her, saying that her husband's conduct was in accordance with "ancient right and custom" (i.e., laws), but the district chief overruled the council, declaring the custom obsolete. The chief thus assumed the status of "appeals-court judge" as well as that of legislator by declaring the old rule outdated. When the father refused to obey the chief's declaration, he was punished severely (clearly, the chief's edict was a law because it was enforced).

Horticulturalists also evidenced a more explicit court structure and, in many cases, a system of courts. For example, among the Kikuyu, disputes within a family were settled by the father, and if members of two families in a dispute could not come to a satisfactory resolution, the family heads of all kin groups within a clan sought to do so. But if the two disputants came from different clans, a council of elders of all the clans within the village, constituting a kind of village council, settled the dispute, and if the disputants were also from different villages, then an intervillage council would act as a court. Thus, we can see that various courts were being assembled in accordance with spheres of jurisdiction as dictated by descent and resident rules.

As simple kin-based horticulture began to move toward a state-based sys-

Table 5.4. Law in Horticultural Societies

	Simple	Advanced
Body of Laws		
Substantive:	Highly variable, from fairly complex system of rules governing family, property, and contracts to very few rules outside those of kinship and normal day-to-day demeanor and ritual	Complex system of rules governing family, property, contract, and other civil matters, but also bodies of laws specifying relationship of individuals, kin groups, and other corporate actors to the emerging state or, in some cases, fully developed state. Laws are increasingly written down, often by religious scribes, and more likely to be codified as a system of rules. Religious prohibitions and prescriptions will often be important elements of law
Procedural:	Highly variable, but most systems have some understanding about how parties are to resolve disputes by bringing in advisors or mediators or by making appeals to local chiefs or councils of elders or elites	Clear rules about what is to be done to resolve disputes. Rules increasingly specify how parties are to make appeals to courts controlled by representatives of the state
Legislation of Laws	Chiefs or councils can suggest new rules that arise from disputes	Paramount chief, king, councils of elites, and at times, councils of religious leaders can all make new rules that are binding and enforced. Court decisions by judges or political leaders frequently involve stating new precedents and, hence, new laws. At times, religious elites can pronounce new laws that are accepted by the state

Table 5.4. (Continued)

	Simple	Advanced
Courts		
Judge:	Chief will often serve as an advisor or mediator of conflict in order to arrive at an acceptable compromise	Kin leaders, local chiefs, paramount chiefs, and kings can all serve as judges. In some systems, full-time judges can be found
Jury/Council:	Elders or elites can serve as either advisors or mediators who help in developing a compromise over a dispute	Councils of elders at the local level, councils of elites at more regional levels can serve as juries. At times, religious councils can impose decisions with respect to religious doctrine
Lawyer/Representative:	Relatives of parties in dispute may seek to represent the claims of their kinsmen to advisors and mediators	Disputants are frequently represented by kindred, or by legal specialists
System of Courts:	Paramount chief and councils may, at times, serve as an "appeals court" for decisions made by kin heads and local chiefs	Relatively clear system of local, regional, and appeals courts composed of local chiefs, regional political leaders, and paramount chief or king as well as their respective councils of elites. Religious courts can, in some systems, exist alongside more secular courts, as can various tribunals of secret societies, merchants, and other groups of actors. Criminal and civil courts may be differentiated
Enforcement of laws/ court decisions	Kin and individual feuds and violent revenge can often occur outside the legal system. Court—and judge—suggested "redress" is still common, although chiefs and councils strive to reach compromises that all parties and their representatives find acceptable. Much enforcement involves shaming, ignoring, and otherwise treating guilty parties as undesirable	Redress is now virtually gone. Revenge and feuds that take place outside the legal system are still frequent but less tolerated by the emerging state. Efforts are still made to reach mutually acceptable compromises, but ultimately coercive force can, and often is, used to enforce laws and court decisions

tem, councils of elites, forming a kind of ruling oligarchy, assumed many legislative and court functions (Kuper 1971; Newman 1983). Membership in these councils was based upon family wealth as much as descent and authority rules; and their capacity to manipulate material incentives or purchase coercive force made their edicts and decisions truly enforceable.

Both kin-based and wealth-based systems revealed a paramount chief who had the right to hear disputes, make decisions, proclaim new laws, and enforce laws and decisions. There was a wide variation in this pattern, however. At times, the paramount chief oversaw just a few villages and his powers were not great, but at other times, the paramount chief was, in reality, a king of a nation. Max Gluckman's (1965:129–272) description of law and politics in old tribal societies captures much of this variation, but the critical point is that the largest of these kingdoms came close to constituting a true state system. In these emerging states, the institution of law was differentiated along several lines. First, the legal system evidenced distinct levels, from village through region to nation; and at each level could be found explicit laws, legislative bodies, courts, and enforcement capacities by local heads and chiefs. Second, at the national level, the elements of the legal system were more elaborated, consisting of more explicit rules, permanent legislative councils of the king or paramount chief, standing courts staffed by administrators and officials, and dramatically expanded enforcement capacities. This more elaborated system often articulated only loosely with local legal systems, but the increased administrative activity at the national level often involved overseeing lower-level laws and decisions, although unless local disputes threatened the power and privilege of national elites, the two systems could operate somewhat independently.

With true state formation with advanced horticulture, the legal system changed by virtue of the concentration of coercive force. As Morton Fried (1967:237) points out, rules within and outside of kinship were now enforced by political leaders; and the centralized state began to manage ever more activity. As it did so, the state developed larger bodies of law, both substantively and procedurally; it expanded courts and related officers for managing the courts, from judges to administrative record-keepers; and it established enforcement procedures, ranging from fines and other material deprivations through imprisonment and banishment to outright execution. In this process the body of laws became more codified, especially as writing was developed and used to record the law (Weber [1922] 1954; Diamond 1971:40–41). These codes, such as the Imperial Codes of the Inca Empire or the Chinese Empire at its moments of dynastic unification, specified crimes and threats against the state; and they began to be applied more uniformly. Local laws and codes still persisted, as did local adjudication, as long as it did not interfere with the Imperial Code's intent to maintain elite privilege, state finances, and state control of coercive power.

But the groundwork for more advanced legal evolution had been laid with state-based horticulture. Rules were increasingly written down and codified in formal and systematic ways; and while local rules existed alongside the codes of the state, conflicts between the two were resolved in the state's favor, further codifying and systematizing the body of laws. Legislative activity existed, once again, at multiple levels, but the council of elites began to look more like a deliberative legislative body. Courts at the state level were supreme, and while their articulation with local adjudicative processes was loose, they often evidenced differentiation of full-time, professional judges, lawyers, and administrative record-keeping staff; and they had the potential, if desired or needed, to protect the interests of elites or the state, to intervene in local courts and, thereby, begin the process of court integration. Most significantly, laws and court decisions were no longer advisory; they were backed by the extensive coercive capacity to fine, confine, or kill litigants. With agrarianism, these features of the legal system were to develop further.

RELIGION

Shamanic religion could be found among most hunter-gatherers, at least among those who had a religion. Somewhat more developed than shamanic are communal religions that were typical of simple horticultural populations (Wallace 1966:86–87). What distinguishes *communal* from the shamanic religions of hunter-gatherers was not so much an increase in complexity of the belief system, but in the complexity of the cult structures. In addition to individualistic and shamanic cults were those that displayed a threefold division of labor (Wallace 1966:87): lay participants; lay organizers, sponsors, and performers; and religious specialists (shamans and magicians). The rituals performed in these communal cults tended to be *calendrical*, with laymen organizing and often performing at least some of the prescribed rituals. Frequently this organization of lay personnel began to approximate a bureaucratic structure with regular technical and supervisory assignments for laymen. Still, no full-time priesthood or elaborate religious hierarchy could be said to exist (Wallace 1966:87). Communal cults varied in size from small groupings to very large structures encompassing the whole community; membership also varied and usually revolved around categoric units such as age and sex or around special corporate units like secret societies or kinship groupings. In these communal regions, however, the cosmology was only slightly more complicated than that in shamanic religions. The pantheon was a loosely structured conglomerate of supernatural deities and spirits, but the mythology surrounding these deities tended to be more elaborate than that of shamanic religions of hunter-gatherers. For example, among the Trobriand Islanders a series of ancestral spirits were postulated, with their genealogy being well known, but the hierarchy of relations and power among these spirits still remained somewhat vague and ambiguous. Moreover, values prescribed by the belief system of communal religions were not clearly articulated or systematized into a moral code, remaining implicit and uncodified (Malinowski 1955). Thus, while the belief systems of communal religions were not greatly evolved beyond those of hunter-gatherers, the cult structure was considerably more complex than in shamanic religions.

As Bronislaw Malinowski's ([1925] 1955) ethnography reveals, the Trobriand Islanders displayed the beginnings of two communal cults: the Technological Magic Cult and the Cult of the Spirits of the Dead. In the Technological Magic Cult, certain ancestral spirit-beings controlled economic activity, and hence, ritual deference had to be paid to these spirits with respect to the main types of economic activity among the Trobriand Islanders: gardening and deep-sea fishing in canoes. No intermediary or spiritual helper was required to communicate with these ancestral spirits, but communal participation was somewhat calendrical, while rituals were supervised by magicians. The second communal cult structure of the Trobriand Islanders—the Spirits of the Dead— relied less on magicians and intermediaries than the Technological Magic Cult. Here, ceremonies and rituals were organized and run principally by lay persons, with the one major calendrical ritual being held at the end of the harvest and involving a prolonged period of food display, consumption, dancing, and sex. Aside from these two communal cults, the religion of the Trobriand Islanders was organized into shamanic cults with professional magicians and sorcerers causing and/or curing misfortune and illness for clients. Also, there were various individualistic cults requiring individual ritual activity with respect to matters such as love, protection from evil, lesser spirits, flying witches, and so on.

Communal religions thus displayed a level of structural organization beyond that of shamanic religions: Cult structures were more varied and began to look like quasi-bureaucratic organizations; and although the belief system was only slightly more elaborate than among hunter-gatherers, the mythology tended to be more extensive. Within communal religions, however, were the seeds of beliefs and cult structures that became more conspicuous features of pre-industrial ecclesiastic religions, especially as societies became more stratified and hierarchical (Swanson 1960).

Traditional ecclesiastic religions were evident in advanced horticultural and early agrarian societies; and they revealed a marked increase in the complexity of both the belief system and cult structure. In examining this type of religion I utilize the extensive ethnographic data on the traditional Dahomey of West Africa during its political independence (Herskovits and Herskovits 1933; Herskovits 1938), as well as Goode's (1951) and Wallace's (1966) secondary analysis of Dahomean religion.

The most notable features of traditional ecclesiastic religions compared to communal religions are the complexity of the cosmology and the emergence of a more bureaucratically organized clergy. With traditional ecclesiastic religions, there was an elaborate pantheon or group of pantheons as well as a relatively clear hierarchical ordering of the supernatural beings in terms of their power and influence. Also, there was usually a creator god—a supernatural being who created both the natural and supernatural. The mythology of the cosmology was well developed and included episodes in the lives of gods, fraternal jealousies, sexual relations, and competition among various supernatural deities. In some traditional ecclesiastical religions, values began to be codified into a religious code of rights and wrongs, although equally frequently, religious values remained only implicit within ritual activity. The traditional Dahomean religion displayed such a belief system. There was a female Sky God—Mawu or Mawu-Lisa (Lisa being the son of Mawu and yet often fused with her). Indeed, depending upon the mythology, Mawu could also be a male. Mawu or Mawu-Lisa was usually believed to have divided the universe and world, because Mawu was the creator of all things, although other myths indicated that additional gods created certain things. And so, there was some ambiguity over just which god was the creator—although in most cases Mawu ultimately held the formula for the creation of humans, matter, and other gods. Although the mythologies surrounding Mawu or Mawu-Lisa were somewhat ambiguous, Mawu was almost always viewed as dividing the supernatural into three giant subpantheons pertaining to the Sky, Thunder, and Earth; and in each of these subpantheons existed a host of deities with an elaborate mythology surrounding all of them. A fourth pantheon revolving around sea gods also existed, but its relationship to Mawu was unclear. Thus, the Dahomean pantheon was extremely complex, containing not only ambiguous but sometimes conflicting mythologies. Yet, despite these ambiguities, there were incipient hierarchies of power and influence extending from Mawu or Mawu-Lisa down to the gods of the various subpantheons. Also, although somewhat clouded, there was a creation myth about Mawu as well as some other gods in the subpantheon. Religions such as the Dahomean were ecclesiastic because of a new form of cult structure, one displaying a professional clergy organized into a bureaucracy. These clergy differed from shamans in that they were not individual entrepreneurs or lay officials like those in communal cults; instead, they were formally appointed or elected as more or less full-time religious specialists (or priests). Relations among these priests usually became somewhat hierarchical in terms of prestige and power. These religious specialists of ecclesiastic cults also performed certain calendrical and noncalendrical rituals in established tem-

Table 5.5.   Religion in Horticultural Societies

	Simple	Advanced
Belief system	Conception of supernatural realm of beings and forces; no clear organization of supernatural into cosmology, but considerable mythology; no explicit religious value system or moral code	Conception of supernatural realm of beings and forces; increased organization of supernatural realm into levels and a hierarchical pantheon of gods and forces; extensive mythology often evident; some indication of explicit values and moral codes
Rituals	Clear and regular calendrical rituals, usually performed by individuals alone or in kin groupings, but at times led by shaman	Regular calendrical rituals, often led by shaman and, in more complex systems, by full-time priests; increased control and mediation of ritual activity by religious specialists
Cult structure	Explicit structures devoted to religious activity, involving (1) division of labor among lay participants, lay organizers-sponsors, performers, and religious specialists (shamans, magicians, and others deemed to have special capabilities to mediate with supernatural); (2) explicit symbols and artifacts representing various aspects of the supernatural, and at times (3) specialized buildings and places where cult members meet to perform religious activity	Explicit structures devoted to religious activity, involving (1) clear division of labor between religious specialists (often full-time) and increasingly less active laypersons, who assume role of worshippers; (2) hierarchy of religious specialists; (3) elaborate symbols and artifacts representing each aspect of the supernatural; and (4) specialized buildings and places (temples) for religious specialists to perform religious activity for laypersons

ple structures, with laypersons increasingly becoming passive respondents rather than active participants (Wallace 1966:88). Furthermore, these religious specialists began to exert tremendous nonreligious influence and perhaps authority in secular (as well as sacred) activities.

Although the Dahomean religion never spread far beyond West Africa, it displayed the incipient structural features of more developed premodern religions such as Islam, Christianity, Hinduism, Buddhism, and Judaism that became typical of full-blown agrarian systems. The Dahomean religion had numerous individualistic cults where members established ritual relations with various minor deities, and the Dahomeans also had a shamanic cult—the Divination Cult—whose professional diviners discovered the proper ritual for certain crucial activities (harvesting, marketing, etc.) as well as illness and misfortune. Various quasi-communal cults—the Ancestral Cults—organized around kinship groupings were also in evidence, with kin members engaging in certain ritual activities, especially those surrounding death. But the distinguishing feature of the Dahomean religion was the emergence of an ecclesiastical cult. Each major pantheon in the belief system—Sky, Thunder, Earth, Sea—had a separate religious order or cult structure, and each of these cults possessed its own temple, professional clergy, and hierarchy of religious specialists. They thus represented different "churches" with related and yet separate cosmologies. What is most significant about the religious system was the quasibureaucratic structure of cults, since religious development into true world religions could not occur without this structural base. And, as advanced horticulture evolved into agrarianism, it became possible to support a fully bureaucratized system of religion.

EDUCATION

As a review of the short contents of table 5.6 underscores, education is a recessive institution up to, and including, advanced horticulture. Most education was informal and, if formal, confined to instruction for scribes, warriors, religious practitioners, and craft apprentices. But once formal instruction outside of kinship is evident, education has become differentiated from kinship. As I

Table 5.6. Education in Horticultural Societies

	Simple	Advanced
Instruction	Most learning by observation and practice. Yet, frequent episodes of explicit tutelage of young by elder kin	Same as simple system, except there are explicit patterns of apprenticeship in crafts. Also, a clear training period for religious practitioners, warriors, and scribes. Clear school structures evident. Tutors also prominent for political and religious elites
Curricula	Technologies, religious beliefs and rituals, kinship history and traditions	Same as simple system, except now various patterns of apprenticeship and school structures impart literacy, arithmetic, religion and history, military skills, religious rituals, crafts, and arts
Ritualized passage	Transition to adulthood always marked. Transitions to age cohorts, to warrior status, to new positions in kinship also marked after a period of instruction	Same as simple, except that clear ceremonies marking completion of apprenticeships and, at times, school-based education are now evident

note in chapter 3, education remained somewhat isolated from the mainstream of the population until industrialization. Even during the agrarian era where full differentiation exists, formal education was confined primarily to elites, with only particular economic specialists in trades and crafts receiving formal instruction and with much of this instruction occurring within the structure of kinship systems, particularly the patrimonial family where apprentices would be taken into families for instruction.

KEY INSTITUTIONAL INTERCHANGES

Although the influence of kinship in organizing other institutional spheres began to decline with advanced horticulture, kinship was nonetheless the principal organizing feature of this stage of human evolution. Thus, we should begin to examine key interchanges among institutional systems with a review of the reciprocal effects between kinship, on the one hand, and the other core institutional systems, on the other.

Kinship and Economy

Economy and Kinship Formation   The formation of the family in human evolution was in response to production and reproduction as social forces that generated intense selection pressures, especially as hominids and eventually humans were forced to live in open-country savanna. Thus, the structure of kinship during early stages of human evolution very much reflected the effects of production and distribution as these pushed humans into economic activities.

The addition of the father to the mother–child bond was, no doubt, selected as a solution to the fundamental economic questions of how to organize gathering, conversion, and distribution of food in ways that promoted reproduction of the species. For once there was a nuclear family unit of mother, father, and offspring, the structure of social life could be more stable and attuned to gathering, producing, and distributing resources. Indeed, the nuclear unit organized technology as well as human and physical capital for gathering and producing, while providing the unit within which distribution was to occur. Without kinship, where individuals would be free to go their own way and where mother and dependent children would be left to fend for themselves, reproduction of the species would be problematic. Thus, the creation of the elementary nuclear unit occurred under selection pressures for stabilizing and coordinating the elements needed in gathering, producing, and distributing in ways enabling the species to survive.

As populations grew and settled down, they needed to gather more, produce more, and distribute to more people. The only structures available to these emerging horticultural populations were the band and kinship. The band was replaced by communities that, in turn, organized groupings of kin, but with selection for more complex social structures to organize production and distribution, kinship was expanded because this was the easiest route to finding a structure capable of organizing larger numbers of individuals. Humans had to reorganize, or die. By elaborating upon blood and marriage ties, selection pressures generated by population, production, reproduction, distribution, and regulation could all be met, although many populations of the past probably failed to do so and, as a result, died out or were conquered by more organized peoples.

Norms of extendedness or polygamy resulted in larger family groups that could perform necessary labor; rules of residence insured that some family members would remain close and that new recruits would be brought by either the daughter or son into the family compound; norms of exogamy forced the incorporation of new members from outside the community into the family labor pool; unilineal descent rules insured that the labor pool would remain loyal and tied to the familial economic unit, while also insuring that capital and property would be concentrated in a particular kin grouping, whether a lineage, clan, or moiety; rules of authority allowed for the coordination and control of the family labor pool and capital, as did unambiguous rules concerning family activity, especially rules concerning the division of household tasks (which often shaded into economic role behaviors); and norms of dissolution kept the labor force intact by spelling out where dependents (future labor) were to reside.

Kinship and the Structure of the Economy   By becoming more elaborate, kinship made it possible for the economy to gather and produce more, while providing a kin-based system for the distribution of increased productivity to larger numbers of people. Figure 5.1 presents in outline form the way in which blood and marriage ties of a unilineal descent system built up a structure that looks very much like the chart of a large corporation in today's world. The similarities between the two structures are not coincidental, because unilineal descent provided a mechanism for creating something that is structurally equivalent to a modern organization for populations without the level of economic surplus to support full-fledged bureaucratic systems.

The major weakness of this form of organization is that it is rife with tensions among kindred because family activities and economic roles are mixed together, as are roles in other institutional domains. When large numbers of kindred are forced to live and work together, while also governing themselves, the potential for conflict is great. And so, people abandoned these systems when new agrarian technologies allowed for sufficient economic surplus to support nonkin corporate units. Yet, all elements of the economy were pro-

Kinship Unit

Moiety

Clans

Sub-clans

Lineages

Nuclear
families

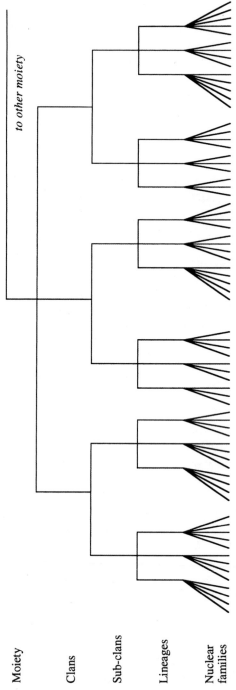

to other moiety

Figure 5.1. Kinship as a Type of Complex Organization

Note: The structure above would represent one-half (the chart flowing down from the moiety is not drawn because of space limitations) of a rather small society, divided into two moieties, three clans, six subclans, and eighteen lineages connecting a larger number of nuclear families. This kind of structure looks very much like the organization chart for a bureaucracy because it is the functional equivalent for a society that does not generate sufficient surplus to create formal organizations.

vided by kinship: technologies were stored in members' brains, at least until writing emerged in very advanced horticultural systems. Physical capital belonged to kin groups, and human capital was allocated by kinship rules to members of various units. Property was generally held by kin groupings, although advanced horticultural systems begin to develop alternative systems for defining and allocating property outside of kinship. And clearly, the entrepreneurial structure organizing all other economic elements was kinship.

Kinship and Polity

Small bands of hunter-gatherers did not need government; people performed traditional economic and familial roles, talking over problematic matters that might come up. If conflict erupted, the band generally split apart, with the antagonistic parties forming new bands. Leaders in these simple systems were informal, noted for their abilities, and followed only if others were so inclined.

Once humans settled down, and populations began to grow, selection pressures emanating from regulation as a macrodynamic force emerged: If protagonists could no longer go their own way, how was conflict to be resolved? If land became property, who was to distribute it and the rights to its use? If surplus food was now produced, who decided what was to be done with it? If outside populations invaded territories, who was to coordinate people for war? These kinds of problems forced people to find ways of consolidating power in order to survive.

One can see beginnings of polity in hunter-gatherers who had settled down, usually near a waterway or ocean that provided food to support a larger, year-round population. Under these conditions, a Big Man often emerged and made decisions for the population as a whole, although once this leader died, there was no clear heir to his position—a situation that often threw villages into conflict (Johnson and Earle 1987:160–93; Boas 1921). As populations grew and moved into full-fledged horticulture, however, the demands or selection pressures for more stable leadership intensified. At the very least, there were more people to coordinate, more property to distribute, more economic surplus to allocate, and more enemies to defend against. And hence, much as economic pressures forced the elaboration of kinship, so these pressures for leadership put pressure on members of populations to use blood and marriage ties to create a kin-based polity. The descent rule became the key to building a system of leaders, primarily because it could provide instructions about lines of authority and was, therefore, the easiest evolutionary path to take.

As lineages, clans, or moieties were constructed in unilineal descent systems, norms designated certain kin as decision makers for the larger kin grouping—usually the eldest and/or ablest male of a descent grouping in a patrilineal system. These norms delineated and delimited the spheres of influence for various decision makers in a society, and coupled with family-authority norms, descent rules could provide an efficient way to delegate authority and establish a chain of command in a society without a governmental bureaucracy and administrative staff. Such rules could resolve administrative problems by indicating which adults in each family unit would possess ultimate authority, and when combined with descent norms, family-authority norms indicated just who the "chief executive" and his "lieutenants" were. Family norms thus promoted clarity in decision making by specifying the sphere of authority possessed by each decision maker within the larger descent grouping.

In indicating where kin were to live, residence norms enclosed kin within various geographical areas, thereby facilitating coordinated decision making by cutting down on geographical dispersion. Too much dispersion would inhibit decision making, especially when systems of transportation and communication were cumbersome and could not effectively unite large territories. Residence rules also sought to stabilize the boundaries and numbers of those in a political sphere by attempting to regularize and keep in balance immigrants and emigrants. Ideally, but rarely in actual practice (because of varying sex ratios, age distributions, and mortality rates), rules sought to assure that for each daughter who left a territory, a new daughter-in-law would come in (assuming patrilocal residence rules). The reverse was attempted in a matrilocal system.

Marriage rules like those for exogamy forced actors outside their kin group or village in search of partners. In gathering partners from other kin groups (or villages), a system of political allegiances and alliances emerged among kin groupings and communities. Exogamy in conjunction with rules of residence forced kin to exchange kindred with other kin groups and villages. To be at war or have strained relations with these other groups or communities would make life miserable for transplanted kin; and so, these cross-cutting kin ties promoted allegiances and some degree of political stability in societies lacking a well-articulated state or military apparatus.

Thus, kinship rules can create a very effective system of authority by establishing a chain of command and a system of political alliances. Yet, as the size and scale of society increased, kinship began to recede as the basis for organizing polity. In its place came the state because the problems of coordination and control, representing selection pressures from the forces of population and regulation, began to exceed the organizational capacities of kinship.

One of the structural problems of kin-based polities is that they were rife with tension (Maryanski and Turner 1992), as I emphasize above. Fights, feuds, and warfare were endemic, primarily because people resented, or were jealous of, control by relatives. Power is always resented by those without it, and when family and power are interwoven, these resentments can take on double intensity.

In addition to this structural weakness, kin-based systems could only work effectively when kinship was organizing economic activity; but as the economy and kinship began to differentiate with advanced horticulture, alternatives to kin-based government were sought. Indeed, there was often intense selection pressure on a population to find alternatives, or face disintegration.

The first states were, no doubt, kin-based chiefdoms organized along the lines of descent rules, with authority, residence, and marriage among elites being very much influenced by the norms of the kinship system. Below the hereditary nobility, however, a less kin-based bureaucracy began to emerge as warfare, tax collection, public works, policing, managing, accounting, recording, law-making, and other activities were performed. This political bureaucracy was, of course, filled with personnel receiving noble favors and with appointments based upon elite patronage—thereby making it rather inefficient and filled with corruption. Yet, the structural form of elites and their administrative staff was set, and as the scale and complexity of tasks increased, an ever-greater percentage of incumbents in polity was from nonelite families.

As this process unfolded, kinship was no longer needed to organize power, authority, and leadership; and indeed kin-based authority, such as a clan in a particular region, would be seen by a monarch as a threat to the emerging state and would be pressured to disband or would be destroyed in conflict with the state. As unilineal kinship was gradually disbanded, descent and residence rules lost much of their power; and people were reassembled in a more feudal pattern on manorial estates as tenant farmers and craftspersons, or they migrated to emerging urban areas to seek new economic opportunities. Advanced horticulture and early agrarianism thus differentiated economy, polity, and kinship from each other, breaking the hold of kinship but imposing the hold of the nobility and state. The cage of kinship was now replaced by the cage of state power (Maryanski and Turner 1992).

As this transition proceeded, kinship ceased to be the structural locus of polity, although families would dominate monarchies for many generations. Still, even in monarchal systems that emerged with agrarianism and, in some cases (like China) with advanced horticulture, kinship increasingly revolved around reproduction rather than production and regulation. For once kinship is differentiated from economy and polity, it is geared primarily for socialization of commitments to play roles in the economy and to provide legitimacy (as a symbolic base of power) for the emerging polity. In turn, the polity through the legal system allocates power within the family, specifying duties and responsibilities of family members. Thus, by the dawn of the agrarian revolution, kinship was reverting to more nucleated forms of households, stripped of the complex structure made possible by descent rules and other kinship norms, and becoming focused on reproduction of people biologically and socioculturally. In this transformation, kinship becomes an important base of symbolic power for polity and human capital for the economy.

Kinship and Law

During early horticulture, the rules of the legal system were often the same as kinship norms, or at least circumscribed by these norms; the courts were built from kin leaders and councils of kin elders; the representatives of litigants were fellow kin members; the enforcement of laws and decisions were by kindred; and even a system of appeals courts was based upon hierarchies of kin lineages and chiefdoms. Thus, in these horticultural societies, where unilineal descent shaped other kinship norms, the structure of the legal system paralleled the structure of kinship groupings created by descent, authority, residence, and activity norms.

As kinship rules were learned, then, many of the specific tenets of the legal system were also acquired, signaling the importance of kinship as a reproductive and regulatory structure. Socialization within the family operated at two levels, one at the level of imparting commitments to basic values embodied in the legal system and another at the level of the specific laws and procedures involved in the operation of the legal system. Family could impart knowledge and commitments as long as the legal system was relatively simple and embedded in kinship, but with differentiation of polity and law from kinship, the reproductive effects of kinship shifted. In general, the simpler the legal system was, the more details of this system were imparted through family socialization, whereas as legal systems became more complex, family socialization imparted commitments to the basic values of the civic culture that eventually became the guiding framework of law. Thus, among hunter-gatherers and simple horticulturalists, socialization in kinship also involved imparting knowledge of basic rules, procedures for their mediation, and perhaps enforcement. With advanced horticulture, however, a trend increasingly evident with agrarianism was initiated: As the legal system became more complex, family socialization emphasized more general premises of law rather than the specifics of law. Still, if local or religious legal systems remained viable, many of the details of local laws, courts, and enforcement continued to be learned within kinship. For often, even as a state-initiated law expanded, systems of local codes, tribunals, and enforcement activities often stayed intact for long periods of time during advanced horticulture and agrarianism.

As law began to differentiate from kinship, however, it abandoned the structural template provided by kinship (and religion as well) and, instead, began to follow the mandates of polity in the face of an increasing volume and variety of new problems of control and coordination. As law became structurally free of kinship, the importance of family socialization of the cultural underpinnings of the evolving legal system was to become ever more significant for sustaining diffuse commitments to law. Such commitments are always critical to the operation of a law as an institution, because the system is too complex for all individuals to understand fully and, more importantly, because individuals may often have disagreements over specific procedures while still remaining committed to the system as a whole. These diffuse commitments also served as a symbolic base of power for polity, which increasingly used law to regulate and coordinate the activities of actors in advanced horticultural populations.

Kinship and Religion

As the purveyor of the supernatural, religion has the power to bestow special meaning—indeed, a sacredness—on norms and behaviors in society. Thus, if the norms of kinship can be made sacred, as embodying the will and wishes of supernatural forces, they will be given additional salience and will be subject to more intense sanctions. For now, to violate a kinship norm is to invite the wrath or intervention of the supernatural (Wallace 1966; Harris 1971). Ancestor worship among hunter-gatherers was one of the first ways in which religious beliefs gave power to kinship norms (although probably less than 25 percent of hunter-gatherers practiced ancestor worship; see Nolan and Lenski 2001).

As kinship systems elaborated during horticulture, however, ancestor worship became much more prevalent, and new religious beliefs enhanced the sacred quality of kinship norms, thereby increasing the chances that kin members would abide by them. More elaborate rituals were directed toward ancestors who were seen to inhabit the supernatural realm, and as these rituals were emitted, they reinforced descent rules and strengthened the sense of kin continuity. Kinship was not just for the living; it reached back and included the dead. Moreover, fears of being labeled deviant, particularly by virtue of special powers such as witchcraft, kept people in line and, in so doing, reinforced key kinship norms (Wallace 1966; Swanson 1960; Whiting 1950).

This kind of supernatural backing of kinship rules was, no doubt, the result of intense selection pressures from regulation and reproduction as macrodynamic forces on unilineal descent systems, because these systems are filled with tension. Aggregating larger numbers of kin related by blood and marriage ties produced tensions and anxiety which, to some degree, could be mitigated by commitments to religious beliefs and values embodied in cult structures organized by kinship and reinforced by rituals.

Religious rituals were also critical to *rites de passage* within kinship, marking transitions to new statuses and roles and, in the process, re-enforcing the norms of kinship. For as children grow they assume new statuses within their family and larger kin grouping; and the new normative obligations accompanying these statuses require a new set of attitudes, dispositions, and self-identity. Religious rituals surrounding such major status transitions generate particular awareness of these new obligations by bringing to bear supernatural forces, and admonishing the young under the threat of supernatural intervention to display the dispositions and behavior appropriate to their newly acquired station in life. The puberty rites of many traditional societies were a conspicuous example of how religious rituals solemnly informed adolescents that they were now close to assuming adult status, marking emphatically the transformed relationship between these new adults and their fellow kinsmen. In this way, internal family reorganization occurred with a minimal amount of internal role strain and conflict among kinsmen who often existed in a steady state of underlying tension. Marriage is another major status transition, for it marks the creation of a new family or the incorporation of new members into an existing family. In either case, a reorganization of the kinship system occurs; and by symbolizing this reorganization with religious or sacred significance, the new obligations attendant on both the marrying partners and their fellow kinsmen are made explicit, if not emphatic. The birth of a child confers another cluster of obligations on parents and surrounding kinsmen and has, therefore, become marked by religious rituals. Since birth is the beginning of social reproduction and ultimately a society's survival, these rituals have often been very elaborate, as in the case among the ZuZi. In delivering her child, a mother called upon a ZuZi priest to enact the appropriate rituals; and at birth, the child was placed in a bed of hot stones covered with sand and then appropriate prayers were offered for a long life and good health. Four days later the child and mother were brought to the Sun Father at dawn to be ritually washed and to be subjects of prayers (Turner 1972:128).

Probably the most dramatic status transition experienced by members of a kinship system is death. A death profoundly reorganizes family and kinship relations, since a person for whom strong attachments and emotions existed is simply removed from the daily life of the kin group; and when a kinship leader dies, reorganization of the larger kin grouping must ensue. It is therefore not surprising that elaborate religious rituals have surrounded death because the removal of a kinsman has always generated both intrapersonal anxiety and the need for structural reorganization of the family. Death rituals have thus provided for the alleviation of anxiety and grief, as well as ritually reintegrating the disrupted kinship group.

With advanced horticulture, religion and kinship became more differentiated. Ecclesiastic cult structures with more permanent temples and with religious specialists interpreting religious beliefs and leading rituals for family members began to emerge and organize religion outside kinship. With renuclearization of the family that was initiated with very advanced horticulture and early agrarianism, this split between religion and kinship continued. Still, even where ecclesiastic cultures dominated, kinship socialization was essential in generating the commitments to religious beliefs and the motivations for performing rituals in temples. Moreover, minor rituals such as praying were still conducted within kinship, thus furthering commitments to religious beliefs.

Even as kinship ceased to be the locus of many religious rituals, however, it became a source of financial support of religious specialists and the temples in which cult activities were organized. In giving support to the cult structure and its activities, commitments to religious beliefs were reinforced, especially since giving is often highly ritualized. In return, religion gave legitimacy to the structure of the family and to the role activities of its members. Thus, the basic exchange between religion and family so evident in the present era—that is, financial support in return for legitimization of familial roles—began with advanced horticulture and accelerated through the agrarian and industrial stages of societal evolution.

Polity and Other Institutions

Polity is a decision-making and implementing system, whose leaders set societal-level goals and, then, allocate and distribute the material and symbolic resources of other institutional systems to realize these goals. Political systems thus depend upon other institutional spheres in order to maintain each base of power, as well as balances among these bases. In a sense power is consolidated and centralized into polity in order to draw upon the organizational outputs of other institutions; and since polity as a differentiated institution makes its appearance with horticulture, it is essential to analyze some of its interactions with other institutional systems that are also differentiating and developing.

Economy and Polity Without the capacity to generate economic surplus, a distinctive polity cannot exist. Thus, the most basic effect of the economy on polity is producing the surplus that enables political leaders and their staffs to consolidate and centralize power; and the greater is the economic surplus, the more power can be mobilized in a society (Lenski 1966). For hunter-gatherers, there was little surplus to support a distinct political system; and only with a more settled existence did Big Men systems of leadership emerge, usurping and distributing the surplus. With horticulture, descent and authority rules of kinship organized the appropriation and redistribution of economic surplus; and as this surplus increased with expanded production, the scale and scope of these kin-based polities also grew, often becoming less kin-based and moving toward state formation.

Yet, the economy not only enables and facilitates the consolidation of power by providing the surplus on which polity survives, the underlying force of production raises valences for regulation as a force and, thereby, increases selection pressures on people to find new ways to mobilize, regulate, control, and distribute human and physical capital, technology, and property so as to sustain the viable economy. Some of these key pressures from the economy on the polity are examined below.

When economies generate a surplus beyond the subsistence needs of the population, problems of who is to get how much of the surplus escalate, often into violent confrontations. There is, then, intense selection pressure to resolve rising distributional problems; and these pressures are one important reason for the emergence of polity. For ultimately, the leaders of government make decisions about the allocation of economic surplus. And as the surplus gets larger with economic development, the complexity and scale of these allocation decisions correspondingly increase.

Allocation depends upon the consolidation and centralization of the bases of power so as to have the capacity to appropriate economic surplus and, then, the administrative facility to redistribute what is expropriated. Big Men and horticultural chiefs usually redistributed all or most of what they collected in order to gain prestige and honor (thereby consolidating their symbolic claims to power). Such "generous" redistribution was also encouraged because much of the surplus could not be stored (it would simply rot) and, hence, could not lead to accumulations of great wealth. With advanced horticulture, however, some surplus could be stored and hoarded; and moreover, the new productive outputs that come with mining and metallurgy, marketing and trade, masonry and building, and many other advances of advanced horticulture allowed for considerable wealth to be amassed. The inequalities generated by the extraction of surplus and its redistribution to the more privileged sectors of the society push for the further consolidation and centralization of power in order to manage and control the growing resentments and internal threats. Yet, in usurping surplus, polities develop *systems of taxation* that institutionalize the appropriation process with taxing formulas and administrative offices for collection. For most of human history, this system of taxation was very simple, as when a headman received ritualistically the economic output of kin units, followed by his giving it back to them. In more advanced horticultural systems, however, the incipient state began to develop a taxation system that would increase (1) the administrative base of power in order to rationalize the collection of taxes, (2) the coercive base in order to enforce the compliance of taxpayers, and eventually, (3) the legal system in order to articulate and adjudicate ever more complex formulas of taxation. At the same time, the legitimacy of the state, an important symbolic base of power, may have eroded if taxation was too severe. Compared to advanced agrarian and industrial societies, however, this system of taxation was still relatively simple, but the basic structural template for systematic taxation had been invented and would, hereafter, assure growth in the size and scale of polity.

In creating a system of taxation, government also began to formalize definitions of property, and property rights. For example, a horticultural chief may have "owned" all land, but he had to allocate gardening plots to kin units in return for their economic outputs, which he then redistributed back to them. In all of this expropriation and redistribution, definitions of property and property rights were being established; and once this process was initiated, it continued so that almost all resources, technologies, physical capital, and even human capital would eventually become defined in terms of property or rights to property. And when defined as property, it is but a short step to viewing these elements of all economies as *commodities* that can be bought and sold in markets. Without establishing a system of taxation, then, notions of property and commodities would be very limited; and when systems of property rights became institutionalized in tradition and law, the scale of government could expand because there is more property to be taxed and commodities to be accumulated.

As definitions of property and tax formulas were more clearly articulated, the state's extraction of economic surplus became more varied. Moreover, in some horticultural systems, the capacity of the state to extract liquid capital (money) existed and could be used to finance new projects. In human history, much of this financial ability has gone to pay for war and military adventurism. Military conquest can, if successful, increase wealth (through plunder and pillage, or tribute), but if unsuccessful, war drains the capital resources of a society and makes it vulnerable to both internal or external threats.

As the economy grows, a larger population can be supported; conversely, population growth places selection pressures for increased gathering, producing, and distributing. Population size, per se, escalates the logistical problems revolving around the coordination and control of the larger population; and when accompanied by a larger number and diversity of economic units engaged in gathering, producing, and distributing, the logistical loads escalate that much further, thereby raising the values of regulation as a macrodynamic force. These mounting problems of coordination and control in economic activity represent selection pressures to consolidate and centralize power. At first, this consolidation involved giving headmen, Big Men, and chiefs rights to coordinate basic tasks, as when the chief assigned gardening plots to kin units or when the Big Man engaged in negotiation and trade with neighboring communities. Later, as power became more consolidated and centralized under a paramount chief or king, power was increasingly used to regulate all economic elements—property, technology, and physical and human capital. Initial involvement of government in economic coordination was relatively limited, assigning tasks and redistributing outputs in a comparatively egalitarian manner; and in this process, the chief heightened his symbolic base of power, instituted the manipulation of material incentives, created the first administrative system, and held the threat of coercion as a possible sanction. From this simple beginning with horticulture, however, the structural template was in place for polity to extract ever more resources to support the privilege of elites, and in the process, polity became capable of (1) building an administrative system for tax collection and for public expenditures, (2) developing effective strategies for material incentives in order to control elites, (3) establishing a permanently mobilized coercive force, and (4) initiating the process of using more secular symbols from law for legitimization.

With advanced horticulture, the force of distribution pushed actors to develop market systems for distribution of economic goods. These markets rarely went beyond Braudel's lower levels (see chapter 2), but larger urban centers using money and credit could be found among the most advanced horticultural systems. These systems, in turn, created selection pressures for their regulation; and polity began very slowly to provide at least some of this needed regulation, although leagues of merchants and traders were often more involved than polity in managing trade and markets. The transactions in markets by traders represented a potentially large source of liquid capital for polity, but surprisingly it was not until late agrarianism and early industrial stages of human evolution that polity fully recognized the potential wealth to be gained by taxing heavily the emerging bourgeoisie. Still, polity in advanced horticultural systems began first forays into coordinating and regulation markets using money, if only to assure the proper coinage of money.

Religion and Polity   In hunter-gatherer and simple horticultural societies, religious ritual and beliefs were often interwoven with most major decisions in the society—when and where to hunt, when to move on, or, in the case of emerging horticulturalists, when and where to plant and harvest. The communal planting rituals associated with major decisions in these simple societies reaffirmed religious beliefs, and in so doing, made rituals even more effective in mobilizing people to engage in necessary behaviors, while alleviating much of the uncertainty and anxiety arising from these behaviors (Wallace 1966:110–27). Sometimes these rituals were performed by special practitioners such as a shaman, while at other times kin leaders doubled as religious practitioners. Thus, one of the major consequences of religion on political decision making in very simple societies was to mobilize the members of the society and to confer legitimacy on leaders. Since decision makers in these systems had a limited capacity to use physical force or coercion, invoking the gods and performing rituals reaffirming beliefs became an effective base of power.

With the emergence of a kin-based polity in full-blown horticultural systems, the legitimating consequences of religion for decision making became even more significant. Societies with kin-based polities displayed a clearly visible locus of power and decision making, for heads of kin groups exerted real control over their fellow kinsmen and, if paramount chiefs existed, the head of one kin grouping had decision-making power over the heads of other kin groupings in the society. Religion often provided the necessary legitimization of these power differentials (Parsons 1966); and although this legitimating consequence of religion could take various forms, leaders were often considered gods or at least as having special powers of communication with the gods, and they were usually charged with preserving the religious dogma and traditions of a society, frequently becoming important religious practitioners in a society. Because religion was an influential and compelling force in these early horticultural societies, the domination of religious roles by political elites enabled them, if they wished, to legitimate inequality by making it seem the mandate of the gods. To rule by divine right thus represented a major basis of power in most pre-industrial societies.

In more advanced horticultural and agrarian systems, where an administrative bureaucracy existed, *literate* religious practitioners often performed many of the administrative tasks requiring expertise in the political bureaucracy. In systems where both extensive political and religious bureaucracies existed, as was the case in pre-modern China, considerable overlap between the emerging secular state and ecclesiastical bureaucracy was evident, but as both the state and church bureaucracies developed, a clear segregation between the institutions of polity and religion ensued (Wallace 1966:261). Usually, but not always, religion still legitimated the right of elites to hold and wield power, but eventually a basic conflict between the more sacred concerns of religion and the secular focus of the emerging state became marked. With advanced horticulture, this tension was clearly evident but it becomes considerably more intense with the advent of agrarianism. But, even in state-based horticultural societies, leaders began the search for new bases of legitimization. One of these bases is law.

Law and Polity   In hunting and gathering as well as simple horticulture, law was a recessive institution, being fused with kinship, religion, and the emerging polity. At times, it became possible to see a glimpse of a separate legal system, as when a council of elders heard the evidence and directed kinsmen to require an offending person to pay compensation for violating a rule. In this example can be found the three basic elements of law: laws, adjudicating structures or courts, and enforcement capacities. And if elders had decided that this case required a new or revised rule, then the fourth element—the legislative function—of all legal systems would surface. With advanced horticulture, the emerging state began to establish a more permanent legal system, and once a legal system was sufficiently differentiated from its political origins, it exerted independent effects back on the polity that had created it (Luhmann 1985, 1982).

As polities have consolidated and centralized power over humans' evolutionary history, the basis of legitimization has shifted, by fits and starts, from religious to secular symbols. Among horticulturalists and early agrarian populations, religious symbols were sufficient, but as polity became more distinct as an institutional system and increasingly intrusive in regulating social action, it inevitably came into conflict with religion which, as noted above, could be a potential source of rival power. Polities thus began to seek alternative bases of legitimization to justify the need, or desire, to intrude into more spheres of social activity.

As this process unfolded, law increasingly became a new legitimating base of power. For law to be an effective source of legitimization, however, it must possess several features: (1) It must codify in some form the emotionally charged values, traditions, and religious dogmas of the population into secular tenets; (2) it must help establish a civic culture that provides basic postulates and principles for law enactment and enforcement; and (3) it must create a system of law-enacting (the legislative function), law-managing (courts), and law-enforcing (police) structures that are perceived as fair and honest by members of the population.

Since state-based polities have supported vast inequalities, the use of law by polity to legitimate itself has not always been successful, and particularly so as advanced horticulture evolves into full agrarianism. Still, in advanced horticultural societies, the beginnings of a movement to embodying traditions in secular tenets were evident. Moreover, in some cases polity began to push for a secular civic culture promoting (usually through symbolic manipulation) perceptions of fairness and honesty among agents and agencies of the emerging legal system. Still, only the bare beginnings of this transition to fully secular bases of legitimization were evident in advanced horticulture. It was only with late agrarianism and the transition to industrialism that this transformation accelerated, and even then secularization of legitimacy is far from complete.

Economy and Religion

Religion is organized around beliefs and rituals directed at a supernatural realm of forces, powers, and deities. Religion deals with many of the nonempirical and cosmic parameters of social life, but this fact does not mean that religious beliefs and rituals cannot have a profound impact on everyday activities within the economy, especially among settled hunter-gatherers and horticulturalists where religious beliefs and rituals could mobilize actors to perform crucial economic roles and, thereby, could reinforce economic norms guiding behaviors.

Religious beliefs can, for example, mobilize actors to engage in economic roles by reducing the anxiety often associated with economic behavior. By making available rituals designed to invoke the benevolence, or at least suspend the malevolence, of supernatural beings and forces, religion reduces the anxiety associated with dangerous economic activity. One of the best illustrations of this comes from Bronislaw Malinowski's ([1925] 1955) account of the Trobriand Islanders' use of extensive magic rites before participating in dangerous deep-sea fishing expeditions. Such rituals alleviated anxiety and thus pushed individuals to engage in this difficult economic activity. Even though technology among the Trobriands had risen after contact with colonial powers of the West to a level eliminating the objective uncertainty of deep-sea fishing, the religious rituals persisted—indicating that, once *institutionalized,* religious rituals endure even as the original conditions generating them have been greatly altered or even eliminated (O'Dea 1966:10). In fact the rituals may have actually increased the level of anxiety associated with economic tasks among the Trobriand Islanders (Radcliffe-Brown 1938), but the rituals also made the activities associated with the rituals sacred and essential, thereby assuring that they would be performed.

Religious beliefs and rituals can also have entrepreneurial consequences for the economy by reinforcing crucial economic norms, as is illustrated by Raymond Firth's (1936) account of Tikopian fishing rituals. One of the more elaborate rituals among the Tikopians revolved around preparation of fishing equipment—especially canoes—for expeditions into the open sea. Preparation for fishing is an obvious way to form capital and mobilize labor, but this activity among the Tikopians was considered particularly necessary because it was a religious ritual having significance for the supernatural. Under these conditions, economic tasks were performed more rapidly, efficiently, and with greater harmony. Even in more agrarian societies with an extensive technology, religious rituals had similar consequences. For example, among the Dahomeans, who displayed certain features of an advanced horticultural and an early agrarian economy with a more complex market structure, religious rituals were intimately involved in cultivation, harvesting, marketing, weaving, woodcarving, and iron-working (Goode 1951:88–89). Through rituals, appeals to deities were made in order to assure the success of parties engaged in the various kinds of tasks of the Dahomeans, despite the fact that considerable technology was utilized in all phases of the Dahomean economy.

In a very real sense, then, religious rituals in "sacredizing" crucial economic norms increased normative conformity. This religious reinforcement of norms, coupled with the mobilizing consequence of religious rituals, represented a major institutional source of entrepreneurship in horticultural societies because religion secured the involvement of labor in key economic activities and made this activity more efficient and harmonious.

CONCLUSION

Horticulture was a major step in human evolution because it led to permanent communities that would, over thousands of years, evolve into larger-scale agrarian societies and empires. The first horticultural societies were small, consisting of a few hundred people gardening in villages that were linked by kinship ties. Some of these kin-based societies became very large, at least for their time, and from these came the state-based systems of advanced horticulture. It is during the period when horticulture spread that the initial wave of institutional differentiation occurred. By the time advanced horticultural systems were in place from 10,000 to 5,000 years ago, economy, kinship, polity, and religion were clearly differentiated, with law just beginning to emerge from polity and kinship as a distinct institution. Education, the last of the early core to differentiate, would wait until more advanced agrarian systems were in place.

Once differentiation had occurred under selection pressures imposed by macrodynamic forces, the structural and cultural base for further evolution was established. The transition to agriculture where animal power and the plow, along with wind and water power, were widely used was just a short step from advanced horticultural systems. The real breakthrough had occurred millennia earlier, when hunter-gatherers first settled—having, in essence, fled their figurative garden of Eden to take up real gardening in the cage of kinship.

As humans settled, polity emerged not only to coordinate and control but also to conquer, and once societies were put on the path of chronic warfare, the winners of wars would become larger, thereby escalating selection pressures from population, production, reproduction, distribution, and regulation. As these pressures mounted, actors sought new ways to increase economic outputs, new ways to use power, and new ways to distribute resources. And as societies were successful, they could grow larger, thus setting into motion a new round of selection pressures. It took thousands of years, but once these cycles were initiated, the scale and complexity of human societies increased as institutional differentiation continued.

NOTES

1. This general description of horticultural populations, or variants such as pastoralism (Evans-Pritchard 1940), is drawn from Maryanski and Turner (1992), Lenski (1966), Nolan and Lenski (2001), Gordon (1914), Malinowski (1922), Landtman (1927), Childe (1964, 1960, 1952, 1930), Herskovitz (1938), Goldschmidt (1959), Leach (1954), Schapera (1956), Sahlins (1958), Sanders (1972), Murdock (1965, 1959, 1953), von Hagen (1961), Mair (1962), Chang (1963), MacNeish (1964), Hawkes (1965), Flannery (1973), Gibbs (1965), Earle (1984), Mann (1986), Johnson and Earle (1987), Bates and Plog (1991).

2. For analyses of these kinship systems, see: Keesing (1975), Schneider and Gough (1961), Fox (1967), Pasternak (1976), M. Ember and Ember (1971), C. Ember et al. (1974), Graburn (1971), 57–67.

Chapter Six

Institutional Systems of Agrarian Populations

Agrarian societies began[1] the process of harnessing nonhuman power to physical capital, most notably animals to the plow but also wind and water power to new types of machines for manufacturing goods and commodities. These new modes of productivity allowed for a significant increase in the level of economic surplus that, in turn, changed the nature of all institutional systems. Because a larger population could be supported, population as a force exerted even more selection pressures on production, distribution, and regulation; and as the respective values of these forces increased, institutional differentiation and development ensued. A state apparatus could now be supported by the economic surplus, leading to more consolidation and centralization of power. With expanded production and power came increased inequality and the emergence of new social classes. Most members of the population belonged to the rural peasant class, and below peasants were the expendable poor. On top of the system of stratification were elites from the land-owning nobility, the leaders of state power, the high priests of religion, and at times, the high-ranking military. Merchants and bourgeoisie classes could now be clearly discerned, ranging from small peddlers and shopkeepers to wealthy merchants, financiers, and other players in the growing system of exchange distribution. And finally, artisans and craft classes could be clearly distinguished. Thus, as the economy and polity differentiated and developed, the scale and scope of inequality and stratification increased, dramatically raising the potential for conflict and revolt within human societies. Moreover, with the wealth to mobilize coercive power, empire-building increased, thereby extending the scale of conflict between populations.

Expanded production, regulation, and distribution not only allowed for population growth and new systems of stratification, the institutional systems

157

that emerged from these forces led to the development of bigger and more permanent settlements that encouraged large migrations to market towns and cities as well as the core capital city (Sjoberg 1960; Hammond 1972; Eisenstadt and Shachar 1987). Simple agrarian systems could remain quite small, however, with perhaps only a few thousand people, but they often had populations numbering into the hundreds of thousands. In contrast, more advanced systems usually ranged from a few million people to many millions. Cities could have up to 100,000 inhabitants in simple systems, compared with as many as one million in advanced ones. Yet even with these larger urban centers, the vast majority of the population (usually over 90 percent) lived in rural areas, working land owned and controlled by elites. Most of the population in agrarian societies was arrayed in small villages and towns connected by extensive road networks to regional market cities that, in turn, were connected to a core capital city. Moreover, agrarian societies used considerably more land than horticultural populations in order to increase the production of food so necessary to support the larger population and the growing privilege of elites. Indeed, resources tended to flow from rural villages to regional centers and market towns, and then, to the capital city as the state and its elites extracted evergreater amounts of surplus from peasants and the local nobility (Nolan and Lenski 2001). Agrarian societies also occupied more territory than typical horticultural systems, not just because of increased population and production but also because of war, conquest, and empire-building (Mann 1986; Skocpol 1979; Giddens 1985; Turner 1995).

Agrarian populations tended to reveal a period of rapid growth, followed by a leveling off as the more densely settled population succumbed to disease, war, and poverty. The population could even decline after particularly violent wars or virulent diseases, and dramatically so in Europe during the successive waves of "the plague." Malthusian processes were thus very evident among agrarian societies, perhaps more than at any other time in human history.

With agrarianism, then, the scale and complexity of human societies dramatically increased. And, as empire-building ensued, horticultural populations came under increasing attack, surviving only in isolated areas of the globe, at least until a large-scale agrarian empire could reach them. Equally significant, the rates of contact among the populations of the world increased with warfare and long-distance trade; and as a consequence, migrations from society to society accelerated. With these migrations came diffusion of ideas and culture, particularly religious ideas that were to undergo transformation during the agrarian era into the world religions—Christianity, Judaism, Islam, Hinduism, Buddhism, and Confucianism.

Some populations remained small, as the scale of other societies expanded, but new technologies and forms of capital formation created a potential for human societies that, with population growth, would increase the complexity of human societies forever. Save for the complete differentiation of education as a mass system of reproduction, all other core institutions were fully differentiated with agrarianism. These would be developed during the Industrial Revolution and supplemented by the differentiation of new institutional complexes; and even these new institutional domains could be seen in agrarian societies. Science and medicine, to give the two most obvious examples, were clearly evident and, like education, would soon differentiate from other institutional systems. Agrarianism was built on new sources of energy coupled with physical capital and specialized human capital; and once these connections were made, slowly accumulating technologies would lead to the harnessing of even more sources of inanimate energy to capital, eventually leading to industrialism and modernity.

ECONOMY

The increase in the size, scale, scope, and reach of agrarian societies was made possible by higher levels for each of the basic elements of the economy, as is summarized in table 6.1 for both simple and advanced agrarian populations. In broad strokes, new technologies, heightened levels of physical capital formation, more complex divisions of labor organizing human capital, new entrepreneurial mechanisms, and increased access to resources greatly expanded gathering and production, with the surplus being usurped as property for the privilege and power of elites (Lenski 1966). As production escalated, new entrepreneurial mechanisms (e.g., markets, chartered corporations, manorial estates, craft factories, law guilds) and the ever-expanding and restrictive hierarchy of state power (local and regional elites connected to a monarch) fully displaced kinship as the organizational basis of the economy. Family structures—mostly nuclear and at times patrimonial family-owned businesses with slaves, workers, or apprentices—still organized many portions of the labor force, such as peasants, artisans, and merchants, but complex structures of kinship receded as an important societywide integrative mechanism. The transformation of kinship from the structural base of society to primarily a reproductive structure was now virtually complete with advanced agrarianism, finishing a trend that had begun with advanced horticulture (Weber [1916–1917] 1958; Laslett and Wall 1972; Collins 1986:267–321).

POLITY

In the place of kinship came the expanding state, with a hereditary monarch at its apex and with expanding administrative and coercive bureaucracies serving

Table 6.1. Agrarian Economies

	Simple	Advanced
Technology	Knowledge of herding, farming with animal-drawn plow, irrigation, fertilization, sailing, wheel and its use on vehicles, orchards, husbandry, ceramics, metallurgy, writing, mathematical notations, and solar calendar; rate of innovation high, but tending to decline as political economy begins to circumscribe activity in more advanced systems	In addition to technology of simple systems, knowledge of smelting and hardening iron mark a significant advance; other innovations include improved harnesses for horses, wood-turning lathe, auger, screws, printing, clocks, spinning and weaving, windmill and watermill technology
Physical Capital	Plow, work animals, wood, ceramic, and sometimes iron tools; large facilities for storage and milling of grains; roads and often large-scale irrigation projects; and most significantly, increased use of money	In addition to capital of simpler systems, widespread use of metal tools marks a significant increase in capital formation; also, larger facilities for storage, transportation, and milling; more elaborate and extensive roads and irrigation projects; light "industry," made possible by new sources of power (water, wind); and most importantly, money becomes fully integrated into the economy
Human Capital	Dramatically increased division of labor as occupational trades expand; continued clear division of labor by age and sex; more merchants and other "trade specialties"; development of "free labor" and artisans who "sell" services in labor markets	Continuing increase in division of labor; peasantry increasingly constrained by slavery and serfdom, but also a growing pool of "free" or unattached laborers (as a result of losing their land or tenancy rights) available for hire, leading to sale of free labor in urban labor markets; the most prominent axes of differentiation are among merchants/traders and artisans, now typically pursuing between 100 and 200 different occupational specialties

Table 6.1. (Continued)

	Simple	Advanced
Entrepreneurship	Kinship and village structures decline as major entrepreneurial mechanisms and are supplemented by new political and economic forms of entrepreneurship; political consolidation of territories creates hierarchies of authority and resource flow; market expansion generates new methods of stimulating production and distributing labor, goods, and services; and merchants, beginnings of banking and insuring, and early craft guilds become evident; but for a given individual, the first entrepreneurial structure is the family, increasingly less connected to larger kinship structures and dramatically more circumscribed by the state, but nonetheless a crucial unit organizing economic activity	Kinship and village as entrepreneurial mechanisms replaced in rural areas by servitude obligations to ruling elites; polity thus becomes a major entrepreneurial structure assuring the flow of resources from poor to rich, and from rural areas to urban centers; dramatic expansion of markets, along with money as a medium of exchange; increasing volume and velocity of goods and services exchanged across ever-larger amounts of territory (in fact, large networks of ties among merchants often develop across an empire, and certainly within a society or region of an empire); artisans and merchants increasingly organized into guilds that coordinate their activity and assure their privileges; law begins to regulate contracts and the enforcement of obligations
Property	Clear system of private property, leading to very high levels of inequality; almost all material resources owned by nobility and church; some material accumulation possible by merchants, bankers/financiers, and craft specialists, but for vast majority (i.e., the peasantry) all surplus usurped by the state and religious elites. Produces system of stratification with very clear class cleavages, each with its own subculture; ruling class (including religious and military elites) clearly distinguished from rest of the population, which has virtually no say in political decisions (except during periodic revolts); urban minority vastly different from large rural majority, and there is a growing split between literate few and illiterate masses; additionally, there are highly salient class distinctions for various occupational specialists, especially for artisans, craft specialists, merchants/traders, and perhaps slaves	Clear system of private property, leading to very high levels of inequality, similar to that in simple systems, but altered somewhat by monarch's increased power to extract surplus and expansion of new trading/merchant occupations permitting accumulation of wealth. Produces system of stratification with very clear class cleavages, similar to those in simple systems, with several modifications: the increased number of occupations allows for expansion of classes between the elites and peasants (and slaves, if still evident); there is increased capacity for some artisans, merchants, and even peasants to acquire wealth exceeding that possessed by some sectors of nobility; and the growing number of state bureaucrats, military personnel, and retainers for the nobility create additional classes, whose members can acquire wealth, power (or at least influence), and some prestige

the interests of the monarch. In centralized polities most typical of advanced agrarian populations, the monarch used the state bureaucracy and the coercive capacity of a professional army (and local enforcement capacities as well) to control territories, other elites, peasants, artisans, and merchants. The burden of financing the state, the army, and the privileges of the monarchy and nobility fell mainly on the peasantry, whose surplus was extracted by the state (usually directly from lands owned and controlled by the monarch, or indirectly, through taxes on other land-holding nobility), although the monarch often turned to the bourgeoisie for additional revenue to finance military adventures and large-scale undertakings such as public works or infrastructural development (Goldstone 1990). In such a system, property became an important element for not only economic activity but also for sustaining inequality and stratification (Turner 1984; Lenski 1966).

Because of the inequality and the constant usurpation of surplus as property for elites, incentives for technological innovation and investment in physical capital could decline (unless the monarch financed "public works" projects), especially as human capital saw little incentive for working hard. As a result, agrarian societies could stagnate and, in the end, disintegrate (Maryanski and Turner 1992:118; Nolan and Lenski 2001). As we see below, inherent in free markets as a major distributive mechanism[2] and in non-kin entrepreneurial structures are highly dynamic qualities that could, at times, overcome the stagnating effects of concentrated power and high levels of inequality. The basic structure of polity in simpler and more advanced agrarian systems is reviewed in table 6.2.

With consolidated and centralized power that could tax surplus wealth, power could be mobilized on a heretofore unprecedented scale. Although war had been, no doubt, a chronic activity among all human populations of the past, its scale and scope could now extend beyond what had previously been possible. Large armies could be mobilized and supported as they sought to conquer not only contiguous populations but also those at ever further distances; and although empires existed during horticulture, the expanse of agrarian empires could now reach several million square miles. As a larger and more diverse population came under the jurisdiction of government, selection pressures from the macrodynamic forces of regulation, production, reproduction, and distribution mounted. Coercive and administrative power had to be consolidated further, and if possible, efforts were made to use symbols and material incentives (more typically, disincentives) to control larger territories and the diverse populations in them. Infrastructural development and exchange distribution had to expand in order to overcome the logistical loads of moving commodities, resources, people, and information about larger territories. Production had to expand to support the state and its military as well as admin-

Table 6.2. Polity in Agrarian Societies

	Simple	Advanced
Centralization of decision-making and leadership	Hereditary monarchy composed of king and other nobility organized into state bureaucracy composed of military officials, administrative bureaucrats and, at times, religious officials	Hereditary monarchy, organized into coercive state bureaucracy, begins to transform relations between king and nobility in favor of ever more centralized control by monarch. Less delegation of decision-making to nobility
Consolidation of bases of power		
Material incentives:	King extracts economic surplus from estates of nobility in accordance with taxation formula. Manipulation of tax formulas and monarchial patronage to elites are common tactics for manipulating conformity	Heavy taxation of peasants, nobility, and growing merchant/artisan sectors to support growing state bureaucracy, army, public works projects, and geopolitical activity. Use of patronage, franchises, and subsidy to other elites as mechanism of social control, coupled with strategic expenditures on public works (roads, ships, ports, and other infrastructural projects)
Symbolic:	Prestige of nobility, per se, but heavy reliance on religion to legitimate power. Success in geopolitics becomes ever more important source of symbolic manipulation of conformity. Less emphasis on redistribution as sources of legitimacy	Prestige of nobility, per se; complete abandonment of redistribution to mass of population as source of legitimation. Growing tension with religious leaders over religious basis of legitimation. Increasing appeals to "nationhood," "ethnicity," and other secular symbols
Coercive:	Very high capacity for coercion by king's army, village and city police, and by armies of nobility	Very high capacity for coercion by king with a fully professionalized army, system of town and city police, with less reliance on armies of nobility
Administration:	Feudal system of relations among monarch, nobility, army, and workers, coupled with King's bureaucrats and, at times, religious officials	Reliance on feudal system of relations continues, but ever more control exercised by state bureaucracy, either directly through bureaucratic system (enforced by laws, courts, police, and army) or indirectly through franchises to other elites

istrative activities, although taxing wealth eventually created disincentives to produce and to innovate, causing most polities of agrarian systems to face grave fiscal crises leading to their collapse (Goldstone 1990).

Empire formation, however, created a template for very large-scale societies; and although a few, such as the Roman Empire, lasted for many centuries, most collapsed because the polity and economy simply could not meet the selection pressures generated by the forces of regulation, production, and distribution. Further, the logistical loads emanating from these forces would always increase dramatically if power was used in ways that increased inequality and, hence, internal threats coupled with external threats from populations that had yet to be conquered. Indeed, as threats to polity increased, it centralized power even more and, in so doing, extracted more surplus to support its military-administrative apparatus and in the end only aggravated threats stemming from increased inequality.

KINSHIP

With agrarianism, sufficient economic surplus could be produced to support non-kin corporate units, such as manorial estates composed of more nucleated tenant farmers, administrative bureaucracies attached to the state, and new organizational forms such as guilds, cartels, and chartered companies. These alternatives could organize far greater numbers of people than kinship alone, and they allowed people to escape the "cage of kinship" (Maryanski and Turner 1992). With these new kinds of corporate units, kinship continued its odyssey back to the simpler system of hunters and gatherers. The descent rule lost much of its salience, except for the inheritance of property and titles, and the construction of lineages and larger structures like clans and moieties became increasingly less viable; larger family units often remained but were not essential, and they were frequently converted to patrimonial structures composed of kin and non-kin workers or apprentices. Residence retained some of the patrilocal bias of horticultural systems, but neolocality became ever more frequent as people migrated to new lands or emerging urban areas. Authority remained patriarchal, and activities of men and women were strictly divided, but as the extended family began to decline in prevalence and as neolocal residence became possible, intergenerational authority and divisions of labor were less explicit and restrictive. Incest rules remained for marriage partners, but rules of exogamy and endogamy declined and, then, disappeared; dissolution often became more difficult, however, as a means for male control of women. Thus, even as the structure of kinship began to evolve back to a more nucleated pattern of hunter-gatherers, the relative equality between males and females of hunter-gatherers was not recreated. Instead, patriarchy remained and, to this very day, persists among most populations, even in the modern post-industrial world.

Table 6.3.   Structure of Kinship in Agrarian Societies

	Simple	Advanced
Size and composition	Larger family units still very evident but decline in frequency and embeddedness in larger kin structures; patrimonial family (male-dominated and including non-kin, such as workers) appears	Patrimonial families frequent among artisans and merchants; larger families still found among peasants, but patterns of political servitude disrupt kinship ties
Residence	Explicit rules begin to lose power, although offspring usually remain close to parents, or even in their household	Few explicit rules, but patterns of servitude in rural areas restrict mobility (although roving landless peasants are, at times, evident); in urban areas patrimonial households organize much economic activity
Activity	Clear division of labor by sex and age in all activities	Same as simple societies
Descent	Increasingly bilateral and truncated	Except for "royal" family, lineage less important, and increasingly bilateral and truncated; only royalty and nobility continue to use descent rules to a high degree
Authority	Male-dominated, and in patrimonial units, considerable male authoritarianism	Male-dominated, especially in patrimonial families
Marriage	Incest prohibited; rules of exogamy and endogamy decline, and dissolution allowed but economically difficult and rarely formal	Incest prohibited, except in a few cases for nobility; rules of exogamy and endogamy decline further; dissolution allowed but difficult and rarely formal

RELIGION

The "world religions"—that is, Christianity, Hinduism, Buddhism, traditional Judaism, Confucianism, and Islam—emerged during the agrarian era and, then, spread to other agrarian populations[3] through combinations of migrations, war, conquest, missionary proselytizing, and colonialism. Indeed, as a result of the organizational base that encouraged their diffusion, these religions are now the dominant cult structures in most of the advanced industrial and post-industrial societies of today. Frequently these religions have been imposed upon—and to some extent amalgamated with—traditional and indigenous religions of a population with the result that somewhat unique versions of each world religion can be found in various societies. Furthermore, these dominant religions often bear common origins, with one being a revolt or break with another: Christianity from Judaism, Buddhism from Hinduism, and Islam from both Judaism and Christianity.

The cosmology of these world religions is greatly attenuated compared to those of traditional ecclesiastic religions typical of horticulturalists and early agrarian populations, revealing a clear tendency toward monotheism or belief in one, all-encompassing god or supernatural force (Wallace 1966:94–101). For example, Islam, Christianity, Judaism, and Confucianism evidence clear tendencies toward monotheism (Allah, God and the Trinity, God, and Tao, respectively, being the all-powerful beings or forces of the supernatural realm). Hinduism reveals a more ambiguous pantheon, however, as does its offshoot, Buddhism. Philosophical Hinduism (Wallace 1966:94) is monotheistic with its all-encompassing supernatural being or force, the "One," whereas Sanskritic Hinduism maintains an elaborate pantheon of gods, including Siva, Krishna, Ram, Vishnu, and Lakshimi. The pantheon of Buddhism is similarly structured with the world being guided by a series of Buddhas (or "Enlightened Ones").

Still, compared to traditional ecclesiastic religions, the mythology of the pantheon of world religions became truncated. Robert Bellah (1964:366) has called this the process of "de-mythologization" because little myth surrounds the creation of the all-powerful god and his court of relatives. Thus, the increasingly elaborate accounts of the jealousies, conflicts, rivalries, and genealogies typical of religious evolution up to this point in societal evolution suddenly began to decline during agrarianism. For example, the myths revolving around Krishna and Vishnu, the historical sequences of Buddhas, the interaction of God and Moses, God and Jesus, Allah, the angel Gabriel, Mohammed, and so on are sparse indeed compared to the myths of other traditional religions.

As Bellah (1964) has emphasized, one of the most distinctive features of what are often called *premodern* religions is the emergence of a series of *substantive beliefs* concerning the supernatural, revolving around the capacity of mortals to become part of the sacred and supernatural realm upon death. These beliefs emphasize for the first time the possibility of understanding the fundamental nature of both natural and supernatural reality (Bellah 1964:367). For instance, Hinduism emphasizes the prospects of not only a better reincarnation in one's next life but also holds out the possibility of becoming a god; Christianity offers salvation in heaven after death; and Islam provides for the attainment of paradise after death. It should be noted that these religious beliefs provide places for the unworthy—hell or a poor reincarnation, for example. Previous traditional religions had offered the chance for humans to maintain only a peace and harmony with the supernatural, but premodern religious beliefs began to provide for the possibility of actually *becoming a part* of this realm.

Under these conditions, religious *values* became explicit, and conformity to these values increases the possibility of salvation after death in the supernatural realm. These values were increasingly codified into a religious code spelling out appropriate behaviors for the members of a society: the Ten Command-ments, the sayings of Confucius, or the Noble Eightfold Path among Buddhists being prominent examples. What is significant about these religious codes is that they specify more than just stereotyped ritual behavior; they also place upon individuals a set of diffuse obligations guiding everyday, nonreligious conduct. Yet these codes tend to emphasize worldly resignation and retreatism; and in order to secure salvation, conformity to religious law must not be too contaminated by worldly passions, actions, and events.

In sum, then, the cosmology of the premodern religions that emerged with agrarianism began to shift toward monotheism, truncating the pantheon and attendant mythology, and highlighting substantive beliefs about the supernatu-ral and salvation. Equally noticeable in these religions was the emergence of a codified value system controlling both ritual and nonritual behavior, while encouraging a kind of retreatism or at least an acceptance of one's fate in this world.

The structural trends evident in traditional ecclesiastic religions continued during the agrarian era, as ecclesiastic cult structures increasingly came to dom-inate over shamanic, communal, and individualistic cults. Usually one large ecclesiastic bureaucracy with an extensive hierarchy of religious specialists became dominant among more advanced agrarian populations: Catholicism in medieval Europe and in many parts of Latin America; Hinduism in India; Con-fucianism in pre-Communist China; Islam in the Middle East; and so on. The specialists within this bureaucracy could claim a monopoly on religious exper-tise and the right to perform major calendrical and noncalendrical rituals. They became permanent residents in large and elaborate temple structures and devoted all their time to operating the church bureaucracy. The influence of this dominant ecclesiastic cult and its bureaucracy was so great that religious elite had high levels of secular power, setting up a mounting tension in agrarian societies between religious and political elites (Bellah 1964:368).

The church and state bureaucracies thus became clearly differentiated in the agrarian era, with the result that the legitimating functions of religion for the polity were no longer automatic and nonproblematic. Sometimes religious beliefs and the organization of a religious cult became the stimulus and locus for rebellious social movements, and so, because of their well-articulated and codified belief system and their high degree of bureaucratic organization, premodern religions could *potentially* become an impetus to social change. As long as cult structures remained loosely organized in a communal or in incipient ecclesiastic form, they lacked the organizational resources to generate major

Table 6.4.   Religion in Agrarian Societies

	Simple	Advanced
Beliefs	Clear conception of supernatural realm of beings, and at times, forces; relatively clear pantheon, hierarchically organized; explicit mythologies as well as values and moral codes sanctioned by the supernatural and used to legitimate privilege of clergy and power of ruling elites	Clear separation of supernatural and natural, but pantheons decline in favor of "universal religions" proclaiming one god or force in the universe; mythology also declines and is simplified; moral codes and values become explicit part of simplified religious doctrines; religious legitimation of elites still prominent, but religions seek to appeal to the "common person"; alongside spread of universal, monotheistic religions exist beliefs in magic and witchcraft tending to be localized in content
Rituals	Regular calendrical rituals, directed and led by full-time clergy; considerable control by clergy of economic production, either through ownership of property or, indirectly, through ritualized rights to economic surplus	Regular calendrical rituals, directed by full-time clergy; but rituals simplified and designed to appeal to mass audiences; clergy still major property holder, but rituals increasingly separated from economic and political spheres, being directed instead to a force/god that can improve life now and in hereafter
Cult structure	Clear structures, housed in elaborate temples of worship supporting full-time, bureaucratically organized clergy; explicit symbols, places, and times of worship evident; cults often control not only economic but also much social and political activity	Clear, bureaucratized structures in elaborate temples/churches; times and places of worship specified, and symbols simplified; cults still own property and exert political influence, but decreasingly so in the political arena; alongside large universal religions exist smaller cults with different beliefs and ritual, although these tend to adopt elements of dominant religion

social change in the face of a well-organized kin- or state-based polity, but as the religious bureaucracy became more organized, controlling financial and symbolic resources, while demanding loyalty from the general population, its power to influence the course of events in societies increased. Still, despite their potential for instituting radical change, premodern religions have historically performed a conservative, legitimating function for the polity and other institutional structures in a society.

Yet within the institution of religion itself, considerable change could occur as lesser cult structures organized and began to challenge the beliefs and organization of the dominant ecclesiastic cult. Religious evolution has documented this process of revolt against the dominant cult again and again, whether it be Catholicism reacting to Judaism, Protestantism from Catholicism, or Buddhism from Hinduism. With further religious development, this pattern of revolt against a dominant cult produced several dominant ecclesiastic cults (e.g., Catholicism and Protestantism in Europe) as well as subcults within these larger cults (e.g., the Protestant denominations). Thus at their most advanced stage, premodern religions displayed several large ecclesiastic cult structures organizing most religious ritual activity in a society, but they also evidenced other forms of cult structures: communal, shamanic, and individualistic. For example, in India where Philosophical Hinduism has dominated since the agrarian era, religion in many rural village cults is still organized into communal cults and utilizes Sanskritic Hinduism and pre-Hindu beliefs and rituals; and in these same villages can also be found various ancestral cults that represent a similar amalgamation of Sanskritic and pre-Hindu beliefs and rituals. Furthermore there are shamanic cults of holy men (gurus and curers, for example) who perform necessary ritual activities for clients. Finally, there are various individualistic cults in which ritual activity revolves around seeking harmony with various personal guardian spirits. Thus, premodern religions of agrarian societies displayed considerable structural heterogeneity, with many different types of cult structures (ecclesiastic, communal, shamanic, and individualistic) whose size and relative influence varied tremendously. These religions were a conglomeration of various cult structures having similar but always somewhat divergent belief systems. The interplay—competition, conflict, assimilation, accommodation, and conquest—among these various cults frequently made these religions highly dynamic. Yet, when one large ecclesiastic cult dominates, a premodern religion will remain comparatively static—unless disrupted by nonreligious institutional influences.

LAW

The level of development in the legal systems of agrarian societies was very much related to the level of state formation. As coercive, administrative, and material incentives were consolidated into a quasi-bureaucratic system, the state used its power to regulate and control ever more activity in the population. As it did so, law became an essential mechanism for exercising this control and for legitimating the self-interested use of power by political elites. Historically, population growth stimulated economic development, and vice versa, which in turn increased the state's interest in regulating activities and legitimating its use of power, especially as this power was used to increase inequalities.

Added to these selection pressures for law was the differentiation of economic activity, the expansion of markets and the resulting increase in the volume of exchange transactions, the constant need to increase tax revenues to support the state's adventurism and the privilege of its elites, and the frequent need to sort out relations and transactions (e.g., citizenship, tribute, taxes, administration, etc.) with conquered peoples. To the extent that, in A. S. Diamond's (1951:303) words, "the law of a people is the instrument by which its orderly activity is maintained and protected," the sheer volume of activity in agrarian populations escalated regulation as a social force and created intense selection pressures on law. Wherever political control of territories could be achieved, law became an instrument of this control. This control was evident by written codes which, to varying degrees, constituted a system of rules for regulating key classes of human activity: marriage, inheritance, property, contract, crime, disputes, taxation, state-church relations, and the like.

The culmination of this development of systematic codes was Roman law, although less systematic legal formations could be found in the various consolidations of power in Egypt, Persia, Greece, and small states in the Middle East as well as in Japan, India, and other agrarian societies of the east. By extending "citizenship" (to all "free men") and applying the law consistently and more or less equally to citizens, a system of laws emerged in Rome specifying rights of persons vis-à-vis government and rights of individuals to one another (Parsons 1966:88). Beginning with the Roman emperor, Justinian, and during the sixth century A.D., a system of codes was legislated and, over the centuries, expanded. The intent was to create a comprehensive body of enacted laws that could regulate and control all essential activities among citizens. No agrarian system went as far as Rome in creating a centralized body of laws; indeed, most simply adapted and adjusted old local codes in an ad hoc manner of issuing degrees and establishing precedents from court decisions, but in all agrarian systems, considerable attention was paid to writing the legal codes down and, in some manner, trying to systematize them into a more coherent whole.

As agrarian societies moved to an advanced profile, the legislative body tended to get larger, with more debate about what the laws should be. In some cases, such as the city-states of Greece and later Rome, a limited form of election or "competitive selection" to such legislative bodies as senates, councils, and forums occurred—although these selection processes were only among elites and, hence, far from representative of the population as a whole.

The court systems of agrarian societies became more developed as the body of laws to be interpreted and applied to ever more diverse contexts expanded. At first, even in the developing Roman system, the officers of the court were part-time and comparatively unprofessional, but as the body of laws became codified and as legislation continually added to this body, a system of courts became more integrated, moving from local tribunals to state-level courts; and the officers of the court—from judges, administrators, and scribes—were increasingly full-time and professional. If a systematic body of enacted laws existed, as was the case in Rome and those societies that adopted Roman civil law, courts were primarily involved in interpreting existing laws. In other societies, such as England and those like India, Canada, Ireland, and America that adopted the English model during their agrarian eras, no coherent body of enacted laws was initially developed. Instead, court decisions at the national level created common-law precedents that became part of a body of laws, but the ad hoc nature of these court decisions produced a less coherent and systematic form of law than the laws originating from legislative enactments within government. In both the civil and common law systems, a hierarchy of courts developed in order to either impose top-down civil law to the local level or to pass up for review and validation or invalidation court precedents from the local level. Moreover, the involvement of courts in an increasing number and variety of actions and transactions generated further selection pressures for their integration into a coherent hierarchy which, in turn, worked to increase the coherence in the body of laws and its legislative enactment.

Enforcement of law and court decisions became more decisive in agrarian populations. The increased economic surplus that could support the coercive base of power, coupled with the need of polity to regulate and intervene in a wider array of actions and transactions, worked to expand not only the total amount of coercive power available to the polity but, more importantly, the actual use or the threat to use coercive power to enforce laws and court decisions. With advanced agrarianism, therefore, came coercive policing, torture, prisons, and executions; and these means of enforcement gave more material sanctions, such as fines, penalties, and compensation in civil matters, an imperative force. Indeed, agrarian polities tended to overuse coercion in order to repress resentments over inequality, to control deviance, to regulate disruptive actions and transactions, and to compensate for weak symbolic legitimacy. Such violence by the state escalated as the expansion of markets and the com-

Table 6.5. Law in Agrarian Societies

	Simple	Complex
Body of Laws		
Substantive:	Highly variable, but there will be explicit rules, often written down, concerning (a) what is defined as a crime, (b) what is the relation among individuals, kin groups, and other corporate actors, and (c) what are the prerogatives of the state and the obligations of actors to the state	Same as simple systems, but the body of written law is much larger and more systematic, although the degree of systematization will vary greatly. Religious laws can exist alongside secular laws. Laws increasingly reflect broad legal postulates that embody the general values of a population but more typically the culture and interests of elites
Procedural:	Clear rules about how to resolve disputes and how parties are to present grievances to courts. Some rules about how officers of the court are to behave, but these vary in salience and in the capacity to generate conformity by court officials	Same as simple systems, but more complex and binding rules on parties, especially court officials
Legislation of Laws	Officials at city, regional, and national level have some capacity to pronounce edicts. Ultimate authority to legislate rests with king and council of elites. At times, forums and other bodies of elite representation may exist and have legislative functions. Court decisions increasingly can become part of law, although the ratio of court-generated to political elite-generated law is highly variable	Same as simple systems, but forums of elites are more likely to be actively involved in legislating new laws; and in the advanced stages before industrialization, legislative bodies of non-elite representation can sometimes be found. Court decisions become an increasingly important source of common law in many systems

Table 6.5. (Continued)

	Simple	Complex
Courts		
Judge:	Political leaders at all levels of government can still double as judges, but increasingly there is a cadre of full-time judges who are more likely to have been formally educated in the law	Except at the highest level, where the king and elite council may operate as judges, courts are staffed by full-time professionals, although at the local level, judges may be part time. But increasingly all judges are educated in the law, both substantive and procedural
Jury/Council:	Juries still tend to be dominated by councils of elites at local, regional, and national levels	Same as simple systems, but emergence of ad hoc juries composed of nonelites and peers become evident
System of courts:	Emerging system of local, regional, and high level (supreme) courts	Relatively coherent system of courts, with increasingly clear rules about procedures for making appeals to higher level courts, culminating with the king (queen) and his (her) council
Bureaucratization of courts:	Expansion of court activity increases number and differentiation of personnel, thereby prompting bureaucratization of courts. Differentiation among civil, criminal, and administrative courts	Full bureaucratization of courts
Enforcement of laws/ court decisions:	Enforcement of laws and court decisions is increasingly performed by full-time agents. Feuds and revenge are punished by enforcement agents because they violate criminal laws	Same as simple systems, but more complex and formal system of enforcement at local, regional, and national levels. Enforcement agents are increasingly organized bureaucratically as police, sheriffs, and military. State claims legitimate use and monopoly of coercion and, therefore, punishes all other actors who use coercion. Much enforcement is administrative in character, as bureaucratic extensions of the state monitor and manage actions and transactions of individual and collective actors in the society

mercialization of the economy aggravated interclass tensions, all of which increased internal threats to the polity.

It is this overuse of the coercive base of power that marked the great weakness of agrarian systems. If coercion rather than law, legislative enactment, legal precedent, and court adjudication were to determine what people must do and what the relationship between state and citizenry was to be, the legal system lost its capacity to create a civic culture in which broad principles—incorporating the values, beliefs, and customs of a population—legitimated the centers of power in society.

Indeed, when the rule of law was easily suspended in the name of short-term crisis management or pursuit of privilege by those controlling the coercive base of power, its effectiveness as a basis for legitimating power and inequality, for preserving and integrating culture, and for coordination was reduced. As agrarian leaders faced chronic fiscal crises, demands for patronage by noble elites, mass protests from peasants and slaves, external threats, and new social constructions like markets that aggravated interclass and intraclass conflicts, these leaders often subverted through arbitrary edict and coercion the very legal system that had enabled them to consolidate power (Turner 1995). This dismantling of legal development helps explain why agrarian systems, and empires composed of agrarian societies, were constantly built up, only to collapse as disintegrative pressures mounted. Ironically, this collapse was the result of the very selection pressures that had caused legal development in the first place—that is, pressures stemming from regulatory and reproductive problems of coordinating and controlling, legitimating power and inequality, and preserving as well as codifying culture. These forces overwhelmed political systems that had imbalanced the consolidation of power toward the coercive-administrative bases, thereby eroding the symbolic base of power provided by law.

EDUCATION

With agrarianism came explicit school structures for training, often constituting the beginnings of a hierarchical system from primary to university-level education, for a select few: those who would be government officials (often in church-sponsored schools or private primary schools), religious practitioners (although their training frequently occurred in religious schools), military officials (again, often in separate military academies), commercial entrepreneurs (although much of this education was by tutors or kin members outside of schools), and members of emerging professions such as law and medicine. Elites were still taught by private tutors; and if they entered private secondary or university-level schools, instruction was nonvocational, emphasizing aes-

Table 6.6.   Education in Agrarian Societies

	Simple	*Advanced*
Instruction	Apprentice-master teaching in all trades and crafts. Private tutors for children of elites. Some schools for imparting literacy. Military academies. Kin-based instruction for commerce. Religious instruction for priesthood. In a few cases, higher education structures for emerging professions and nonvocational elite instruction	Same as simple system, except primary schools more prevalent (both private and state-financed), secondary schools for elites, and beginnings of universities for professions (law and medicine) and for nonvocational training of elites. Private tutors for children of elites is still the dominant form of instruction, and for religious priesthood. A vast majority of population never goes to school and is illiterate. System of church schools for admittance to priesthood or positions in government bureaucracy can also exist
Curricula	Depending on instructional venue, economic technology, literacy and counting, military skills, religious beliefs and rituals, commerce, and crafts are taught	Same as simple system, but primary, secondary, and university-level schools will have a diverse curriculum revolving around writing, arithmetic, history, languages, geography, and classic literatures
Ritualized passage	Ceremonies marking completion of apprenticeships, military training, and religious training	Same as simple system, except that some school structures will tend to have grades, examinations, and graduations

thetics over practical skills. Religion still exerted an enormous influence on education, and in fact, if religion was as bureaucratized and as powerful as the state, religious instruction would dominate all levels of the educational hierarchy (Collins 1977). As states gained power relative to religion, however, education became more secular. Still, the vast majority of the population remained illiterate in agrarian societies, learning what they required in family and apprenticeships. Education would fully differentiate from other institutions only with advanced industrialization.

KEY INSTITUTIONAL INTERCHANGES

With agrarianism, kinship no longer represented the solution to higher valences for population, production, distribution, regulation, and reproduction as social forces. New kinds of corporate and categoric units emerged within institutional domains in response to selection pressures from these macrodynamic forces. As the influence of kinship declined, selection pressure on polity increased; and thus, the key institutional interchanges of agrarian societies revolved around the rise of polity and the fall of kinship as the institutions involved in coordinating and controlling the population.

Kinship and Other Institutional Systems

With agrarian modes of production, kinship began its odyssey back to a more nuclear form, where descent rules no longer organized families into complex systems of kindred that, in essence, were the structural backbone of horticultural societies. Kinship was no longer needed as new kinds of corporate and categoric units emerged with the clear differentiation of economy, polity, law, religion, and even education from kinship. As this differentiation occurred, selection pressures were placed on kinship to alter its structure so that differentiation and development of alternative institutions could proceed. As a consequence, kinship reverted to its initial place among human populations as a structure responding to selection pressures from reproduction as a social force.

Economy and Kinship   As the economy developed during the agrarian era, new kinds of entrepreneurial structures emerged—polity, law, markets, manorial estates, businesses, guilds, and other corporate structures—to coordinate technology, physical and human capital, and property. As these new structures emerged, they exerted selection pressures against unilineal descent systems. These systems were no longer required, but more fundamentally, they worked against development of the economy by confining economic activity to kinship roles. Each new form of entrepreneurship, from free markets, to leagues of traders, through regulatory activities of the emerging state and legal system, on to the expansion of manorial estates, all worked against larger kinship systems. At times, kinship and these alternative corporate units could coexist, as was the case with guilds and patrimonial families, but in the end, kin structures began to lose their complexity and move back to nucleated families.

This scaling back occurred as the forces of production, regulation, population, and distribution pushed for the formation of new corporate structures organized into new institutional systems, but as this process occurred, reproductive forces increasingly drove the selection pressures, pushing kinship toward a structure primarily concerned with socialization. At some point, of course, additional structures like education emerged in response to these selection pressures stemming from reproductive forces, but during agrarianism, kinship reverted back to being a reproductive structure for sustaining the commitments of individuals to play roles in the corporate units of the diverse institutional systems that were differentiating and developing. For the economy, kinship thus became the primary source of human capital, socializing motivational dispositions to play roles in the economy and many required skills.

Polity and Kinship   With institutional differentiation that accompanied the capacity of the economy to generate a large surplus, the emergence of the state in response to selection pressures emanating from regulation as a force also generated selection pressures for kinship to recede. At some point, kinship systems become incapable of coordinating and controlling a larger population engaged in diverse economic activities generating an economic surplus and the inequalities that inevitably come with this surplus. For most of the agrarian era, however, political leaders were chosen on the basis of their place in the kinship systems (as was the case for succession of the nobility in general), but this system no longer organized the whole society. Rather, the descent rule provided instructions to kin members about who would inherit property and, potentially, power if the family was part of the political elite. In a sense, the kinship system provided the human capital necessary for leadership and succession of political leaders, but it did not organize other institutional activities including those in the emerging state bureaucracy. Outside of elite circles, of course, pressures from new forms of economic activity were pushing the reorganization of kinship back to a more nucleated profile independently of the effects of new forms of political organization.

As this transformation occurred, kinship became primarily devoted to generating commitments to the political system, obviously to widely varying degrees in light of the fact that revolts were very common among the agrarian peasantry. In return, the emerging state increasingly defined the relevant activities, rights, and obligations of various family members, heavily loading the kinship system to the rights of males over those of females. Indeed, the patriarchal bias of most kinship systems was enforced by the state, leaving females in a highly vulnerable and dependent situation.

Law and Kinship   In horticulture, laws were very often coextensive with the rules of kinship, but with the emergence of the state, the polity would legislate laws to realize its goals and interests. Kinship rules were successively replaced by edits and other law-making activities of elites, and as this process occurred, the system of unilineal descent was replaced by norms applicable to more nucleated families. Even within the family, law often became the mechanisms for assigning rights, duties, and obligations to family members. Indeed, patriarchy was very much supported by laws regarding who could own and inherit property. These laws often resurrected old biases of patrilineal kinship rules, but more fundamentally, they were distinct from these rules and, potentially, enforced by officers of the administrative branch of the state rather than by kindred. As the legal system evolved, kinship increasingly provided only a diffuse commitment to this system, and even here, this commitment was often very weak since the law was often perceived, quite correctly, as biased toward elites and those with wealth and power.

Religion and Kinship   With the loss of its entrepreneurial consequences for the economy and polity in agrarian societies, the rules of kinship no longer needed to be sanctioned by supernatural forces because they were not the rules that organized broader societal activities. Moreover, religious differentiation from kinship and the formation of large cult structures changed the relation between kinship and religion forever. Kin members could financially support cult structures, and they would often use these structures to make appeals to supernatural forces and beings in the increasingly simplified pantheons of premodern religions. Furthermore, the value premises of religious belief systems often served as moral underpinnings of kinship rules and role behaviors among family members. Thus, religion often provided moral and spiritual guidance to family members; in return, the family generated commitments to religious beliefs, while often supplying a significant portion of the financial resources necessary to maintain differentiated cult structures and their functionaries. Moreover, religion still provided many of the ceremonies marking passages through kinship—for example, birth, death, and marriage—but with advanced agrarianism, there were secular alternatives to these ceremonies offered by the state and legal system. Nonetheless, as is evident today, religion was to remain involved in reinforcing key points of passage through the kinship system.

Education and Kinship   For most members of the population, all education occurred within the family or on the job. Education was still a very recessive institutional system, operating primarily to train elites, religious specialists, or a few skilled positions in the economy. With the emergence of formal school structures with agrarianism, this system of formal education, as small as it was, could be expanded when selection pressures from reproduction, production, and regulation pushed for the development of new skills for economic roles and new forms of secular commitments to the political system.

Polity and Other Institutional Systems

During agrarianism, the rise of the state to coordinate and control ever more activities was as dramatic as the decline of kinship as the organizational base for society. As power was consolidated along its four bases—coercion, symbols, material incentives, and administration—it generated selection pressures against kinship as a locus of counterpower. If kinship systems were large and well organized, they always could pose a threat to state power, and so, the emerging state often pushed for the destruction of unilineal descent systems in order to eliminate rival bases of power formation. Even without active persecution of kinship systems, other selection pressures from the economy were working to break the older unilineal descent system down. And as noted above, kinship was transformed into nucleated families whose political loyalty was sought by the state, often unsuccessfully, in return for allocation by the state and legal system of authority and rights within the family. As the influence of kinship declined, the dynamic interchanges of polity with other institutions became increasingly significant, as is explored below.

Economy and Polity Without an economic surplus beyond meeting the subsistence needs of the population, polity cannot differentiate from kinship. Once this surplus exists, however, polity depends upon the economy to generate the resources that it needs to consolidate each base of power. And, as centralization of power occurred in agrarian states, the need for resources increased as polity generally began to build larger-scale administrative and coercive structures, while at the same time keeping resources available for manipulating material incentives (through patronage to elites and upwardly mobile bourgeoisie) and for propagating symbols. Because of this dependence on economic outputs, polity had an interest in influencing all economic elements, particularly capital formation that could become a source of revenue to sustain the state.

Physical capital is formed as production increases and as markets expand and generate profits, and hence, liquid capital or money. These forms of capital can be taxed by polity, and so, the state in agrarian societies soon began to define property in ways that gave it the right to expropriate some portion of this property or the income from property. The state also had an interest in new technologies that could increase production and, hence, wealth, but sectors of the agrarian polity often feared innovations that could cause social change in the elites' bases of power; and as the state became more centralized, it increasingly created disincentives for innovation because it feared change and, more importantly, because it overtaxed productive output to the point of discouraging innovative efforts to increase these outputs.

While increased surplus provided the means for the consolidation and centralization of power, there were also intense selection pressures pushing actors to consolidate power in non-kin structures. Higher levels of production are both a response to, and cause of, population growth. Population growth may stimulate actors to find new technologies and forms of capital to expand production so as to meet the needs of the larger population; and conversely, once productive outputs increase, it becomes possible to support a larger population. Out of this cycle, populations grew in agrarian societies, and this growth generated selection pressures for coordinating and controlling members of a society. For a time, kinship could segment and provide the necessary structures for coordination and control, but eventually, the force of regulation reached such high levels that selection favored the consolidation of power among non-kin leaders and the centralization of power in the state. Thus, through its effects on population as a social force, production indirectly created selection pressures for political formations in agrarian societies.

More directly, expanded production created new kinds of corporate structures that needed coordinating. For a time, informal and formal agreements among households, guilds, vendors, estates, and other new forms organizing production could provide the necessary coordination, but as markets expanded and as differentiation among corporate and categoric units increased, particularly if inequalities and class tensions rose, selection pushed for the consolidation of power in the form of the state. The state and the legal system thus became critical entrepreneurial structures for the economy, particularly as they defined property rights, taxed capital, and regulated labor.

With expanded production, the valences for distribution as a social force increased, generating selection pressures for new infrastructures and systems of exchange. These selection pressures became even more intense in agrarian societies as a population grew and became densely settled in urban areas and as the size of territories expanded as a result of conflict and empire building. As new infrastructures—roads, ocean ports, river transport systems, and the like—first developed, they often did so out of the purview of polity. Communities or elites within the economy often financed such structures in order to increase their wealth, but over time, the scale of infrastructural needs surpassed the capacities of individuals, households, and other corporate units to finance and administer infrastructures, thereby generating intense selection for political financing (from tax revenues) of these infrastructures. Similarly, market systems at the lower level in Braudel's hierarchy could operate quite efficiently without government, and even long-distance trade could be coordinated through agreements among traders. Eventually, markets became too complex and extended in the agrarian era for nongovernmental actors; and as result, government began to regulate, often through the legal system, key aspects of markets. In particular, government had an often unrecognized vested interest in maintaining the money supply that fueled market transaction, since ultimately this could be taxed to support the state. Indeed, without money, inflation is less likely because traditional exchange systems, such as barter, tend to keep prices stable. However, with currency as the marker of value and medium of exchange, suddenly the relative supply of commodities and money began to influence their value. With the widespread use of money, inflation became a distinct possibility; and inflation was particularly hard on traditional elites or landed estates who were less likely than the urban bourgeoisie to have money to purchase more expensive goods. As a consequence, the wealth contained in the holdings of the manorial estates declined. This regulation of currency also became increasingly important as a symbol of the state's legitimacy because the purchasing power of money was often seen as a marker of the state's effectiveness and, hence, its legitimacy. Rapid inflation decreased purchasing power and individuals' sense of value; and as this occurred, people often became less willing to support the state. Thus, the use of money often eroded the support of the old landed aristocracy for the state, as inflation reduced their wealth and imposed higher costs on their activities. In fact, the state itself would experience fiscal crises with inflation and, as a result, was often unable to respond to traditional elites' needs for patronage. And, if this crisis was severe, both elites and peasants could revolt. Thus, money as a symbolic source of the polity's hold on power became visible for the first time during the agrarian era as money increasingly became the marker of value and the medium through which exchange transactions were conducted; and as this transformation ensued, the state's monetary policies, if any, began to influence its legitimacy.

Moreover, beyond the effort to control the supply of money, other instruments of trade like contracts, insurance, banking, and other services needed for dynamic markets increasingly had to be regulated by polity in order to assure their implementation; and once the state intervened in the services surrounding trade, these services could expand. Such was particularly likely to be the case as the polity came to realize that the wealth created by the operation of the service sector could be taxed, although this recognition tended to come only in late agrarianism. For a long time, it appears, elites in the polity continued to see the landed aristocracy as their source of tax revenue (even as the latter's wealth declined), but eventually, the wealth being created by market activity—both the profits from trade and from services like banking facilitating trade—was seen by polity for what it was: a source of revenue. Often elites in the states of agrarian societies would borrow money from the market sector, only to worsen their financial situation (Goldstone 1990) and eventually cause a fiscal crisis that would threaten the viability of the state. Eventually, tax formulas were adjusted to extract capital being generated in markets, but this transition occurred only just before industrialization in Europe.

Human capital was, to an extent, regulated by the emerging state. As labor markets expanded in urban areas, entirely new mechanisms for inserting human capital into the economy emerged. As the landed estates of the agrarian era broke up or became commercialized, peasants were pushed off the land, forcing them to migrate to urban areas where they always posed a threat to the state. The state thus had a vested interest in controlling what potentially could prove to be a revolutionary force in urban areas, and as a result of efforts to control the unattached masses, the state began to regulate pools of labor. Labor could be compelled (conscripted) to join the coercive branch of the state; it could be imprisoned in ways that increased or decreased the activities of the labor market; it could be banished from urban areas; and it could experience many other direct interventions by the state. Still, the state's control over labor was limited; and indeed, urban and rural uprising often placed heavy financial burdens on polity as it sought to quell these uprisings.

Religion and Polity   During agrarianism, both the state and religion became fully differentiated and, in advanced agrarian systems, highly bureaucratized. As the source of access to supernatural and sacred forces, religious elites yielded considerable power among those who belonged to the cult structures and who were committed to a particular set of beliefs about the nature of the supernatural realm. This power always posed a threat to the emerging state, which was trying to consolidate power, especially if cults had a coercive capacity of their own. Moreover, because religion often legitimated polity in agrarian societies, providing it with one of its principal bases of symbolic power, this dependency of the state on religion furthered the potential threat posed by religion. As a consequence, there was almost always considerable tension between religious and political elites in agrarian societies. This tension was often aggravated as emerging world religions spread, thereby undermining the religious beliefs on which the state had previously based its symbolic power. Open conflict between the armies of the state and religious cults was not uncommon during the agrarian era, and there was a constant competition between elites in the two institutional systems for the loyalty of the nobility and for the financial resources of both the nobility, emerging middle classes, and even peasants.

These tensions, coupled with the broad array of secular activities performed by the state's administrative and coercive arms, increasingly led leaders of the state to seek alternative sources of legitimization outside religion. Typically, an official state religion remained and was involved in visible ceremonial rituals; and in fact, kings may have ruled by so-called divine right from their special connection, mediated by clerics of religious cults, to the supernatural. Still, leaders increasingly sought a more secular basis of legitimization in many advanced agrarian societies in order to free themselves from dependency on religious practitioners. Thus, by the time industrialization secularized ever more aspects of social life, the separation of polity and religion was well under way at the end of the agrarian era in many societies.

Law and Polity   The secular basis of legitimization that the state sought was to be found in law. Because the leaders of the state controlled the legislation of new laws, the courts, and enforcement of laws, the emerging legal systems of advanced agrarian societies could serve as a more reliable and less problematic source of legitimization of polity. Moreover, because law became one of the primary vehicles by which the state regulated and coordinated activity in other institutional spheres, law could potentially legitimate the state at the level of daily transactions. For, as individuals use the law to engage in exchange, to negotiate contracts, to define property, to stabilize family relations, and to regulate much of their daily conduct, the law as an extension of state power is given honor and prestige and, by extension, so is the state.

Political elites also sought to enshrine cultural traditions, even those embodied in religious values, in higher-order postulates of the legal system. Constitutions existed in only a few agrarian societies, but there were consistent efforts to create high-sounding principles of governance that could provide a more diffuse basis of legitimacy for polity. If the polity could be seen by the general population as the embodiment of cherished cultural traditions, then it could more effectively consolidate symbolic power.

The major obstacle in all agrarian societies to the success of these efforts by polity to secularize its symbolic base of power was inequality and abusive practices by the state and the elites whom it supported. As long as the state was perceived as the tool of elites against the larger masses, it was difficult to secure a stable basis of symbolic power. The state's need to manipulate material incentives through patronage of elites, who could mobilize counter-power, pushed polity to engage in tax practices that angered the vast majority of members of agrarian societies. Without a firm symbolic base of power, whether in religion or law, the state had to rely excessively on its coercive powers and on the monitoring capacities of the administrative bureaucracy; and the mobilization of these latter bases of power was very expensive, forcing the state to engage in more resentment-generating expropriation practices. These practices would dramatically escalate if the state was engaged in military adventurism in order to deflect attention from internal tensions. Indeed, agrarian states often initiated war with neighbors to create a sense of threat to unify a restive population while at the same time trying to extract resources from those populations that it could conquer. However, as Theda Skocpol (1979) following Max Weber (1922) documents, should an agrarian state lose a war under these conditions, its legitimacy is rapidly eroded, leading to revolutionary movement that could topple state power. Thus, with only a few exceptions, such as periods during the Roman Empire and at times during various Chinese dynasties, did the state effectively legitimize itself with law alone. Inequalities in agrarian societies generated too much conflict potential for the state's extractive practices to be smoothed over by manipulations of symbols.

Education and Polity   Education was still recessive in agrarian societies, being confined to elites, religious specialists, and some technical economic roles. Yet, in some societies such as traditional China, performance of examinations at the local level led to placement in the imperial bureaucracy, thus initiating what increasingly would become a trend: incumbents in the bureaucracies of the polity being trained by formal school structures. This trend could be found in many agrarian societies, but the scale of the state in most agrarian societies was not sufficient to need larger numbers of literate personnel.

In addition to these reproductive functions of education, the state in many societies increasingly came to see state-sponsored education as a means to socialize individuals into a secular political culture, thereby generating political loyalty to the state. This kind of deliberate use of the education system, however, was to be more typical of contemporary agrarian societies initiating industrialization whereby the state has sought to expand the skill of human capital while at the same time creating political commitments to the state. In more historical agrarian societies of the past, education did not reach the masses of the population, and so, it was not used in this deliberate effort to create commitments to the civic culture of the state.

CONCLUSION

By the end of the eighteenth century, advanced agrarian societies had evolved to the threshold of industrialism. Although the transition to industrialism is often proclaimed as a "revolution," it was as much a process of cumulative evolution. Technologies had been slowly accumulating with, for example, the use of nonhuman energy and the coupling of energy with simple machines or the ability to engage in extensive metallurgy; capital formation was ever more intensive, and especially so with the widespread use of money in domestic and international markets; labor was highly diverse; property was clearly defined by tradition and law; and new entrepreneurial mechanisms—from markets and law through bureaucracies and chartered corporations to the use of state power—were in place. As a consequence, production had increased, and distribution was dynamic in free markets using money, credit, and other financial instruments. The older landed aristocracy was in decline, and the bourgeoisie was emerging, especially in western Europe. Religious values and beliefs, such as Protestantism, were pushing for hard work, rationality, and other orientations appropriate to industrial capitalism. Larger cities grew where trade, financial servicing, and production were common. Further, some movement toward democratization of polity on a limited basis could be seen in parts of Europe.

Thus, much of the structural and cultural framework for the Industrial Revolution had been built during the agrarian era. Max Weber appeared to argue that, without some extra stimulus, industrialization would not have occurred at all in human history; agrarian societies would continue to rise and fall without taking the final step into industrialism. It seems inevitable, however, that this transition would have occurred eventually, perhaps not in Europe at the beginning of the nineteenth century but eventually at some place. The agrarian era was indeed locked into a pattern of concentrated power, high inequality, tension and revolt, and declining rates of technological innovation. Yet, changes had been slowly accumulating that would form the structural base of early industrial societies in Eurasia, and so, I think, industrialization was inevitable once advanced stages of agrarianism had been reached.

NOTES

1. This description of agrarian populations is drawn from Maryanski and Turner (1992), Lenski (1966), Nolan and Lenski (2001), Childe (1953), Kramer (1959), Mellaart (1965), Eberhard (1960), Sjoberg (1960), Clough and Cole (1941), Blum (1961), Curwen and Hatt (1961), Wolf (1982), Bloch (1962), McNeill (1963), Cambridge (1963), Wolley (1965), Moore (1966), Bender (1975), Hammond (1972), Postan (1972), Anderson (1974), Moseley and Wallerstein (1978), Tilly (1975), and Johnson and Earle (1987).

2. For descriptions of markets in such systems, see Silver (1985), Oates (1978), Kohl (1989), and Braudel (1982).

3. For a readable review of these and other "world religions," see Mathews (1991), and Yates (1988). For even more detail in all religions of the world, see the fifteen-volume set compiled by Eliade (1987).

Chapter Seven

Institutional Systems of Industrial and Post-industrial Populations

Industrialization revolves around the harnessing of fuels to machines. For most of human history, human power had been the fuel of the economy; and with advanced horticulture and agrarianism, inanimate sources of power like wind and water were also used, as was fire to melt metals. It was perhaps only a short step, but a fundamental one nonetheless, to using fossil fuels to drive engines that, in turn, would power machines. This Industrial Revolution occurred first in England, and it was the result of many events, including the relative toleration of religious pluralism, the emergence of new cosmologies provided by astronomy and Newtonian physics, the acceptance and indeed competition over building science machines like the telescope that, in turn, led to the dissemination of mechanical knowledge to larger numbers of individuals, the emergence of an urban bourgeoisie who mixed freely with artisans and natural philosophers, the expansion of markets with discoveries of the raw materials in the New World and the needs of colonialists for finished goods, and the formation of new kinds of corporate units within differentiating institutional spheres. Many have argued that this confluence of events was a chance event, but I see these events as inevitable because the agrarian world had been slowly changing for many centuries, even with the de-evolution from Rome into the European "Dark Ages." What, then, were some of these changes that would cause the Industrial Revolution, or in my view, the industrial *evolution* of society?

THE BREAKTHROUGH TO INDUSTRIALISM

The level of technology, the amount of physical capital, the skill of human capital, the dynamism of entrepreneurial mechanisms, and the complexity of property systems had been slowly changing for several centuries, reaching a threshold point in the early nineteenth century. The technological, capital, and entrepreneurial base of large-scale agrarian systems had in fact been produced by advanced horticultural and small-scale agrarian populations—harnessing of animal power, artificial irrigation, the simple plow, fermentation, sail power, production of copper and bronze, firing of bricks, use of mortar, techniques of glazing, and reliance on calendars, writing, and numerical notation. Indeed, add to this list knowledge of how to construct capital infrastructures—roads, ports, canals, walls, buildings—and the feats of the larger agrarian systems seem less fundamentally new and less spectacular. Yet, large agrarian populations expanded the scale and scope of these technologies, and added several key breakthroughs: the knowledge of how to smelt iron on a large scale, the knowledge of how to construct a true alphabet for creating and storing information, the knowledge of decimal notation for more accurate counting, and the knowledge of how to construct aqueducts for supplying water in support of larger cities (Childe 1964; Nolan and Lenski 2001:186).

For industrialization to emerge, one additional step was required: a source of energy beyond animals, wind, water, and fire, along with the capacity to harness this energy to physical capital (machines) and to human capital (labor). With this breakthrough came the Industrial Revolution, and the potential capacity to gather, produce, and distribute on a monumental scale.

Technology alone does not drive an economy, although it is perhaps its most important element because it provides the knowledge base for other elements of the economy. For technology to be *used*, however, there must be organizational forms or entrepreneurial mechanisms that connect technology to physical and human capital. Several are crucial: (1) the development of market systems, (2) the existence of non-kin corporate structures, (3) the consolidation of power and administrative systems, (4) the nature of organized religion, and (5) the redefinition of property. Each of these is examined below.

The Evolution of Market Systems

Gathering and production are greatly influenced by the capacity to distribute what is produced. As I emphasize in earlier chapters, Fernand Braudel ([1979] 1985, 1977) has visualized the markets of agrarian systems in terms of "lower" and "upper" levels. Let me repeat some of the arguments developed above in order to emphasize how critical new market systems as a kind of entrepreneurial mechanism were to the Industrial Revolution. As I note in chapter 2, Braudel included in his typology of lower markets: (1) person-to-person barter in terms of commodities, (2) person-to-person exchanges using money, (3) peddlers who make goods and sell them for money and who extend credit, and

(4) shopkeepers who sell goods that they do not make for money and on credit. The vast majority of transactions in agrarian systems occurred in these lower markets, and the limitations of these markets placed restrictions on the level of gathering and production.

Yet, two critical features of levels (3) and (4) represented important break-throughs: the use of money, and the extension of credit. These breakthroughs would ultimately be the sociocultural fuel that drove the Industrial Revolution. Without these breakthroughs, markets could not become more complex, nor could markets generate the physical capital necessary for industrialization. As early sociologists like Georg Simmel ([1907] 1978, 1903) and Max Weber ([1922] 1978) recognized, the use of money dramatically alters exchanges, because it is a neutral medium that can be used to express a wider range of preferences and, hence, demand in markets. As such, money can encourage the production of ever more varieties of commodities to meet more individu-alized tastes, needs, and preferences that can now be expressed by the expendi-ture of money in markets. Credit was also crucial to early market exchanges because it enabled buyers and sellers to conduct transactions without full pay-ment, thereby accelerating exchanges as the buyer need not delay in making purchases for lack of funds. Moreover, once interest was charged for credit, it became yet another way to accumulate physical capital that could be used to expand production or to finance further extension of credit so as to accelerate distribution.

Money and credit also transformed the economy as a whole (Turner 1995). First, the widespread use of money and credit created selection pressures for their regulation because if money inflates (and loses value) and if credit obliga-tions are not honored, markets collapse. Such pressures have brought govern-mental power into distribution processes, especially with respect to maintaining the stability of money. For increasingly, the legitimacy of political authority has rested upon its capacity to sustain the value of money and the corresponding security of those who use it. Second, money and credit became the basis for expanding government in several ways: it was easier to collect taxes in money than hard goods; payment of administrative staff in money enabled government to grow beyond kin-based nepotistic and elite-based patronage systems of recruitment; and government could borrow money to sustain itself (often to excess, creating fiscal crises) and to support larger-scale projects (and, of course, elite privilege). And as government grew, it became an important entrepreneurial mechanism as well as a source of technology and capital. Third, the use of credit and money initiated the production of services in banking, insuring, mortgaging, and other activities that money and credit stimulate. And fourth, the existence of money as a neutral and generalized marker of value that is not tied to a specific good or commodity enabled value to be potentially bestowed on all objects, behaviors, symbols, and organizations, thereby increasing the capacity to denote and differentiate new forms of property (Marx [1867] 1967; Harvey 1989:100–102).

Thus, contained in lower market activities of agrarian societies were the beginnings of important dynamics that became the mainstay of upper markets and, eventually, prime movers of industrialization and post-industrialization. These upper markets in Braudel's analysis of agrarian systems were of varying types: (1) fairs or relatively stable geographical locations where higher volumes and varieties of goods were exchanged in terms of money and credit; (2) permanent trade centers where brokers sold goods and services, including credit and other financial instruments; and (3) private markets where merchants engaged in high-risk and high-profit speculations involving long chains of exchange between producers and buyers. For Braudel, and others as well (Verlinden 1963; Moore 1966; Hall 1985; Mann 1986; Wallerstein 1974), the existence of the last two kinds of markets became critical for industrialization in the West, although such markets existed in many parts of the world where industrialism did not spontaneously emerge (Abu-Lughod 1989). The coexistence of a relatively nonintrusive state, along with a system of brokers, a stable currency, and an efficient set of credit mechanisms, enabled parts of Europe to engage in long-distance buying and selling, which would eventually become the basis for commercial capitalism, which initiated the Industrial Revolution. Without markets that could extend across territories, use stable currencies, employ credit mechanisms, and evidence brokerage, banking, insuring, and other servicing activities, industrialization could not occur, nor could it ever reveal the dynamic qualities that led to post-industrialism (White 1988, 1981).

The Evolution of Non-Kin Corporate Structures

The kin-based organization of horticultural economies broke down in agrarian systems, forcing the development of alternative corporate structures (Laslett and Wall 1972). The manorial estate—with a mass of tenant peasants, with overseers such as the squire reporting to the "lord" of the manor—was the basic economic unit organizing most gathering processes in advanced agrarian systems. In urban areas as well, non-kin structures emerged—guilds of craftsmen, "patrimonial" families (of kin and non-kin apprentices running a business or performing a craft), bankers and brokers, government officials (as part of emerging governmental bureaucracies), warehousing organizations, business cartels, and chartered (by government) companies. All of these non-kin structures, including even the patrimonial household, which only partly housed kindred, provided a structural base from which industrialization could emerge, and on which it could build.

As long as kinship and, hence, restrictive norms and traditions were the sole entrepreneurial structures organizing economic activity, change was difficult, although small kin-based "cottage industries," such as weaving, were important in the beginning of the Industrial Revolution in England (Smelser 1959). Moreover, once kinship no longer dominated entrepreneurship, it became possible for money, markets, and growth of government to stimulate alternative entrepreneurial structures that were increasingly freed from constraining networks of kindred.

The Consolidation of Power and the Evolution of Its Administrative Base

Agrarian societies (and advanced horticultural as well) all revealed a state, usually comprised of a monarch and land-owning nobility organized in a feudal pattern (Tilly 1990). Hereditary descent lines, or violent takeovers by other kin leaders, controlled the succession of elites at the top of the state bureaucracy, but the day-to-day administration was often organized in a quasi-bureaucratic form where incumbents were paid a salary and recruited for their competence as much as their kin affiliation or other ascriptive criteria. The existence of this structural form, even when revealing kin-ascription or nepotism and patronage to members of elite families, provided a model or template for organizing economic activity for a larger, more productive economy. Furthermore, the state had some interest in economic growth to support its privileges and projects, often leading the state to subsidize economic units, such as chartered companies or franchises to particular organizations.

The Nature of Religion

Religion was often a source of resistance to change, since it is the keeper of traditional values and beliefs. In the west, the Roman Catholic Church became a wealthy bureaucratic structure, thereby providing another template for bureaucratization. More significantly, the church was a land-owning and productive unit, organizing agricultural activity in a more bureaucratic pattern, especially when compared to the feudal manor; and once again, it could serve as a model for the accumulation of physical capital and organization of non-kin human capital (Hall 1985).

Additionally, the Protestant Reformation altered the religious belief system in ways encouraging accumulation of physical capital and its use to expand productive activity (Weber [1904–1905] 1958). While the Catholic Church clearly evidenced the capacity for capital accumulation and large-scale production, the Protestant Reformation shifted the Christian belief system toward an emphasis on secular and productive economic activity by individuals outside of the church. Whether this shift ultimately caused the Industrial Revolution or simply removed a potential barrier is debated, but there can be little doubt that Protestantism emphasized values—individual accumulation of physical capital and hard work—which were to foster capitalism.

In addition to religious encouragement of accumulation, religious toleration of secular activities, especially those in science and instrumentation of scientific inquiry, was also critical. For the goal of science is to accumulate knowledge, and if this accumulation is to occur through measurements by scientific instruments, both technology and machine capital formation are more likely to increase. Once individuals begin to experiment with machines, and indeed are encouraged to do so, it is a short step to harnessing fuels to these machines.

The Redefinition of Property

In feudal agrarian systems, property was controlled by the nobility, and the great mass of the population was propertyless. The widespread use of money and credit in markets began to change not only the distribution of property but also how it was defined. Great wealth could be accumulated by merchants, brokers, and bankers in markets, and this wealth was more than purely monetary; it was also attached to an ever increasing variety of objects—ships, warehouses and other buildings, rights to paid labor, roads, shops, houses, ports, and the like—and to financial instruments—mortgages, bonds, and insurance premiums—that contained rights to property and income from property. What Karl Marx ([1867] 1967) called "commodification"—indeed, a "fetishism of commodities" for workers in industrial societies—was well under way in agrarian systems with upper market activity. This development was crucial to capitalism because without the capacity to possess property and to enjoy its rewards, there was no incentive for developing technologies and new forms of gathering and producing. As long as most property was controlled by elites and used for their privilege, the diversity of property and its distribution to those who could develop new technologies and modes of gathering, producing, and distributing were constrained. Without increases in the diversity and distribution of property, then, capitalism could not flourish.

Industrialization and the Transformation of Societies[1]

Once technology, property systems, capital formation, and non-kin entrepreneurial mechanisms had reached the levels typical of late agrarianism, industrialization was inevitable. Although a precise date is impossible to pinpoint, the application of steam to gathering and producing processes initiated the Industrial Revolution in Europe around two hundred years ago. The nature of the economy was forever changed in fundamental ways, as was the structure of human societies. As a population industrializes, all core institutional systems become fully differentiated, and new institutions like science and medicine move into dominant positions. Older ones like education become ever more prominent, whereas others like religion and kinship no longer dominate as they once did. Polity becomes larger and, typically somewhat more democratized, which in turn, reduces the level of inequality in society. Concentrations of capital lead to large-scale urbanization, culminating in the world cities of tens of millions of people. And, technological developments and capital investments in new communication and transportation technologies make possible a global system.

ECONOMY

Industrial Economies

Several features typify industrial and industrializing economies. These include: (1) the dynamic relations between machines and technology; (2) the emergence of the factory system as a key corporate unit, (3) the expansion of bureaucratic forms of corporate unit organization, and (4) the development of markets.

Machines and Technology   The historical consequences of steam technology for generating a physical capital base that could expand gathering and producing processes were immense. Steam eliminated the exclusive reliance not only on human and animal power but wind power as well (Cottrell 1955); steam enabled the construction of powerful pumps and drilling shafts in mines, thereby generating access to resources such as coal and iron ore; steam power also enabled the development and operation of blast furnaces, automatic hammers, and rollers for converting iron ore into more refined metals.

With these advances in conversion of resources, new and more efficient machines for expanding resource extraction and conversion could be built. A machine capital base not only produces goods at a rapid rate but also generates new knowledge or technology about how to make more extensive and efficient machinery—thereby expanding further the processes of gathering and conversion. For example, the original blast furnaces provided for the large-scale conversion of iron ore into metal, but they also generated a legacy of knowledge and experience that could improve production to make steel with the Bessemer converter and open-hearth process. Similarly, through trial and error, other sources of power such as oil, electricity, uranium, and hydrolysis were discovered and applied to the revolution ushered in by the application of steam and resulting mechanization of gathering and producing.

Some of the commodity outputs of an industrializing economy are machines that come back into the economy via markets for factory equipment. Driven by the motive for profits, this marketing of machine capital stimulates constant innovation in machines, thereby increasing access to natural resources and the capacity of converting resources into more goods and commodities. And so, once well-developed and specialized markets exist for new types of machines, incentives for their production and distribution continually accelerate the accumulation of a machine capital base. The same is true of knowledge. Experience in machine producing and gathering can generate new knowledge about how to expand these processes which, if a market exists, can be sold, thereby creating incentives to expand the technological storehouse.

Without markets for distributing machine capital and technology, these elements accumulate slowly. New machines, or refinements of existing ones, stay in the local area where they are created; and new ideas, similarly, only diffuse gradually. With markets, there is a mechanism for the broader distribution of capital and technology, and moreover, if the market is profit-oriented, there is incentive for such distribution. Thus, once markets for capital and technology exist, they provide the means for the spread of capital and technology to ever wider circles of potential users at ever accelerating rates.

The level of technology available to an industrial and post-industrial economy has also been dependent upon the organization of science, or the systematic search for knowledge. The organization of science has varied in different societies. In the United States, for example, the research-oriented university, coupled with publicly funded laboratories and with private research in market-oriented firms, became the pattern, with the greatest proportion of pure research being conducted by graduate faculties and students of research universities. In other societies, primarily those in eastern Europe, national academies of science operating as politically sponsored organizations are the predominant locus of scientific research. Other societies, such as western Europe, Japan, and China, reveal a pattern that falls between those of eastern Europe and the United States.

What emerges is "Big Science" or a set of organizations, funded primarily by governments and, to a lesser extent, by private capital in market-driven economies. Big Science will generate new technologies (Price 1982, 1963). In some, much of this technology is military and, as a consequence, can distort production toward military ends. Even with the end of the Cold War and corresponding downsizing of many military programs, the United States still devotes a considerably higher proportion of its science and productive capacities to "defense."

When this occurs, as was dramatically evident in the case of the old Soviet Union, technology loses much of its stimulus effect on gathering, producing, and distribution. Such technology must be kept secret and, hence, remains unavailable as a source of innovations for the domestic economy. Even when made available as is the case today in the post–Cold War era, it is often unusable or, if ultimately usable, difficult to translate from military to domestic applications. The rise of Japan and Germany as serious economic competitors to the United States was partly the result of the greater proportion of investment of American technology (and capital), especially of the high-technology end, to military ends. In the case of the Soviet Union, which had a far less productive economy than that in the United States, the technological and capital drain were so great as to stagnate the economy by the end of the 1960s.

Thus, modern Big Science is very much a result of perceived needs for military technologies, and these needs affect the nature of science and the total technology available to the domestic economy (Price 1963). But Big Science is also stimulated by economic forces, especially the need for innovations by corporate units and their government sponsors in an increasingly competitive world system. And in the post–Cold War era, science will be increasingly tied to the demand for economic innovations. We could expect, then, the research in academies of science and graduate programs in research universities to meet this demand; and to the extent that they do, gathering, producing, and distributing will increase.

The Factory System   The initial expansion of gathering and producing processes with the application of new technologies and new forms of physical capital has usually resulted in centralization of the domestic economy, especially its physical capital base of machines and money. Machines and other capital resources increasingly become located near sources of fuel, resources, transportation, and commerce; and as capital becomes concentrated, so must the labor force. Moreover, workers must now schedule, pace, and standardize their work in specialized ways to the requirements of machines. Work that must be highly coordinated tends to become hierarchically organized, with work at one level being supervised and coordinated by work at higher levels, resulting in the proliferation of foremen, supervisory, and managerial roles in the factory system.

The factory system allows for the organization of larger numbers of employees around networks of machines. Once this system is established, it facilitates the concentration of more human capital around even bigger machines, resulting in expansion of the factory system—at least up to the point that the very size of the factory creates inefficiencies and increases costs. In general, larger machines are usually cheaper to run, while increasing productivity and profits, although there are limits to this process, as large factory systems can become inefficient because supervising functions begin to drain resources from manufacturing and create rigidities that reduce innovation and flexibility. Still, enlarging the factory also has advantages in obtaining resources and other materials, thereby stimulating greater industrial productivity, and in so doing the factory system generates positive feedback that often encourages its own expansion up to the point where it becomes so large as to be less efficient than smaller, niche-oriented manufacturers.

Larger factories are most typical of early industrialization, especially state-managed patterns but more market-driven forms as well. Larger factories are, however, only part of a system of factories, some of which are rather small and oriented to the manufacture of specialized products. There is always a tension in free market systems between large-scale factories and smaller, niche-oriented factories. This tension runs along several fault lines: (1) smaller factories are often suppliers of parts and materials for larger ones, becoming dependent upon them and always fearful of cost-cutting competition from other suppliers; and (2) smaller and larger factories can also be in direct competition—as is the case with steel production in the United States—where the economics of scale that large factories can generate must compete with the flexibility, quality control, and lower administrative overhead of smaller "mini-mills." Increasingly, with the clear exception of capital-intensive mass-market goods, such as automobiles, chemicals, airplanes, and the like, it appears that large factories in the most economically advanced societies are losing ground to smaller centers of manufacturing operating in specialized niches, although this trend may be only an oscillation in the Darwinian competition between larger and smaller factories.

Smaller factories also allow for the deconcentration of physical and human capital, thereby encouraging movement of labor to new areas and away from the early large industrial cities. Yet, equally often smaller factories are clustered together in industrial zones in, or near, older cities, thereby having less impact on geographical dispersion.

The factory system helps create a labor market of wage employees; and once a mobile and semi-skilled pool of workers is available, unencumbered by kinship and traditional trades or farming, this pool of labor encourages the development of the factory system. In early state-managed industrial economies, such as those in the former Soviet Union and post-revolution China, the labor market was regulated by the state, with the result that wages were set in terms of political policies rather than supply and demand for various skills. In contrast, early industrialism in free markets tends to create exploitive tendencies by capital, which seeks to maximize profits by paying workers as little as possible, especially when the supply of labor can be manipulated to remain in excess of demand for this labor (Braverman 1974). In so doing, capital encourages labor to organize (into unions and other collective-bargaining bodies) and exert both political pressure on the state and on corporate managers to give workers more favorable wages and benefits. In the more mature industrial nations, after a period of conflict and turmoil, this negotiation is well institutionalized, although the import of lower-priced labor and the export of physical capital (and hence jobs) to other countries have created new points of tension as capital seeks to bargain down the price of domestic labor by threatening to import workers or export jobs.

The Growth of Bureaucratic Formations   Accompanying the factory system is bureaucracy, whether as the administrative component of the factory or as separate structures producing services, such as banking, insuring, advertising, marketing, engineering, accounting, and many other service functions required by an industrial economy. Although bureaucracies are often portrayed as inefficient and rife with "red tape," especially as they become large, they are essential to large-scale administrative activity. They facilitate coordination of specialists by organizing them into offices, which in turn are arranged into hierarchies of offices; and in so doing, they focus activity on specific goals. As long as the economy is small with low productivity, limited market facilities, and few servicing requirements, large bureaucracies are unnecessary, but when the economy becomes large and complex, the scale of activity eventually stimulates bureaucratization.

Once large-scale bureaucratization occurs, it feeds back and allows for the further expansion of the factory system, markets, and service organizations. In this way bureaucratization actually provides the structural base for growth and development in an economy, although if bureaucratization is "undisciplined" by market competition, as is the case in state-owned corporations or market-controlling oligopolies and monopolies, it can stagnate the economy by increasing the proportion of administrative roles and hierarchies of authority to the point where the efficiencies of the bureaucratic system are undermined by rules, regulations, administrative infighting, and pursuit of short-term interests of bureaucrats rather than the preferences of consumers. Still, without bureaucratization, there is an inadequate structural base for economic development.

The degree of bureaucratization can vary enormously in different sectors of the economy. The more professional and skilled are tasks, the less rigid is the bureaucratic system. Moreover, the full effects on the future of bureaucratization of the current information revolution—from computers to the worldwide Internet—are difficult to forecast. There will, no doubt, be considerable leveling of authority systems in some bureaucracies as well as a horizontal stretch in space of economic activity as information networks allow some workers to work at remote distances, even in their homes. Only the most elite workers today, or those providing highly skilled contracted services to bureaucratic organizations, exhibit this horizontal dimension in work patterns. Indeed, some analysts have predicted the end of traditional bureaucracies with the information revolution, but thus far, computers have simply changed how human capital sits at its desk and how it performs its administrative functions. For the present, the often-predicted demise of bureaucracy is a perhaps premature obituary.

Like the factory system, bureaucracies generate a new labor market and, moreover, a differentiation of this market in terms of skill and training requirements for human capital. Once such a market exists, it facilitates the development of new bureaucratic systems in ever more economic arenas (and other institutional arenas organized bureaucratically, such as the state and the educational system). Indeed, despite incessant public criticisms of bureaucracies by members of industrial and post-industrial populations, alternatives will have to prove more efficient than bureaucracies—a transformation that has yet to occur even in the most advanced post-industrial society.

The Expansion of Markets   Markets pervade all aspects of industrialization. Internal to the economy, they determine the distribution of technology, capital, and labor; and externally, they distribute goods, services, resources, and materials to the population as a whole. Without the expansion and differentiation of markets, industrialization is not dynamic, and for this dynamism to be sustained in terms of developing new technologies, new forms of capital, higher wages and living standards, and new products and services, markets must have the capacity to stimulate *new kinds of productive outputs* of both goods and services. Many of the problems of state socialism before the Soviet collapse and before recent Chinese reforms inhere in the nature of their markets, which were guided by state edicts and production quotas rather than consumer needs, tastes, and interests. Such state-controlled production and markets worked well (ignoring, of course, the human costs of the corresponding political repression) in jump-starting industrial development, but all of these economies were stagnant by the mid-1960s because without incentives for private profit among producers and without a well-cultivated freedom among consumers for expressing their preferences in market demand, markets cannot grow, proliferate, and develop in ways that encourage new kinds of production. They simply become dreary state-run distribution depots.[2] In contrast, when property and profits can be owned, there are incentives for developing new technologies, new concentrations of physical capital, new skills and types of human capital, and new entrepreneurial systems so that profits can be realized as preferences are expressed.

The problem with such dynamic markets in capitalism is that they are inherently unstable, along several fronts. First, these markets tend to pyramid into hierarchies of metamarkets where the terms and instruments of exchange in a lower market become themselves objects of highly speculative trade in a higher-order market (Collins 1990)—a trend that has been facilitated by globalization of markets for capital. For example, instruments facilitating exchange in one level of market, such as money, credit contracts, mortgages, stocks, bonds, and futures on commodities, become themselves the objects exchanged in a higher-order market; and such exchanges are often highly speculative and leveraged (that is, bought and sold on credit). The recent advent of "derivatives" and their marketing takes this speculation to yet another level whereby financial instruments from different metamarkets are co-mingled in ever further speculation, as when bonds are purchased by borrowing in money markets, or stocks traded for futures on commodities. All these processes eventually cause reversals that reverberate across metamarkets, and down to lower-level markets in which the instruments of exchange in a metamarket (say, credit and money) become less available to facilitate exchange, thereby sending the lower market into instability or at least retraction.

A second problem with these more dynamic markets of capitalism is that, short of collapse through overspeculation, they oscillate between periods of high demand, production, and employment to episodes of lower demand, decreased production, and layoffs of human capital that further dampen demand (since workers have lost income and, hence, purchasing power). Indeed, left to themselves, free markets produce periodic depressions and corresponding social chaos, especially when oscillations are stimulated or accelerated by speculation and collapse in higher-order metamarkets.

A third tendency of free markets is that they tend to produce oligopolies, hidden networks, and monopolies of corporate control within a sector of production and marketing, As a result, competition is reduced or eliminated, enabling corporations to charge prices that no longer correspond to demand. Prices are, as a consequence, fixed in much the same way that state-run enterprises fix prices, except private corporations will tend to fix prices that are artificially high whereas those in state-run markets tend to charge prices that are artificially low.

A fourth problem occurs when markets remain truly competitive and avoid oligopoly and monopoly control. Under these conditions, cutthroat competition tends to generate a decline in the rate of profit as producers constantly cut prices to gather market share from competitors (Marx [1867] 1967; Applebaum 1978). If this process continues unabated, profits cease to exist, thereby forcing the liquidation of physical capital and leading to the unemployment of human capital.

A fifth problem, noted earlier, is that production for open and free markets also creates a labor market for human capital in which conflict between owners and managers of capital, on the one side, and the wage employees, on the other side, escalates as owners and managers of capital attempt to keep wages low while human capital seeks to do the reverse. Such conflict can often turn violent, unless a system of labor-management negotiation can be institutionalized.

A sixth problem is that unregulated markets are invitations for fraud, corruption, abuse of occupational and environmental hazards, and other ills as drives for profits at any cost, and in any way, create incentives for doing social harm. Thus, the dynamism of capitalist markets is not without its problems, and they raise the values for regulation as a social force. As selection pressures increase, centers of power are pulled into gathering, producing, and distributing processes.

Industrial capitalism is built on the constant expansion and differentiation of markets.[3] For without the capacity to expand existing markets or create new ones, incentives for capital investment are dampened because, in the end, it is the drive for higher profits that sustains capitalism. As Marx ([1867] 1967) recognized, there is only a limited number of ways to increase profit—eliminate competitors and fix prices, pay labor as little as possible, develop new technologies that provide more efficient machines, and expand or differentiate markets.

The need of capital to expand markets makes capitalism global, always reaching out beyond nation-state boundaries. Historically, in early phases of capitalism during the nineteenth century, a kind of coercive laissez-faire was practiced (first by Britain and later other European powers), whereby raw materials were extracted (often under coercive threats or control) from less developed countries, shipped home for conversion into manufactured goods, and then distributed on both domestic and international markets (Gereffi 1994:207–8). The coercive side of this internationalism led to the partitioning of the nonindustrial world into colonial spheres of influence by dominant powers. Between the World Wars in the twentieth century this system was disrupted by the Depression and the wars themselves; and in the aftermath of World War II, a "monopoly capitalism" (Baran and Sweezy 1966) phase emerged as transnational corporations invested capital and technology abroad (at first, disproportionately by the United States but, increasingly, by all other industrial nations). More recently, a new phase of "global capitalism" where the organization of capital and technology either within the boundaries or at least under the guidance of nation-states is giving way to more fluid patterns where capital (money and machines) and technology move easily across nation-state boundaries and, increasingly, out of the control of the state (Gereffi 1994:208).

Markets are now truly global, as are the corporate actors in them. Over the last thirty years, very rapid development of the nonindustrial world has ensued as technology and capital from foreign corporations, often in partnerships with domestic governments or private companies, have been invested in order to secure indigenous natural resources or to take advantage of lower priced labor (Gereffi and Wyman 1990). Thus, when a country possesses natural resources, such as oil, minerals, or agricultural lands, that can be extracted and marketed to other nations, and when a country is inhabited by lower-priced human capital than in developed nations, incentives exist for manufacturers to relocate their manufacturing operations. As markets have become global this process enabling all elements of economic activity to be bought and sold across nation-state boundaries has accelerated. Development of this kind, however, is always uneven, with some sectors of physical and human capital changing, while others remain undeveloped (Frank 1980, 1975, 1969; Amin, [1973] 1976, [1970] 1974); and development that is dependent on foreign capital and technology is often exploitive as resources and productive outputs are sold overseas for profits that do not come back to the producing nation.

Still, the incentives to the global markets for generating profits have worked to transform capital flows throughout the world (Mizruchi and Stearns 1994). Liquid physical capital or money and other financial instruments move very rapidly through international metamarkets, especially as deregulation of national money and financial markets has occurred. Much of this money is simply shifted from one short-term speculative financial instrument to another, but much is also invested in technology and manufacturing physical capital in foreign countries—a situation that accelerates economic development and, in more advanced economies, increases the interconnections among corporations and governments.

Post-industrial Economies

As those involved in services surpass those in manual labor connected to gathering, producing, and distributing, post-industrialism supplants industrialism (Bell 1973; Block 1990; Harvey 1989; Lash 1990). As is evident in the advanced economies of the world today, primarily in North America, Western Europe, and Japan, nonmanual service positions far outnumber those in agriculture and factory system production; and consumption levels of goods, services, and energy are very high because per capital income is high relative to industrial societies.

This shift is due to the increasing automation of gathering and production, as machines and information systems made possible by the computer organize and perform many of the routine gathering and production processes formerly conducted by less sophisticated machines and labor. This process of reducing the manual work force can be accelerated with the export by advanced economies of manual-machine labor to less developed economies where labor costs are low, or if labor costs are not lower, where markets are closer.

This shift in the relative proportions of manual and nonmanual work reflects other economic forces beyond mechanization or export of manual work. Accompanying mechanization, and the information systems that make automation possible, are changes in (1) the organization of production, (2) the outputs of production, and (3) the distribution of outputs. Each of these alterations is examined below.

The Reorganization of Production The corporate units in which production occurs undergo important transformations with post-industrialization. First, as noted earlier, smaller manufacturing units, involved in flexible production of specialized goods, become as prominent as the large-scale factory. Second, in both large and small factories, many changes are occurring in their operation, including: new systems of managing inventories ("just-in-time" stocking, for example, which eliminates the need for large inventories), new procedures for quality control (at the point of error rather than after the product is finished), new systems of contracting and subcontracting (increasingly, parts supply, accounting, maintenance, sales, and other functions are turned over to subcontractors), new planning procedures (whereby longer-term assessment of markets occurs), new procedures for ownership and regulation by the state (with states increasingly deregulating private corporations and privatizing state-owned corporations), new patterns of planning and subsidy by the state (increasing reliance on indirect subsidies through government purchases and taxing policies rather than direct state subsidies), new levels of competition among smaller, niche-oriented companies, and renewed emphasis on technological innovation as the means to maintain, or increase, market share. Third, a greater proportion of production is export-oriented, seeking markets in other nations, while attempting to deal with competition from imports. Fourth, as noted earlier, the global orientation of the large multinational company and many more moderate-sized companies make them truly multinational and increasingly involved in production outside national boundaries.

The Production of Services All of these changes increase reliance on service production for sustaining flexibility, for planning, for innovation, for marketing, for information systems, for managing subcontracting, and for providing the administrative and fiscal infrastructure—accounting, banking, computing, selling of financial instruments (stocks, bonds, futures), advertising, marketing, insuring, capitalizing, managing, and so forth—on which manufacturing depends. Separate companies producing these and many other services now become as numerous as those manufacturing hard goods and products. Many of these companies, especially at the high-technology and high-skill end, have begun to adopt less bureaucratized work settings, offering flexible working hours, horizontal dispersion via information nets, less rigid authority, and more collegial teamwork.

The Expansion of Markets   Distribution processes reflect and, at the same time, cause transformations in production. As markets expand, differentiate, and globalize, demand drives production more than the reverse. When market demands for goods and services dictate what is produced, the diversity and volume of production escalate because consumers can create ever more market niches that serve as incentives for producers. Conversely, once well-developed markets exist they can be used to create new needs in consumers that determine what will be produced. For example, most advertising is directed at consumers to generate a need, often one consumers did not know they had. Moreover, once needs are widespread, such as a desire for video games or high-technology skate boards, consumers and manufacturers begin to seek variants of these products, like home computer games and in-line skates. Thus, as consumers become conditioned to being stimulated by marketing ploys, their desires and needs for new products are constantly escalating, stimulating ever more diverse market demand. And, as manufacturers become dependent upon shifts in the needs and preferences of consumers, they take the risks in producing new outputs.

As markets become the driving force of the economy in post-industrial systems, the production of services for facilitating the constant reformation of capital for new market niches and for conducting transactions in more differentiated and global markets increases. This production of services is also market driven, and it tends to create metamarkets in which financial instruments—stocks, bonds, money, mortgages, insurance premiums, pools of debt and capital—are themselves marketed in increasingly complex ways. This complexity furthers demand for services—from computer systems, sales brokers, and highly trained analysts to clerks and secretaries. Thus, as physical capital in both its more liquid forms or in actual productive implements moves about domestic and world economic systems, markets for servicing this flow expand and differentiate in ways escalating demand for more services. Just how far this process can go is uncertain, but it is clear that the servicing revolution is not over.

The net result of these forces is for some pools of human capital to find themselves in a more vulnerable market position. High-skill service positions are less vulnerable, although efforts of corporations to "downsize" and become more efficient in world-level economic competition can make even this sector of the labor market vulnerable. Moreover, corporate mergers have a similar effect as redundancies are eliminated after two corporations have merged into

Table 7.1. Industrial and Post-industrial Economies

	Industrial	Post-industrial
Technology	Harnessing of inanimate sources of energy to machines creates search for more efficient fuels (resulting in heavy reliance on fossil fuels, supplemented by water-generated electricity, nuclear power, and for limited application, solar energy) and leads to mechanization of all productive sectors and generates both new social technologies—the factory system, assembly line, and corporation—and new productive technologies, especially with respect to new materials (metals and synthetics), new machines (machine tools, robotics), new modes of transportation (trains, ships, cars, airplanes), and new capacities to store, process, and send information; technological innovation becomes institutionalized in the education system, the scientific establishment, secularized values and beliefs, economic/political competition, research and development by corporations and government, and laws (i.e., patents)	Same as industrial societies, except for increasing emphasis on developing ways to make new materials (especially synthetic products), to use information in the production process (robotics, computers, communication networks), and to reduce time and cost of transportation; institutionalization of innovation proceeds, increasingly driven by world-level economic competition
Physical Capital	Capital formation and accumulation increase dramatically, with money used to buy and construct tools, machines, factories, and large-scale infrastructural projects (revolving around transportation, energy, and communication); capital may be heavily concentrated in either the private sector or the state; new mechanisms—bond, stock and money markets—are used to concentrate capital coming from ever more diverse sources, including taxes, pension funds, mutual funds, individual investors, and corporations	Same as industrial societies, except that capital formation and accumulation increase and become increasingly global, involving multinational corporations, foreign governments, and private investing consortiums

Table 7.1. (Continued)

	Industrial	Post-industrial
Human Capital	Division of labor becoming dramatically more differentiated and complex, while revolving less around primary industries (farming, mining and other basic producer sectors) and more around secondary industries (mills, factories, construction) and tertiary industries (services, such as retailing, banking, insuring, education, health care, police, social welfare, government, and managing); women increase their nonhousehold economic roles; and self-employment decreases as a proportion of work force; labor increasingly allocated to economic positions by a labor market guided by expertise as determined by educational credentials	Division of labor increases in complexity, along with a marked shift from secondary to tertiary industries as machines coupled with information-processing computers increasingly perform many routine activities in the secondary sector; women continue to increase as proportion of non-household work force, and self-employment continues to decline; educational credentials and labor markets increase as criteria for allocating workers to economic positions
Entrepreneurship	Household and family lose virtually all their integrative functions, except for the remaining family-run businesses; markets, corporations, law, and state become principal entrepreneurial structures, with law and state predominating in some systems, and private corporations in others	Same as industrial societies, except that there are more differentiated and varied markets (labor, money, commodities, bonds, precious metals, etc.), larger corporations, more extensive bodies of law, and increased state regulation of markets and corporations; increasing use of markets, combined with state regulation, evident in all post-industrial systems; world-level economic integration by global markets; world-level banking, international economic alliances (partnerships, joint ventures, stock purchases, and government-to-government cooperative agreements) become increasingly evident
Property	Most material things and labor activities defined as property and assessed in terms of monetary value. Decreased inequality compared with agrarian systems as result of governmental tax-redistributive policies, increased productivity (making distribution less of a zero-sum game), and episodes of political-economic-social conflict between privileged and nonprivileged sectors, but still considerable material inequality. Nobility as a class virtually disappears, although continuing in some systems as symbols and in some cases as holders of considerable wealth; very clear modal differences in behavior, culture, and income, and sources of power and prestige among elites, high education/salaried professionals, small business entrepreneurs, white collar workers, blue collar workers, and the poor; but considerable income overlap among members of different classes; higher rates (compared with agrarian systems) of mobility (both individual and structural) also work against maintenance of hard class barriers; the few continuing cultural differences between rural and urban mitigated by smallness of rural population, with ethnic and urban-suburban differences becoming more salient than rural-urban distinctions	Same as industrial societies, except that cultural capital (in the form of educational credentials as property to be sold) becomes more salient for making class distinctions. Virtually all material things, labor activities, and cultural symbols defined as property or as property rights and assessed in terms of monetary value. Material inequality about the same as in industrial systems, except for widening gap between unskilled and skilled, especially information-literate

one. Semi-skilled clerical labor becomes even more vulnerable with downsizing and mergers, increasingly pushed into a reserve labor pool of "temporary" workers who work for subcontractors. The semi-skilled workers in manual manufacturing are the most vulnerable, as automation and export of their jobs shrink demand relative to supply in this portion of the labor market. Labor markets thus are driven by changes in productive forces in several directions: (1) the loss of lower- or semi-skilled manufacturing jobs, even as the factory system differentiates; (2) the gain in high-technology, high-skill service positions, such as research and engineering, brokering, accounting, computer science, education, banking, finance, insuring, and the like that require advanced educational credentials and that cannot be exported; and (3) manual and non-manual service positions, such as secretaries, care taking, retail sales, and the like that are necessary to keep the domestic economy operating. The dilemma for such systems is twofold: (1) can the low and semi-skilled pool of human capital be fully employed? (2) can corporate units increasingly involved in world-level gathering, manufacturing, and distribution be controlled by national-level political, social, and economic forces?

Post-modernization

Post-industrialization can be seen as inherent in industrialization, per se. In the eyes of many, however, the processes of industrialization and post-industrialization have created a fundamentally new kind of society—indeed, a new phase in societal evolution. If new technologies attaching inanimate sources of energy to machines and labor in factory systems, new non-kin organizational forms like corporate bureaucracies, new systems of private property, new and differentiated markets, and new service-oriented production were all the mark of modernization driven by industrialization and post-industrialization, then these forces have reached such high levels that a new "post-modern" stage in human development has begun (e.g., Crook, Pakulski, and Waters 1992; Harvey 1989; Lash 1990; Lash and Urry 1987; Seidman and Wagner 1992; Touraine 1988). There is no clear consensus on just what distinguishes modernization from post-modernization, but certain trends in economy are viewed as particularly important driving forces in reorganizing human societies.

Commodification   Once open markets become highly differentiated and dynamic, virtually every domain of the social world can be viewed as a commodity that has a "price" and that can be bought and sold. Even arenas of social life previously immune to such market forces, such as personal feelings, lifestyles, values, and traditions, can now be invaded and "colonized" (Habermas [1973] 1976). When virtually all things, persons, relationships, behaviors, activities, symbols, thoughts, and ideas can be bought and sold, the social order is fundamentally changed—at least, according to those who see a new post-modern phase to have evolved.

Commodification is not only the result of free, open, and profit-driven markets, it is also the result of media processes that give individuals access to the symbols, lifestyles, behaviors, traditions, tastes, and preferences of others. Advertising is built upon these media processes, and its effectiveness depends upon stimulating consumers to want new products and services. But advertising must constantly create "newness" to exert its effects on market demand, sometimes through repackaging and recycling the old, other times by actually making something innovative and original, and frequently by usurping the symbols, tastes, lifestyles, and traditions of other nations, communities, ethnicities, and classes. In this escalating process, little is sacred or off-limits, and all can be used to make advertising pitches or to make products. Such commodification, it is argued, makes traditions, ethnicity, community, tastes, lifestyles, behaviors, dress, symbols, and ideas less real, less powerful, and less attached to the social structures in which they were once embedded. These new commodities that previously marked important social activities and structures can now be purchased and used as lifestyle props or as expressions of taste in ways that dilute their original meaning and significance. These commodities become symbols that float free from their origins, thereby losing their significance and making social life an incessant consumption of superficial markers of once important realities.

Hyperdifferentiation and Dedifferentiation   For some, differentiation of activities, symbol systems, organizations, and other activities reaches such high levels that a kind of *de*differentiation occurs (Crook, Pakulski, and Waters 1992). The idea here is that as culture and social structure become hyperdifferentiated, incessantly splitting into ever more distinct types of symbols, categories, and economic specialties, the boundaries among these hyperdifferentiated dimensions of social life are weakened and, in fact, become open to all and easily penetrated. The result is that any person or group can usurp the symbols, dress, mannerisms, and organizational forms of other persons and groups, especially in an economy that makes everything available for purchase and that produces media access to virtually any aspect of culture, activity, or organization. As partitions break down, cultural symbols marking these boundaries have been disconnected from the structures that generated them; and as a result, symbols become free-floating and easily adopted by others. Social life becomes a collage of symbols with little capacity to inspire and even less capacity to denote and mark points of difference and differentiation; and as hyperdifferentiation, coupled with commodification, produce this outcome, social life loses texture, substance, and meaning.

Hyperrationalization   Rational calculation of costs and benefits comes to dominate a society as profit-oriented markets extend to virtually all spheres of life. Increased levels of impersonality, formality, technical specialization, and cost calculations all become essential features of social relations as bureaucratization prevails in economic and other arenas of social organization. As these processes continue, they generate a hyperrationality—a concern with efficiency, speed, and profit—that, ironically, can generate less efficiency, speed, or profit (Ritzer 1993). For example, "fast food" restaurants are often not very fast because they attract too many customers at peak times and force them to line up and wait; bureaucracies can become big, bloated, inflexible, and inefficient; and computer trading in stocks, using programmed "rationality," can cause the collapse of markets when all programs simultaneously seek to "sell."

Hyperrationality also invites countermovements in art, alternative lifestyles, and religious fundamentalism that seek to overcome or even to attack the impersonality of cost-benefit calculations. Rationality thus invites its opposite—social movements against rationality—and these movements can often seek to destroy what is rational.

More significantly, the recognition of the imperfections of rationality leads some corporate units to reduce hierarchy, to extend boundaries via information hookups, to require flexible and generalized skills of human capital, and to construct more flexible, fluid, and informal work networks, all of which discourage precise cost-benefit analysis, speed at all costs, and impersonality in favor of less calculable informal and personal work relations. Or, because economic activities can often be performed more efficiently and cheaply outside a corporate structure, subcontracting to small-scale specialists increases, creating cadres of self-employed providers of services (from computer consulting, engineering, payroll, and finance to maintenance and transportation) that are less bureaucratically organized, especially if they remain small. Thus, some argue that the "irrationality of hyperrationality" creates fundamentally new forms of economic organization, revolving around teamwork, flexibility, reduced authority, temporary employment, and contracting services to outside providers (Kanter 1989).

Just whether these transformations represent a new type of society, as distinguishable from the industrial as the industrial was from the agrarian, is difficult to tell. There can be little doubt that certain trends are going to change the organization of human economies (Block 1990), but with less hyperbole than post-modernists, let me conclude by listing some of these changes:

1. Increased production of services as a proportion of economic output, and increased reliance on computer-driven machines or less expensive human capital outside an economy's borders,

2. Mass and differentiated marketing, with niche markets for an increasing variety and volume of goods, services, symbols, or virtually anything,
3. Globalization of all economic activity so that gathering, producing, and distributing of all goods and services will involve the economies of other nation-states,
4. Bifurcation of human capital into an elite, highly skilled, and high-wage labor pool, on the one side, and a vulnerable, less skilled, and lower-wage labor pool, on the other side,
5. Restructuring of gathering, producing, and distributing corporate units toward less hierarchy, more extension of boundaries across space (through information technologies), more flexible and changeable team-work activity, and more reliance on outside service providers,[4] and
6. Ever greater reliance on new technologies for gathering, producing, and distribution, especially as world-level competition among corporations and their nation-state sponsors intensifies.

Industrialization and post-industrialization dramatically change the nature of selection pressures in human societies. Darwinian selection becomes more prominent as markets institutionalize competition. For most of human history, many major transformations have come from Spencerian selection in which the absence of relevant structures to resolve problems has pushed actors to create new institutional systems or alter older ones to fit new circumstances. These Spencerian pressures continue with industrialization, but societies driven by market dynamics will reveal considerably more Darwinian selection as individuals and various types of corporate units compete with each other for resources; and as the more fit of these units reproduce themselves and the less fit disappear or find new niches, the nature of the institutional order is changed. Moreover, as the economy becomes so dynamic, production and distribution as social forces increasingly impose selection pressures on other institutional systems to adapt to the new economic conditions. Thus, as we move to other institutional domains in post-industrial societies, we should pay particular attention to how the economy imposes new selection pressures on them.

KINSHIP

Industrialization completes the odyssey of kinship back to the basic structure of hunting and gathering, primarily because kinship is no longer needed to organize societal activities. In fact, large kinship systems would get in the way of rational and efficient corporate units and market mechanisms for distributing goods, services, and human capital; and as a result, they are increasingly eliminated in favor of small, mobile nuclear families that are unencumbered by uni-lineal descent and mandatory residence rules. Authority remains somewhat patriarchal, although as women enter the labor force, a more egalitarian pattern of authority and family activities begins to emerge (but vestiges of patriarchy remain, especially among manual, nonprofessional labor). Marriage is still guided by incest, but exogamy rules disappear, and endogamy is purely infor-mal, being guided more by categoric unit memberships—social class, ethnicity, and other non-kin criteria. Divorce becomes easier to get, and rates of divorce and nonmarital childbearing begin to rise with post-industrialization.

Several trends have accompanied the structural transformation of kinship to truncated bilateral descent, isolated nuclear units, and neolocal residence. These revolve around (1) the changing authority relations within nuclear units; (2) the division of labor for family activities; and (3) the patterns of marriage dissolution. Although there are large differences among post-industrial systems, especially between the Eastern and Western Hemispheres, there is some con-vergence of these trends in the western post-industrial societies—the United States and western Europe. These converging trends in the Western Hemi-sphere are the result of pressures that have yet to exert great influence on Japa-nese kinship and other eastern industrial societies, although I would speculate that they will become more manifest in the decades ahead.

Changing Authority Relations

As the family unit became ever more nuclearized beginning with late agrarian-ism (Flandrin 1979; Laslett and Wall 1972) and increasingly with industrializa-tion and post-industrialization, norms of patriarchy have not gone completely back to a more egalitarian pattern evident among many hunter-gatherer popu-lations. The horticultural-agrarian system of male control has persisted, primar-ily because it was in the male's interest to have such norms and because women were not in an economic position to demand changes, especially as they remained burdened with household-domestic obligations.

Those under authority always resent it, and so, as women have begun to participate in the labor force and to command economic resources, they have been able to make claims for egalitarian decision-making—much like many hunter-gatherers of the past. If they too are "bread winners," then there must be a sharing of power. A complete shift to egalitarianism has not occurred, however. Males have resisted, and although there is a trend in the direction of egalitarianism, norms have not completely gone over in this direction (Hoch-schild 1989; Hertz 1986). Indeed, there is considerable normative ambiguity over authority, especially with respect to who has it in what domestic spheres.

Table 7.2. Structure of Kinship in Modern Societies

	Industrial	Post-industrial
Size and composition	Extended kinship virtually disappears except for various ethnic migrants/businesses and for some portions of agricultural sector; decrease in birth rates reduces family size to nuclear units	Same as industrial societies, except modal family size decreases and number of childless families increases
Residence	Neolocal, with freedom to move in accordance with labor-market opportunities; multiple-family residence typically only of poor underclass, ethnic migrants, and portions of agricultural sector	Same as industrial societies
Activity	Increasingly ambiguous division of labor by sex and age as women enter nonhousehold labor force and children become integrated in peer cultures	Same as industrial societies, with considerable ambiguity over division of labor by sex and age; incipient trend toward increased egalitarianism by sex and, to a lesser extent, by age; also, increased activity by all family members outside family
Descent	Unilateral descent virtually disappears in favor of a truncated, bilateral system	Same as industrial societies
Authority	Still male-dominated but with less clarity and decisiveness	Still male-dominated but with considerable ambiguity and with trend toward egalitarian or, at least, sharing of authority between males and females
Marriage	Incest prohibited; no explicit rules of exogamy or endogamy; dissolution allowed and increasingly easy to secure; rising rates of divorce and dissolution initially but tending to level off	Same as industrial societies, except divorce rates increase again

This ambiguity will, no doubt, persist well into the twenty-first century, even in the West and certainly in the eastern industrial systems.

Changing Division of Labor

As with authority relations, and in fact, as a partial reflection of authority norms, the divisions of labor in industrial and post-industrial kinship systems reveal considerable ambiguity. Even as women have entered the labor force, they are more likely to feel obligated to perform domestic chores than men— that is, socialization and nurturance of the young, food preparation and cleanup, and housework. Indeed, men actively resist performing these chores, or if avoidance is not possible, they seek to minimize their involvement (Robinson 1988). Such a situation generates considerable tension in families as women resent having to perform a "second shift" of domestic chores (Hochschild 1989). Norms are clearly changing to a more equitable division of labor in the West among families where women work. But change is slow; and in families where women do not work, the older patriarchal pattern prevails. Thus, there is not only ambiguity in norms, there are multiple normative systems in the division of labor. The existence of the traditional division of labor norms for nonworking women often makes it difficult to substitute a more liberal and egalitarian normative profile in families where women work. Indeed, women themselves may feel caught between the two normative systems, moving back and forth between them and trying to create a viable normative system for their own families.

Changing Marriage Dissolution

With post-industrialization, marriage occurs later in life, childbearing often occurs outside of formal marriage, and dissolution rates increase. These latter two trends—childbearing out of wedlock and high divorce rates—potentially pose problems.

Childbearing outside of marriage has increased throughout the West, but particularly in the United States. If the father is in the household, this trend need not cause problems, especially since the couple usually gets married eventually. It is when fathers never become part of the household, or soon leave it, that a special burden is placed upon the nuclear unit: earning an income, providing adequate child care, and giving nurturance and guidance all become problematic. And, the younger the mother in this situation is, the more problematic are these necessities. As a result the basic functions that family has always provided in human societies are abrogated, often forcing the bureaucratic structures of the state to intervene in an area where it is ill suited. In

American society, especially among some poor minority populations, rates of out-of-wedlock birth are extremely high, causing severe problems for children and the broader society in which these children cannot always participate.

Rates of divorce increase with post–industrialization, although rates of remarriage are also high. But the breakup of families, per se, creates many of the same problems that out-of-wedlock families reveal: problems of adequate income, child care, and nurturance and guidance. And if children of divorced parents become part of a reconstituted family through remarriage, then problems of integrating stepparent(s) and stepsibling(s) can become acute, placing considerable tension on all family members. There are no well-institutionalized norms for either single-parent or stepfamilies, and as a result, families must cope and grope to find solutions, often compromising some of the critical functions of kinship systems in the process.

All of these trends are the result of the changing institutional environment of kinship. For as kinship has lost most of its social coordination functions and has become just one subsystem in a complex of differentiated institutional subsystems, the dynamics of these other subsystems exert ever more influence on the organization and operation of kinship. For now, kinship is not the organizational backbone of the entire society, as it was in hunting and gathering as well as horticulture. Indeed, kinship becomes a reactive institutional system, trying to sustain a viable operation as the dynamic forces of other institutions, especially economy, polity, and education, increasingly dictate how kinship is to be structured and what functions it is to retain in the fast-changing industrial and post-industrial eras.

RELIGION

Religion in Industrial and Post-industrial Societies

Early Modern Religions The Protestant Reformation marked the emergence of what can be termed "modern religion." Until recently—and even now the matter is ambiguous—the great premodern religions of Islam, Buddhism, Catholicism, Hinduism, and Confucianism resisted changing; and in fact, early reform movements within these religions did not have the widespread appeal or far-reaching consequences of the Protestant Reformation (Bellah 1964). Even today, under massive selection pressure from other institutional systems in industrial and post-industrial societies, these stable premodern religions are not easily changed. Yet, with industrialization, early modern religions can begin to shift to the pattern described below.

The cosmology of early modern religions becomes even more attenuated than that of premodern religions, especially under the impact of industrialization. The trend toward monotheism is more evident, and the cast of supporting gods and deities decreases. Myths become comparatively unimportant and are de-emphasized. More revolutionary than these extensions of trends evident in premodern religions is the emergence of a new set of substantive beliefs about the supernatural, and humans' relation to the supernatural. A clear separation of the natural and supernatural realms is maintained, but the premodern emphasis on the hierarchies within either of these realms is eliminated. God and humans now stand in direct relation to each other and mediating religious specialists (priests) are essentially excess baggage. Such substantive beliefs result in a reorganization of religious values that still stress the importance of salvation, but through a new route. For now, religious values emphasize the importance of *individual* faith and commitment to God, rather than ritual performance or conformity to strict ethical codes. Values also emphasize the necessity for God's work to be done in this world, which in Bellah's (1964:369) words, becomes "a valid arena in which to work out the divine command." Moreover, a wide variety of secular beliefs—"capitalism," "democracy," "nationalism," "humanism," and the like—begins to compete with religious beliefs as providers of meaning, thereby increasing the Darwinian competition between these "civil religions" and beliefs about the sacred and supernatural.

What distinguished the Protestant Reformation from reform movements in other premodern religions was that the new emphasis on individualism and de-emphasis of ritual and priestly mediation between God and humans became *institutionalized into strong ecclesiastic cult structures*. These structures were and are bureaucratized, with a hierarchy of religious specialists and with requirements of religious orthodoxy for lay members. Yet typical features of premodern ecclesiastic cults, such as compulsory membership, high authoritarianism, ritual emphasis, and *elaborate* hierarchy, were not evident in these early Protestant cult structures, such as Calvinism, Methodism, Pietism, and Baptism. Thus a curious accommodation between new religious beliefs within a somewhat watered-down form of ecclesiastic cult occurred during early modernization. The failure of other premodern religions to change resided not so much in the lack of reform movements similar to those that eventually spawned the Protestant Reformation, but rather in the incapacity to institutionalize these reforms into an ecclesiastic cult structure (Bellah 1964:369). Still, early modern cult structures were not loosely structured or entirely permissive; on the contrary, the early Protestant cults required much orthodoxy and conformity to church rules, with this conformity extending beyond the church doors into everyday life. But within these cults, the de-emphasis on ritual, the decreasing role of the clergy as intermediaries, and the emphasis on individual relations between

Table 7.3. Religion in Modern Societies

	Industrial	Post-industrial
Belief system	Clear separation of supernatural and natural, domination by universal religions proclaiming one god and/or force in their sparse pantheon and very little mythology, explicit codes of ethics and systems of values persist; new secular ideologies using referents to the supernatural further secularize religious beliefs, creating "civil religions"—e.g., nationalism, capitalism, humanism—that are not so much religious as advocacies of particular secular activities and social forms	Same as industrial societies, but with further diminution of pantheon and mythology as well as some questioning of separation between natural and supernatural realms. Emphasis on personal interpretation of nonempirical and sacred in some cults. Less pronounced and rigid moral codes in beliefs of some cults. Secular ideologies and "civil religion" compete with religious beliefs
Rituals	Some calendrical rituals, certain of which lose their religious significance (e.g., Christmas gift giving); private rituals also encouraged; mass media increasingly a vehicle for observing and expressing religious sentiments	Same as industrial societies, except that religious rituals often supplemented/supplanted by secular rituals (e.g., "meditation," "daily workouts," "weekly therapy"); mass media increasingly important as means for ritual enactment
Cult structures	Bureaucratized structures in variety of temples/churches (from large and grand to simple); times and places of worship specified but less regularly followed and/or enforced; little political influence, except through capacity to mold public opinion; some trends for consolidation of cults, counteracted in some systems by new, splinter cults; in democratic systems, cults may become political interest group/party lobbying for particular legislative programs	Same as industrial societies, except that new national cult structures are created through market forces and mass media, particularly TV (in those societies allowing private TV), and cults increasingly involved in political lobbying and party activity

God and person generated a whole series of contradictions between tightly organized ecclesiastic cults and a loosely organized belief system. With industrialization, these contradictions become increasingly evident to both the clergy and laity, with the result that a loosening of religious orthodoxy and cult structure as well as a further individualization of the religious belief system has occurred.

Modern Religion The label *modern religion* is only a convenient term for describing religious activities in a few post-industrial, western societies with a Protestant tradition. Societies dominated by one of the large premodern religions do not display this "modern" religious type; and in societies that do, it exists alongside premodern and early modern forms of religion. Thus, what I am labeling "modern religion" is neither widespread nor even dominant in those post-industrial societies where it is found.

Modern religion is marked by the destruction of a coherent cosmology, as the supernatural mythologies and substantive beliefs increasingly all become ambiguous and unsystematic. Perhaps the most dramatic manifestation of the de-cosmologicalization of religion is reflected in the ambiguity over whether or not there is a god or a clearly distinguishable supernatural (Wuthnow 1988:485). Bellah (1964:370–71) has referred to this process as the breakdown of the basic dualism that has been central to all religions through history and throughout most of the world today. The belief in forces beyond humans' control remains in modern religions but the clear-cut differentiation between the sacred and profane or supernatural and natural diminishes. Substantive beliefs begin to emphasize individualistic or personal interpretations of the nonempirical and sacred, with ever more concern over searching for truths that fit one's actual conditions of living. To the extent that salvation remains a tenet within the belief system, it is likely to emphasize multiple and personal paths to life in another world, with these paths to salvation always involving enhanced adjustment and happiness in this world. These alterations of the cosmology are reflected in a new, emerging set of religious values. Rigid moral codes become less pronounced and are replaced by values directing worshippers to seek adjustment, happiness, and self-realization with others and the world around them (Bellah 1964:363; Berger 1963; Luckmann 1967). Thus in modern religious belief systems, the elaborate cosmology typical of traditional ecclesiastical religions has crumbled, while the explicit and rigid moral code of premodern religions has become loose and highly flexible, emphasizing adjustment to the secular rather than to the sacred or supernatural.

With this flexible and individualistic form of religious belief system, cult structures in post-industrial societies are altered, although the tight cult structures of premodern and early modern religions still persist and outnumber the more loosely organized modern cults. And, in the near future, structures embracing the more flexible belief system of modern religions will remain ecclesiastical, but these ecclesiastical structures are somewhat fluid, adjusting themselves to the needs of their clients. Such is particularly likely to be the case as mass electronic media and market forces organize a significant amount of religious activity. There are many subunits and organizations within any cult that cater to diverse groups of clients; and as the needs of clients change, the lower-level organizational units of the ecclesia servicing the membership will also change. Cults—churches, denominations, sects, and the like—come to provide more of a place or location where individuals work out their own solutions to ultimate questions about the cosmos and supernatural rather than a rigid orthodox structure where these solutions are prefabricated in the form of an established belief system and ritual pattern (Bellah 1964:373; Lenski 1963:59–60). This is increasingly the trend, especially among Protestant cults (denominations) in post-industrial western societies (Wuthnow 1994; Berger 1969; Lenski 1963:59), but these cult structures are a curious hybrid or cross between an ecclesiastic cult structure at their top and a more flexible, almost individualistic structure at their bottom or local membership level. As media ministries proliferate, a further contradiction becomes evident as conservative beliefs are marketed to a diffuse and mass audience whose members can remain isolated from each other, rarely engaging in collective ritual activity (Hadden and Swann 1981).

Indeed, media-driven cults tend to be more "evangelical" and fundamentalistic, placing them in a Darwinian competition with more traditional religious cults and with the modern cults in which individuals engage in their own search for, and interpretation of, the supernatural. In fact, in many western countries, especially the United States but European countries as well, a variety of religious movements appear to be in motion—movements such as the Promise Keepers and other Protestant cults advocating a strict moral code. These movements are gaining members, while more traditional premodern cults are losing members, indicating that the enhanced religiosity has wide appeal even in a post-industrial society. Part of this appeal is to those who feel left out of the transformative effects of a high technology society, but this alone cannot explain the appeal of this form of fundamentalistic cults. Thus, religion in contemporary post-industrial societies is in flux, and there is considerable Darwinian competition among cults for members.

Trends in Religion

Historically, religious evolution through shamanic, communal, and traditional ecclesiastical religions involved an increasing codification and complexity of the cosmology: the number of deities in the pantheon, their degree of definition, the myths relating them and accounting for their emergence, and substantive beliefs about levels or planes in the supernatural realms all became more clearly articulated and codified into a comparatively unambiguous hierarchy of gods and supernatural forces. With the emergence of premodern religious forms, however, the number of deities decreased as a tendency toward monotheism became evident, although relations among supernatural beings as well

as planes of supernatural existence remain clearly articulated. With the emergence of early modern religions, these trends in cosmological development
decelerated and began to be reversed: mythology became attenuated; the size
of the pantheon decreased; and the various hierarchical levels within the supernatural realm were eliminated. And with post-industrialization, many cults
further diminish the cosmology as beliefs come to emphasize personal interpretations and relationships with the supernatural. Increasingly, religious beliefs
about the sacred and supernatural must compete with "civil religions" revolving around secular beliefs dressed up in "god language" that provide meaning
and purpose to individuals.

Similarly, religious values display a parallel curvilinear trend: from the shamanic to the premodern stage religious values became increasingly more
explicit, culminating in the strict moral code of most premodern religions. This
code persists with early industrialization—although in a somewhat less compelling form. With post-industrialization, the rigid moral code in many cults
becomes relativistic as values stress a more flexible relationship between individuals and the supernatural as well as a more accommodating mode of adjustment in the natural world.

At the structural level, religious development entailed an increasing bureaucratization up to the early modern stage. Early religions displayed only individualistic and shamanic cult structures; traditional communal religions evidenced
communal cults with some degree of a division of labor among the lay membership; and traditional ecclesiastical religions revealed cults with a bureaucratic
structure revolving around a clear division of labor between laity and specialized clergy as well as a hierarchy of control among the clergy itself. Premodern
religions had an even more elaborate and extensive church bureaucracy with a
high degree of centralization of its religious specialists, as is exemplified in the
Catholic Church, which has a world bureaucracy culminating in the Pope as
its head. Early modern religions, however, began to decentralize their bureaucracies as smaller, geographically dispersed, and local bureaucracies evidence
only loose administrative ties to a central staff of clergy and as strict relationships of authority among units within the religious bureaucracy decline. And,
as media ministries and alternatives to traditional ecclesiastic cults have prolifer-
ated with post-industrialization, the structure of cults has undergone further
transformation as membership often remains outside of the bureaucratized central headquarters of those who run and market the ministry.

With these changes in beliefs and cult structures has come some degree of
secularization among a greater proportion of religious cults. Of course, to speak
of a trend toward secularization of religion represents a contradiction in terms,
because religion revolves around the nonsecular—the ultimate, the cosmos,
the supernatural, and the sacred. To a great extent religion has always been

secular, since religious beliefs and rituals in traditional societies have had consequences for economic, political, educational, and familial structures and processes, but in traditional societies, religious rituals—whether calendrical, noncalendrical, or magical—have always made direct and strong appeals for the intervention of supernatural forces into everyday affairs. Many cults in modern religions decreasingly make such appeals. Moreover, while operating on a supernatural or sacred set of premises, the actual role behavior of modern clergy in a myriad of secular activities such as social work, the leisure sphere, criminal corrections, youth programs, athletic leagues, marriage counseling, and group therapy frequently make little or no reference (much less an appeal) to the supernatural. Since the supernatural realm in modern religions has no clear-cut or elaborate cosmology or strict moral code, this is to be expected, especially as religion now must compete in a market-driven economy with many secular organizations. And when beliefs begin to emphasize the importance of each individual establishing his or her personal relationship with the ultimate conditions of life, direct and strong appeals of clergy for divine intervention become less appropriate. There is, however, only a trend toward increased secularization of religious activity, because if religious behavior completely loses sight of the supernatural and sacred premise, then it would cease to be religious. And if all cult structures become organized solely for secular activities, then the institution of religion would no longer exist. Twenty-five years ago, many analysts predicted this fate for religion, but these predictions were premature, because the organization of rituals directed at the supernatural is still a most prominent form of human activity in even the most advanced post-industrial society. Moreover, various movements toward a new fundamentalism speak to the far-reaching effects of more traditional religious appeals on even the most modern populations, indicating that most post-industrial societies have a diversity of religious formations.

Religion has changed in response to transformations in other institutions, but even as it has had to adapt to external selection pressures from other institutions, important dynamics internal to the religious institutional system operate in industrial and post-industrial societies. These dynamics revolve around religious movements producing diversity in beliefs, cults, and rituals.

This diversity runs a full range (Kurtz 1995:167–209). On one end are "popular religions" where beliefs in such matters as the occult, astrology, lucky numbers, extrasensory perception, trances, mystical experiences, out-of-body experiences, powers of nature, and magic are still widely held and provide guidance for people over such fundamental issues as food, sickness and health, death and the dead, and transitions in the life cycle (Williams 1980:65; Wuthnow 1988:481). Such beliefs are organized in a wide variety of cults, from individual practitioners to secret societies, most of which are on the margins and fringes of religion in industrial and post-industrial societies. At the other end of the religious spectrum are the established cult structures that dominate religious life in a society. Sometimes these are sanctioned by the state but whether or not this is the case is less essential than the fact that a vast majority of the population seeking religion belong to the cult structures of these established religions, all of which are the descendants of premodern religions in the agrarian era.

It is the in-between areas of these end points where the interesting dynamics are occurring. Successive religious movements in which new beliefs, rituals, and cult structures are invented take up much of this intermediate space, and the result in post-industrial societies is to increase religious diversity (Stark and Bainbridge 1985). Religious movements occur when subpopulations feel deprived relative to others in a society (Stark and Bainbridge 1980; Bainbridge and Stark 1979; Glock 1973) and when moral definitions of behavior and relationships are changing (Wuthnow 1988:478). Under either or both of these conditions, especially when deprivation and moral uncertainty are experienced collectively by members of a subpopulation, new religious beliefs are articulated, new leaders emerge, and new cults are formed. There are usually multiple religious systems emerging under these conditions, setting them into Darwinian competition over symbolic and ideological resources, financial resources, and members (Wuthnow 1988, 1987). This competition focuses beliefs and rituals while defining the boundaries of cult structures; and in the end, some movements are more successful than others, thereby shifting the distribution and relative members of cults organizing the religious activities of a population. As noted earlier, religious movements are more "evangelical" than established religions or popular religion, and through more cohesive cult structures and emotionally laden rituals, they produce a number of potential outcomes: (1) They can generate more fundamentalistic beliefs than established religions, which have been evolving toward less rigid belief systems; (2) they can create entirely new beliefs and rituals; or (3) they can advocate a revitalization of the moral principles that have been lost. Each of these alternatives is briefly discussed below:

1. Religious fundamentalism advocates a strict interpretation of the texts in which beliefs were first written down; at the same time, fundamentalism also demands a rigid morality, an adherence to rituals, and an intolerance for relaxing orthodoxy. In some societies, such as the United States, these sects are gaining membership because their members' birth rates tend to be high, their emotional and evangelical appeal is often effectively packaged through the video mass media or through high-solidarity cults attracted to local communities, and their message responds to the sense of deprivation, marginality, and

fears of moral decline among significant sectors of post-industrial societies (Marty and Appleby 1993). Not only in the United States, but elsewhere in the world, as is evident in the Islamic nations, similar fundamentalistic movements are underway (Hiro 1989).

2. Religious innovations often come from the same conditions that cause fundamentalism, but more typically, these advocate new religious beliefs rather than a renewed adherence to old ones. Historically this process has involved incorporating older religious ideas into a new set of beliefs—as is evident for Judaism, Islam, and Christianity, which ultimately involve variants and elaborations on the Book of Abraham; as is the case for Buddhism, which reacted to Hinduism; or more recently, as was the case with Mormonism, which involves an elaboration and change of ideas from Christianity. In more industrial and post-industrial societies, the new religions can be conservative but most are more liberal, advocating secular adjustment and personal growth in their beliefs. And some, such as Scientology, are only marginally religious.

3. Revitalization movements involve efforts to recapture a way of life that has been lost through the articulation of beliefs and rituals. Relatedly, millenarian movements postulate a future state when things will be better and people will once again live in peace and harmony (Cohn 1957). These movements usually occur among those whose modes of existence have been uprooted by external forces and whose life is now insecure and anxious. Under these conditions, religious beliefs, rituals, and cults that promise hope of a return to the way it was or, alternatively, to the dawning of a new millennia of happiness in the future, have widespread appeal. For example, in the latter part of the nineteenth century among conquered Native Americans, a number of millenarian movements emerged in which beliefs emphasized that the old ways would return and whites would be vanquished.

Thus, social change where moral definitions are altered and where people feel deprived are the breeding grounds for religious movements. These movements can go in many directions, but in the end they must compete for limited resources. Some are successful, as is evident for the great premodern religions (e.g., Hinduism, Buddhism, Christianity, Islam, Judaism) that still dominate the globe; others die out; and still others find viable niches in which they can sustain cult structures. Thus, as long as there is social change in the broader institutional systems of a society, religious movements will emerge, compete, die, and selectively survive (Stark and Bainbridge 1985; Robbins and Anthony 1990).

At one time, many were predicting the demise of religion, or at the very least, its secularization and compartmentalization from the institutional mainstream. Yet, religion has remained a central institutional system, even in highly secular, post-industrial societies. True, except in a few theocracies like those in some Arab countries, religion no longer penetrates the political and legal systems as it once did in agrarian systems, nor does it dominate daily social life for most members of post-industrial societies. But it is still salient, and as can easily be seen, it is an important source of conflict in many societies of the world. Religion is thus an important dynamic in all societies.

Yet, religion is now reactive, having to cope with changes in its institutional environment. For as science and technology dominate economic activity, as political systems use legal-constitutional principles for their legitimization, as secular education for trade skills is extended to the masses, as kinship becomes nucleated and mobile in search of economic opportunities, and as medicine reduces some of the uncertainty over health, the nature of religion must change. This change in religion's institutional environment sets into motion many of the dynamics evident in religion today.

POLITY

Industrialization, Post-industrialization, and the State

Industrialization has generated a sufficient economic surplus to support a large bureaucratic state in which power is, to varying degrees, centralized and which reshuffles the four bases of power toward somewhat diverging patterns of consolidation. In democratic states, where incumbents in the decision-making bodies of government (the chief executive and legislative bodies) are selected in contested elections by a population that enjoys political freedoms and citizenship rights, the consolidation of power revolves around (1) minimal and selective use of coercion, (2) symbolic legitimization in terms of secular legal principles usually embodied in a constitution, (3) manipulation of material incentives through tax and redistribution policies for broad segments of the population, and (4) reliance on an extensive administrative bureaucracy whose officials are recruited and promoted for their expertise and whose heads are ultimately responsible to the elected executive and to members of representative bodies. In less democratic and in totalitarian states, where contested elections are not held or, if held, are mechanical confirmations of decisions made by those who hold power, the consolidation of power is skewed toward (1) extensive use of coercion or threats of coercion, (2) legitimization in terms of secular constitutional principles that are frequently ignored by those holding power (a religious variant is for legitimization to come from religious doctrines that are also subject to manipulation), (3) selective use of material incentives to "buy off" the masses (through state-run job, education, and recreation programs) and to support the privilege of elites, and (4) extensive intrusions of the state bureaucracy into the daily affairs of actors, coupled with high degrees of regulation of other institutional systems.

Industrialization creates selection pressures for democratization, and the corresponding profile of consolidation and centralization of power, under several conditions: First, a relatively free and open market system encouraging the entrepreneurial activity must exist. Second, a large bourgeoisie who are willing to mobilize politically to support their interests in market-oriented activity must be in place (Moore 1966; Szymanski 1978). Third, a large, industrially oriented working class must exist that, despite opposition by the bourgeoisie (who want to keep wages down by politically disenfranchising workers), must be able to mobilize politically to press for the right to vote (Rueschemeyer, Stephens, and Stephens 1992). Conversely, when markets are not well developed, when the bourgeoisie is small relative to the land-owning aristocracy of the agrarian era, and when the industrial working class is small, or politically inactive, a more totalitarian form of state is likely to emerge with industrialization, as was the case for early phases of industrialization in Russia and its satellites, eastern Europe, Germany in the west, and most of Latin America, Africa, and Asia. However, as these less democratic societies have sought to compete in the world system by expanding their free markets, encouraging entrepreneurship, and developing a working class, pressures mount for the democratization of the state, although it is not clear that these pressures can always shift the pattern of centralization and consolidation of power toward a more democratic profile. China and Russia, for example, are interesting test cases as they undergo transformation to market-driven systems.

The Dynamics of Power

The Self-Escalating Nature of Power   Polity originally emerged as a visible institutional force when populations grew and settled down, thereby escalating regulation as a force and increasing selection pressures arising from problems of coordination and control (Turner 1995; Maryanski and Turner 1992; Carneiro 1973, 1970, 1967; Fried 1967; Johnson and Earle 1987; Earle 1984). Once leaders possessing power came into existence, the dynamics of power were initiated. When set into motion by population growth, consolidation takes on a life of its own because as legitimating symbols, coercive capacities, manipulation of material symbols, and administrative forms are brought together, the short-term interest of those involved in each of these bases of power is to expand their base. Controllers of symbols want to persuade more to follow their lead; forces of coercion wish to increase their readiness; administrative factions want to extend their prerogatives; and holders of material

Table 7.4. Polity in Modern Societies

	Industrial	Post-industrial
Centralization of decision-making and leadership	Disappearance of monarch, except as figurehead in some societies. Centralized state bureaucracy of civil servants, sprinkled with patronage, and clear tendency toward election of legislative and executive decision makers, although the number of parties and freedom of the electorate varies enormously	Same as industrial societies, except for dramatic increase in democratic systems in which legislative and executive leaders are selected in elections, with varying degrees of true competition among candidates. Varying patterns of centralization of legislative, administrative, and judicial functions of government
Consolidation of bases of power		
Material incentives:	Extensive system of progressive income (and at times, wealth) taxation, coupled with systems of sales and property taxes. Manipulation of taxes themselves for distinct subpopulations, or redistribution of tax revenues to targeted sectors of the population become common bases for manipulating the material base of power. The welfare state emerges	Same as in industrial societies, with ever more complex system of taxation and redistribution through tax subsidies or tax expenditures and direct budgetary expenditures on targeted sectors of the population. The welfare state expands, although there is considerable variation in its size and scope
Symbolic:	Decreased reliance on religious symbols and increased reliance on secular symbols: ideologies and democracy, citizenship rights, constitutional and legal principles, ideologies of welfare activities, nationalism, and beliefs associated with geopolitical activities	Same as industrial, with ever more reliance on secular systems of symbols
Coercion:	Very high capacity with professional army and police, used strategically and, to greatly varying degrees, constrained by laws	Same as industrial with legal constraints on coercive actions ever more evident
Administration:	Vast state bureaucracy controlling virtually all institutional spheres, staffed increasingly by professionals certified by educational credentials and regulated by civil service systems of promotion	Same as industrial societies, with some efforts (often unsuccessful) to "privatize" activities previously controlled by administrative system

resources want to have more. Thus, as the bases of power are brought together, or consolidated, there are pressures for the mobilization of more power. This process began slowly in human history, primarily because the size, density, and diversity of the population did not increase the valences for regulation beyond a minimal threshold. But once this threshold was reached, usually with advanced horticulture, polity became a distinctive institutional system as selection pressures from regulation increased (Easton 1965). As polities have grown, however, maintaining balances among the bases of power has proven ever more difficult.

Industrialization and particularly post-industrialization will inevitably increase the values for regulation as a force and, hence, the consolidation of more power along each base. The complexity of society generates selection pressures for coordination and control of diverse activities among individuals and collective units. As a result, the administrative base of power grows, as does the coercive base as a means to enforce administrative decisions. The material incentive base also increases because the exercise of power increasingly involves incentives and subsidies for actors to engage in particular lines of conduct. The symbolic base expands the least because much of this base is passed to the legal system that, in turn, provides the symbols legitimating the rights of leaders to make binding decisions.

Democratization of polity has the ironical consequence of consolidating more power in the administrative and material incentive bases. As various interests gain access to leaders, or force leaders to be responsive to their interests, each interest group makes demands on polity to respond with incentives or administrative structures to deal with their concerns. And, the more open the democracy, the greater are these pressures to expand centers of power. In a very real sense, then, democracy creates bureaucracy in industrial and post-industrial societies.

Balances of Power   Governments rarely achieve stable balances among the four bases of power—symbolic, coercive, material, or administrative. As holders of any one base seek to extend their influence, the bases of power often come into conflict. For example, those who hold material wealth are rarely willing to give this control of the material riches of the population over to the state; those who control coercion are often frustrated by what they perceive as the incompetence of the administrative wing of the state; those who control important symbols, such as religious leaders, typically resist state's efforts to develop alternative symbols; and those who run the administrative apparatus fear the coercive branch of the state, while seeking the material resources of others to sustain their operations and the systems of symbols to legitimate these operations. The history of all societies, therefore, has been littered with the debris left over from the conflicts among those holding differing bases of power.

Still, without some balance, even if somewhat distorted, polity cannot function; and as a consequence, disintegration of a population can follow. Users of power recognize, at least implicitly, that they must control all bases if they are to lead effectively; and so, many of the dynamics of power revolve around contests among those from one base trying to dominate the others. The controllers of religious symbols sometimes win, as was the case in Iran in 1979; at other times it is the forces of coercion who win, as is evident for virtually any nation experiencing a coup d'etat; more infrequently, holders of material wealth win, as was the case with the "Merchant of Venice"; and generally in the long run, it is the civil administrators who come to dominate the state, at least in its day-to-day operations. In fact, the long run of human history is a documentary on how power has become ever more concentrated and centralized in the administrative base, which has then sought to maintain some pattern of accommodation to the other bases of power that are not directly under its control.

Industrialization and especially post-industrialization generally shift the configuration of power toward the administrative and material incentive bases. These are the bases that can regulate complex activities and markets, whereas coercion will work against complexity and free markets. And, with the symbolic base lodged in the postulates of the legal system, this base resides, to some degree, outside of polity proper. Yet, high levels of inequality or other internal threats and external threats can dramatically raise the coercive and administrative bases as leaders mobilize resources. But in general, the volume of activity and the diversity of actors involved biases consolidation toward the administrative-material incentive end, with only episodic and tactical use of coercion and with key symbols residing in legal postulates.

Consolidation and Centralization of Power   As power is consolidated, pressures emerge for its centralization because, as actors holding different bases compete, the winners come to control the losers. Thus, built into the very process of consolidating power is its centralization, whether as a headman or an elected prime minister. Centralization of power, however, presents problems in maintaining balance among the bases. If symbolic leaders hold the most power, then the centers of controlling coercion, administration, and material incentives will be distorted by the need for symbolic orthodoxy. If the coercive base wins, then all other bases will be directed toward facilitating coercive repression. If controllers of material wealth dominate, then the other bases will be used to augment and further concentrate material wealth. And, if the administrative base overly dominates, then a dreary world of bureaucratic administration of everything emerges. But we should note that this last scenario seems more stable and, hence, less volatile and out of balance; and it is for this reason that selection has favored the administrative base, tempered by and integrated with the other bases (Weber [1922] 1978). Indeed, the great accomplishment of democratic forms of government in industrial and post-industrial societies has been the particular blending of the bases of power: (1) the effective use of administrative structures, whose ultimate leaders are elected, to monitor and control the coercive base; (2) the secularization of symbols legitimating the administrative and coercive components of government and, at the same time, restricting the use of coercion (Weil 1989); and (3) the sharing of control of material resources and incentives between the state and actors outside the state.

There is, however, considerable variation in the centralization of power in industrial and post-industrial societies. Many industrializing societies reveal highly centralized and often authoritarian polities that tightly regulate activities with a combination of administrative and coercive bases. This profile of regulation increases with either internal or external threats. Another source of variation comes from the symbols legitimating power. Some societies like the United States with powerful symbols emphasizing freedom from governmental control will be less centralized than other societies like France and Germany with cultural symbols emphasizing the expansive functions of government.

Production, Distribution, and Power As noted earlier, increased production and market distribution create wealth that can be used to sustain the polity, but aside from this enabling capacity, production and distribution increase the values for regulation as a social force and, thereby, activate selection pressures for the expansion of the state. The basic dilemma of the state is how to tax surplus wealth in a way that mitigates against the hostility of those who must pay and, at the same time, how to use these taxed resources to address the problems of coordination and control generated by increased production and market activity. Rarely has this dilemma been resolved without generating conflict, but it has been the basic problem that all polities have had to manage, or face the disintegrative consequences. Centers of power in agrarian societies simply taxed their populations to the point where the privilege of other elites was threatened and indirectly, to the point where the well-being of peasants who depended on the resources of these elites was undermined. In agrarian systems without a large commercial class, the resulting conflict was typically intraclass, with elites fighting each other for resources and privilege and with peasants "revolting" in efforts to restore the old order where they at least had some security. With commercialization of the agrarian economy, however, the conflict became increasingly interclass, as the commercial class's wealth posed threats to traditional landed elites. Moreover, in order to meet their tax obligations as well as their needs for privilege, elites began to impose on peasants more profit-oriented practices, such as higher rents, demands for larger shares of harvest, and even displacement from estates (Lenski 1966; Nolan and Lenski 2001; Kautsky 1982; Goldstone 1990). Industrial and post-industrial polities have taxed and redistributed wealth in ways that have reduced interclass hostilities and allowed for government to address the problems of coordinating productive and market processes in ways that encourage economic innovation and growth (Turner 1995). Yet, there is considerable variation among industrial and post-industrial societies in taxation rates and in redistribution. In the United States, for example, much subsidy to actors comes through the tax system in which taxes are not collected because of loopholes and other features of the tax codes that individuals and corporate units use to avoid paying taxes. In contrast, most European societies actually collect taxes and then selectively redistribute the revenue. These differences reflect, to some extent, the symbols legitimating polity: In the United States, beliefs about "the government that governs least is best" lead polity to hide subsidies in tax codes, whereas in Europe, beliefs generally emphasize the activist role that government should take in managing a society, thereby encouraging higher tax rates and more extensive use of directly-administered material incentives.

Inequality, Stratification, and Power   When power is consolidated and concentrated, inequalities increase (Lenski 1966; Moore 1977), for power is not only a resource in itself; it can be used to extract the resources of others. Those who can coerce, symbolically control, materially manipulate, or administratively dictate are all in a position to increase their resources at the expense of others. Those who come out in the short end of these power dynamics are rarely content; indeed, they are almost always hostile and, hence, are a potential source of internal threat.

This existence of hostility and internal threat typically has had the ironical consequence of mobilizing additional power to control the threat that, in turn, leads to more inequality, internal threat, and concentration of power to manage the escalated threat (Turner 1995, 1984). If this cycle is continually ratcheted up, a society can fall apart as hostilities build to the point of open revolt, as was chronic in agrarian societies (McCarthy and Zald 1977; Tilly 1978; Davies 1962). The constant peasant revolts, coupled with periodic rebellion by some nobility, of agrarian societies, especially those with a growing commercial class, were a good indication that these highly stratified societies were at the high end of this cycle (Goldstone 1990; Tilly 1990), whereas the comparative stability of advanced industrial and post-industrial societies indicates that they have found a way, at least for the present, to keep this cycle somewhat in check.

With industrialization come efforts at redistribution of wealth through the activities of the state (Lenski 1966). Thus, if the power of the state can be used to extract resources from the more privileged segments of the society and, then, redistribute these resources in the form of education, health care, welfare, and other benefit programs for the masses, then the tension associated with inequality can be mitigated. Much as the headman in a simple horticultural society had to redistribute most of what he took from others, so the modern state must redistribute to sustain its legitimacy and viability. But still, inequality persists in these more developed societies; and hence, power remains concentrated to manage the hostility that is inevitably generated by such inequality. This management can take many forms—administrative cooptation through social programs (e.g., welfare, medical care), ideological manipulation (e.g., nationalism, or scapegoating of particular sectors of the society), material buy-outs (e.g., subsidies, tax credits, special tax rates), or strategic coercion (e.g., selective enforcement of laws, massive mobilization of armed forces at "flash points" of conflict). No matter what the profile or configuration among these forms, power is more concentrated as a consequence. Power and internal threats arising from inequality are, therefore, inevitably interrelated.

Geopolitics, Geoeconomics, and Power When distinct populations or societies come into conflict, the values for regulation as a social force escalate dramatically, setting into motion selection pressures to centralize power so as to mobilize and organize resources to deal with the conflict (Webster 1975). Whether this centralization has involved giving power to a Big Man in a settled hunting and gathering population, clarifying descent and authority rules among lineages of horticulturalists, or creating an army of mass destruction, external conflict with other populations will always concentrate power. Even less severe forms of conflict, such as economic competition, will consolidate and centralize power to manage more effectively the competition.

And once power is concentrated to confront conflict, its symbolic legitimacy becomes more dependent upon being successful in the conflict (Weber [1922] 1978). Political leaders have thus faced an interesting dilemma: they could gain power through external conflict and through creating a sense of external threat, but they would set themselves up for an erosion of their symbolic base of power if they were to "lose" in the external confrontation. When centers of power are seen by the population, or some of its strategic segments, to "lose," then other bases of power—coercion, administration, or material manipulation of incentives—often must be mobilized to compensate for symbolic delegitim-ization, thereby setting into motion the conflict-producing cycles of inequality and internal threat discussed earlier. Thus, as Skocpol (1979) observed for agrarian societies, revolutions were more likely to occur in agrarian societies *after* the loss of a war in the geopolitical arena.

Industrial and post-industrial polities are not immune to these forces, but democracy mitigates against the disintegrative effects of geopolitics. The existence of more democratic profiles can help leaders deflect some of the negative sentiments for a lack of success in war or economic competition to those who elected them, or alternatively, if they are blamed, then democratic elections will allow the population to replace their leaders, thus making it less likely to engage in revolt. Yet, geopolitical problems do not disappear with post-industrialization, nor do threats from inequality. Local and regional wars often pull democratic polities into geopolitics, and leaders are vulnerable to popular sentiments about their effectiveness (e.g., the Vietnam War, or the "war" against terrorism). Moreover, all industrial and post-industrial societies are part of a geoeconomic system; and perceived success in this arena affects the legitimacy of government in general and leaders in particular. Still, with the capacity to elect new leaders in democratic systems, geopolitics and geoeconomics need not lead to a revolt against the structure of polity, per se, but only a dissatisfaction with particular leaders who can be turned out of office.

Democratization of Polity   It appears that the process whereby decision-makers are selected has become more democratized, although this is, at best, a very uneven and variable trend in the world's societies. Internal conflict and threats and external geopolitical threats—whether real or manufactured by elites—are often a reason for suspending democratic processes. But it is nonetheless clear that all post-industrial societies are comparatively democratic, and many industrial and industrializing societies are beginning to move in this direction, but again at a highly variable and episodic pace.

Before examining why democratization of polity occurs, we should define some of its essential features: (1) the rights of citizens to vote for key decision-makers in free elections, (2) the existence of parties who place candidates and policies before voters, (3) a distinctive arena of "politics" in which issues are debated and in which parties and individuals supporting candidates are willing to confine their disagreements and conflicts to this political arena, and (4) a willingness by all participants in the arena of politics to abide by the results of elections. These features of democracy, however, depend upon a delicate balance among the bases of power.

At the symbolic level, government must enjoy a diffuse legitimacy in the eyes of the population—that is, a legitimacy that transcends specific issues and disagreements about government's actions (Turner 1995; Weil 1989). This diffuse legitimacy needs to be based upon secular idea systems—nationalism, constitutional principles, historical traditions—rather than religious beliefs, which can arouse intense and uncompromising orientations. With diffuse, secular legitimacy, government is not held accountable for each and every action with which segments of a population may disagree. Without this reserve of legitimacy, each decision or action by government can become a potential stimulus to de-legitimization.

In terms of coercive bases of power, force must only be periodically used, for if each decision by leaders must actively mobilize coercion, or threat of coercion, resentments soon accumulate to the point that de-legitimization will occur. To paraphrase Edmund Burke, "no nation is ruled which must be perpetually conquered."

The use of material incentives by government must be viewed in a general sense as "fair" (whether this is actually so is less relevant than the perception of fairness). Specific uses of material incentives can be viewed as unfair and as debatable points in the arena of politics, but overall, the public must see government use of material incentives as basically and fundamentally "fair." Taxing policies, redistribution, and subsidies must also be perceived as in the national interest. Without these perceptions, the use of incentives becomes, itself, a source of resentment that undermines the symbolic base of power and often prompts the overuse of the coercive base of power by polity to compensate for its loss of legitimacy—a tactic that only inflames resentments.

Finally, the administration of decisions must not be seen as a spoils and patronage system; instead, the public must perceive that, whatever the merits of specific administrative programs, these programs are designed for the good of the society as a whole. It is when the public perceives administration as corrupt and as a source of privilege for elites that this base of power becomes a source of resentment. Even if administration is seen as inefficient or as implementing flawed policies, it generates less resentment because these issues can become points of debate in the arena of politics. But if administration is seen as yet another source of inequality, resentments dramatically escalate.

Maintaining this broad profile among the bases of power as they support and sustain the features of democracy listed earlier is difficult, and especially so when internal inequalities or external enemies create perceptions of threat that distort the balance toward a coercive-administrative profile of power. For once coercion is overused, it bends administrative processes to its ends and, thereby, begins to limit the rights of citizens as voters, the activities of opposition parties, the integrity of a separate arena of politics, and the willingness of participants in politics to abide by the results of elections or to even allow elections to express the preferences of the public. Democracy is thus a most delicate political dynamic—one that, since humans left hunting and gathering, has only recently re-emerged in the institutional order.

The End of History?

Recently, a kind of "end of history" argument has been proposed, arguing that a long-run convergence of the world's societies toward a post-industrial profile and democratic forms of government will somehow achieve a permanent and self-correcting balance among the bases of power. In this scenario, redistribution through the tax and subsidy programs of the welfare state mitigates against the resentments and internal threats that come from inequality as well as per-ceptions of injustice and corruption; and movement after the end of the Cold War toward resolution of external economic and political conflicts decreases the imbalances that come from external threats. Although the achievements of democratic forms of government have, in a relatively short span of human his-tory, been rather spectacular, it is not clear that these balances among the bases of power mark so much an end of history as merely a chapter in the evolution of human societies since hunting and gathering.

There are clearly forces at work that can make polity less benign: one is the fact that the use of power is *always* resented by some who become potential sources of conflict; still another is persisting inequalities that generate conflict; yet another force is the persistence of religious-ethnic symbols as bases for con-flict-group formation; and still another is points of geopolitical tension among societies in every part of the world that inevitably generate a less benign polity. Thus, the history of polity is not at an end. The dialectics that inhere in the consolidation and centralization of power into polity are still very active, as they have been throughout human history since horticulture.

LAW

Legal Systems in Industrial and Post-industrial Societies

The Body of Laws   Bodies of law in modern legal systems are extensive networks of local and national statutes, private and public codes, crimes and torts, common law precedents and politically enacted civil laws, and procedural and substantive rules. One of the most distinctive features of modern law is the proliferation of public and procedural laws, especially *administrative* law. With expansion and then bureaucratization of both the polity and legal subsystems, much law is designed to regulate and coordinate activity within and between bureaucracies as well as between individuals, on the one side, and governmen-tal and legal bureaucracies on the other. Another feature of law is the increasing proportion of civil to common law, for with the consolidation and centraliza-tion of power legislation becomes a more typical way of adjusting law to social conditions. Common law precedents from court decisions remain prevalent and actually increase even in systems with long histories of civil law; yet, as a codified system of law emerges, civil law as a proportion of all laws dominates over common law in all industrial or post-industrial societies.

As enacted laws come to dominate, the expanding body of laws constitutes a more well-defined system in which clear hierarchies of laws, from constitu-tional codes to regional and local codes, become evident.[5] There is some degree of consistency in these hierarchies of laws, although many ambiguities remain, especially in societies like England and the United States with long common law traditions, or in societies like Russia that were formed from empire-building and only partially incorporated local laws of conquered territories into a societywide legal system. As law develops a more consistent internal structure, it becomes more autonomous and differentiated from culture. Laws still preserve basic values and ideologies, thereby having many consequences for reconciling conflicts among cultural components, but the corpus of laws is more autonomous, possessing its own distinct logic. This autonomy is amplified as the practitioners of law—lawyers, judges, and police—become more professionalized, since professionalism inevitably generates its own norms, values, ideologies, and traditions that often deviate significantly from those of the broader society and culture.

Still, even as the details of laws become somewhat detached from culture, the broad legal postulates and associated civic culture of the legal system reflect the traditions, customs, and values of the population; and where they have not, as was the case in the aftermath of the Russian and Chinese revolutions, the polity purges dissidents and engages in massive resocialization and indoctrination of the population. As long as these broad postulates are considered legitimate, the laws will also be seen as legitimate, at least in the diffuse sense of legitimacy.

Indeed, as the complexity of laws increases, there is no option but to turn the specifics of law over to professionals trained in the law and to focus the public's attention on broad legal principles and precedents. However, when professionals in the legal system act in ways that generate disrespect from the public—a phenomenon that appears to be occurring for lawyers in the United States—there is a corresponding loss of respect for laws and, eventually, for the broad legal (constitutional) principles on which laws rest.

The underlying principles organizing a body of laws have an enormous influence on the nature of law as well as on how the legal system will operate. Four basic types of legal systems, evidencing distinctive types of laws, are often noted by legal scholars (see Vago 1994:10–13 for a summary). These are: (1) the Roman civil law system in which comprehensive laws are enacted by political bodies; (2) common legal systems based upon case law, relying upon precedents set by judges in deciding on a case; (3) socialist legal systems based upon socialist principles of (a) providing for people on the basis of their needs and (b) using the state to define, interpret, and provide for people's needs; and (4) Islamic or religious law where the sacred texts provide the basic guidelines for all laws, law-enactment, and court decisions. As noted above, civil law becomes ever more prominent in industrial systems, even those with long traditions of common law.

More interesting are socialist and Islamic systems. In the case of former socialist states, such as Russia, the body of laws was ill-suited for a market-driven, contract-oriented, and profit-making economic system. Profits as well as private property and private ownership of economic units were repressed for most of the twentieth century by the legal system in favor of collective owner-ship or, in reality, state ownership. Thus, the laws, as well as the principles of the civic culture imposed by heavy-handed indoctrination and enforced by Joseph Stalin's purges, were simply not designed to regularize market transac-tions or to redefine individual freedoms vis-à-vis the state. The result has been chaos, corruption, and violence in Russia in an effort to regularize actions and transactions in a new, market-oriented system. Indeed, the "Russian mafia" of illegal syndicates controls much of what occurs in market transactions, because without a viable body of laws, selection forces work to create order through the use of informal "laws" and "rules" of organized criminal syndicates.

The Islamic system of law poses fewer problems because the economies of these societies are not highly industrial, save for the extraction and export of oil. The religious nature of the laws will create problems for further modern-ization, however, since traditional sayings, acts, and proclamations, coupled with "the word of God" in the Koran, limit what can be legislated and what common law precedents can be set in the courts. Indeed, the nature of law is more reminiscent of simpler economic forms, such as horticulture and early agrarianism, than a modern commercial system. Still, this system has proven viable in coordinating activities and transactions in the Islamic world, although much of this viability is the result of the capacity of oil profits to insulate these populations from patterns of full-scale industrialization and internal market development that might clash with the restrictions of religious-based legal codes. And, in countries like Afghanistan that are not resource rich, Islamic law has worked against economic development.

Legislation of Laws   In industrial and post-industrial societies, legislative bodies within the political subsystem increase in size and power, becoming responsible for the vast majority of law enactment in the legal subsystem. Just how free the legislatures (or assemblies, congresses, parliaments, or equivalent bodies) are to enact law differs greatly from society to society, depending upon answers to such questions as the following (Turner 1972:238): (1) How estab-lished is the constitution of the legal system? The more established the consti-tution—as in the United States, but not in England—the more constraint on law enactment. (2) How many and how powerful are the higher courts of the legal system? Do they have the power to interpret the constitutionality of laws? To the extent that they do, constraint on legislators increases. (3) How exten-sive and effective are the enforcement agencies of the legal system? The more extensive and effective, the greater are the law-enacting powers of the legislature. (4) How extensive, professional, and integrated is the court system in a society? The more courts are an integrated and institutionalized mechanism for applying laws, the more effective law enactment can be. (5) How strong is custom and tradition in society? How much value and ideological consensus is there? The stronger custom and the more consensus over values and ideology, the greater is pressure on legislatures to enact laws not deviating too far from these cultural components and the associated civic culture. (6) How responsive to public opinion must the legislature be? Are legislatures elected in free elections? If they are, the more law enactment must reflect the fads and foibles of public opinion and sentiment. (7) And most importantly, how autonomous from rulers is the legislature? To the extent that power lies with a small number of elites, the greater is the political constraint on legislatures. All of these conditions affect the legislative processes in industrial and post-industrial societies, and by establishing the weights and relative influence of each factor, predictions about exact legislative structures and processes could be made for each particular legal system.

Despite all the potential variability, several overall generalizations about legislation in modern systems can be made: Legislation is not piecemeal but comprehensive; law enactment increasingly tends to cover large areas where disputes and integrative problems are evident (or at least perceived as problematic by legislators and political elites), thereby making bodies of civil laws a more prominent part of the legal system, even where—as in England—a long tradition of common law exists. Once legislative enactment becomes prominent, a more consistent and stable body of laws emerges; and although laws will always contradict and overlap each other in any legal system, comprehensive enactment tends to generate a discernible *system* of laws. And with the emergence of a stable legislature, comprehensive law enactment can become a mechanism of social change, establishing new structures and relationships, especially when effective court and enforcement systems exist to enforce the changes dictated by laws.

Courts and Adjudication   Modern courts reflect the complexity—and resulting regulatory problems—of industrial and post-industrial societies. With high degrees of differentiation, there are many more disputes and considerably higher rates of deviance than in traditional societies (Black 1976). By necessity, then, the courts come to have ever more consequences for mediating and mitigating conflicts, disputes, deviance, and other sources of malintegration, especially as kinship, community, and religion no longer exert the pervasive influence and control typical in pre-industrial societies.

The roles of court incumbents—for example, judge, lawyer, litigant, juror, and administrator—become more distinct and clearly differentiated from one another, and the positions of judge and lawyer become highly professionalized and, hence, licensed, sanctioned, and guided by professional organizations. As the volume of codified law in any particular area expands, court officials become specialists, dealing only in certain types of cases such as family, tax, bankruptcy, real estate, corporate, or criminal law. Since modern courts must handle a tremendous volume of cases, they reveal problems of coordinating; and as a consequence, administrative positions—clerks, bailiffs, stenographers, and public prosecutors—proliferate, specialize, and become heavily bureaucratized.

Just as the structure of courts becomes increasingly differentiated and specialized, so do the courts themselves, with particular courts—like their incumbents—often mediating only certain kinds of disputes. For example, in the United States courts can usually be distinguished in larger urban areas along at least domestic (family and divorce), criminal, and civil (or more accurately, torts) lines. Probably the distinctive feature of courts in industrial and post-industrial societies is that they constitute a clear-cut system of community, regional, and national mediation and adjudication structures. The jurisdiction of each court is better articulated (Parsons 1962), and the hierarchy of control is less ambiguous than in agrarian and early industrial legal systems. Cases unresolved in lower courts are argued in higher courts, with these courts having the power to reverse lower court decisions.

One of the serious problems facing modern courts is case overload. Courts cannot properly handle the volume of cases needing mediation and adjudication. One of the consequences of this fact is that litigants often settle out of court in order to avoid delays created by case overloads and backlogs. Such proceedings further the normative obligations on lawyers, who must negotiate for a client out of court as often as plead and argue a case inside the court. Another problem endemic to modern courts is a result of bureaucratization. Bureaucratization tends to make the process of adjudication somewhat invisible; within vast hierarchies of bureaucratic offices much hidden mediation occurs that is not carried out in accordance with procedural laws, or made public. Since modern legal systems usually attempt to implement some view of "justice," such proceedings can severely threaten this implementation. In fact, administrative bureaucracies are often judge and jury without many of the procedural (and professional) safeguards required within a courtroom. Yet, with extensive court backlogs, this kind of "administrative mediation" is perhaps necessary in modern legal systems.

Enforcement   The enforcement of laws and court decisions in modern legal systems is performed by a clearly differentiated and organized police force. In most industrial and post-industrial societies, there are several different kinds of enforcement agencies with separate and yet somewhat overlapping jurisdictions—typically, a trilevel system consisting of a community-based force, another district or regional force, and a national police force. Each police force possesses its own internal organization that becomes increasingly bureaucratized; and between forces there are relatively clear lines of communication, power, and control.

Police forces at all levels are heavily bureaucratized because of the volume and complexity of their functions in modern legal systems. Moreover, the police are guided by many procedural laws, especially those labeled administrative laws, that regulate and control the way in which enforcement can occur. But since police bureaucracies are large, they can hide many violations of these procedural laws; and because they can do so, the police can maintain considerable autonomy from laws, courts, and even the political bodies supposedly controlling their activities. These facts always pose the problem of unequal or arbitrary enforcement of laws, denying rights of due process (and all industrial and post-industrial systems, even totalitarian ones, articulate such rights), and concealment of illegal police action.

Enforcement of laws often is a more purely administrative process in industrial and post-industrial societies; and indeed, the administration of laws becomes as important as the coercive enforcement of laws, as is evidenced by the growing number of regulatory agencies in modern societies. In the United States, for example, agencies such as the Federal Communications Commission, Federal Trade Commission, Federal Reserve Board, Food and Drug Administration, Federal Aviation Agency, Environmental Protection Agency, and others oversee and regulate conformity to laws. These agencies cannot be considered a police force in the strict sense, but they do enforce laws—calling in police and courts if necessary. Much law enforcement in modern societies is of this kind: administrative agencies interpreting laws for various corporate actors, while constantly checking on these actors' degree of conformity to laws. The emergence and proliferation of these strictly administrative enforcement agencies continue the bureaucratization of law enforcement in the legal systems of advanced industrial and post-industrial societies. In a sense, administrative enforcement underscores the basic structural dilemma of all legal systems: the legislative and enforcement components are lodged primarily in the polity, which can come into conflict with more independent adjudicative (court) components of the legal system proper.

Trends in Legal System Evolution

Bureaucratization Because of intense selection pressures emanating from regulation as a macrodynamic force, the legal subsystem becomes large. Size

Table 7.5. Law in Modern Societies

	Industrial	Post-industrial
Body of Laws		
Substantive:	Written body of laws organized along one of four patterns: (a) civil law, (b) common law, (c) socialist law, (d) religious law. Each type has rules that denote crimes, specify relations between actors and the state, and mediate relations among actors. All systems reveal general legal postulates that reflect a mixture of cultural values and traditions of the masses and elites, as these have led to the articulation of a "civic culture"	Same as industrial, except that a combination of the "civic culture," broad legal postulates, and electoral political pressures exert more constraint on the body of substantive laws
Procedural:	Clear body of rules, specifying how all agents in the legal system are supposed to act as well as how disputants are to prepare and present cases in courts. Procedural laws, specifying rights and duties of all actors in the system, increasingly are used to guide the formulation of substantive laws	Same as industrial system, except that procedural laws are even more constraining on substantive laws
Legislation of Laws	Elected representatives at most levels of government enact new laws, although the degree of freedom and choice in "elections" varies. The nature of representative bodies differs, but often two elected bodies of legislators jointly enact laws. Except in civil law systems, court decisions also contribute to body of law	Same as industrial systems, except that elections are more likely to be free and, because of active and diverse political parties, to offer a wider range of choice among potential candidates

Table 7.5. (Continued)

	Industrial	Post-industrial
Courts		
Judge:	Increasing separation of position of judge from political offices, although judges are constrained by the state, and vice versa. Professionalization of judges in terms of education, experience, and competence, although in those systems where judges are elected (usually at local levels) both separation of judges from politics and professionalism decline. Depending on system of law, judges have autonomy and power, with most power given in common law systems, somewhat less in civil and social systems, and even less in religious systems	Same as industrial, except that judges are more autonomous from political or religious centers of power
Jury:	Juries of peers, judges, and experts become common, replacing juries dominated by elites. Councils of advisors and elites disappear as major court agent	Same as industrial
Lawyers:	Full professionalization of legal profession, with examination systems and sanctioning associations	Same as industrial
System of courts:	Clear hierarchy of courts, from local to regional to national; system of appeals up to supreme tribunal of judges. Clear differentiation of criminal, civil, administrative, and military courts (and at times, other courts, such as maritime courts)	Same as industrial
Bureaucratization of courts:	Full bureaucratization and professionalization of courts, involving use of educational credentials, examinations, and civil service systems for placement and promotion, although if judges are elected, professionalization suffers	Same as industrial
Enforcement of laws/court decisions	Differentiated by geographical jurisdiction (e.g., local, regional, state, nation) and by function (investigative, coercive, spying) at each level. Fully professionalized. Enforcement agents often become an active vested interest in the political arena	Same as industrial systems, except procedural laws are more likely to be invoked, often creating conflicts between enforcement agents and courts/legislatures imposing procedural constraints. Such conflicts often cause police, sheriffs, troopers, and other enforcement agents to become political lobbies

inevitably generates second-order logistical loads that are partially resolved through bureaucratization. Not only is there bureaucratization of courts, police forces, and various administrative or regulatory agencies, but similarly, as legislatures increase in size, they too become administrative hierarchies. One consequence of this trend is for each bureaucracy of a modern legal system—that is, courts, police, and legislatures—to achieve considerable autonomy from other elements because what occurs within each bureaucracy can be hidden. Such autonomy can protect and insulate the respective components of the legal system from excessive manipulation by either the public or political elite, but this autonomy from supervision and control also enables courts, police, and regulatory agencies to engage in de facto legislation—independently of the legislature and political elite. Within and behind the vast maze of bureaucratic offices in the courts, police, and regulatory agencies, differential and preferential enforcement, or lack of enforcement, of laws can be hidden—a trend that amounts to law enactment, since only some laws are enforced. For example, the common process of "copping a plea" in American courts violates the spirit of American procedural law, but by threatening delays, expense, and the risks of court trials, defendants can be pushed by court officials to plead guilty to a lesser charge. American police have been likely to treat violators of laws in an urban ghetto much differently than they do a white, middle-class violator of the same law in a suburban community. Thus, differential enforcement of laws across social classes and ethnic categories amounts to police enactment of new substantive and procedural laws (Black 1993, 1976).

Similar processes occur behind the administrative bureaucracies of other modern legal systems, and particularly so for those societies without a democratic political tradition and civic culture. While bureaucratization is inevitable and necessary for the reasonably smooth functioning of a legal system, it grants legal structure considerable autonomy, and in some cases, excessive license.

Professionalization   Specialized training, regulation by professional associations, and the utilization of expertise for the welfare of clients is an increasing trend in legal systems. Professionalism first emerged as courts become prominent and distinguishable elements; and by the Middle Ages in Europe, lawyers' behavior involved the roles of *agent* representing a client in court in various legal matters, *advocate* pleading a case before a judge and perhaps jury of peers, and *jurisconsultant* advising, teaching, consulting, and writing. The final criterion for professionalization is an active regulatory professional association, and in modern systems lawyers are usually regulated by such associations. Furthermore, because judges in most modern legal systems are lawyers, judges can be considered quasi professionals in all respects except the formal regulatory capacity of an association, and even here, judges are often part of voluntary associations that have influence but typically little direct power. However, much informal regulation can still occur through judges' contacts with periodicals and members of the legal profession.

Once the profession of law becomes established, legislators in law-enacting bodies tend to be drawn from the profession; and to the extent that this occurs, law-enacting structures become indirectly professionalized. This professionalization of law occurs for several reasons. (1) Modern legal systems are complex, with vast bodies of substantive and procedural laws, and such complexity necessitates considerable expertise and competence of court and legislative personnel, a necessity that can be best achieved through extensive professional education. (2) Professionalism also stabilizes law—giving it a tradition that is passed from one generation of professionals to another; and although laws constantly change, they are best altered by courts and legislatures in light of existing traditions and precedents, a necessity that, once again, can be achieved by expert training. (3) Since so much legal activity occurs outside courts and legislatures in administrative hierarchies, considerable knowledge and expertise are required to carry out administrative adjudication. As a consequence, professional staffing of the bureaucracies and professional counseling of individuals negotiating within the bureaucracy become requisites for the smooth functioning of a modern legal system.

In all industrial and post-industrial legal systems, then, legislative, court, and administrative structures always possess a high proportion of professional incumbents. The last element of the legal system to professionalize is the police, but as procedural laws begin to take hold, some professionalization of police forces occurs through training in specialized academies. Professionalization of the police probably increases its enforcement effectiveness, but for which client: the state or the police themselves? Since professional norms usually emphasize flexibility in the name of service for the client, it makes a great deal of difference just whom the police define as a client. If the client of the police is the state, then individual rights guaranteed under procedural law will be violated in service of this client, a fact best illustrated in most totalitarian societies where a highly professionalized police force views the state as its client. If the police themselves become their own client, as they develop collective bargaining agreements and associations in pushing their own agenda, the enforcement of law becomes biased toward the interests of the police.

Systematization and Centralization   Law in industrial and post-industrial societies is a *system*, indicating a high degree of interrelatedness among its component parts. A national system of codified laws setting general guidelines for state, regional, and local laws emerges; and while laws at each level display some autonomy from each other, they begin to approximate a reasonably consistent and coordinated body of rules. Courts also become systematized, with the jurisdictions of local, state, regional, and national courts becoming clearly delimited; and they begin to form an explicit hierarchy of control and decision making. Enforcement structures similarly evolve clear boundaries of jurisdiction with a clear hierarchy of power and control.

Much of the systematization of the legal system is a reflection of the consolidation and centralization of power. Until the exclusive use of force can be concentrated into a legitimate political structure, legal system development will remain somewhat disorganized at a national level. Nor can law become a system until clear legislative bodies emerge. Without a national legislature, law remains tied to the scattered common-law precedents of local and regional courts, the enactments of local legislatures, or the arbitrary dictates of local or regional centers of power. Once national legislative enactment of laws exists and once there is a centralized source of force to back such enactment, a comprehensive body of rules and courts to mediate them can develop. Conflicts, anachronisms, and gaps in the law can be remedied by enactment of civil codes and statutes. These comprehensive codes and statutes help standardize both the procedures and substance of court and police actions into a more integrated whole, and once mediation and enforcement agencies have a common set of procedural and substantive laws guiding their actions, consistency in enforcement and court processes across diverse regions can occur.

A major force promoting systematization and centralization of the legal system is the polity's use of law to effect social change. Law becomes the means for implementing the plans and programs of the polity. For example, in Russia after the communist revolution, legislative enactment drastically changed not only the structure of laws but the courts, police, and administrative agencies. These changes were deliberately made to effect alterations in conditions of production, transactions, and the nature of legal ownership and contract (Friedman 1959). Law also radically changed the kinship structure by making marriage more of a legal contract, by creating "on paper" egalitarianism among men and women in and out of the family (although in actual practice relations in Russia remained highly patriarchal), by removing much of the stigma of illegitimate children, and by the legislation of liberal abortion laws. Utilizing legislation this way necessitates centralizing police, courts, and administrative agencies because these must become integrated and centralized in order to enforce, administer, and mediate the new programs of the polity. To have courts, police, and other legal structures decentralized would make societal planning through legislation ineffective.

Systems without this capacity to centralize and coordinate their legal subsystems cannot implement planned social change through legislation. There are, however, many limitations on how much the legal system can be used as an agent of planned social change, including the following. (1) How much do changes deviate from custom, tradition, and deeply held values? The more deviations, the greater will be resistance to planned change through law enact-ment. (2) How drastic are the structural rearrangements demanded by new laws? The more drastic, the greater resistance will be. (3) In what structural areas are changes legislated? It is probably easier to legislate change in the eco-nomic and educational spheres than in either the familial or religious spheres where values, traditions, and emotions run deep. Finally, (4) how much force does the polity possess and how great is its capacity to apply that force? The more the polity has the sole possession of force and capacity to use it, the more it can overcome cultural and structural resistance to legislated changes.

These trends—bureaucratization, professionalization, and systematization along centralized lines—appear ubiquitous in industrial and post-industrial societies. Some legal systems such as those in continental Europe evidenced these trends early in their development because they adopted the Roman tradi-tion of civil law. In other systems, such as in England, the use of common law worked against these trends, at least for a while. Yet eventually as selection pressures for regulation mount, all legal systems will move toward a higher degree of bureaucratization, professionalization, systematization, and central-ization.

From very modest beginnings, law evolved into a complex system that regu-lates just about every facet of social life in post-industrial societies. Indeed, under intense selection pressures generated by regulation as a social force, law has become the principal integrative structure of a society that preserves, codi-fies, and translates key cultural symbols into specific rules defining what is devi-ant, while coordinating transactions among actors. Without law, each differentiated institutional complex in a modern society could not operate, nor could relations among institutional subsystems proceed smoothly. In the absence of law, then, a large and differentiated social structure is not viable; and if a specific legal system proves incapable of managing internal actions and relations within an institutional subsystem, as well as external relations among institutional subsystems, social structures and the cultural codes that guide them begin to disintegrate.

When institutions remain undifferentiated and simple, law is not needed most of the time, but as institutional growth and differentiation occur—that is, as economy, kinship, religion, polity, education, and newer institutional com-plexes like science and medicine separate from each other and begin to elabo-rate their structure and culture—law becomes ever more essential if a population is to remain organized. And add to these selection pressures those revolving around the inequalities that institutional growth and differentiation inevitably produce, and it is clear that law becomes ever more critical to main-taining order.

Of course, in maintaining order, law generates its own disintegrative pres-

sures. When law coordinates contracts that exploit others, when law legitimates an oppressive polity, when law differentially punishes criminals by social
class, when law selectively enacts or enforces laws in terms of ascriptive criteria,
such as gender and ethnicity, when law protects the privilege of elites, when
law sanctions an unfair system of taxation or is perceived to do so, then the
legal system may generate the seeds for its own destruction and the broader
society that it seeks to keep together.

In the end, law always fails because all known societies have collapsed, or
been weak enough to be conquered. But out of the rubble of a former society,
new institutional systems are built up; and as these institutional systems are
constructed, regulation as a social force generates selection pressures for law.
Thus, once again law becomes a means for societal integration, however problematic and temporary.

EDUCATION

Industrialization dramatically changes the educational process, not so much
because selection pressures emanating from reproduction generate demands for
new kinds of human capital (which can perform industrial activities without
formal education in schools) but more because the state seeks to consolidate its
symbolic base of power through instruction into a civic culture. Of course,
with advanced industrialism and post-industrialism, values for reproduction
and regulation push for expansion of education as an institutional system. The
correlation between universal literacy and schooling that exists for early industrializing societies, most of which are now post-industrial, has become translated into a worldwide ideology that economic development follows from
expansion of the education system. Hence, currently industrializing societies
seek to develop an educational system for economic reasons, whether or not
there is a real basis for this faith in education's power to generate economic
development (independently of technology, physical capital, and entrepreneurship). As the state takes over education, it initiates a number of dynamic trends
revolving around extending education to the mass of the population in the
name of increasing equality of opportunities and, at the same time, political
loyalty as well as economic development. As it does so, the entire educational
process is bureaucratized; and as bureaucratization occurs, grading, examining,
sorting, and tracking of students emerge as the means to "rationalize" assessment of students' performance. Credentials marking movement through the
educational hierarchy increase in salience as determinants of changes in labor
markets and status groups.

Table 7.6.   Education in Modern Societies

	Industrial	Post-industrial
Instruction	Learning now occurs in bureaucratized and hierarchical system of primary, secondary, and university-level schools (some private, but mostly state-sponsored). Nearly universal primary and secondary education. University-level instruction for a minority. Private tutors exist for specific skills, but decline as a base for instruction	Same as industrial, except university-level instruction reaches a larger proportion of secondary school graduates, but this is highly variable (ranging from 25% to 65% of secondary school graduates)
Curricula	Basic skills in reading, writing, and arithmetic. History and civil culture. Vocational skills in secondary schools for some, university-oriented curriculum in literature, mathematics, science, arts, history, and social sciences for others	Same as industrial, with increased emphasis on science, computer-based skills
Ritualized passage	Extensive and incessant system of grades and examinations, punctuated by periodic graduations and movements to educational tracks	Same as industrial, except that there are efforts to mitigate against the discriminatory effects on the disadvantaged of grading, testing, and tracking systems. Also, increased efforts to provide disadvantaged with cultural and financial resources necessary to compete in school hierarchy

Massification

By almost any measure—years of schooling, proportion of population completing primary and secondary schools—education now reaches a greater percentage of all the world's populations. In 1950, about 60 percent of the young enrolled in primary schools, a figure that was an average between the near 100 percent figure for industrial and post-industrial societies and the 44 percent for the poor, still–industrializing societies of the Third and Fourth World. By 1975, this average had climbed to 86 percent (Ramirez and Boli 1987:152) and by the year 2002 it was over 93 percent (UNESCO 2002). Secondary education (junior high school and high school) showed a similar increase, from around

11 percent in 1950 to 41 percent in 1975, and well over 50 percent in the first decade of the twenty-first century. Even college-level education expanded, although more of this increase occurred among industrial and post-industrial societies than those still industrializing. Indeed, in societies like the United States and Canada, over 60 percent of secondary school graduates at least begin college (for most other post-industrial societies the percentage is between 20 percent to 35 percent).

This dramatic extension of education has occurred for two basic reasons: (1) the world-level ideology uncritically accepted by most political regimes that the education of human capital is a key to economic development, and (2) the desire of political regimes to socialize the young into a legitimating civic culture (Braungart and Braungart 1994). Thus, the massification of education is a political process, one initiated and financed by government (Meyer, Ramirez, and Soysal 1992).

This massification of education presents a number of dynamic dilemmas. First, it may not be possible for other elements of the economy (technology, physical capital, and entrepreneurship) to keep pace with the education of human capital, which may become overeducated for the economic positions available in the labor market. The result can be an educated, restive, and resentful subpopulation who blames the state for its plight. Second, education tends to enhance critical thinking, especially higher education, in ways that can be directed at the polity, especially if the polity is perceived to violate the ideals of the civic culture learned in schools. These two dilemmas can become volatile when combined; and thus, massification of education rarely resolves either the economic or political problems of industrializing nations; indeed, massification can aggravate them. In fact, authoritarian leaders in industrializing societies have often reduced funding for schools, fired teachers, and closed universities because these are seen as threats to traditional elites. In South America, for example, military regimes of the mid-twentieth century were most likely to work against massification—although as these regimes have given way to more democratic forms of government in recent decades, massification has resumed (Brint 1996; Hanson 1995; Levy 1986).

Equalization

Accompanying the massification of education is typically an ideology of equalization in which the schools are to give all future citizens rights to achieve their aspirations in a fair and open process. Old patterns of ascription and inequality are now to be eliminated as performance in schools is to determine how one will fare in the labor market and, ultimately, in status group membership. The problem with this ideology is that it can never be realized in practice because

(1) students bring to schools varying advantages and disadvantages associated with family socialization and family resources, (2) schools themselves always vary in terms of the resources that they can provide students, and (3) older patterns of ascription (by gender, ethnicity, region, and class) are not eliminated in schools.

This difficulty of realizing in practice what is preached in educational and political ideologies can be a volatile force in a society because individuals' rising aspirations must confront the reality of an uneven playing field, a confrontation that can disproportionately escalate people's sense of deprivation and make them willing subjects in mobilizations against polity. Indeed, education can become yet another way of sustaining older patterns of inequality; for as educational credentials become tickets to entrance into occupations and status groups, those without the ticket become resentful. Such was especially likely when education was perceived by lower class and status group members as a way to be economically and socially mobile.

Evaluating, Sorting, and Tracking

All educational systems today engage in systematic processes of (1) evaluating the performance of students (through grades, teacher assessments, and standardized examinations) and, then (2) sorting students into different tracks of education leading them into varying niches in the labor market. There is, however, a great deal of variability in how and when sorting and tracking occur.

In older societies with a long agrarian history where secondary and university education were for the hereditary aristocracy and the upper bourgeoisie, with some sponsorship of exceptional lower class students in secondary schools and universities (R. Turner 1960), the evaluation and tracking of students toward either vocational careers or university-level studies occur early. In societies with a less entrenched aristocracy, whether because of its displacement through conflict or because of the newness of the society itself, testing and sorting come later in a student's career. Among post-industrial societies, Germany and the United States are at the extreme poles of these differences (Brint 1996). Germany tracks students into different schools early, whereas the United States does so very late; and even if American students are tracked into vocational programs, they can still enter a college or university. Other post-industrial societies, such as Japan, Sweden, France, Italy, Canada, and Australia fall between these poles, with most moving toward the American pole, although both Sweden and England remain like Germany in severely limiting college enrollments.

Less developed societies send far fewer students to universities, primarily because of comparatively low secondary enrollments and, also, because of the relative scarcity of universities. Sorting occurs early, sometimes by default as poorer students drop out of school after their primary education is complete and at other times as a result of examinations in which they are at a disadvantage when competing with sons and daughters of higher social classes.

Even in the most open systems, such as that in the United States, Canada, and the other English-speaking democracies outside of England, the grading, sorting, and tracking processes tend to follow class boundaries because people of higher classes have the cultural capital and financial resources to sponsor their children in school. Still, in most post-modern societies, there are efforts to implement compensatory education—special classes, scholarships, and other mechanisms for helping children from less advantaged environments—but these still must overcome serious obstacles stemming from the lower cultural capital of parents and early socialization by family and peers.

Because educational credentials become ever more critical to placement in an occupation and to gaining access into status groups, political pressures for making the system more open and fair always exist. But just how this political pressure changes tracking varies enormously. In Sweden, for example, these pressures led to intense efforts for finding talented students from lower class backgrounds early in their school careers and, then, helping them pursue a university-oriented secondary career, but the percentage of all students actually entering college still has remained rather low in Sweden. In England, the exam system was modified and pushed back in a student's career, and the "red brick" university system was expanded (that is, those universities besides Oxford, Cambridge, and perhaps the London School of Economics), but the rates of college entrance still remain much lower than most other post-industrial societies. And, in the United States, not only were the university and college systems dramatically expanded with the creation of land grant universities from the 1860s onward and with the emergence of community colleges in the second half of the twentieth century, but the testing and tracking systems were pushed back further in a student's career; and, moreover, the consequences of tests and grades on a student's ability to enter college were less determinative (except for elite universities). Moreover, government and universities in the United States established a wide variety of special loan, scholarship, and admission programs for students from disadvantaged backgrounds.

Credentialism and Credential Inflation

The demand to reduce the effects of early testing, sorting, and tracking on access to colleges and universities has had the ironical consequence of encouraging credentialism and credential inflation (Collins 1979; Dore 1976). In demanding access to credentials, the credentials themselves are given more credence and are viewed as accurate markers of ability by potential employers. As a result, alternative ways of assessing the abilities of workers are abandoned in favor of their educational credentials, as these are brought to a highly competitive job market. In turn, this credentialism has produced "standardized membership categories," such as high school graduate, college graduate, or post-graduate, which gloss over the wide variations in abilities and knowledge of individuals in these categories (Brint 1996). A more damaging effort has been to exclude from portions of labor markets those who do not have credentials that put them into a standardized category. Since it is the disadvantaged who are most likely to lack credentials, pressures by disadvantaged subpopulations to open access to credentials—which, in turn, help spawn credentialism—can backfire against those among the disadvantaged who fail to get these now mandatory credentials.

Another ironical consequence of political pressures for access to credentials is credential inflation. If virtually all members of a post-industrial society belong to a standardized membership category like "high school graduate" and if credentialism diminishes efforts to assess the wide variations in knowledge and talent of people in this category, the credential loses its value in the labor market, and students must now seek additional credentials, such as a "college degree," to distinguish themselves. If enough individuals get this new credential, however, it too loses value, forcing those who want to distinguish themselves in a labor market to seek even more educational credentials.

One effect of such credential inflation is that the disadvantaged are the least likely to have the resources to pursue additional credentials. Another effect is the overproduction of credentials and standardized categories like "college graduate," with the result that workers must seek jobs that do not require the skills associated with such credentials. Indeed, as more and more credentialed individuals must take jobs formerly held by those with fewer credentials, the latter are pushed out of these jobs, thereby deflating their credentials further. Since these displaced individuals are likely to be from lower and disadvantaged classes, credential inflation hurts them more than those who have the resources to stay in the credentials race. Yet another effect of credential inflation is to raise pressures for the credentials to be defined as entitlements, regardless of whether or not students have earned them. A high school degree is now a virtual certainty for any student who stays in school in post-industrial societies; and the grade inflation in universities of many societies like the United States makes getting a college degree considerably easier than previously.

Bureaucratization

Massification of education inevitably generates bureaucracy as a means to coordinate and control a large-scale activity. Equalization of education also generates bureaucracy as a means to implement, administer, and monitor programs that further equality of opportunity. As the state initiates both massification and the ideology of equalization, it furthers bureaucratization of the educational system, since states always seek to create bureaucratic structures to consolidate power and to regulate their institutional environment.

This last force is perhaps the most significant because when states have been centralized, they have extended their administrative base of power over other institutional spheres, especially those crucial to consolidating the other bases of power—symbolic, coercive, and material. Thus, when states have sought to impose a new civic culture, or revitalize an old one, they massify and bureaucratize the educational system. When they have needed committed military officers and mass conscript armies, as was the case in early eighteenth-century Japan, Denmark, and Prussia or early twentieth-century Russia, in order to expand their coercive base of power, they have massified and bureaucratized the school system (Collins 1977). When states have sought to provide material incentives as a base of power, they have often done so indirectly by providing educational opportunities that, in turn, will bring material payoffs to graduates.

Once bureaucratized, an educational system shifts toward grading, sorting, and tracking because bureaucracies are record-keeping structures. The goal is to rationalize instruction, keep records on performance, and promote on the basis of performance; and once this organizational form is imposed upon educational systems, grades, tests, required sequences, set time periods, and certification become prominent. Historically, this change occurred in advanced agrarian societies, like China, and agrarian societies such as Japan and the Roman Empire, once the state bureaucratized the educational systems (Collins 1977), although not to the degree of contemporary industrial and post-industrial societies because education was still oriented to elites. With industrialism and post-industrialism, however, the state massifies the system and, hence, extends the educational bureaucracy and the accompanying emphasis on grades, tests, sequences, and certification. And with these as organizational tools, sorting and tracking are inevitable, despite emerging political pressures to provide equalities of opportunities through delaying or weakening the criteria (grades and examinations) used to sort and track students.

Centralization

Educational systems vary enormously in the degree of centralization of the bureaucracy at the national level. Highly centralized systems, such as those in post-industrial France, Sweden, Japan, and most industrializing societies, will vary in how much they each spend as a whole on education, but within a given society, per-student expenditures will tend to be equal across the entire student population. In contrast, highly decentralized systems, like that in the United States where much financing and control are local, spend widely varying amounts on students. For example, affluent school districts in Texas spend as much as nine times more on students than poorer districts (Kozol 1991). Between these extremes are societies like Germany and Canada where education is centralized at regional levels (e.g., provinces, states); and in these systems expenditures on students are approximately the same within regions but can vary across regions.

Thus, the degree of centralization has important effects on the equality of expenditures for education. With the exception of the United States, where beliefs in local control of schools are intense, political pressures for equalizing expenditures on students and, presumably, equality of opportunities for students bring the state into financing schools. Once financing passes to the national level, so will administrative control over the purse strings. Centralization of educational systems is, therefore, a general tendency, unless powerful ideological pressures such as those revolving around ethnicity (such as the French-speaking in Quebec province of Canada) or politics (such as beliefs in so-called state's rights and local control in America) override efforts to pass financing and control of schools to the national governments.

Professionalization

School bureaucracies are complicated by the fact that instructors define themselves as professionals who have a higher obligation, above and beyond the bureaucratic mandates of the schools. As such there is often a tension between the professionalism of instructors and the bureaucratic demands of the school system to process and promote students in standardized ways. This tension is complicated because the clients of this profession and the school bureaucracy are nonadults, at least up to the college or university level, who do not directly purchase a school's and a teacher's services and who are not readily able to evaluate the competence of the services received. Furthermore, these clients are usually not in a position to take their business elsewhere. The end result is for the school to have a level of control over its clients that resembles a coercive bureaucracy, such as a prison, but this bureaucratic control is mitigated by and frequently in conflict with the professionalism of teachers. At the same time, teachers are often unionized, which makes them contract workers pulled toward the imperatives of a union bureaucracy as much as a profession.

This mix of conflicts is further confounded by the size of teaching as a profession, or as a unionized group of workers. For example, teaching is by far the largest profession in America, with some 4.4 million members; and if college instructors are added, the profession constitutes well over five million. As a

large interest group, teachers can exert considerable political power in democratic societies; and when teachers strike, they disrupt other institutional systems such as the family (which must reorganize its scheduling) and the polity
(which needs schools to push its political agendas). Yet, despite this potential
power, teachers rarely exert as much power as much smaller, high prestige professions like medicine and law, nor even as much as industrial unions. Part of
the reason is that professionalism and the helplessness of their clients make
teachers reluctant to strike as an industrial union would. Another part is that
the professional organizations of teachers are often not well organized as an
effective lobby in national politics, although in some countries such as the
United States teacher organizations have begun to exert a considerable influence on state and national politics. Still, the potential for mass political influence by teachers exists; and should it be mobilized, it could disrupt the state's
control of education.

Privatization

Through the agrarian era, virtually all schools were private, but as the state
began to finance education with industrialization, the proportion of private
schools declined, even in societies like Spain and France with a long tradition
of Catholic education. At the primary and secondary levels of education, societies rarely have over 10 percent of the student population in private schools.
At the higher educational level, societies vary in the number of private colleges
and universities. The United States has many, whereas Germany and most
European societies have virtually none; England and Japan have a few (in the
case of England, the separate colleges of Oxford and Cambridge are private,
but each of the universities as a whole is public); and in most developing
nations, universities are almost exclusively public.

For most of the world the historical trend has been toward government
financed and administered schools. Only in the United States does a large private sector of education exist; and it should not be surprising, therefore, that
advocacy for creating open competition between public and private schools is
intense (through such mechanisms as vouchers in which parents would be
given money to use in their school of choice, whether public or private). But
only in societies with intense ideological commitment to local control of
schools, or where religion is still a dominant force, will this long-term historical
trend away from government-controlled schools be challenged.

Although it was the last of the core institutions to differentiate as a distinctive
system, education is now at the center of the institutional order. In a sense,
education has forced its way into this order, pushing on and assuming functions
of other institutions. These institutions in the environment of education have

thus had to adjust and adapt to the spread of education, especially when this expansion has been backed by the state in its efforts to consolidate power. Even if schools become antiestablishment in their mission, they threaten the power of the state and bring state regulation into education. Thus, the institutional environment of education presents an interesting set of dynamics. Education has been pushed by the state; and as systems of education have grown, other institutional systems have all had to accommodate education.

CONCLUSION

With post-industrialization, all core institutions are clearly differentiated from each other. Other institutions like science and medicine are also differentiated, but the original core—economy, kinship, religion, polity, law, and education—are what allowed populations to adapt to their environments, both the external environment and the environment created by the growing complexity of society itself. These core institutions represent responses for the macrodynamic forces of production, reproduction, distribution, regulation, and population as they have exerted selection pressures, both Spencerian and Darwinian, on individual and collective actors. In this sense, then, institutions have evolved.

In previous chapters, I have moved into an analysis of key interchanges among institutions at this point, but since all of the institutions are now differentiated among post-industrial populations, I think it best to devote an entire chapter to these interchanges, exploring the reciprocal effects of institutions on each other in a more systematic way. Such an exercise can enable us to appreciate the extent to which institutions represent environments for each other and how they exert selection pressures on each other's culture and structure.

NOTES

1. This discussion on industrialization draws upon Turner (1972:30–42), R. Heilbroner (1985), Hilton (1976), H. Davis and Scase (1985), Chirot (1986), Beaud (1983), Kumar (1992), Smelser (1959), B. Turner (1990), and S. Sanderson (1995a, 1995b). The notion of *post-industrialization* is perhaps vague, but it is intended only as a rough distinction between early industrial and currently industrializing societies, on the one hand, and those where more than 50 percent of the workforce is employed in services, gross domestic product is very high, per capita incomes are high, and per capita use of energy is very high, on the other.

2. For a review of the literature on this issue—a more sympathetic one than presented here—see Szelenyi, Beckett, and King (1994). See also Nee (1989).

3. For a review of the sociology of markets, see Swedberg (1994). Also see on Swedberg (1994:272–74) an interesting typology on the social structure of markets. Another interesting typology on modes of exchange can be found in Sanderson (1995a:120). See also White (1988, 1981).

4. For a review of the various views of organizational structure, especially "post-bureaucratic" forms, see Nohria and Gulati (1994).

5. The approach taken in this chapter is functionalist, but with a conflict theory slant. I draw from my own work (Turner 1980, 1974, 1972); Fuchs and Turner (1991); and William M. Evan's (1990:222–23) theoretical model; also, elements of Black's (1993) theory. For reviews of theoretical approaches to the sociology of law, see Rich (1977), Selznick (1968), Reasons and Rich (1978), Vago (1994), Evan (1990, 1980, 1962), Chambliss (1976), and Black and Mileski (1973).

Chapter Eight

Fundamental Interchanges Among Institutions

THE EVOLUTION OF COMPLEXITY

Among hunter-gatherers, institutions were folded into kinship because selection pressures from macrodynamic forces were relatively low, save for production and reproduction. With only these two forces operating at higher valences, family and band were sufficient to sustain populations in their environments. When populations became sedentary, however, they also began to grow; and as a result, population as a macrodynamic force increased, thereby also raising the values of production, reproduction, regulation, and distribution which, in turn, set into motion selection pressures for more elaborate social structures and systems of cultural symbols. At this point in humans' long evolutionary history, distinctive institutions began to become visible inside and outside of kinship. Yet, most institutional activity was still performed within the elaborated kinship system of horticulturalists, because creating a more complex kinship system to house and organize economic, political, religious, legal, and educational activity was the easiest way to respond to selection pressures emanating from population, production, reproduction, regulation, and distribution.

Although kinship provided much of the organizational setting for other institutions among hunter-gatherers and early horticulturalists, new and differentiated economic structures, especially non-kin corporate units and markets, began to develop with advanced horticulture and agrarianism. As this development occurred, the economy was freed from the restrictions of kinship which, by its nature, is a conservative institution. Yet, for thousands of years, human populations could not get past the barriers imposed by economic organization in agrarian societies. By fits and starts, new technologies, new forms of physical capital, new skills among human capital, new entrepreneurial mechanisms, and new systems of property were slowly emerging, to be sure, but the vast inequalities in agrarian systems made them unstable. Societies would develop to a point of potential breakthrough to a new form of economic organization but, in the end, they would collapse back under the pressures of internal conflict and fiscal crises. Even evolving market structures that, by their very nature, are highly dynamic could not make the breakthrough to a new economic form. When this breakthrough finally came in western Europe, it forced all institutional systems to adapt to these changes, accelerating the process of institutional differentiation.

Along with economic activity within kinship, religion was one of humans' first institutional systems. Not all hunter-gatherer populations had strong beliefs about the sacred and supernatural, nor did they necessarily have cult structures organizing rituals directed at supernatural forces. But most did, at least in some incipient form; and by the time human populations settled down, religious activity was prominent in these sedentary societies. Although much of this religious activity was conducted within kinship structures, separate religious practitioners were also evident, even among hunter-gatherers and always among horticulturalists. Religion thus began to differentiate from kinship early in humans' long evolutionary history; and as it continued to do so through horticulture and agrarianism, religion increased in complexity, elaborating the cosmology of supernatural beings and forces and creating larger and more elaborate temples to house leaders of cult rituals. Then, with advancing agrarianism, a sudden simplification of religion began. The cosmology became more simplified, lay persons could participate more in religious rituals, hope for a life hereafter among the gods themselves became a possibility, and cult structures became organized for proselytizing new converts. These new religions spread over the world and are still with us today as the dominant religions, although older cult structures as well as new modern ones exist alongside the descendants of these agrarian religions.

As religion differentiated, however, it had to accommodate the expanding secular economy and the emergence of a distinct system of political power. The struggle with centers of secular power was long, typifying advanced horticulture and agrarian systems, but in the end under intense selection pressures emanating from regulation, polity has generally been able to segregate, at least to a degree, the sacred concerns of religion. Yet, even in the more modern world, this segregation is often overcome as religious movements exert political influence or, as was the case in parts of the Islamic world, take the reins of power. Thus, the long-term evolutionary trend was for religion to elaborate and gain power through the agrarian era, only to be pushed from the center of institutional order by secularizing forces in market-driven economies and by pressures mobilizing state power. Religion has nonetheless persisted as a dynamic institution, even in the most advanced post-industrial societies.

With expanded economic production, coupled with a growing population, regulation as a force caused selection to favor the development of polity. Concentrations of power were required to coordinate and regulate the larger social mass in ways that religion and kinship could not; and those populations that could not consolidate and concentrate power were selected out, falling apart from within or being conquered from without. At first, polity was housed in the elaborate kinship system of horticulturalists, but with agrarianism and even advanced horticulture a distinctive state system emerged, organized around an administrative bureaucracy and backed up by the mobilization of coercive power. Religion was at first the major source of legitimization for these new centers of power, but over time, law and a broader civic culture became an even more significant source of legitimization, except in the few remaining theocracies. With concentrations of power, inequality increased dramatically as those with power extracted the resources of others. And so, the regulatory force that generated selection pressures favoring the emergence of polity also increased inequality and, thereby, raised the values for regulation as a force. Once this cycle was initiated, it operated to expand polity until disintegration occurred. Power as a response to regulation as a force thus created disintegrative tension within human societies; and moreover, it was used to conquer other societies, thus increasing the values for regulation (coordination and control of conquered territories) and, hence, selection pressures for more power. With polity, then, came not just the capacity to coordinate and regulate, but also the ability to exploit and destroy. Over time with industrial and post-industrial production, the democracies of the early industrializing societies have mitigated against the disintegrative tendencies inherent in the concentration of power. Moreover, the now democratic polities of early industrializing societies have often served as a template for many of the late industrializing societies, although this path to democratization is hardly smooth or clear. But there are powerful economic processes, especially free markets and information systems operating at a world system level, that may force liberalization of power toward more democratic forms.

Much like other institutions, law was buried within kinship during hunting and gathering as well as early horticulture. But, even among hunter-gatherers, it is possible to see rules that were applied to problematic situations and that were enforced, if only by public opinion and threats of sanctioned revenge. These rules and their application represented the first signs of legal system differentiation from kinship. As problems of coordination and control, or regulation, escalated with population growth and as the values for production and distribution also increased with this growth, selection pressures pushed actors to develop a system of rules, adjudicative procedures, and enforcement capacities. As polity and religion evolved into more complex forms, law was typically affiliated with both, and only when polity became dominant over religion did law become clearly differentiated. Even then, however, law was often used as a tool by the powerful to sustain their privilege; and only when law could become more autonomous from polity, separating its adjudicative functions from centers of power and placing legislative and coercive functions under the review of courts, could it facilitate rapid differentiation of other institutional systems. Once a relatively autonomous legal system was in place, new rules and adjudicative procedures could respond to, as well as facilitate, institutional differentiation, elaboration, and coordination.

Among the institutions examined in this book, education was the last to differentiate. For most of human history, education was performed in kinship and, if it existed as a separate structure, it was confined mostly to elites. Only slowly did schools imparting secular content begin to reach the masses, although early religious movements such as the Protestant Reformation could accelerate the development of education. Societies were well into industrialism before polity created a national school system to promote indoctrination into a civic culture, to impart trade and interpersonal skills to human capital, and to develop and disseminate new technologies. Today, education is often viewed by political leaders in industrializing societies as the key to economic development and political stability, since it performs such critical functions for political legitimization and for developing human capital. As education has differentiated and elaborated, many reproductive activities—socialization and social placement, for example—have been taken from kinship by schools. Moreover, education has increased its effects on production as a source of human capital and technology as well as on polity as a source of symbolic power for political legitimization.

In sum, then, the long-term evolutionary history of humans has revolved around the differentiation of distinctive institutions from kinship—economy, polity, religion, law, and education—as the valences for population, production, distribution, reproduction, and regulation have escalated. Other institutions such as medicine and science are still in the process of differentiating, although it could be argued that they are now fully differentiated systems of the institutional order. The differentiation of institutional subsystems of this order presents problems of how to integrate these discrete subsystems. That is, how are the various institutions that have become distinctive systems to fit together? Over the long course of evolution, the relations among the systems of the institutional order have changed somewhat, as each new institution became differentiated and as some institutions, such as economy and polity, have become more dominant. Indeed, I have tried to document these shifting patterns of interrelations among institutions during societal evolution. Yet, beneath these shifting relationships are certain fundamental interchanges among institutional subsystems.

KEY DYNAMICS AMONG
SOCIAL INSTITUTIONS

In societies where the institutional order is fully differentiated, it becomes possible to see the basic nature of the connections among the separate institutions comprising this order. As long as institutions were fused with kinship or overlapping in their structure, the nature of the interchanges among them was obscured, but with some degree of separation between their structures, the consequences of institutions for each other become more readily apparent. These consequences constitute interchanges in the sense that each institution provides for the others certain resources on which their operation depends and, reciprocally, receives from these other institutions resources that shape its workings. In table 8.1 these interchanges are summarized in abbreviated form; this chapter elaborates upon the brief descriptions in table 8.1.

Economy and Polity

For much of human history, societies had economies but no polity because the values for regulation as a macrodynamic force were not as high as those for production. The consolidation and concentration of power were not possible, nor needed among small bands of hunter–gatherers. But, as problems of coordination and control escalated, selection favored the emergence of the polity or government as the force of regulation increased. From this point in human societal development, the relationship between economy and polity has been fundamental to the viability of a society. What, then, is the basic relationship between polity and economy?

At the most generic level, this relationship revolves around physical capital. A political system cannot become complex without a stable and sufficient economic surplus to support political leaders; and so, the productivity of the economy determines whether or not a polity can exist, and just how elaborate it can become. Without forms of liquid capital to finance political functionaries and to enforce decisions of leaders, a political system remains merged with kinship. At times, Big Men systems developed among settled hunter–gatherers but their leaders always confronted the problem of extracting surplus and then redistributing it in ways that maintained their prestige; and when the use of coercive force became necessary, they often called upon their kindred and

Table 8.1. Brief Summary of the Dynamic Interchanges Among Social Institutions

	Economy	Kinship	Religion	Polity	Law
Kinship	Kinship provides human capital for gathering, producing, and distributing Economy provides consumer goods and services necessary to sustain family members				
Religion	Religion provides mechanisms for alleviating economic insecurities, as well as reinforcement of economic norms Economy provides resources and opportunities for religious mobilization	Religion provides resources for alleviating family members' tensions, for reinforcing kin norms, and for marking status transitions of family members Kinship provides commitments to religious beliefs, opportunities to engage in religious rituals, and financial resources to support cult structures			
Polity	Polity regulates the level of physical capital available for gathering, producing, and distributing Economy provides physical capital, especially liquid capital, to support and sustain the polity	Polity allocates power and authority within kinship Kinship provides loyalty to polity, thereby consolidating the symbolic base of power	Polity provides conditional autonomy to religion to organize rituals in cult structures Religion provides contingent support to polity, especially for the consolidation of the symbolic base of power		
Law	Law provides external entrepreneurial services to coordinate gathering, producing, and distributing Economy generates problems of coordination that stimulate demand for law, while providing (via the polity) resources to sustain the legal system	Law provides external rules, as well as procedures for their adjudication and enforcement, that define and regulate family organization Kinship generates commitments to general tenets of the legal system	Law assures rights of cult structures, while specifying their obligations Religion provides moral premises of law, while ceding to law regulatory authority	Law provides contingent support for the consolidation of power, especially its symbolic base but other bases as well Polity generates demands for secular basis of legitimation, while providing resources to sustain the legal system	
Education	Education provides human capital for gathering, producing, and distributing Economy generates financial resources, directly and indirectly (through polity and kinship), to sustain education, while generating demand in labor markets for credentialed human capital	Education assumes some of the socialization and social placement functions of kinship, thereby altering kinship norms Kinship provides many of the financial and cultural resources for performance by students in school system	Educational system of polity determines curriculum requirements of religious schools Religion provides financial support for some schools, while ceding state-controlled system regulatory authority	Education generates loyalty to the civic cultural legitimating polity, thereby consolidating the symbolic base of power Polity creates and finances public education, while regulating private education	Education socializes commitments to, while providing training for incumbents in, the legal system Law provides rules for formation and operation of school systems, both public and private

related allies. Thus, even Big Men systems were not wholly differentiated from kinship, nor were they particularly stable because, in a sense, they were premature; the economy has not developed to the extent that it could support and sustain a distinct political system.

The invention of money—the most liquid form of capital—dramatically accelerated political development because now it was possible to pay administrative functionaries in the polity with a resource that could be used elsewhere. Moreover, an effective coercive force is best mobilized when its key members are paid professionals. Equally important, money becomes an ever more important basis for consolidating the symbolic base of power; if money retains its value, it becomes a symbol of the effectiveness of a political regime, whereas if money loses value or is unstable, its instability highlights the ineffectiveness of the political regime. Finally, without money, the amount of manipulation of material incentives is limited; true, a polity can grant lands, let out franchises, and bestow honor that can indirectly give elites material benefits, but without money, material manipulation is limited to land, favors, and honor which, although highly rewarding, are not as flexible as monetary material manipulation. Indeed, if nonmonetary incentives cannot ultimately bestow money on those receiving lands, franchises, and other favors, its effectiveness as a source of power is reduced. Thus, the capacity of the economy to generate physical capital, and most significantly, liquid physical capital like money, determines how the administrative, coercive, symbolic, and material incentive bases of power are mobilized.

Once a political system develops, its policies have effects on the level of physical capital available to the economy. These effects operate on a number of fronts. First, the taxation and appropriation policies of the polity determine how much liquid physical capital can be retained for reinvestment in gathering, production, and distribution. These policies operate directly and indirectly; taxation of productive output or the capital used to generate outputs, such as land in an agrarian system, directly reduces the amount of capital available for reinsertion back into the economy, whereas more indirectly, taxation policies influence incentives for innovation, capital investment, and entrepreneurial activity. When taxation policies create disincentives for hard work, for capital investment, for innovation, and for entrepreneurial creativity, they stagnate or even decrease gathering, producing, and distribution processes. Second, the expenditures of polity on infrastructural projects—roads, ports, canals, airports, information systems, and other projects—greatly influence the level of activity in the economy. If the appropriated monies are used in this way, rather than to support elite privilege and geopolitical adventurism, then taxation policies become strategies for capital reinvestment in accordance with the goals of the polity. However, infrastructural projects are often designed for defense and war-making, and under these conditions, they have a less dynamic effect on economic productivity, unless they facilitate conquest and plunder of capital from other societies. Third, geopolitical policies, from conquest to open trade, influence how much access to resources and markets in other societies is possible which, in turn, determines the level and profile of gathering, producing, and distributing processes. Relatedly, the boundary maintenance activities of polity beyond sustaining territorial integrity also determine the level and nature of capital, as is the case when government imposes protective tariffs, institutes export-import subsidies, and employs similar procedures for monitoring the flow of goods and services across borders.

Polity has a number of indirect effects on other economic elements, all of which ultimately influence the amount of physical capital available as private wealth or, more importantly, as sources for investment in gathering, producing, and distributing. With respect to property, it is the coercive arm of the polity—as it overlaps with the enforcement wing of the legal system—that sustains definitions of property. With respect to human capital, it is the investments of polity in education that can dramatically reshape the pool of human capital available to the economy. With regard to technology, taxation policies not only influence the incentives for technological innovation, but direct investments in research and science or subsidies through the tax code can have important effects on the amount and rate of technological development. Finally, with respect to entrepreneurial activity, polity is always involved in coordinating human and physical capital, technology, and property systems in an effort to increase productivity that it can then appropriate.

These additional effects do not, however, obviate the basic relationship between economy and polity. For in the end, it is physical capital that is being exchanged in the many transactions of economic and political actors. The productivity of the economy, particularly its capacity to generate liquid capital, determines the size and shape of polity, whereas the policies of polity affect how much physical capital is available for gathering, producing, and distributing processes.

Economy and Kinship

Until the economy fully differentiates from kinship during agrarianism, kinship remains the primary entrepreneurial structure for organizing technology, human and physical capital, and property rights. As differentiation between economy and kinship occurs, however, the more basic and fundamental relationship between these institutional systems is exposed. This relationship involves the exchange of human capital from kinship in return for consumer goods and services from the economy (Parsons and Smelser 1956).

In simple economies the provision of human capital to the economy also involves the technological knowledge that individuals have learned, as well as the physical capital, such as tools and implements, that labor brings to the economy, the rights to property contained in kinship rules, and the entrepreneurial consequences of unilineal descent for organizing all of these elements of an economy. As other structures emerge to provide technology, to pool physical capital, and to organize economic activity, kinship retains its functions as the provider of human capital to the economy.

Socialization in kinship generates the commitments, interpersonal skills, and initial knowledge base for labor to be inserted directly into the economy, or more indirectly it supports and sustains the movement of the young through educational structures that, in turn, impart much of the skill and knowledge (or at least the credentials) necessary for participation in the economy. Whether directly or indirectly through its effects on school performance, kinship is nonetheless the key source of human capital. It is in kinship that future human capital is born; it is in kinship that early socialization establishes basic behavioral patterns; and it is in kinship that the resources and support necessary for school performance ultimately reside.

As kinship and economy differentiate, kinship is transformed from both a producing and consuming unit to one revolving primarily around consumption. It is the members of the family, and the family as a whole, who generate the demand for consumer goods and services. Much of this demand is direct, as when families purchase basic consumer goods or services in a market, but much of the demand is more indirect as goods and services are produced for other economic units that, in turn, provide families with basic consumer goods and services. Even when economy and kinship are not differentiated, this fundamental relationship between the two institutions is paramount. Economy would not even exist unless members of families required life-sustaining commodities; and so the initial selection for economic organization came from reproduction as a social force. As economy and kinship become more elaborated during horticulture, this fundamental connection becomes somewhat obscured as kinship served as the entrepreneurial basis for the economy, but the more the economy differentiated from kinship, the more apparent is this underlying relationship between the two institutions.

Economy and Education

Much like the kinship system, education provides human capital for the economy, and in societies where research is performed in universities, some technology as well. Reciprocally, the effects of economy on education tend to be somewhat indirect. One effect is via the polity; as productivity increases the amount of economic surplus, some of this surplus is used in industrializing and industrial systems to finance education, particularly as the polity seeks to generate a legitimating civic culture and to stimulate economic development. Another effect is through the labor market in more developed economies where educational credentials are used to sort and place human capital; such usage generates a market demand for the expansion of the educational system, generally through political pressures on polity to extend educational opportunities but also through direct purchases of education by consumers in both private and public education markets (creating consumer demands for education at all levels and in all forms).

The effects of education on economic development are somewhat ambiguous, but generally, investments in educating human capital do not pay off unless there is a corresponding investment by the private sector and government in physical capital, technology, and entrepreneurship. Thus, expansion of the educational system is driven by perceptions of the population and political leaders that the education of human capital will inevitably increase economic productivity. Indeed, the expansion of the educational system is as much driven by an ideology stressing the relationship between economic and educational development and by political necessity to meet the populace's demand for signs of new opportunities as by real labor market demand in the economy.

Yet, in the long run advanced industrial and post-industrial economic development cannot occur without formal education of human capital that can be coordinated with higher levels of technology and complex forms of physical capital. Moreover, as the scale and scope of education expand, the educational system becomes a major economic actor. For example, the combined income of those working within the educational establishment or those involved in building the physical structures of the educational system generates a tremendous demand for consumer goods and services which, in turn, stimulates the economy.

The basic relationship between economy and education is thus somewhat similar to that between family and economy. Education is a source of human capital for the economy; and the economy provides the resources via the polity to expand the educational system as well as many of the consumer goods and services necessary to build and maintain the educational infrastructure. And, as the labor market begins to utilize educational credentials for sorting and placing human capital and as both the general population and the government perceive that there is a relationship between education and economic growth as well as personal prosperity, the economy begins to generate a high demand for expanding the educational system.

Economy and Law

Law remained a recessive institution for much of humans' evolutionary history, although all societies have revealed rules that were subject to adjudication and enforcement. But law often emerged only in moments of crisis and conflict. Still, the effects of even these incipient legal systems on coordinating and regulating social relations were clear, even in very primitive form. With differentiation of the economy from kinship, and then its elaboration into a more complex and dynamic system, economy began to evidence severe problems of internal coordination and control, thereby raising the values of regulation as a macrodynamic force. Exchange in markets is perhaps the key dynamic, because once relatively free and open markets emerge, selection pressures are intense for new rules about exchange, new rules about property, new rules about the relationship between human capital and those who employ this capital, new rules about physical capital formation, and eventually, new rules about the rights to, and uses of, technology. Thus, the fundamental relationship between economy and law revolves around entrepreneurial problems inherent in economic differentiation and the capacity of law to provide an array of external entrepreneurial services to the economy.

Even when law and kinship rules overlap, the entrepreneurial consequences for the economy of implicit bodies of law (within kinship rules) are evident. These rules define property rights, specify what human capital is to do, indicate uses of physical capital, and regulate the application of technology. Such entrepreneurial functions became more explicit as market systems emerged, and as the economy began to differentiate from kinship. Once the rules of unilineal descent could no longer organize economic activity, intense selection pressure to create new rules ensued. Sometimes these rules could not be created, and conflict destroyed the economy or significant portions of the economy. At other times in history, informal and formal "merchant laws" have emerged as a way to regulate exchange and to sanction those who do not abide by the rules. Eventually, the developing polity becomes involved in regulating economic activity because, as emphasized above, the viability of the polity depends upon the productive outputs of the economy. This process of political intervention has rarely been smooth, but over time, polity has increasingly come to use the legal system as a tool for regularizing and coordinating relations in the economy.

Until an autonomous legal system is in place, however, economic development is inhibited because there is no coherent and consistent way to define property rights, uses of physical and human capital, or access to technologies. As markets become ever more dynamic, selection for this external force escalates under pressures from regulation. Through a series of crises—ranging, for example, from definitions of the rights of corporate actors through labor-management disputes and concerns over concentration of capital in oligopolies to concerns about the environment and genetic engineering—increasing values for regulation as a force place upon the legal system pressures to provide rules, adjudicative procedures and, if necessary, enforcement capacities to resolve and regularize these crises. Thus, inherent in a dynamic economy is a constant demand for external regulation by law; and despite conservative ideologies like those in the United States stressing free enterprise and laissez faire, the reality is that the economy generates ever new crises of entrepreneurship that cannot be managed by economic actors themselves.

As a result, the body of tort law in a society expands, the civil court system grows, and the legislative activities within polity or in separate administrative bodies accelerate. In societies without this capacity to use tort laws effectively in regulating a market-driven economy, such as in Russia in the first decade after the collapse of the Soviet Union, the economy often remains chaotic with regulation coming from corruption, threats, and coercive activities of criminal syndicates. There is, then, nothing inevitable about the evolution of law to meet these entrepreneurial demands of the economy; indeed, economies have often stagnated or fallen apart. Yet, because the economy is so vital to the viability of polity and the members of kinship units, pressures to develop and use laws come from these institutional sectors.

Polity and Law

As polity became differentiated from kinship, problems of consolidating power were more acute. For, without kinship rules to organize administrative tasks, to provide enforcement coalitions, to regulate the distribution of material incentives, and to legitimate the use of power with the symbols of kinship, all of these bases of power had to be rebuilt and reestablished. Rarely is this a smooth process, especially when polity competed with well-organized religious cult structures for power. Over time as values for regulation as a macrodynamic force increased, selection favored the polity creating, or usurping from religion or economic actors, a system of laws that would enable it to legitimate itself with secular symbols, that would provide broad rules by which to administer decisions and manipulate material incentives, and that would give the polity the right to use coercive power. Law thus emerged not only from economic demands for entrepreneurial resources, but also from escalating pressures from regulatory forces to consolidate the bases of power in order to control and coordinate activities in the broader society. Conversely, once law exists as a distinctive system, it could provide support for the legitimating, administrating, manipulating (material incentives), and coercing activities of the polity.

This support is, however, contingent, limiting the actions of the polity by rule and court decision; and should a government ignore the law, as has often been the case in the history of human societies, political regimes have undermined the law's all-important capacity to provide a symbolic basis of legitimization. Thus, the basic relationship between polity and law revolves around a legal system's capacity to provide contingent support for the consolidation and use of power and a polity's need for a system of rules, adjudicative procedures, and enforcement capacities that can facilitate this consolidation and use of power. In return, the legal system is supported by the polity and granted a degree of autonomy.

This basic exchange is complicated by the fact that the legal and political systems overlap. The legislative process of law-making resides primarily in the political system, as do many of the enforcement capacities of the legal system. This overlap often leads political leaders to use, in an arbitrary fashion, the legal system for their own narrow purposes; and to the extent that polity uses the legal system in this way, it becomes less effective as a resource in consolidating power for polity and as a mechanism of societywide integration and coordination. The law, in essence, simply becomes a cynically imposed tool for the use of power.

The key problem in the relationship between polity and law is thus one of how to create and sustain a relatively "autonomous" legal system at the very same time that the elements of the law remain partially lodged in polity. Historically, relatively few societies have ever been able to achieve a balanced interchange where an autonomous legal system could provide contingent support for polity in its consolidation and use of power, on the one side, and where the polity would provide resources for maintenance of a system that will limit how power is to be exercised, on the other side. The key event is for the polity to give up some of its power to the legal system in exchange for secular legitimating symbols and rules for guiding the use of power. Actors in government have rarely been willing to do so voluntarily, but demands from economic actors or rumblings from the discontent in a society have often forced the polity's hand.

Once the polity has given over some of its power, the legal system must, in return, provide the primary basis for legitimization of polity (often expressed in a constitution) as well as the flexibility to generate new rules for guiding the use of power as changing circumstances dictate. Law must become "positive law" in two senses (Luhmann 1985). First, the legal system must create procedural rules to regulate legislation, adjudication, and enforcement laws. If these procedural rules are accepted by members of the population, then they further legitimate polity and, at the same time, guide the implementation of political decisions. Second, the legal system must have the capacity to change laws as new demands for coordination in the society emerge, but such changes must be performed in accordance with procedural law. If laws become enshrined and too conservative, they lose the ability to coordinate flexibly social action, and eventually, rigid legal rules begin to erode the legitimacy of the polity. So, a positive legal system must have the capacity to legislate new rules, or alternatively, to adjudicate them from court decisions, if it is to be effective. These two conditions are, in historical reality, difficult to achieve; and only the political democracies of the contemporary world have come close to meeting these conditions.

As societies have differentiated, increasing valences for regulation have generated selection pressures for an autonomous and positive legal system to manage problems of coordination among diverse institutional subsystems and the many actors in these systems. For once the rules of kinship could no longer provide the basis of coordination and once the power of religion to dictate daily routines declined, an alternative source of coordination and controls was needed, if a society was to remain viable in its environment. The consolidation and centralization of power is the easiest route to developing this alternative source of control and coordination, but soon the abuse of power erodes its legitimacy and effectiveness in regulating social activity. As a result, legal systems expand, and in a few historical cases, they have become sufficiently autonomous to provide both legitimization of polity and the tools for the effective administration of power and enforcement of political decisions. In turn, because these legal systems are effective, the polity has been willing to provide the resources sustaining the system and, most importantly, to grant it a certain degree of autonomy.

Polity and Kinship

Among hunting and gathering bands, polity is hardly noticeable. Only with settled gatherers did clear leadership begin to emerge, typically in the form of a Big Man system. As polity became distinctive, and even when lodged in the kinship systems of horticulturalists, the basic exchange between polity and kinship emerged. Kinship produced political loyalty in exchange for the allocation of power and authority within kinship (Parsons and Smelser 1956).

As the principal agent of reproduction—indeed, for most of human history, the only agent—kinship imparts to the young basic values, beliefs, and commitments; and in this process of socialization, members of a society can acquire commitments to leaders, or at least to the broader system of consolidated power. In horticultural systems, where the descent and authority rules also determined the distribution of power, political commitments were the natural by-product of socialization and generally gave to senior kin the right to power. When there is a clear structural division between kin units and those holding power, however, the socialization of political loyalties is not so automatic. In fact, even among horticulturalists, feuds within clans and lineages or between them could make the socialization of loyalty problematic, but the problem became ever more evident with a clear differentiation between polity and kinship. As the consolidation and centralization of power are used to perpetuate vast inequalities, this problem of assuring political loyalty escalates; and under these conditions, kin socialization could not only fail to impart the appropriate loyalties, but actually work to produce the opposite. Revolutionaries are often raised in kin structures that are unsupportive of political regimes, and to the extent that socialization works against imparting political loyalties, it destroys the symbolic base of power so necessary for the consolidation of power.

It is this vulnerability of government to the erosion of its symbolic base of power that frequently brings its intrusion into the family system. There are, of course, limits as to how far polity can intervene in the private lives of family members, but at a minimum, the polity and legal system operate to define marriage and dissolution rules as well as the distribution of property among family members. In so doing, power and authority are also allocated to the family as a whole (as a legal corporate unit with rights, obligations, and responsibilities) and to its individual members. For example, for much of the agrarian era, wives in many societies could not own property, hold contracts, litigate in court, or exercise their political will (through voting and other means of political expression); and as a result, the polity and the legal system allocated power disproportionately to men. In more recent years, polity has extended the rights of women in the family, although these vary enormously even in political democracies (as a comparison of the industrial powers of the West and Asia would make clear), but nonetheless, as polity and law have redefined the rights of women, shifts in authority relations within the family have become possible.

The polity changes the allocation of power in the family for a simple reason: to accommodate potential shifts in political loyalties. If, for example, wives are politically restive or if members of lower-class families are dissatisfied, the potential for socializing disloyalty increases. Of course, even as socialization erodes the symbolic base of power, the other three bases can typically compensate—at least for a time until the pressures on the government to change the allocation of authority increase to the point where they overcome the other bases of power. Indeed, those who have power within kinship will often be supportive of the political system that supports their family authority, even at the cost of tension with other family members.

It is this dynamic and potentially problematic exchange of political loyalty for authority in kinship that often leads the polity in industrializing societies to expand the educational system as an alternative to exclusive reliance upon family socialization. Here, the goal is to impart a political culture to the young that reaffirms the symbolic base of power; and if family socialization supports the reaffirmation, then polity further consolidates its symbolic base of power. Alternatively, if family socialization contradicts educational socialization, then polity will have difficulty in legitimating itself in terms of a political culture.

Polity and Education

Political regimes have, historically, not encouraged the education of the masses, either because they could not afford it or, more typically, because they considered it a threat to the system of privilege and status group membership of elites. Indeed, up to the industrial era, most education was privately financed and acquired, with the vast majority of students coming from families of elites. When polity has become involved in education, it almost always is designed to create political loyalties and firm up its symbolic base of power. In return, as polity establishes a state-run bureaucratic system of schools, it reallocates authority among key socializing agents.

The use of education to create political loyalty is a complicated process in post-industrial, industrial, and industrializing societies. There is the obvious civics curriculum of schools that imparts the (distorted) history of the society, that requires classroom rituals (such as pledges to the flag) directed at affirming political loyalty, that creates historical heroes who symbolize the political culture, and that presents the rudiments of the legal system supporting the polity. Less directly, the polity uses the expansion of primary and secondary education to the masses (and eventually higher education as well) as a sign that economic opportunities are increasing. In this way, the polity also manipulates the material aspirations of the populace; in return, the government expects loyalty from citizens whose opportunities for a better life are increasing. If, however, people's aspirations are raised beyond the capacity of the economy to absorb and reward its increasingly educated population, then much of the effort of civics training by schools can be undone. Moreover, the literate population is now in position to receive and communicate written messages questioning the policies of the political regime.

Another less direct effect of polity on education comes from its capacity to employ in the state bureaucracy the educated labor pool; and it is no coincidence that governmental bureaucracies are often bloated as the state seeks to absorb its educated members and, in the process, co-opt them and make them loyal to the political system. Such employment practices often divert capital from the economy, and thereby act as a drag on productivity, although the purchasing power of state bureaucrats creates market demand which, in turn, stimulates production. In the end, despite the depletion of liquid capital involved, the state often has little choice but to employ its educated workforce in order to affirm that opportunities are increasing, especially when the economy cannot absorb a significant portion of credentialed human capital.

Thus, the polity's investment in education is often a high stakes game of diverting capital from the economy to education in an effort to increase political loyalties. In making this investment, polity is reallocating power and authority to agents of socialization. For, as education becomes compulsory and as opportunities for success are determined by educational credentials, some of the authority of parents and control of family over children is lost and reallocated to the schools. Education can thus become a threat to the traditional authority system of kinship, leading parents to pull their children out of school. In the long run, however, the growing use of educational credentials by employers in the economy overcomes the threats experienced by parents who also desire expanded opportunities for their children. Yet, until the economy can absorb a high proportion of the better educated population, the creation of the education system will not have dramatic effects on shifting power and authority from family to schools. And even when this shift occurs, schools do not supplant kinship; rather, children are typically subject to increased regulation by virtue of the interpersonal authority of the family and the bureaucratic authority of the schools. In creating a school system, the polity has reallocated authority to socializing agents who are more reliable than the kinship system in imparting political loyalty.

Law and Kinship

Kinship provided the template for much of the legal system through horticulture; the substance of laws as well as their adjudication and enforcement followed the rules of kinship and designated kin as judges and enforcers of rules. Still, even when heavily fused with the kinship system, elements of laws, adjudication, and enforcement were also evident outside the template of kinship. As kinship has become nucleated and law increasingly autonomous as an institutional system, the basic exchange between law and religion has become more evident. The legal system provides the rules, as well as their adjudication and enforcement, that define and control family organization. In exchange, family provides the socialization of commitments to the general tenets of the legal system. This interchange always existed, even when law and kinship overlapped, but the exchange has become more pronounced as kinship and law have become differentiated from each other. Moreover, as the influence of religion on the institutional order has declined, law has taken over many of the tasks formerly performed by religion. Furthermore, the polity has a clear interest in controlling the family as a source of political loyalty, and to realize this interest, governments have used the legal system to define and organize family and, in the process, have usurped many of the functions formerly performed by religion.

As the legal system has increased its regulatory consequences for the society as a whole, it has developed specific laws, courts, and enforcement procedures for regulating the basic functions of the family, such as sex, marriage, biological support, reproduction, dissolution, and social placement of the young. In many societies, separate bodies of laws and courts devoted exclusively to family processes have evolved, but whether or not such separate systems of family law have emerged, the legal system regulates family organization and activity by specifying rules about sex and premarital sex (often ignored and violated), marriage, dissolution, child care and support, child and spousal abuse, family authority (via gender-oriented laws), and child placement (via compulsory education laws and their consequences for acquiring credentials and jobs). And as rates of family dissolution, child and spousal abuse (or at least awareness of these), and out-of-wedlock childbirth have increased throughout the developed world, but especially in the West, the legal system has sought to intervene further into kin activities.

Intervention is possible because family socialization, as reinforced by school indoctrination, generally supports the rights of the legal system to regulate institutional activity. The broad philosophical tenets of the legal system, as well as a smattering of knowledge about substantive bodies of laws and courts, are learned in family interactions. Schools provide a more structured indoctrination into the civic culture that ultimately frames the legal system, but family socialization is crucial in reinforcing commitments to the legal system. As a consequence, with each new "crisis" of the modern family, legal intervention is either demanded (as is the case with child and spousal abuse) or at least tolerated, although highly contentious issues, such as rights to abortions, often undermine the legitimacy of the legal system (by those who view the law, whichever side it falls on, as "immoral"). This intervention, and even the controversy that the legal system can generate, only serve to highlight the exchange between law and family whereby law regulates and controls basic family processes and family provides diffuse commitments to the legal system.

Law and Education

Even before law was clearly differentiated from kinship, socialization of commitments to both the broad legal tenets and the specifics of law were essential; conversely, the process of socialization was assured by the rules of kinship. As law became increasingly differentiated and autonomous from kinship, the basic nature of this exchange remained the same, except now it was an exchange between two distinct institutional systems. Educational socialization in schools generates commitments to the broad civic culture framing the legal system, as well as some knowledge of key laws, court decisions, and enforcement precedents. Reciprocally, law regulates the formation and operation of school structures, both state-mandated and private.

Since law has become the basis for the consolidation of the symbolic base of power, the state has an active interest in assuring that members of the population are socialized into the tenets and procedures of the legal system. Thus, a large portion of the curriculum in both public and private schools is devoted to history and civics, as these have influenced, and been influenced by, the operation of the legal system. Moreover, as the law becomes complex, education is increasingly involved in the training of those who legislate, adjudicate, and enforce the law. Initially, much of this training was by apprenticeships to practitioners, but over time, formal credentials were increasingly required of many incumbents in the legal system. For example, those who advise legislators (as well as the legislators themselves) and those who are involved in adjudication (judges, attorneys, and barristers) generally require law degrees, and specialized training (often in state-run academies) is often required for those who enforce the law.

Law regulates the educational system by defining the obligations of public and private schools; and with industrialization and post-industrialization, law increasingly specifies the minimum years of schooling that all citizens must have. Moreover, as educational credentials become both the symbol and reality of economic opportunities, the legal system is often used by segments of the population to gain rights to educational opportunities. For example, in the United States, court decisions, legislative enactments, and presidential or executive orders have all been involved in increasing the access of minorities and other subpopulations who have been the victims of discrimination in education (as well as other institutional spheres). Indeed, as educational credentials become the defining criterion for opportunities, pressures on the legal system to guarantee these opportunities mount. The legal system thus moves beyond establishing minimal requirements; in post-industrial societies, it increasingly defines the rights of individuals in gaining access to all levels of the educational system.

Polity and Religion

Throughout much of humans' evolutionary history, political and religious leaders have overlapped; those who held political power were often religious elites. Yet, more typically, there was some differentiation of political and religious functions; and this division became more evident as societies increased in complexity. Indeed, advanced horticultural and agrarian societies generally experienced conflict and tension between religious and political elites, and their corresponding organizational systems; and in the end, the state-based polity won this contest, with some notable exceptions such as Iran after the revolution in 1979 or Afghanistan in the 1980s and 1990s before the American invasion in 2001 and 2002. Throughout evolutionary history, however, the basic exchange between polity and religion has remained fundamentally the same: religion provides contingent support to government, offering a symbolic basis of legitimization for the polity, whereas the polity provides religion with a certain autonomy to control nonsecular symbol systems and to organize the population in cult structures. In a few cases, such as the old Soviet Union's unsuccessful attempt to create an atheist society, the state has discouraged religion, but more typically, the state and religion have reached a compromise, with the state using some religious symbols for legitimization, and religion supporting such usage of its symbols in exchange for the right to organize ritual activities.

With a few exceptions such as the theocracy that emerged in Tibet and some societies of the Middle East, the exchange between polity and religion has evolved toward less reliance by the polity on the legitimating symbols of religion. Because religion can mobilize emotions and because of past war-making by religious organizations in many societies, the state has sought alternatives that it can more readily control. The development of a legal system is the most obvious of these alternatives, because such a system provides the polity with a secular basis of legitimization (again, except in a few societies with a religious legal system). States generally attempt to develop a civic culture that may include some religious symbols and mythologies, but which for the most part is secular, emphasizing the history, heroes, legal principles, and other secular matters that highlight the centrality of the state. In this process, religious beliefs can still provide a diffuse legitimacy, but more typically, religious symbols are restated in a more secular form so as to become integrated into the civic culture.

As religion becomes somewhat segregated from direct legitimization of the polity, the state still allows religious organizations some autonomy and often protects them through the legal system. In this way, religion is co-opted in supporting political regimes, although religious cults have often been actively involved in political movements (as was the case in America with the civil rights movement in the 1960s or with the current political mobilization of Conservative Protestant cults into the "Christian Coalition"). Religious activism is, however, usually practiced within the legitimate arena of politics and in accordance with the rules of the legal system; and if this activism exceeds these boundaries, then the state typically crushes, if it can, religious social movements that could undermine the legitimacy of polity. Thus, when religion ceases to offer contingent support to the symbolic base of power, the polity often begins to invade the autonomy of religion. The state usually prevails in this contest, but as the revolution in Iran underscored, religion can sometimes win this contest, at least for a time.

Religion and Law

Religious ethics and codes have always been partly fused with secular laws, but as a distinct legal system has emerged, this fusion has become less obvious, and at best, religious symbols provide some of the moral premises on which more secular laws are based. Through agrarianism, however, religious law was often more dominant than emerging secular law; and even in some contemporary Islamic societies, religious law remains central. However, as the force of regulation has escalated with population growth and increased production and as states have sought a secular basis of legitimization, selection has favored legal system development. As the body of secular laws, courts, and enforcement agencies has grown, the exchange between law and religion has increasingly involved legal system protection for the autonomy of religion and religious support for the autonomy of the legal system.

Thus, laws generally specify the rights of religious cult structures to operate, while the beliefs of dominant cults typically become the underlying value premises for at least some of the constitutional principles and higher-order laws in the legal system. At times, as was the case with the old Soviet Union, law took little from religion and gave religion very little support and, in fact, often persecuted religious cults. More common has been the use of law to provide religion with certain rights and prerequisites, while at the same time limiting the extent to which religion can become involved in the affairs of the state. The state almost always views religion suspiciously as a source of counterpower; and so, it uses the legal system to grant religion a certain autonomy that is highly constrained by law. In exchange, religion offers contingent support to polity and the autonomy of the legal system.

Religion and Education

The first teachings of formal education were, in all probability, religious in nature, as instructors passed on to their successors the beliefs and ritual practices of religion. Up through the agrarian era, most universities were affiliated with religion in some way; and a considerable portion of the curriculum was religious. At times, religious support for education of the masses occurred, although these efforts did not fully massify the educational system. Still, for the vast majority of the population, education in school structures was confined to perpetuating elites' status group membership or to impart skills to a few who needed these secular skills for trade and commerce. It is only with industrialization that massification of education accelerates; and this expansion of education is part of the segregation of religion from ever more spheres of secular life. Even as religion establishes its own school system, such as the Catholic schools, the curriculum is, for the most part, secular and matches the curriculum of state-financed schools. As segregation of religion from schools, or secularization in religious schools, occurs, religion is excluded from much of the socialization of children. Moreover, religion becomes less relevant to social placement in the labor market of the economy; and it must adjust beliefs in ways that make them more compatible with the civic culture imposed by the state on the school curriculum.

The exchange between education and religion is thus very imbalanced. The evolving state-financed educational system simply removes much religion from its curriculum, or waters it down and incorporates it into civics training. In exchange, religion is allowed to create its own educational system, ranging from Sunday school through ad hoc Christian academies to full educational hierarchies like the Catholic school system. Yet when this religious system becomes involved in mandatory training of children, it must generally meet the same curricular requirements imposed by the state on the public educational system. Thus, religion is given some autonomy to teach dogma and ritual in its own system, but this instruction is constrained by the requirements to teach the state-mandated secular curriculum. The expansion of the educational system thereby grants some autonomy to religion as it segregates it from the institutional mainstream.

Religion and Economy

Ultimately, religion provides a sense of meaning to individuals and, in the process, alleviates anxieties and reinforces crucial institutional norms. In so doing, religion responds to selection pressures emanating from regulation and reproduction as social forces. In contrast, economies organize natural, physical, and human resources for distribution as goods and services to members of a population; and as a consequence, the economy responds to selection pressures stemming from production as a social force. The basic exchange between religion and economy has thus revolved around the capacity of religion to alleviate the anxieties associated with economic activity and to reinforce crucial economic norms; reciprocally the economy has provided the resources and opportunities for religious mobilization. The way in which this basic exchange has been carried out in the history of human societies has, however, varied enormously as economies have moved from a hunting and gathering to an industrial and post-industrial profile.

Among most hunter-gatherers, the level of uncertainty in securing sufficient resources for survival was generally low; and as a result, religion was not a dominant form of activity in most of these early societies. Yet, where there was danger and uncertainty in economic activity, as was the case with the Eskimo, selection worked to produce clear signs of religion. From hunting and gathering to advanced agrarianism, there was considerable economic uncertainty, aggravated by war, internal conflict, and crushing inequality. And so, it is no surprise that religion became a prominent institutional system during this phase of human evolution. Moreover, the economic surplus of more advanced economies provided the resources to build and sustain elaborate cult structures.

Beginning with the commercial revolution of advanced agrarianism and accelerating with industrialization, the secularization of social activity spread. Technologies transformed the process of production, and the emergence and extension of science questioned many traditional religious beliefs. State-sponsored education increased the salience of secular educational credentials on life chances in competitive labor markets. And in the end, market-driven economies tended to commodify and, hence, secularize virtually everything, including services to alleviate anxiety. Thus, as the economy has industrialized, religion has been forced to adjust to Darwinian selection pressures.

This adjustment represents an accommodation to several changes in the organization of resources and opportunities in the economy. First, a market-driven economy drives all providers of services to compete for market shares, thereby pushing religion to become more market-oriented in its provision of services. Second, market economies tend to secularize goods and services since they must be bought and sold with a neutral medium like money, requiring religion to repackage its message in ways that accommodate or compensate for this reality. Third, market economies generate new kinds of insecurities, such as unemployment in a competitive job market, obsolescence of skills in a market that constantly upgrades its credential requirements, or marginality for unskilled in a credentially inflated labor market, thereby creating opportunities for religion to market its message. Fourth, the availability of mass media making it possible to communicate with large numbers of individuals transforms the way goods and services are marketed, thus providing religion with a potentially very effective tool for disseminating its message and securing resources for its survival.

The end result of these changes in the economy is for religion to niche-market itself within the broader market for human services. Traditional religions generally opt for providing a wider range of secular services, such as youth programs, counseling, and recreational facilities, to compete with more secular economic actors. More evangelical religions market themselves, often through the mass media, to the chronically insecure who may feel vulnerable in a highly dynamic post-industrial economy. Through effective marketing, religions have remained viable; and among some evangelical cults, their numbers have increased. Thus, as industrial and post-industrial economies secularize the orientations of the population, they also create the resources and opportunities for religion to sustain itself in highly competitive markets for human services.

Moreover, although religious dogmas are no longer the direct inspiration for institutional norms in industrial and post-industrial societies, religious values and beliefs are part of these norms. It would be hard to deny that the norms of western capitalist societies—individual hard work and accumulation of wealth, for example—are not reflections of Protestant values and beliefs. And even as nonwestern societies have industrialized, derivatives of Protestant values have been imported in more secular formulations. Moreover, variations from western norms among these late industrializing societies often follow the premises of their dominant religions, albeit in muted and highly secularized form.

Religion and Kinship

Religion originally emerged within kinship systems, probably in the form of ancestor worship; and so, there has always been an important interchange between religion and kinship. Even as the influence of religion has been segregated with institutional differentiation, and as kinship has become nuclearized with agrarianism and industrialism, the basic connection between kinship and religion has remained the same, despite dramatic alterations of these two institutional systems. From the kinship side, this interchange involves socialization of commitments to religious beliefs, the practice of rituals reinforcing these beliefs, and the willingness to commit household surplus to support cult structures. From the religious side, religion provides the means for alleviating tensions in the family, for reinforcing crucial norms, and for marking status transitions (e.g., marriage, dissolution, birth, puberty) in family life.

As kinship has become nucleated and as it has moved from a unit of both production and consumption to primarily one of consumption, this interchange has also been transformed. In the traditional kinship systems of horticulture and early agrarianism, kinship organized considerably more of the institutional activity of the society; and as a result, the influence of religion in reinforcing important norms and alleviating sources of tension and anxiety was more consequential. As other institutions differentiated from kinship, and with the successive segregation and compartmentalization of religion, socialization by family into religious beliefs has declined, ritual practices have been attenuated or eliminated, and contributions from households have become less certain. Indeed, in post-industrial societies, religion now has to compete with secular organizations in markets offering tension management and recreational diversions. Moreover, law now regulates marriage, dissolution, and support activities within the family.

Thus, only in some families does religion retain its former influence as the principal source of anxiety reduction and normative control; and only some families are willing to socialize intense commitments to religious beliefs and to contribute financially to the maintenance of cult structures. In fact, as family members have begun to move in diverse directions in their daily routines in post-industrial societies, the family unit as the source of collective commitment to religion has diminished, with individual members of the family increasingly making their own personal choices about religious beliefs, rituals, and cults.

Still, among a very significant portion of the population in post-industrial and industrializing societies, the basic interchange between religion and kinship is retained. In some cases, as with the societies of the old Soviet Union, religion has reasserted its influence on kinship as political and economic insecurities have risen; and in many societies, such as those in the Middle East, this influence has never been lost. Thus, despite the emergence of a secular market economy and the efforts of polity to create a civic culture, religion remains viable and visible because of the commitments generated by kin socialization.

Education and Kinship

For most of human history, education occurred within kinship. When separate educational structures did emerge, they were generally confined to the socialization of religious practitioners and elites, although religious instruction did reach the masses in some societies. Even in this incipient state, however, the basic interchange between education and kinship was evident: Education would assume some of the socialization functions as well as many of the social placement (in occupations, professions, and status groups) functions of kinship; and kinship would provide the financial and cultural resources for students moving through the educational system.

The establishment of a state-mandated educational system has often posed a threat to the family, since the socialization of children outside the home can reduce the control of parents over children. Moreover, the schools can take needed sources of labor or income from the family (in fact, summer vacation is a holdover from the agrarian era when students were needed to harvest crops). In rapidly changing societies, education can create large knowledge gaps between parents and children that, in turn, alter balances of power and authority in the family. Only when universal education is mandated by the state and when it is seen to increase economic opportunities is this tension between schools and kinship reduced. As this transition in school-family relationships occurs, families seek to provide the financial and cultural resources that can improve school performance, although vast disparities by social class location influence the capacities of families to do so.

These disparities generated by stratification eventually begin to change the perceptions of lower-class families who increasingly pressure the state to provide financial and cultural resources that will increase educational opportunities. These pressures become intense as placement in the post-industrial societies is increasingly determined by the acquisition of educational credentials. Indeed, one of the sources of the credential inflation that has spread among many post-industrial societies like the United States is family pressures to equalize opportunities for less advantaged students.

Thus, as education becomes a central institution, kinship adjusts to the fact that it must lose some socialization and social placement functions. At the same time, kinship becomes ever more willing to provide the resources for students to move up the educational hierarchy; and if the family cannot mobilize the resources, pressure is put on the state to do so. The state generally responds because it seeks to quiet tensions with the lower classes by co-opting their young members into the educational system that, in turn, will indoctrinate students into the political culture legitimating the polity.

CONCLUSION

As institutions have differentiated from kinship, the institutional order has become increasingly complex. Just the cursory review in this chapter of the basic interchanges among six institutions makes clear how complex this web of interrelations among social institutions can become. And, if more fine-grained and secondary interconnections are added to the analysis, the complexity of the institutional order is even more apparent. This complexity can obscure the fundamental relationships among institutions, but in this chapter I seek to cut through some of the complexity.

Although the precise empirical form of these interchanges has varied historically, the more fundamental relationships among institutions have, I believe, remained much the same. These connections among institutions constitute an institutional order, driven by the macrodynamic forces summarized in chapter 2. This order is fundamental to the survival of humans as a species; indeed, it is the result of selection processes as these have been generated by macrodynamic forces.

Most macrolevel sociological analysis examines a piece or portion of the institutional order (for example, "political" and "economic" sociology; or the sociology of "family," "religion," "education," or "law"), but rarely does this analysis step back and view the larger complex of institutions *as a whole*. When this step is taken, the institutional order comes into focus, revealing a distinct and important level of sociological analysis.

My goal in this book is to take not only a panoramic view of the institutional basis of human societies, but also to zoom in on the key elements of each institution, the variations in the organization of these elements in long-range societal evolutionary history, and the dynamic interchanges among these elements. Other units of sociological inquiry—from groups and organizations through communities and stratification systems to societies and world-systems—are constrained by these institutional elements and the order that they create. Indeed, institutions impose parameters on all social processes and structures. To be sure, in some ultimate sense, institutional systems are composed of individual interactions, but one cannot fully understand the substance of these interactions without viewing them in their institutional context and without seeing institutions as driven by macrodynamic forces unique to the macro realm of human social organization. In my view, then, a microlevel focus on interactions among individuals cannot reveal the dynamics of the macro level of social organization and, hence, the dynamics of human social institutions. Only by moving away from micro- and mesolevel processes are some of the most important forces structuring the social universe exposed.

In these pages, I seek to emphasize the regularities, along with historical variations of the regularities, in the institutions that organize the social universe. Of course, only a partial and incomplete look at the institutional order as it evolved is presented here, but even this cursory overview reveals the potential of a purely institutional level of inquiry for expanding knowledge about the dynamics of human societies.

Bibliography

Aberle, David F., A. K. Cohen, A. K. Davis, M. J. Levy, and F. Y. Sutton. 1950. "The Functional Requisites of Society." *Ethics* LX (January):100–11.

Abu-Lughod, Janet. 1989. *Before European Hegemony: The World System A.D. 1250–1350.* New York: Oxford University Press.

Almond, Gabriel, and Sidney Verba. 1963. *The Civic Culture.* Princeton: Princeton University Press.

Amin, Samir. 1976 [1973]. *Unequal Development: An Essay on the Social Formations on Peripheral Capitalism.* New York: Monthly Review Press.

———. 1974 [1970]. *Accumulation on a World Scale.* New York: Monthly Review Press.

Anderson, Perry. 1974. *Passages from Antiquity to Feudalism.* London: New Left Books.

Anyon, J. 1981. "Schools as Agencies of Social Legitimation." *International Journal of Political Education* 4 (2):42–61.

———. 1980. "Social Class and the Hidden Curriculum of Work." *Journal of Education* 161 (1):67–92.

Apple, Michael W. 1988. *Teachers and Text.* London: Routledge and Kegan Paul.

———. 1982a. *Education and Power.* Boston: Routledge and Kegan Paul.

———, ed. 1982b. *Cultural and Economic Reproduction in Education.* Boston: Routledge and Kegan Paul.

———. 1979. *Ideology and Curriculum.* Boston: Routledge and Kegan Paul.

———. 1978. "The New Sociology of Education." *Harvard Educational Review* 22 (6):10–32.

Applebaum, Richard. 1978. "Marx's Theory of the Falling Rate of Profit: Towards a Dialectical Analysis of Structural Social Change." *American Sociological Review* 43:64–73.

Arjomand, Said. 1988. *The Turban for the Crown: The Islamic Revolution in Iran.* New York: Oxford University Press.

Aung, Maung Htin. 1962. *Burmese Law Tales: The Legal Element in Burmese Folklore.* London: Oxford University Press.

Bainbridge, William Sims, and Rodney Stark. 1979. "Cult Formation: Three Compatible Models." *Sociological Analysis* 40:283–95.

Baran, Paul, and Paul M. Sweezy. 1966. *Monopoly Capital: An Essay on the American Economic and Social Order.* New York: Monthly Review Press.

Barton, Roy. 1969. *Ifugao Law.* Berkeley: University of California Publications in Archaeology and Ethnology, volume 15.

Bates, Daniel, and Fred Plog. 1991. *Human Adaptive Strategies.* New York: McGraw-Hill.

Beaud, Michel. 1983. *A History of Capitalism, 1500–1980.* New York: Monthly Review Press.

Becker, Howard. 1950. *Through Values to Social Interpretation.* Durham, NC: Duke University Press.

Bell, Daniel. 1973. *The Coming of Post-Industrial Society.* New York: Basic Books.

Bellah, Robert N. 1970. *Beyond Belief: Essays on Religion in a Post-Traditional World.* New York: Harper and Row.

———. 1967. "Civil Religion in America." *Daedalus* 96:1–21.

———. 1964. "Religious Evolution." *American Sociological Review* 29:358–74.

Ben-David, Joseph. 1971. *The Scientist's Role in Society: A Comparative Study.* Englewood Cliffs, NJ: Prentice-Hall.

Bender, Barbara. 1975. *Farming in Prehistory.* London: Baker.

Berger, Peter L. 1969. *The Sacred Canopy: Elements of a Sociological Theory of Religion.* Garden City, NY: Anchor Books.

———. 1963. "A Market Model for the Analysis of Ecumenicity." *Social Research* 5:21–34.

Berk, Sara Fenstermaker. 1985. *The Gender Factory: The Appointment of Work in American Households.* New York: Plenum.

———. 1980. *Women and Household Labor.* Newbury Park, CA: Sage.

Bicchieri, M. G., ed. 1972. *Hunters and Gatherers Today.* New York: Holt, Rinehart and Winston.

Binford, Lewis R. 1968. "Post-Pleistocene Adaptations," in *New Perspectives in Archaeology,* eds. S. R. Binford and L. R. Binford. Chicago: Aldine.

Black, Donald. 1993. *The Social Structure of Right and Wrong.* San Diego: Academic Press.

———. 1976. *The Behavior of Law.* New York: Academic Press.

Black, Donald, and Maureen Mileski, eds. 1973. *The Social Organization of Law.* New York: Academic Press.

Blalock, Hubert M. 1989. *Power and Conflict: Toward a General Theory.* Newbury Park, CA: Sage.

Blau, Peter M. 1994. *Structural Context of Opportunities.* Chicago: University of Chicago Press.

———. 1977. *Inequality and Heterogeneity: A Primitive Theory of Social Structure.* New York: The Free Press.

Bloch, H. 1973. "The Problem Defined." Introduction to *Civilization and Science: In Conflict or Collaboration.* Amsterdam: Elsevier.

Bloch, Marc. 1962. *Feudal Society,* trans. L. A. Manyon. Chicago: University of Chicago Press.

Block, Fred. 1994. "The State and the Economy," in *Handbook of Economic Sociology,* eds. N. J. Smelser and R. Swedberg. New York: Russell Sage Foundation.

———. 1990. *Postindustrial Possibilities: A Critique of Economic Discourse.* Berkeley: University of California Press.

———. 1980. "Beyond Relative Autonomy: State Managers as Historical Subjects." *Socialist Register:* 227–42.

Blum, Jerome. 1961. *Lord and Peasant in Russia from the Ninth to the Nineteenth Century.* Princeton: Princeton University Press.

Blumberg, Rac Lesser. 1984. "A General Theory of Gender Stratification." *Sociological Theory* 2:23–101.

Blumberg, Rae Lesser, and Robert F. Winch. 1977. "The Curvilinear Relation Between Societal Complexity of Familial Complexity," in *Familial Organization*, ed. R. F. Winch. New York: Free Press.

Boas, Franz. 1921. *Ethnology of the Kwakiutl*. Washington, D.C.: Smithsonian Institution Press.

Bohannan, Paul. 1968. "Law and Legal Institutions," in *International Encyclopedia of the Social Sciences*. New York: Free Press.

———. 1964. *Africa and Africans*. Garden City, NY: American Museum Science Books.

———. 1957. *Justice and Judgement Among the Tir*. London: Oxford University Press.

Bohannan, Paul T., and K. Hickleberry. 1967. "Institutions of Divorce, Family and Law." *Law and Society Review* 2:81–102.

Boli, John. 1989. *New Citizens for a New Society: The Institutional Origins of Mass Schooling in Sweden*. Oxford: Peragamon Press.

Boli, John, Francisco Ramirez, and John W. Meyer. 1985. "Explaining the Origins and Expansion of Mass Education." *Comparative Education Review* 29:145–70.

Boserup, Ester. 1981. *Population and Technological Change: A Study of Long-term Trends*. Chicago: University of Chicago Press.

———. 1965. *The Conditions of Agricultural Growth*. Chicago: Aldine.

Bourdieu, Pierre. 1984. *Distinction: A Social Critique of the Judgement of Taste*. Cambridge: Harvard University Press.

Bourdieu, Pierre, and Jean-Claude Passeron. 1977. *Reproduction: In Education, Society and Culture*. Newbury Park, CA: Sage.

Bowles, Samuel, and H. Gintis. 1976. *Schooling in Capitalist America: Educational Reform and the Contradictions of Economic Life*. New York: Basic Books.

Braudel, Fernand. 1982. *The Wheels of Commerce*, volume 2, *Civilization and Capitalism 15th–18th Century*. New York: Harper and Row.

———. 1977. *Afterthoughts on Material Civilization and Capitalism*. Baltimore: Johns Hopkins University Press.

Braungart, R. G., and M. M. Braungart. 1994. "Political Socialization." *The International Encyclopedia of Education*, second edition, eds. T. Husén and T. N. Postlethwaite. London: Pergamon Press.

Braverman, Harry. 1974. *Labor and Monopoly Capital*. New York: Monthly Review Press.

Bredemeier, Harry C. 1962. "Law as an Integrative Mechanism," in *Law and Sociology Exploratory Essays*, ed. W. J. Evan. New York: Free Press.

Brint, Steven. 1996. *Schools and Society*. Newbury Park, CA: Pine Forge Press.

Bronfenbrenner, Urie. 1968. "Soviet Methods of Character Education," in *Comparative Perspectives on Education*, ed. R. J. Havighurst. Boston: Little, Brown.

Burt, Ronald S. 1992. *Structural Holes*. Cambridge: Harvard University Press.

Cain, Maureen, and Alan Hunt. 1969. *Marx and Engels on Law*. London: Academic Press.

Cambridge University Press. 1963. *The Cambridge Economic History of Europe*. London: Cambridge University Press.

Carniero, Robert L. 1987. "Further Reflections on Resource Concentration and Its Role in the Rise of the State," in *Studies in the Neolithic and Urban Revolutions*, ed. L. Manzanilla. Oxford: British Archaeological Reports. International Series, No. 349.

———. 1981. "The Chiefdom: Precursor of the State," in *The Transition to Statehood in the New World*, ed. R. R. Kantz. New York: Cambridge University Press.

———. 1973. "Structure, Function, and Equilibrium in the Evolutionism of Herbert Spencer." *Journal of Anthropological Research* 29 (2):77–95.

———. 1970. "A Theory of the Origin of the State." *Science* 169:733–38.

———. 1967. "On the Relationship of Size of Population and Complexity of Social Organization." *Southwestern Journal of Anthropology* 23:234–43.

Carnoy, M. 1989. "Education, State, and Culture in American Society," in *Critical Pedagogy: The State and Cultural Struggle*, eds. H. Giroux and P. McLaren. Albany, NY: SUNY Press.

Carnoy, M., and H. Levin. 1985. *Schooling and Work in the Democratic State.* Palo Alto: Stanford University Press.

———, eds. 1976. *The Limits of Educational Reform.* New York: Longmans.

Chafetz, Janet. 1990. *Gender Equity: An Integrated Theory of Stability and Change.* Newbury Park, CA: Sage.

Chagnon, Napoleon A. 1968. *The Fierce People.* New York: Holt, Rinehart and Winston.

Chambliss, William. 1976. "Functional and Conflict Theories of Crime: The Heritage of Émile Durkheim and Karl Marx," in *Whose Law? What Order? A Conflict Approach to Criminology*, ed. William Chambliss and Milton Mankoff. New York: John Wiley.

Chambliss, William, and Robert Seidman. 1982. *Law, Order, and Power*, second edition. Reading, MA: Addison-Wesley.

Chang, Kwang-chih. 1963. *The Archeology of Ancient China.* New Haven: Yale University Press.

Chase-Dunn, Christopher. 2001. "World Systems Theory," in *Handbook of Sociological Theory.* New York: Kluwer Academic/Plenum Publishers.

Chase-Dunn, Christopher, and Thomas D. Hall. 1997. *Rise and Demise: Comparing World Systems.* Boulder, CO: Westview.

Childe, V. Gordon. 1964. *What Happened in History.* Baltimore: Penguin.

———. 1960. "The New Stone Age," in *Man, Culture and Society*, ed. H. Shapiro. New York: Oxford Galaxy.

———. 1953. *Man Makes Himself.* New York: Mentor Books.

———. 1952. *New Light on the Most Ancient East.* London: Routledge and Kegan Paul.

———. 1951. *Man Makes His Way.* New York: Mentor Books.

———. 1930. *The Bronze Age.* London: Cambridge University Press.

Chirot, Daniel. 1986. *Social Change in The Modern Era.* San Diego: Harcourt, Brace, Jovanovich.

Claessen, H., and P. Skalnick, eds. 1978. *The Early State.* The Hague: Mouton.

Clark, Grahame, and Stuart Piggott. 1965. *Prehistoric Societies.* New York: Knopf.

Clark, J. G. D. 1952. *Prehistoric Europe: The Economic Basis.* London: Methuen.

Clough, S. B., and C. W. Cole. 1941. *Economic History of Europe.* Boston: D. C. Heath.

Cohen, Mark N. 1977. *The Food Crisis in Prehistory.* New Haven: Yale University Press.

Cohen, Ronald, and Elman Service, eds. 1977. *Origins of the State.* Philadelphia: Institute for the Study of Human Issues.

Cohn, Norman Rufus Colin. 1957. *The Pursuit of the Millennium.* Fairlawn, NJ: Essential Books; revised and expanded in 1970 by Oxford University Press.

Coleman, James S. 1990. *Foundations of Social Theory.* Cambridge, MA: Belknap.

———, ed. 1965. *Education and Political Development.* Princeton: Princeton University Press.

Collins, Randall. 1990. "Market Dynamics as the Engine of Historical Change." *Sociological Theory* 8:111–35.

———. 1988. *Theoretical Sociology*. San Diego: Harcourt, Brace, Jovanovich.

———. 1986. *Weberian Sociological Theory*. New York: Cambridge University Press.

———. 1979. *The Credential Society*. New York: Academic Press.

———. 1977. "Some Comparative Principles of Educational Stratification." *Harvard Educational Review* 47:1–27.

———. 1975. *Conflict Sociology: Toward an Explanatory Science*. New York: Academic Press.

———. 1971. "Functional and Conflict Theories of Educational Stratification." *American Sociological Review* 36:1002–19.

Comte, Auguste. 1898 [1830–1842]. *The Course of Positive Philosophy*. London: Bell & Sons.

Coon, Carleton S. 1971. *The Hunting Peoples*. Boston: Little, Brown.

Cotgrove, S., and S. Box. 1970. *Science Industry and Society*. London: Allen and Unwin.

Cottrell, William Frederick. 1955. *Energy and Society: The Relation Between Energy, Social Change and Economic Development*. New York: McGraw-Hill.

Crook, Stephan, Jan Pakulski, and Malcolm Waters. 1992. *Postmodernization: Change in Advanced Society*. London: Sage.

Curwen, Cecil, and Gudmund Hatt. 1961. *Plough and Pasture: The Early History of Farming*. New York: Collier.

Darwin, Charles. 1958 [1859]. *On the Origin of Species*. New York: New American Library.

David, Rene, and John E. Brierley. 1985. *Major Legal Systems in the World Today*, third edition. London: Stevens and Sons.

Davies, James C. 1962. "Toward a Theory of Revolution." *American Sociological Review* 27:5–19.

Davis, Howard, and Richard Scase. 1985. *Western Capitalism and State Socialism: An Introduction*. Oxford: Basil Blackwell.

Davis, James F. 1962. "Law as a Type of Social Control," in *Society and Law: New Meanings for an Old Profession*. New York: Free Press.

Davis, Kingsley. 1949. *Human Society*. New York: Macmillan.

Davis, L. B., and O. K. Reeves. 1990. *Hunters of the Recent Past*. London: Unwin Hyman.

Dawson, R. E., and K. Prewitt. 1969. *Political Socialization*. Boston: Little, Brown.

Diamond, Arthur S. 1971. *Primitive Law, Past and Present*. London: Methuen and Co.

———. 1951. *The Evolution of Law and Order*. London: Watts and Co.

Dore, Ronald. 1976. *The Diploma Disease: Education, Qualification and Development*. Berkeley: University of California Press.

Duke, James E. 1976. *Conflict and Power in Social Life*. Provo, Utah: Brigham Young University Press.

Durkheim, Émile. 1965 [1912]. *The Elementary Forms of the Religious Life*. New York: Free Press.

———. 1938 [1895]. *The Rules of the Sociological Method*. New York: Free Press.

———. 1947 [1893]. *The Division of Labor in Society*. New York: Free Press.

Earle, Timothy, ed. 1984. *On the Evolution of Complex Societies*. Malibu, CA: Undena.

Earle, Timothy, and J. Ericson, eds. 1977. *Exchange Systems in Prehistory*. New York: Academic Press.

Easton, David. 1965. *A Systems Analysis of Political Life*. New York: John Wiley and Sons.

Eberhard, Wolfram. 1960. *A History of China*, second edition. Berkeley: University of California Press.

Eibl-Eibesfeldt, Irenäus. 1991. "On Subsistence and Social Relations in the Kalahaic." *Current Anthropology* 32:55–57.

Eisenstadt, S. N., and A. Shachar. 1987. *Society, Culture and Urbanization*. Newbury Park: Sage.

Ekholm, Kajsa, and Jonathan Friedman. 1982. "'Capital' Imperialism and Exploitation in Ancient World-Systems." *Review* 4:87–109.

Eliade, Mircea. 1987. *The Encyclopedia of Religion*, fifteen volumes. New York: Macmillan.

Elkin, A. P. 1954. *The Australian Aborigines*, third edition. Sydney: Angus and Robertson.

Ember, Carol, Melvin Ember, and Burton Pasternak. 1974. "On the Development of Unilineal Descent." *Journal of Anthropological Research* 30:69–94.

Ember, Melvin, and Carol R. Ember. 1983. *Marriage, Family and Kinship: Comparative Studies of Social Organization*. Princeton, NJ: HRAF Press.

———. 1971. "The Conditions Favoring Matrilocal vs. Patrilocal Residence." *American Anthropologist* 73:571–94.

Esping-Andersen, Gøsta. 1994. "Welfare States and the Economy," in *The Handbook of Economy*, eds. N. J. Smelser and R. Swedberg. New York: Russell Sage Foundation.

Etzioni, Amat. 1961. *A Comparative Analysis of Complex Organizations*. New York: Free Press.

Evan, William M. 1990. *Social Structure and Law: Theoretical and Empirical Perspectives*. Newbury Park, CA: Sage.

———. 1980. *The Sociology of Law*. New York: Free Press.

———, ed. 1962. *Law and Society: Exploratory Essays*. New York: Free Press.

Evans, Peter, Dietrich Rueschemeyer, and Theda Skocpol, eds. 1985. *Bringing the State Back In*. New York: Cambridge University Press.

Evans-Pritchard, E. 1940. *The Nuer*. Oxford: Oxford University Press.

Faia, Michael A. 1986. *Dynamic Functionalism: Strategy and Tactics*. New York: Cambridge University Press.

Firth, Raymond. 1970. *Preface to Ancient Law*. Boston: Beacon Press.

———. 1939. *Primitive Polynesian Economy*. London: Routledge and Kegan Paul.

———. 1936. *We the Tikopia*. New York: American Book Company.

Flandrin, Jean-Louis. 1979. *Families in Former Times: Kinship, Household and Sexuality*. Cambridge: Cambridge University Press.

Flannery, Kent V. 1973. "The Origins of Agriculture." *Annual Review of Anthropology* 2:271–310.

Fock, Niel. 1974. "Mataco Law," in *Native South Americans: Ethnology of the Least Known Continent*, ed. P. Lyons. Boston: Little, Brown.

Fortes, Meyer. 1953. "The Structure of Unilineal Descent Groups." *American Anthropologist* 73:571–94.

Fox, Robin. 1967. *Kinship and Marriage*. Baltimore: Penguin.

Frank, Andre Gunder. 1980. *Crisis in World Economy*. New York: Holmes and Meier.

———. 1975. *On Capitalist Underdevelopment*. Oxford: Oxford University Press.

———. 1969. *Capitalism and Underdevelopment in Latin America*. New York: Monthly Review Press.

Freese, Lee. 1997. *Evolutionary Connections*. Greenwich, CT: JAI Press.

Fried, Morton H. 1978. "The State, the Chicken, and the Egg: Or, What Came First?" in *Origins of the State*, ed. R. Cohen. Philadelphia: Institute for the Study of Human Issues.

———. 1967. *The Evolution of Political Society*. New York: Random House.

———. 1957. "The Classification of Corporate Unilineal Descent Groups." *Journal of the Royal Anthropological Institute* 87:1–29.

Friedman, Lawrence M. 1977. *Law and Society: An Introduction.* Englewood Cliffs, NJ: Prentice-Hall.

———. 1975. *The Legal System: A Social Science Perspective.* New York: Russell Sage.

———. 1969a. "On Legal Development." *Rutgers Law Review* 24:11–64.

———. 1969b. "Legal Culture and Societal Development." *Law and Society Review* 4:29–44.

Friedman, William. 1959. *Law in a Changing Society.* Berkeley: University of California Press.

Fuchs, Stephan, and Jonathan H. Turner. 1991. "Legal Sociology as General Theory." *Virginia Review of Sociology* 1:165–72.

Fuller, Bruce. 1991. *Growing-Up Modern: The Western State Builds Third-World Schools.* New York: Routledge.

Fuller, Bruce, and Richard Rubinson. 1992. "Does the State Expand Schooling? Review of Evidence," in *The Political Construction of Education*, eds. B. Fuller and R. Rubinson. New York: Praeger.

Garnier, Maurice, and Jerald Hage. 1990. "Education and Economic Growth in Germany." *Research in Sociology of Education and Socialization* 9:25–53.

Gereffi, Gary. 1994. "The International Economy and Economic Development," in *The Handbook of Economic Sociology*, eds. N. J. Smelser and R. Swedberg. New York: Russell Sage.

Gereffi, Gary, and Donald Wyman, eds. 1990. *Manufacturing Miracles: Paths of Industrialization in Latin America and East Asia.* Princeton: Princeton University Press.

Gibbs, James, ed. 1965. *Peoples of Africa.* New York: Holt.

Giddens, Anthony. 1985. *The Nation State and Violence.* Cambridge: Polity Press.

Gills, Barry K., and Andre Gunder Frank. 1992. "World System Cycles, Crises, and Hegemonial Shifts, 1700 B.C. to 1700 A.D." *Review* 15:621–87.

Gintis, H. 1972. "Toward a Political Economy of Education." *Harvard Educational Review* 42:100–15.

Giroux, H. A. 1990a. *Schooling and the Struggle for Public Life.* Minneapolis: University of Minnesota Press.

———. 1990b. *Teachers as Intellectuals: A Critical Pedagogy for Practical Learning.* South Hadley, MA: Bergin and Garvey.

———. 1981. *Ideology, Culture, and the Process of Schooling.* Philadelphia: Temple University Press.

Glock, Charles Y. 1973. "On the Origins and Evolution of Religious Groups," in *Religion in Sociological Perspective*, ed. C. Y. Glock. Belmont, CA: Wadsworth.

———. 1964. "The Role of Deprivation in the Origin and Evolution of Religious Groups," in *Religion and Social Conflict*, eds. R. Lee and M. Marty. New York: Oxford University Press.

Glock, Charles Y., and Rodney Stark. 1965. *Religion and Society in Tension.* Chicago: Rand McNally.

Gluckman, Max. 1965. *Politics, Law and Ritual in Tribal Society.* Chicago: Aldine.

———. 1955. *The Judicial Process Among the Barotse of Northern Rhodesia.* Manchester: Manchester University Press.

Goffman, Irving. 1967. *Interaction Ritual.* Garden City, N.Y.: Anchor Books.

———. 1961. *Encounters: Two Studies in the Sociology of Interaction.* Indianapolis: Bobbs-Merrill.

Goldschmidt, Walter. 1959. *Man Makes His Way: A Preface to Understanding Human Society.* New York: Holt, Rinehart and Winston.

Goldstone, Jack. 1990. *Revolution and Rebellion in the Early Modern World, 1640–1848.* Berkeley: University of California Press.

Goode, William J. 1951. *Religion Among the Primitives.* New York: The Free Press.

Goodhale, Jane. 1959. The Tiwi Women of Melville Island. Ph.D. dissertation, University of Pennsylvania.

Gordon, R. T. 1914. *The Khasis.* London: Macmillan.

Graburn, Nelson, ed. 1971. *Readings in Kinship and Social Structure.* New York: Harper and Row.

Gramsci, A. 1972. *Selections from Prison Notebooks.* New York: International Publishers.

Granovetter, Mark. 1985. "Economic Action and Social Structure: The Problem of Embeddedness." *American Sociological Review* 91:481–510.

Gurvitch, George. 1953. *Sociology of Law.* London: Routledge and Kegan Paul.

Haas, Jonathan. 1982. *The Evolution of the Prehistoric State.* New York: Columbia University Press.

Habermas, Jurgen. 1979. *Communication and the Evolution of Society.* Boston: Beacon Press.

———. [1973] 1976. *Legitimation Crisis*, trans. T. McCarthy. London: Heineman.

Hadden, Jeffrey K., and Charles E. Swann. 1981. *Prime Time Preachers: The Rising Power of Televangelism.* Reading, MA: Addison-Wesley.

Hall, John A. 1985. *Powers and Liberties: The Causes and Consequences of the Rise of the West.* Berkeley: University of California Press.

Hammond, Mason. 1972. *The City in the Ancient World.* Cambridge: Harvard University Press.

Hannan, Michael, and John H. Freeman. 1977. "The Population Ecology of Organizations." *American Sociological Review* 82:929–64.

Hanson, Mark E. 1995. Educational Change Under Autocratic and Democratic Governments: The Case of Argentina. Masters thesis, UC Riverside School of Education.

Harner, M. 1970. "Population Pressure and the Social Evolution of Agriculturalists." *Southwest Journal of Anthropology* 26:67–86.

Harris, Marvin. 1971. *Culture, Man and Nature: An Introduction to General Anthropology.* New York: Crowell.

Hart, C. W. M., Arnold Pilling, and Jane Goodhale. 1988. *The Tiwi of North Australia.* Chicago: Holt, Rinehart and Winston.

Hart, H. L. A. 1961. *The Concept of Law.* London: Oxford University Press.

Harvey, David. 1989. *The Condition of Postmodernity: An Enquiry into the Origins of Cultural Change.* Oxford: Basil Blackwell.

Hawkes, Jacquetta. 1965. *Prehistory: UNESCO History of Mankind*, volume 1, part 1. New York: Mentor.

Hawley, Amos. 1986. *Human Ecology: A Theoretical Essay.* Chicago: University of Chicago Press.

Hayden, B. 1981. "Subsistence and Ecological Adaptations of Modern Hunter/Gatherers," in *Omnivorous Primates*, eds. R. Harding and G. Teleki. New York: Columbia University Press.

Haydon, E. S. 1960. *Law and Justice in Buganda.* London: Butterworths.

Hays, H. R. 1958. *From Ape to Angel: An Informal History of Social Anthropology.* New York: Capricorn Books.

Hechter, Michael. 1987. *Principles of Group Solidarity*. Berkeley: University of California Press.

Heilbroner, Robert L. 1985. *The Making of Economic Society*, seventh edition. Englewood Cliffs, NJ: Prentice-Hall.

Herskovits, M. J. 1938. *Dahomey*. Locust Valley, NY: J. J. Augustin.

Herskovits, M. J., and F. S. Herskovits. 1933. "An Outline of Dahomean Religious Belief." *Memoirs of the American Anthropological Association* 41:10–25.

Hertz, Rosanna. 1986. *More Equal than Others: Women and Men in Dual-Career Marriages*. Berkeley: University of California Press.

Hess, R. D., and J. V. Torney. 1967. *The Development of Political Attitudes in Children*. Chicago: Aldine.

Hilton, Rodney, ed. 1976. *The Transition from Feudalism to Capitalism*. London: New Left Books.

Hiro, Dilip. 1989. *Holy Wars: The Rise of Islamic Fundamentalism*. New York: Routledge and Kegan Paul.

Hochschild, Arlie R. 1989. *The Second Shift: Working Parents and the Revolution at Home*. New York: Viking Press.

Hoebel, E. Adamson. 1968. *The Law of Primitive Man: A Study in Comparative Dynamics*. Cambridge: Harvard University Press.

———. 1954. *The Law of Primitive Man: A Study in Comparative Legal Dynamics*. Cambridge: Harvard University Press.

Holmberg, Allan. 1950. *Nomads of the Long Bow: The Siriono of Eastern Bolivia*. Washington, D.C.: Smithsonian Institution, Institute for Anthropology, #10.

Hose, Charles, and William McDougall. 1912. *The Pagan Tribes of Borneo*. London: Macmillan.

Howell, Nancy. 1988. "Understanding Simple Social Structures: Kinship Units and Ties," in *Social Structures: A Network Approach*, eds. B. Wellman and S. D. Berkowitz. Cambridge: University of Cambridge Press.

Huff, Toby E. 1993. *The Rise of Early Modern Science: Islam, China, and the West*. Cambridge: Cambridge University Press.

Hultkrantz, Ake, and Ornulf Vorren. 1982. *The Hunters*. Oslo: Universitets-Forlaget.

Iannaccone, Laurence R. 1992. "The Consequences of a Religious Market Structure: Adam Smith and the Economics of Religion." *Rationality and Society* 3:156–77.

Ichilov, O., ed. 1990. *Political Socialization, Citizenship Education, and Democracy*. New York: Teachers College Press of Columbia University.

Johnson, Allen W., and Timothy Earle. 1987. *The Evolution of Human Societies: From Foraging Group to Agrarian State*. Palo Alto: Stanford University Press.

Johnson, Harry M. 1960. *Sociology: A Systematic Introduction*. New York: Harcourt, Brace, Jovanovich.

Juegensmeyer, Mark. 1993. *The New Cold War: Religious Nationalism Confronts the State*. Berkeley: University of California Press.

Kanter, Rosabeth Moss. 1989. *When Giants Learn to Dance: Mastering the Challenges of Strategy, Management and Careers in the 1990s*. New York: Simon and Schuster.

Kautsky, John H. 1982. *The Politics of Aristocratic Empires*. Chapel Hill: University of North Carolina Press.

Keesing, Robert. 1975. *Kin Groups and Social Structure*. New York: Holt, Rinehart and Winston.

Kirch, P. 1984. *The Evolution of Polynesian Chiefdoms*. Cambridge: Cambridge University Press.

―――. 1980. "Polynesian Prehistory: Cultural Adaptation in Island Ecosystems." *American Scientist* 68:39–48.

Kohl, Philip. 1989. "The Use and Abuse of World Systems Theory: The Case of the 'Pristine' West Asian State," in *Archaeological Thought in America*, ed. C. C. Lamberg-Kavlovsky. Cambridge: Cambridge University Press.

Kolata, Gina. 1974. "!Kung Hunter-Gatherers: Feminism, Diet, and Birth." *Science* 185:932–34.

Kozol, Jonathan. 1991. *Savage Inequalities: Children in American Schools*. New York: Crown.

Kramer, Samuel Noah. 1959. *It Happened at Sumer*. Garden City, NY: Doubleday.

Kroeber, Alfred. 1926. *Law of the Yurok Indians*. Washington, D.C.: International Congress of Americanists, Proceedings 22, volume 2.

―――. 1925. *Handbook of the Indians of California*. Washington, DC: Bureau of American Ethnology.

Kumar, Krishan. 1992. "The Revolutions of 1989: Socialism, Capitalism, and Democracy." *Theory and Society* 21:309–56.

Kuper, Adam. 1971. "Council Structure and Decision-making," in *Councils in Action*, eds. A. Richards and A. Kuper. Cambridge: Cambridge University Press.

Kuper, Hilda, and Leo Kuper, eds. 1965. *African Law: Adaptation and Development*. Berkeley: University of California Press.

Kurtz, Lester. 1995. *Gods in the Global Village: The World's Religions in Sociological Perspective*. Thousand Oaks, CA: Pine Forge Press.

Lambert, A. E. 1956. *Kibuyu Social and Political Institutions*. London: Oxford University Press.

Landtman, Gunnar. 1927. *The Kiwi Papuans of British Guinea*. London: Macmillan.

Lash, Scott. 1990. *Sociology of Postmodernism*. London: Routledge.

Lash, Scott, and John Urry. 1987. *The End of Organized Capitalism*. Cambridge: Polity Press.

Laslett, Peter, and Richard Wall. 1972. *Household and Family in Past Time*. Cambridge: Cambridge University Press.

Leach, E. R. 1954. *Political Systems of Highland Burma*. Boston: Beacon Press.

Lee, Richard. 1979. *The !Kung San*. Cambridge: Cambridge University Press.

Lee, Richard, and Irven DeVore, eds. 1976. *Kalahari Hunter-Gatherers*. Cambridge: Cambridge University Press.

―――, eds. 1968. *Man the Hunter*. Chicago: Aldine.

Lenski, Gerhard. 1966. *Power and Privilege*. New York: McGraw-Hill, reprinted by the University of North Carolina Press.

―――. 1963. *The Religious Factor: A Sociologist's Inquiry*. Garden City, NY: Anchor Books.

Levy, Daniel C. 1986. *Higher Education and the State in Latin America*. Chicago: University of Chicago Press.

Linton, Ralph. 1936. *The Study of Man*. New York: Appleton-Century Crofts.

Lipset, Seymour Martin. 1960. *Political Man*. New York: Doubleday.

Llewellyn, K. N., and E. A. Hoebel. 1941. *The Cheyenne Way*. Norman: University of Oklahoma Press.

Lloyd, D. 1964. *The Idea of Law*. Baltimore: Penguin Books.

Loftland, John, and Rodney Stark. 1965. "Becoming a World-Saver: A Theory of Conversion to a Deviant Perspective." *American Sociological Review* 30:862–74.

Lowie, Richard H. 1966. *Social Organization*. New York: Holt, Rinehart and Winston.
Lowie, Robert H. 1948. *Primitive Religion*. New York: Boni and Liveright.
———. 1937. *The History of Ethnological Theory*. New York: Holt, Rinehart and Winston.
Luckmann, Thomas. 1967. *The Invisible Religion: The Transformation of Symbols in Industrial Society*. New York: Macmillan.
Luhmann, Niklas. 1985. *A Sociological Theory of Law*. Boston: Routledge and Kegan Paul.
———. 1984. *Religious Dogmatics and the Evolution of Societies*. New York: Edwin Mellen.
———. 1982. *The Differentiation of Society*. New York: Columbia University Press.
MacNeish, R. 1964. "Ancient Mesoamerican Civilization." *Science* 143:531–37.
Mair, Lucy. 1962. *Primitive Government*. Baltimore: Penguin Books.
Malinowski, Bronislaw. 1944. *A Scientific Theory of Culture and Other Essays*. London: Oxford University Press.
———. 1955 [1925]. *Magic, Science, and Religion*. Garden City, NY: Doubleday.
———. 1926. *Crime and Custom in Savage Society*. London: George Routledge and Sons.
———. 1922. *Argonauts of the Western Pacific*. London: George Routledge and Sons.
———. 1913. *The Family Among the Australian Aborigines*. New York: Schocken.
Malthus, Thomas. [1798] 1926. *First Essay on Population*. New York: Kelley.
Mann, Michael. 1986. *The Social Sources of Power*, volume I. Cambridge: Cambridge University Press.
Marty, Martin E., and R. Scott Appleby, eds. 1993. *Fundamentalism and Society: Reclaiming the Sciences, the Family, and Education*. Chicago: University of Chicago Press.
Marx, Karl. [1867] 1967. *Capital: A Critical Analysis of Capitalist Production*. New York: International Publishers.
———. 1965. *Pre-capitalist Economic Formations*. New York: International Publishers.
———. [1843] 1963. *Karl Marx: Early Writings*, ed. T. Bottomore. New York: McGraw-Hill.
Maryanski, Alexandra, and Jonathan H. Turner. 1992. *The Social Cage: Human Nature and the Evolution of Society*. Palo Alto: Stanford University Press.
Massell, G. J. 1968. "Law as an Instrument of Revolutionary Change in a Traditional Milieu: The Case of Soviet Central Asia." *Law and Society Review* 2:179–228.
Mathews, Warren. 1991. *World Religions*. St. Paul, MN: West Publishing Co.
McCarthy, John D., and Mayer Zald. 1977. "Resource Mobilization of Social Movements." *American Journal of Sociology* 82 (6):1212–41.
McNeill, William. 1963. *The Rise of the West*. Chicago: University of Chicago Press.
Mellaart, James. *Earliest Civilizations of the Near East*. London: Thames and Hudson, 1965.
Mensching, Gustav. 1959. *Die Religion*. Stuttgart: Curt E. Schwab.
———. 1947. *Soziologie der Religion*. Bonn: Ludwig Rohrscheid.
Merton, Robert K. 1957. *Social Theory and Social Structure*. New York: Free Press.
Meyer, John. 1992. "The Social Construction of Motives for Educational Expansion," in *The Political Construction of Education*, eds. B. Fuller and R. Rubinson. New York: Praeger.
———. 1977. "The Effects of Education as an Institution." *American Journal of Sociology* 83:340–63.
Meyer, John W., Francisco O. Ramirez, and Y. N. Soysal. 1992. "World Expansion of Mass Education, 1870–1980." *Sociology of Education* 65:128–49.
Mizruchi, Marks, and Linda Brewster Stearns. 1994. "Money, Banking, and Financial Markets," in *The Handbook of Economic Sociology*, eds. N. J. Smelser and R. Swedberg. New York: Russell Sage Foundation.

Moberg, D. O. 1962. *The Church as a Social Institution.* Englewood Cliffs, NJ: Prentice-Hall.

Moore, Barrington, Jr. 1966. *Social Origins of Dictatorship and Democracy.* Boston: Beacon Press.

Moore, John H. 1977. "The Evolution of Exploitation." *Critique of Anthropology* 8:33–58.

Moore, Sally Falk. 1978. *Law as Process: An Anthropological Approach.* London: Routledge and Kegan Paul.

Moseley, K. P., and Immanuel Wallerstein. 1978. "Precapitalist Social Structures." *Annual Review of Sociology* 4:259–90.

Murdock, George Peter. 1965. *Culture and Society.* Pittsburgh: University of Pittsburgh Press.

———. 1959. *Africa: Its Peoples and Their Culture History.* New York: McGraw-Hill.

———. 1953. "Social Structure," in *An Appraisal of Anthropology Today*, eds. S. Tax, L. Eiseley, I. Rouse, and C. Voegelin. Chicago: University of Chicago Press.

———. 1949. *Social Structure.* New York: The MacMillan Company.

Murphy, W., and J. Tannenhaus. 1968. "Public Opinion and the United States Supreme Courts." *Law and Society* 2:357–84.

Murra, J. 1980. *The Economic Organization of the Inka State.* Greenwich, CN: JAI Press.

Nee, Victor. 1989. "A Theory of Market Transition: From Redistribution to Markets in State Socialism." *American Sociological Review* 81:1408–18.

Newman, Katherine. 1983. *Law and Economic Organization: A Comparative Study of Preindustrial Societies.* Cambridge: Cambridge University Press.

Nohria, Nitin, and Ranjay Gulati. 1994. "Firms and Their Environments," in *Handbook of Economic Sociology*, eds. N. J. Smelser and R. Swedberg. New York: Russell Sage.

Nolan, Patrick, and Gerhard Lenski. 2001. *Human Societies: An Introduction to Macrosociology.* New York: McGraw-Hill.

Norbeck, E. 1961. *Religion in Primitive Society.* New York: Harper and Row.

Oates, Joan. 1978. "Comment on 'The Balance of Trade in Southwest Asia in the Mid-Third Millennium.'" *Current Anthropology* 19:480–81.

O'Dea, Thomas F. 1970. *Sociology and the Study of Religion.* New York: Basic Books.

———. 1966. *The Sociology of Religion.* Englewood Cliffs, NJ: Prentice-Hall.

O'Dea, Thomas F., and Janet O'Dea Aviad. 1983. *The Sociology of Religion*, second edition. Englewood Cliffs, NJ: Prentice-Hall.

Parsons, Talcott. 1990 [1935]. "Prolegomera to a Theory of Social Institutions." *American Sociology Review* 55 (June):319–33.

———. 1971. *The System of Modern Societies.* Englewood Cliffs, NJ: Prentice-Hall.

———. 1966. *Societies: Evolutionary and Comparative Perspectives.* Englewood Cliffs, NJ: Prentice-Hall.

———. 1962. "The Law and Social Control," in *Law and Sociology: Exploratory Essays*, ed. William M. Evan. New York: Free Press.

———. 1951. *The Social System.* New York: Free Press.

Parsons, Talcott, and Neil J. Smelser. 1956. *Economy and Society.* New York: Free Press.

Pashukanis, Eugenic. 1978. *Law and Marxism: A General Theory.* London: Ink Links.

Pasternak, Burton. 1976. *Introduction to Kinship and Social Organization.* Englewood Cliffs, NJ: Prentice-Hall.

Pfautz, H. W. 1955. "The Sociology of Secularization: Religious Groups." *American Journal of Sociology* 61:121–28.

Pospisil, Leopold J. 1978. *The Ethnology of Law,* second edition. Menlo Park, CA: Cummings Publishing Co.

———. 1974. *Anthropology of Law: A Comparative Theory.* New Haven: Yale University Press.

———. 1958. *Kapauku Papuans and Their Law.* New Haven: Yale University Press.

Postan, Michael. 1972. *The Medieval Economy and Society.* Berkeley: University of California Press.

Powell, Walter W., and Paul Damaggio. 1991. *The New Institutionalism in Organizational Analysis.* Chicago: University of Chicago Press.

Price, Derek J. de Solla. 1986. *Little Science, Big Science . . . And Beyond.* New York: Columbia University Press.

———. 1982. "The Parallel Structures of Science and Technology," in *Science in Context: Readings in the Sociology of Science,* eds. B. Barnes and D. Edge. Milton Keynes, UK: Open University Press.

———. 1963. *Little Science, Big Science.* New York: Columbia University Press.

Quinney, Richard. 1974. *Critique of Legal Order: Crime Control in Capitalist Society.* Boston: Little, Brown.

Radcliffe-Brown, A. R. 1952. *Structure and Function in Primitive Society.* Glencoe, IL: Free Press.

———. 1938. *Taboo.* Cambridge: Cambridge University Press.

———. 1935. "On the Concept of Function in Social Science" (reply to Lesser, 1935), *American Anthropologist* 37:394–402.

———. 1930. "The Social Organization of Australian Tribes." *Oceana* 1:44–46.

———. 1914. *The Andaman Islanders.* New York: Free Press.

Ramirez, Francisco O., and John Boli. 1987. "Global Patterns of Educational Institutionalization," in *Institutional Structure: Constituting State, Society, and the Individual,* eds. George M. Thomas, John W. Meyer, Francisco O. Ramirez, and John Boli. Newbury Park, CA: Sage.

Rattray, R. S. 1978. [1929]. *Ashanti Law and Constitution.* London: Oxford University Press.

Reasons, Charles E., and Robert M. Rich, eds., *The Sociology of Law: A Conflict Perspective.* Toronto: Butterworths.

Rich, Robert M. 1977. *The Sociology of Law: An Introduction to Its Theorists and Theories.* Washington, D.C.: University Press of America.

Riches, David. 1982. *Northern Nomadic Hunter-Gatherers.* London: Academic Press.

Rick, J. 1978. *Prehistoric Hunters of the High Andes.* New York: Academic Press.

Ritzer, George. 1996. *The McDonaldization of Society.* Thousand Oaks, CA: Pine Forge Press.

Robbins, Thomas, and Dick Anthony, eds. 1990. *In Gods We Trust: New Patterns of Religious Pluralism in America,* second edition. New Brunswick, NJ: Transaction Books.

Robinson, John. "Who's Doing the Housework?" *American Demographics* 10:24–28.

Roth, H. Ling. 1890. *The Aborigines of Tasmania.* London: Kegan Paul, Trench and Trubner.

Rubinson, Richard, and Irene Browne. 1994. "Education and the Economy," in *The Handbook of Economic Sociology,* eds. N. J. Smelser and R. Swedberg. New York: Russell Sage.

Rueschemeyer, Dietrich, Evelyne Huber Stephens, and John D. Stephens. 1992. *Capitalist Development and Democracy.* Chicago: University of Chicago Press.

Sahlins, Marshall. 1972. *Stone Age Economics.* Chicago: Aldine.

———. 1968a. *Tribesmen.* Englewood Cliffs, NJ: Prentice-Hall.

————. 1968b. "Notes on the Original Affluent Society," in *Man the Hunter*, eds. R. Lee and I. DeVore. Chicago: Aldine.

————. 1963. "Poor Man, Rich Man, Big Man, Chief: Political Types in Melanesia and Polynesia." *Comparative Studies in Society and History*, volume 5. Cambridge: Cambridge University Press.

————. 1958. *Social Stratification in Polynesia*. Seattle: University of Washington Press.

Salisbury, W. S. 1964. *Religion in American Culture*. Homewood, IL: Dorsey Press.

Sanders, J. 1992. "Short- and Long-Term Macroeconomic Returns to Higher Education." *Sociology of Education* 65:21–36.

Sanders, William T. 1972. "Population, Agricultural History, and Societal Evolution in Mesoamerica," in *Population Growth: Anthropological Implications*, ed. B. Spooner. Cambridge: MIT Press.

Sanderson, Stephen K. 1995a. *Macrosociology: An Introduction to Human Societies*, third edition. New York: Harper/Collins.

————. 1995b. *Social Transformations: A General History of Historical Development*. Cambridge, MA: Blackwell.

Sawer, G. 1965. *Law in Society*. Oxford: Clarendon Press.

Schapera, Isaac. 1956. *Government and Politics in Tribal Societies*. London: C. A. Watts and Co.

————. 1930. *The Khoisan Peoples of South Africa: Bushmen and Hottentots*. London: Routledge and Kegan Paul.

Schneider, David, and Kathleen Gough, eds. 1961. *Matrilineal Kinship*. Berkeley: University of California Press.

Schrire, Carmel, ed. 1984. *Past and Present in Hunter Gatherer Studies*. Orlando, FL: Academic Press.

Schwartz, Richard D., and James C. Miller. 1964. "Legal Evolution and Societal Complexity." *American Journal of Sociology* 70:159–69.

Scott, Richard. 1995. *Institutions and Organizations*. Thousand Oaks, CA: Sage.

Scott, Richard, and John W. Meyer, eds. 1994. *Institutional Environments and Organizations: Structural Complexity and Industrialism*. Thousand Oaks, CA: Sage.

Seidman, Steven, and David G. Wagner. 1992. *Postmodernism and Social Theory*. Oxford, UK: Blackwell.

Selznick, Philip. 1968. "Law: The Sociology of Law." *International Encyclopedia of the Social Sciences*, No. 9:50–59.

Service, Elman. 1975. *Origins of the State and Civilizations: The Process of Cultural Evolution*. New York: W. W. Norton.

————. 1966. *The Hunters*. Englewood Cliffs, NJ: Prentice-Hall.

————. 1962. *Primitive Social Organization: An Evolutionary Perspective*. New York: Random House.

Silver, Morris. 1985. *Economic Structures of the Ancient Near East*. London: Croom Helm.

Simmel, Georg. [1907] 1978. *The Philosophy of Money*, trans. T. Bottomore and D. Frisby. Boston: Routledge and Kegan Paul.

————. 1903. "The Sociology of Conflict." *American Journal of Sociology* 9:490–525.

Singer, Charles. 1954–1956. *A History of Technology*, 2 volumes. Oxford: Clarendon Press.

Sjoberg, Gideon. 1960. *The Preindustrial City*. New York: Free Press.

Skocpol, Theda. 1979. *States and Social Revolutions*. Cambridge: Cambridge University Press.

Smelser, Neil J. 1959. *Social Change in the Industrial Revolution: An Application of Theory to the British Cotton Industry.* Chicago: University of Chicago Press.

Smith, Adam. [1776] 1937. *An Inquiry into the Nature and Causes of the Wealth of Nations.* New York: The Modern Library.

Smith, W., and J. Roberts. 1954. *Zuni Law: A Field of Values.* Cambridge: Harvard University Press.

Spencer, Baldwin, and F. J. Gillen. 1927. *The Arunta: A Study of a Stone Age People.* London: Macmillan.

Spencer, Herbert. [1874–1896] 1898. *The Principles of Sociology*, 3 volumes. New York: D. Appleton.

Spiro, M. E. 1956. *Kibbutz, Venture in Utopia.* Cambridge: Harvard University Press.

Stark, Rodney, and William Sims Bainbridge. 1985. *The Future of Religion: Secularization, Revival and Cult Formation.* Berkeley: University of California Press.

———. 1980. "Towards a Theory of Religious Commitment." *Journal for the Scientific Study of Religion* 19:114–28.

Stearns, Linda Brewster. 1990. "Capital Markets Effects on External Control of Corporations," in *Structures of Capital: The Social Organization of the Economy*, eds. S. Zukin and P. DiMaggio. Cambridge: Cambridge University Press.

Stephens, W. N. 1967. "Family and Kinship," in *Sociology*, ed. N. J. Smelser. New York: John Wiley and Sons.

———. 1963. *The Family in Cross-Cultural Perspective.* New York: Holt, Rinehart and Winston.

Steward, Julian. 1930. "The Economic and Social Basis of Primitive Bands," in *Essays on Anthropology in Honor of Alfred Louis Kroeber*, ed. R. Lowie. Berkeley: University of California Press.

Swanson, Guy E. 1967. *Religion and Regime: A Sociological Account of the Reformation.* Ann Arbor: University of Michigan Press.

———. 1960. *The Birth of the Gods: The Origin of Primitive Beliefs.* Ann Arbor: University of Michigan Press.

Swedberg, Richard. 1994. "Markets as Social Structures," in *The Handbook of Economic Sociology*, eds. N. J. Smelser and R. Swedberg. New York: Russell Sage.

Szelenyi, Ivan, Katherine Beckett, and Lawrence P. King. 1994. "The Socialistic Economic System," in *The Handbook of Economic Sociology*, eds. N. J. Smelser and R. Swedberg. New York: Russell Sage Foundation.

Szymanski, Albert. 1978. *The Capitalist State and the Politics of Class.* Cambridge, MA: Winthrop.

Thompson, E. P. 1966. *The Making of the English Working Class.* New York: Random House.

Tilly, Charles. 1990. *Coercion, Capital and European States, A.D. 990–1900.* Oxford: Blackwell.

———. 1978. *From Mobilization to Revolution.* Reading, Mass: Addison-Wesley.

———, ed. 1975. *The Formation of Nation States in Western Europe.* Princeton: Princeton University Press.

Tonkinson, Robert. 1978. *The Marduojara Aborigines.* New York: Holt, Rinehart and Winston.

Touraine, Alan. 1988. *Return of the Actor; Social Theory in Postindustrial Society.* Minneapolis: University of Minnesota Press.

Troeltsch, Ernst. [1911] 1960. *The Social Teachings of Christian Churches*, 2 volumes, trans. O. Wyon. New York: Harper and Row.

Turnbull, Colin. 1961. *The Forest People*. New York: Simon and Schuster.

Turner, Bryan S., ed. 1990. *Theories of Modernity and Postmodernity*. London: Sage.

Turner, Jonathan H. 2003a. "A New Approach for Theoretically Integrating Micro and Macro Analysis," in *Handbook of Sociology*, eds. C. Calhoun, C. Roject, B. S. Turner. London: Sage.

———. 2003b. *The Structure of Sociological Theory*, seventh edition. Belmont, CA: Wadsworth.

———. 2002. *Face to Face: Toward a Theory of Interpersonal Behavior*. Palo Alto: Stanford University Press.

———. 2000. *On the Origins of Human Emotions: A Sociological Inquiry into the Evolution of Human Affect*. Palo Alto: Stanford University Press.

———. 2001a. "A Theory of Embedded Encounters." *Advances in Group Processes* 17:285–322.

———. 2001b. "Can Functionalism Be Saved?" in *Talcott Parsons Today*, ed. A. J. Treviño. Lanham, MD: Rowman & Littlefield.

———. 1999. "The Formation of Social Capital," in *Social Capital*, eds. I. Serageldin and P. S. Dasgupta. Washington, D.C.: The World Bank.

———. 1997. *The Institutional Order: Economy, Kinship, Religion, Polity, Law, and Education in Evolutionary and Comparative Perspective*. New York: Longman.

———. 1995. *Macrodynamics: Toward a Theory on the Organization of Human Populations*. Rose Monographs. New Brunswick, NJ: Rutgers University Press.

———. 1984. *Societal Stratification: A Theoretical Analysis*. New York: Columbia University Press.

———. 1983. "Theoretical Strategies for Linking Micro and Macro Processes." *Western Sociological Review* 14:4–15.

———. 1980. "Legal System Evolution: An Analytical Model," in *The Sociology of Law*. New York: Free Press.

———. 1974. "A Cybernetic Model of Legal Development." *Western Sociological Review* 5:3–16.

———. 1972. *Patterns of Social Organization: A Survey of Social Institutions*. New York: McGraw-Hill.

Turner, Jonathan H., and David E. Boyns. 2001. "The Return of Grand Theory," in *Handbook of Sociological Theory*, ed. J. H. Turner. New York: Kluwer Academic/Plenum Publishing.

Turner, Jonathan H., and Alexandra Maryanski. 1979. *Functionalism*. Menlo Park, CA: Benjamin-Cummings.

Turner, Ralph H. 1960. "Sponsored and Contest Mobility and the School System." *American Sociological Review* 25:855–67.

Underhill, Ralph. 1975. "Economic and Political Antecedents of Monotheism: A Cross-Cultural Study." *American Journal of Sociology* 80:841–61.

UNESCO. 2002. *Statistical Yearbook*. Paris: UNESCO.

Vago, Steven. 1994. *Law and Society*, fourth edition. Englewood Cliffs, NJ: Prentice-Hall.

Verlinden, O. 1963. "Markets and Fairs," in *The Cambridge Economic History of Europe*, volume 3, eds. M. M. Postan and E. E. Rich. Cambridge: Cambridge University Press.

Vernon, G. M. 1962. *Sociology of Religion*. New York: McGraw-Hill.

von Hagen, Victor. 1961. *The Ancient Sun Kingdoms of the Americas*. Cleveland, OH: World Publishing.

Wallace, Anthony F. C. 1966. *Religion: An Anthropological View*. New York: Random House.

Wallerstein, Immanuel M. 1974. *The Modern World System: Capitalist Agriculture and the Origins of the European World Economy in the Sixteenth Century*. New York: Academic Press.

Washburn, Sherwood, ed. 1961. *Social Life of Early Man*. Chicago: Aldine.

Weber, Max. [1922] 1978. *Economy and Society: An Outline of Interpretive Sociology*, eds. G. Roth and C. Wittich. Berkeley: University of California Press.

————. [1922] 1954. *Law in Economy and Society*, trans. E. Shils and M. Rheinstein. Cambridge: Harvard University Press.

————. [1917–1920] 1952. *Ancient Judaism*, trans. Hans H. Gerth and Don Martindale. New York: Free Press.

————. [1916–1917] 1958. *The Religion of India: The Sociology of Hinduism and Buddhism*, trans. Hans H. Gerth and Don Martindale. New York: Free Press.

————. [1915] 1951. *The Religion of China: Confucianism and Taoism*, trans. Hans H. Gerth. New York: Free Press.

————. [1904–1905] 1958. *The Protestant Ethic and the Spirit of Capitalism*, trans. Talcott Parsons. New York: Charles Scribner's.

Webster, D. 1975. "Warfare and the Evolution of the State." *American Antiquity* 40:467–70.

Weil, Frederick D. 1989. "The Sources and Structure of Legitimation in Democracies: A Consolidated Model Tested with Time-Series Data in Six Countries Since World War II." *American Sociological Review* 54:682–706.

Wells, Alan. 1970. *Social Institutions*. London: Heineman.

White, Andrew Dickson. 1896. *A History of the Warfare of Science with Theology in Christendom*. New York: D. Appleton and Co.

White, Harrison C. 1988. "Varieties of Markets," in *Structural Sociology*, eds. B. Wellman and S. D. Berkowitz. New York: Cambridge University Press.

————. 1981. "Where Do Markets Come From?" *American Journal of Sociology* 87:517–47.

White, Leslie. 1959. *The Evolution of Culture*. New York: McGraw-Hill.

Whiting, Beatrice. 1950. *Paiute Sorcery*. New York: Viking Press.

Williams, Peter W. 1980. *Popular Religion in America: Symbolic Change and the Modernization Process in Historical Perspective*. Englewood Cliffs, NJ: Prentice-Hall.

Williams, Robin M., Jr. 1970. *American Society: A Sociological Interpretation*. New York: Alfred Knopf.

Wilson, Bryan. 1969. *Religion in Secular Society*. Baltimore: Penguin Books.

Winterhalder, Bruce, and Eric Alden Smith, eds. 1981. *Hunter-Gatherer Foraging Strategies*. Chicago: University of Chicago Press.

Wolf, Eric. 1982. *Europe and the People Without History*. Berkeley: University of California Press.

Wolley, Leonard. 1965. *The Beginnings of Civilization, UNESCO History of Mankind*. New York: Mentor Books.

Woodburn, J. 1968. "An Introduction to Hadza Ecology," in *Man the Hunter*, eds. R. Lee and I. DeVore. Chicago: Aldine.

Wuthnow, Robert. 1994. "Religion and Economic Life," in *Handbook of Economic Sociology*. New York: Russell Sage Foundation.

————. 1989. *Communities of Discourse: Ideology and Social Structure in the Reformation, the Enlightenment, and European Socialism*. Cambridge: Harvard University Press.

————. 1988. "Sociology of Religion," in *Handbook of Sociology*, ed. N. J. Smelser. Newbury Park, CA: Sage.

————. 1987. *Meaning and Moral Order: Explorations in Cultural Analysis*. Berkeley: University of California Press.

————. 1980. "World Order and Religious Movements," in *Studies of the Modern World System*, ed. A. Bergesen. New York: Academic Press.

Yates, Kyle M., ed. 1988. *The Religious World: Communities of Faith*, second edition. New York: Macmillan.

Yinger, Milton J. 1970. *The Scientific Study of Religion*. New York: Macmillan.

Author Index

Abu-Lughod, J., 190
Amin, S., 201
Anderson, P., 185n
Anthony, D., 221
Anyon, J., 190
Apple, M., 90, 93
Applebaum, R., 199
Appleby, S., 221

Bainbridge, W., 220–21
Baran, P., 200
Bates, D., 155n
Beaud, M., 253n
Becker, H., 96n
Beckett, K., 253n
Bell, D., 201
Bellah, R., 104, 166, 213–16
Bender, B., 185n
Berger, P., 216
Binford, L., 124
Black, D., 80–81, 97n, 235, 240, 254n
Blalock, H., 9
Bloch, M., 185n
Block, F., 201, 208
Blum, J., 185n
Boli, J., 94, 245
Boserup, E., 24
Bourdieu, P., 89
Boyns, D., 3
Braudel, F., 34–35, 46–47, 180, 188, 190

Braungart, M., 246
Braungart, R., 246
Braverman, H., 197
Bredemeier, H., 82
Brint, S., 246–47, 249
Burke, E., 231

Cain, M., 81
Cambridge, 185n
Carneiro, R., 128, 223
Chambliss, W., 97n, 254n
Chang, K., 155n
Chase-Dunn, C., 25, 54
Childe, V., 75, 185n, 188
Chirot, D., 253n
Cohen, M., 124
Cohn, N., 221
Cole, C., 185n
Coleman, J., 14–15
Collins, R., 9, 46, 70, 88–89, 92, 159, 175, 199, 248, 250
Comte, A., 8
Cottrell, W., 193
Crook, S., 206
Curwen, C., 185n

Darwin, C., 11, 15–16, 24
Davis, H., 253n
Davis, J., 81–82
Davis, K., 61–62

301

Subject Index

authority, 67

beliefs: religious, 70–71, 105, 107, 134–36; substantive, 71
Big Man/Men systems, 77–78, 108–9, 111, 113, 117, 120, 149, 259, 261, 268
bureaucracy, 197–98

capital, 7, 31, 58, 102–03,120; and distribution, 47–48; and technology, 47
categoric units, 4
clan, 67
commodification, 192, 206–7
corporate units, 4, 164, 176, 190–91; and competition, 48; differentiation of, 28; and exchange, 42, 48–49; and markets, 28; and power, 28; and production, 28, 48; and reproduction, 50; segmentation of, 28–29
cosmology, 70–71, 166, 213–14
courts, 81–82, 113, 171, 235–36
credentialism, 248–49
cults, 71, 105–6, 134–36, 168

demographic transition, 23–24
descent, 66–67, 124–26, 164, 176–77
differentiation, 207; of corporate units, 28, 48; and distribution, 48–49; and economy, 59–60; and human capital, 48; hyperdifferentiation, 207; institutional,

255–59; and kinship, 62–69; and law, 42, 243; and markets, 46–47, 51; and physical capital, 47–48; and population growth, 17–19, 30, 44–45; and power, 37–38
distribution, 16–17; definition of, 6; elements of, 10–11; as a force, 6, 10

economy: agrarian, 159–62; definition of, 58–60; and education, 263–64; elements of, 58–60; horticultural, 119–22; hunting and gathering, 102–4, 114–15; industrial, 187–93; and law, 265–66, 274; and polity, 179–80, 259–62; and population growth, 179; and religion, 116–17, 276–78; selection pressures on, 57–60
education: bureaucratization of, 249–50; centralization of, 250; credentialing in, 248–49; definition of, 95; and economic development, 263–64; and economy, 244; elements of, 87–88; equalization of, 246–47; and kinship, 116, 178, 279–80; and polity, 183–89, 270–71; professionalization of, 251–55; privatization, 256; and religion, 275–76; selection pressures on, 88–95; tracking in, 247–48
embedding, 3
empires, 159–64
encounters, 4

societies, 222–31; and kinship, 115–16, 126–27, 141–44, 176–78, 268–70; and law, 151–52, 242–43, 266–68; and religion, 115–16, 181–82, 273–75; selection pressures on, 77–78, 86; and taxation, 148, 261
polyandry, 64
population, 6, 8, 24, 117–18; and distribution, 44–45, 47; diversity of, 30; growth of, 27–29; law of, 25; and logistical loads, 44; and markets, 27–28, 30; mobility of, 30; and power, 28, 30, 39–40; and production, 27, 30, 45; and reproduction, 50–51; and selection pressures, 9; settlement of, 26–27; urbanization of, 29–30
post-industrialization, 201–6
post-modernization, 206–9
power: bases of, 9, 76–77; centralization of, 9, 20, 39–40; consolidation of, 9, 29, 37, 40, 77; and distribution, 39–40; dynamics of, 223–31; and economy, 117; and inequality, 41; and institutional differentiation, 37–38; law of, 37; and markets, 38; and population growth, 28–29, 39–40; and production, 35–41, 39; and property, 32; and regulation, 9; and reproduction, 52
production, 6, 30–31; and capital, 31, 33–34; and corporate units, 31, 34; definition of, 6–7; elements of, 7, 31; law of, 31; and markets, 31, 34–35; and population, 26–27, 31, 37; and power, 35–39, 41; and reproduction, 51; and resources, 31, 33–34; of services, 46–47; and technology, 31, 33–34
property, 7, 31, 58, 123, 149, 192

rationality, 208
rational choice, 14–20
regulation, 6, 9, 36–42; definition of, 6; and law of, 37; and power, 6, 9–10, 36
reproduction, 6, 11–12; definition of, 6; and differentiation, 52; and economy, 50–51; and education, 89–90; law of, 49; and markets, 51; and polity, 50–51;

and population, 50; and power, 55; and production, 55
religion: in agrarian societies, 165–70; bureaucratization of, 218; communal, 133–34; definition of, 76; early modern, 213–15; ecclesiastical, 134–35, 147; and economy, 116–17, 276–78; and education, 275–76; elements of, 69–72; fundamentalism, 220–21; in horticultural societies, 133–36, 145–47, 152–53; in hunting and gathering societies, 104–07, 115; and industrialization, 191–92; in industrial societies, 191–92, 213–22; and kinship, 115, 178, 278–79; and law, 275; and markets, 216; and media, 217; modern, 216–22; monotheism, 214; and polity, 150–51, 182, 273–76; popular religions, 219; Protestant Reformation, 213–14; religious movements, 220; revitalization, 221; secularization of, 219; shamanic, 104, 107; and the state, 128–29
rites de passage, 88, 91, 146
rituals, 70, 73, 107, 135–36, 218–19

sacred, 69–70
segmentation, 29
selection pressures, 53–54, 81; and demand, 24; and differentiation, 17, 18, 24; Durkheim's model of, 16–17, 24; first-order, 19; and forces, 19, 53; and functional needs, 13–14, 19; and logistical loads, 24; and negative externalities, 15, 19; second-order, 19, 53, 59, 79, 81, 84; Spencer's model of, 18, 24
services, 202–3
settlements, 29
the state: democratic, 222–23; and economy, 180–81; and education, 183; emergence of, 78, 128–29, 132, 142, 148, 162–63, 178–79; and geopolitics, 228; and inequality, 228; and law, 168–69; and markets, 180; and money, 180–81; and religion, 182; and taxation, 148–49; totalitarian, 222
status groups, 91–92

About the Author

Jonathan H. Turner is Distinguished Professor of Sociology at the University of California, Riverside. Among his many influential books is the recently published *Face to Face: Toward a Sociological Theory of Interpersonal Behavior* (2002).

Human Institutions